SHUNTERS AT WORK

creating a world in a railway yard

SHUNTERS AT WORK

creating a world in a railway yard

Birgitta Edelman

Stockholm Studies in Social Anthropology
1997

SHUNTERS AT WORK
creating a world in a railway yard

Doctoral dissertation

Stockholm Studies in Social Anthropology, 37

© Birgitta Edelman

Photographs by the author

Department of Social Anthropology
Stockholm University
S-106 91 Stockholm

ISBN 91-7153-604-3   100183710

Cover picture: The shunting team leaving the New Hall; C-member on the engine, B-member on the bicycle, and shunt leader on the look-out.

Printed by Gotab, Stockholm 1997

To Johan and Elsa
who are
growing up in Tromsø
a town with no railway yard

CONTENTS

Shunting engine with driver and C-member.

PREFACE

"The preface", Anthony Giddens writes, "is normally the place where the author, surveying the results of his labours, tells the reader about the volume he would have written if only he had been able to overcome the manifest inadequacies of the work now in front of him."[1] Like Giddens I will, however, resist the temptation to elicit sympathy from the reader by describing any imaginary volume and instead express my gratitude to all people who have helped me during the process of producing this one, regardless of its shortcomings. Especially as these people have given their support without knowing what result to expect.

My foremost and deepest gratitude goes to the shunters. They always treated me fairly and convivially (and they just smiled when I crashed three engines in one go).

Apart from the good laughs and the good memories, and the lasting friendships, the shunters gave me another kind of souvenir; the insight that their work should not be described by words like 'merely' or 'just'. I hope that my respect for the shunters, and shunting, will become apparent in the following pages.

In connection with the shunters I also want to stress that SJ and the local union have been extremely helpful. I was met by a positive attitude and even when I was thrown out of the course for work leaders it was done very politely and apologetically. Otherwise all records have been open to me and I have been met with welcoming smiles from the very start and – what is perhaps more significant – to the very end!

My work was made possible by financial support from The Swedish Council for Work Life Research (*Rådet för Arbetslivsforskning*, formerly *Arbetsmiljöfonden*). In my dealings with this large organization I was always met by a friendly and supportive attitude, especially from Jan-Eric Degerblad, who administered my project .

My supervisors during my fieldwork and the period of writing were Dr. Kristina Bohman and, later, Prof. Ulf Hannerz at the Department of Social Anthropology at Stockholm University. Kristina's ability to keep up her enthusiastic and patient listening to my 'on the one hand...but on the other hand'-type of ponderings is in itself worth a medal. Ulf has supervised me

---

[1] GIDDENS 1978, 9.

from a more 'global perspective', as we have been separated by anything from 500 miles to half a globe during the last years. Ulf has treaded with softs paws over the pages, scratching only where details were 'a bit overwhelming'. I realize that a less gentle 'wolf' could have scratched with less mercy.

I also want to thank Prof. Frederick C. Gamst, Department of Anthropology, University of Massachusetts, Boston, for giving me a 'highball' at an early stage, when my only credit was to have arranged the letters A-I-L-and R in the right order. He kindly sent me railway material which I would otherwise have never been able to get hold of and he gave me a lot of advice, of which I have followed some, but not all. I have retained a lot of Swedish, or translated Swedish, terms instead of using American 'equivalents', as suggested by Prof. Gamst. This I have done in order for the reader to see differences which otherwise might have been veiled behind familiar American terminology. The resulting jumble is therefore entirely of my making, not of Prof. Gamst's.

Monica Lindh de Montoya has been 'our woman in Stockholm' duirng the last hectic moments. She has informed me about how to get the thing printed and answered my desperate e-mails with comforting words. (Thank you also for the advice that books can be used as pedestals for plants. That will probably come in handy.)

Patrik Bye has tried to correct my idiosyncratic English, but I am sure that I have managed to add some mistakes in the last minute. Not your fault, Patrik! The linguists Peter Svenonius and Curt Rice have also been attacked when they have been busy. They have answered patiently, saving me some embarrassment.

Anders Holmberg, my poor dear husband, has helped me in a myriad of ways. Above all he has always tried to make me finish this book. He succeeded at last. His name should really be on the cover.

1. INTRODUCTION

"We lived in a railway street; the sidings, with a slag-heap mound, were at our back gate. Those black shunting engines with the interminable back and forth movement instilled no romantic admiration in me. If I stared through my bedroom window when rain flooded the pane and the wind rattled the frame, the supposed objects of my admiration could be seen crouching wretchedly, dripping, cold, but vigilant for hand signals that never came, or fixed signals that tarried. My drowsy last minutes were spent under the counterpane on many nights, to deaden the crash of buffers – the 'ouch' of drawbars protesting."
(Frank Mason, who started his service with British Rail soon after WWI)[1]

'How on earth can you write a whole **book** about this job?' one of the shunters exclaimed as we sat in the switchboard plant watching the shunting locomotive hurriedly moving carriages to and fro in a seemingly endless zig-zag pattern across the yard. I was grasping for a good explanation, but all I came up with was that shunting, as well as all other tasks, entails much more than you think, and that she probably took her skills and what she knew for granted without realizing that it constituted 'knowledge,' and...

I was obviously not very convincing. She just opened her eyes wide and interrupted me by exclaiming: 'I couldn't fill **one page** if I tried!'

Having worked myself as a shunter for two years I do, however, understand her perplexity, as, on the one hand, shunting seems to be a job which can be described in a few words – as assembling carriages into trains –, while on the other hand, it is one which hardly can be explained, but only learned through practice. The practical understanding one aquires at work can be discussed, but it seems that the only persons who really can take part in and understand, not to say enjoy, such a discussion are other shunters. So what is the point of writing a book about shunting?

~~~

Admittedly, not all shunters would subscribe to the view that one could not write a book about shunting. Some shunters took it that I was writing railway history, some that I was doing 'something for the company', others that I was looking for a sensational story worthy of the evening papers – and then there

---

[1] Mason quoted from McKENNA, 175.

1

was Pelle, who announced to all and sundry that: 'She is writing a book about my sexual escapades!' (my ritual response being that half a page would not suffice for a Ph.D.)

Two shunters, who interestingly enough refused to be interviewed, showed a natural inclination for theorizing about different aspects of work.[2] Social relations as well as questions of skill and competence came constantly to the fore when we were talking. We did not necessarily agree, but we observed things (not necessarily the same things) and tried to see patterns, meanings, and causes in the everyday world around us. These two people had what I consider to be a deep interest in and talent for social observation. (I have reason to suspect that there were several such 'naturals' among the seniors, but the ones I spotted were about to retire and I never got the opportunity to talk to them about the events that took place during my fieldwork.)

One of these two 'main informants' of mine declared on the first day of my fieldwork that he did not want my work to interfere with our friendship, and from that point on he never referred directly to what I was doing, but went on presenting his thoughts about everything just as before.

The other one took a more positive view of my project and saw it as important that shunting finally would 'be put on the map'. I sometimes had a feeling that he deliberately provoked people in my presence, expressing views which he knew they would object to, just in order for me to make a note of it. This may of course have been a product of my imagination, but I do know that there was an understanding between us, which made it possible for me to check my views with him, without having to resort to long explanations.

During my writing up I sometimes felt that I was losing touch with the world of the shunters and that I, sitting all alone at my desk, perhaps was 'seeing things'. I would then go down to the yard, hoping to bump into one of these shunters and quickly go through the issues that worried me.

I always felt great relief when I heard their comments – regardless of whether they supported my views or corrected and modified what I had to say. The fact that we could discuss so easily implied that we were talking the same language.[3] It was equally encouraging to realize that there were other persons with a serious interest in reflecting about the same issues. I had not gone mad in my lonely chamber – at least not yet.

---

[2] When declining to be interviewed one of them said that he thought we 'were chatting so much anyway', 'satt och spånade så mycket ändå'. (Spåna = 'think or converse in a free and improvised manner, see brainstorming'. Cf. SO. Transl.: BE. Brainstorming is indeed a term which might describe some of the conversations we had.)

[3] Another expression for this would be that we 'intersubjectively shared the same expert's model'. Cf. D'ANDRADE, 168.

2

Some of the main questions of our discussions concerned competence or skill. What is skill in shunting, who is a competent shunter, and how do you learn to become such a shunter? Boiling it down to one question, we could say that we tried to find out what constituted good shunting. This is also what this book is all about.

~~~

Good shunting implies – among other things – skilful shunting. I have set out to explore skill from several angles. We must first consider the shunters' conceptions of skill.

What are the different views about skill (as we may assume that there are different views) and how are they constituted? Do they change when people advance in their careers, such as when they leave active shunting outdoors and become 'office-shunters'? Do old and young, men and women perceive and come to be perceived differently?

But we must also consider the larger issue concerning how these concepts of skill relate to the social context of working life. I am here thinking about the way in which skill comes to mould personal relations and positions as well as colleagueship and antagonism between categories or groups. We could consider relations of solidarity and belonging on the one hand and separation and exclusion on the other.

In such a perspective, skill (including its acquisition) becomes a meeting point for many other aspects, such as acceptance, dominance and power and, what is often called 'socialization', but which I like to think of as incorporation.[4]

~~~

I have preferred to use the word 'skill' – rather than 'competence' or 'expertise' – since these latter terms seem to imply the mastery of a specific task or field of knowledge. I take the word 'competence'[5] (at least the Swedish equivalent) to refer to proficiency rated according to an accepted standard, a performance which is sufficient and adequate, but not necessarily more than that. This is a limitation I would like to avoid, as I prefer a concept which connotes virtuosity and even excessive display of dexterity.[6]

---

[4] I am following Bourdieu in this respect. See discussion of Bourdieu's usage of this concept in Broady. Cf. BROADY, 228 ff.

[5] The words 'competent' and 'competition' both stem from the latin verb *petere*, which means 'to fall upon' or 'to aim at'. I would not, *per se*, object to an association to 'competition', but the modern meaning of 'competent' does not seem to entail such a connection. Cf. CCE.

[6] Stephen Wood has a different, but not necessarily conflicting view. I can agree when he writes: "Competence is the certain ability to complete a given task; whilst skill is about managing uncertainty." WOOD, 40.

Similar objections can be made against the word 'expertise'. It is too narrowly focused on the mastery of a circumscribed area. In addition, it has a mind-over-body bias, which is unfortunate in this case.[7]

The 'competence' or 'expertise' I discuss is one which goes beyond the successful completion of a task, it is something of *l'art pour l'art*, and as such it is a means of expressing individuality and personality and a way to gain influence and dominance. At the same time it is shaped as part of a collective enterprise. I have therefore decided to use the term 'skill', which I think catches this broader idea beautifully. One can be a skilled painter as well as a skilled shunter – although painting is often done in solitude, while shunting is hardly ever done alone.

My ambition has thus been to use a concept which is as general and comprehensive as possible, postulating and assuming as little as possible. My aim will not be to arrive at a definition of the concept 'skill', but to describe what skill means in the context of this particular shunting yard. My recommendation to the reader is to start with an open mind and read skill much in the sense it is being used in everyday language while hopefully arriving at a deeper understanding of its specific implications for shunting during the reading.

This approach must, however – and particularly as I write this *post factum* – be considered to be programmatic rather than chronological, and I can consequently already disclose certain features resulting from my search.

~~~

Skill, in the way it materializes in the shunting yard, is **not uniform and fixed**. There is a great deal of consent about what properties a 'good shunter' should possess, naturally, but there is likewise disagreement, personal preferences as well as change over time.

As shunting is a **cooperative** task, a considerable part of it cannot be seen as individual mastery, but as a function of adjustment and mutual understanding in practice. Personal preferences concerning the identification of skill are neither fixed once and for all, but rather contextually determined and situation-dependent. Skill will always depend on external evaluation and therefore lies in the eye of the (co-worker) beholder to a considerable extent.

---

[7] My proof-reader, Patrik Bye, refutes this statement. I assume that my misinterpretation stems from the fact that 'expert' in Swedish has a clear reference to scholarly knowledge as opposed to manual skills. A 'football-expert', for example, would then in Swedish be a person who knows a lot about soccer-theory, -rules, -results, -teams and the like. A good football-player would not necessarily qualify as an 'expert' on football. Another linguist tells me, however, that in English one can distinguish between 'expert on' and 'expert at', the former referring to scholarly learning, while the latter embraces dexterity and practical skills. (Curt Rice, personal communication.)

Skill is nearly always acquired in an asymmetrical relationship, in this case initially in an apprentice-master relation. The learning process is therefore also an arena in which power and dominance are established as well as questioned. The path to mastery is, as we shall see, also one of struggle and **reconceptualization**. Gradual learning, through passive drilling or internalization of experience, therefore must be seen as a secondary process.

These three points of my thesis (variance, cooperation, reconceptualization) echo the critique Yrjö Engeström has directed towards what he calls 'two dominant approaches in expertise'. One of these is the 'algorithmic' approach, which concerns itself with defining expert attributes in specific knowledge-based domains, while the other is the 'enculturational' approach, which stresses tacit knowledge, embedded in social practices. Both approaches see expertise as universal, individual, and communicated in an unquestioned master-apprentice continuum. Engeström then develops his view as a counterproposal to these two approaches. [8]

I had already finished the greater part of my book when I realized that my main ideas actually could be formulated as an answer to Engeström's call for a different approach. I do not therefore claim that Engeström necessarily will agree with what I have to say, but I do find it reassuring that there is a call which I have been able to respond to, however insufficiently.

~~~

As stated, my two main informants' pondering about social relations at work and about matters of skill and dexterity has coloured this work to a large extent. They might not agree with all I have to say and this is (partly, but significantly so) caused by the break between lived experience and objectified knowledge, the latter term referring to the different spectacles that the anthropologist must don when translating lived experience into a systematized and structuralized whole. There is a tendency to see human interaction as "...a system of objective relations independent of individual consciousnesses and wills."[9] Such a view stresses the sealed and completed character of the analyst's model, while the openended and unfinished character of the 'insider's' position is neglected and veiled.

My ambition, however, has been to extend my analysis beyond such a structural view and I have tried to present my description in a fashion which unites the 'phenomenological' view of the lived experience with the structural,

---

[8] Cf. ENGESTRÖM, 1 ff.
[9] BOURDIEU, 1977, 4.

objectivist one.[10] Bourdieu calls this a 'second break' (the first break being the one which separates the structural view from the phenomenological one), but I see it rather as a fusion, where the certainty, the *fait accompli*-character, of the structural view is supplemented with the uncertainty which comes from seeing social life as irreversible and subject to the passing of time. In order to illustrate this, Bourdieu contrasts the phenomenological view of how the gift is (or is meant to be) experienced with the unconscious principles of the obligation to give, to receive and to give in return – the 'objective' truth of the gift.[11] One realizes that this closed reciprocal system is abstracted from the subjective experience, which always bears the mark of uncertainty.

Any theory of practice must allow for the fact that every act along the line might 'misfire'. There is a temporal aspect involved, which lends the gift such an uncertain character – again referring to Bourdieu's famous example. The full meaning of the gift can never be established, as later acts in the chain of reciprocity may reflect back upon and colour the meaning of the original act. The full meaning of the gift is thus drawn from the structural, reciprocal pattern of obligations **at the same time** as it can exist only by denying and suppressing that very pattern. If I give expensive gifts to my rich old aunt, it is not because I want anything in return, I claim, but because I like her. When I find that she left me out of her will, I realize, however, that my gifts were obviously not appreciated, and I feel somehow offended. Why should this be?

It is then the retrospective force of the meaning of the gift which creates the uncertainty and cuts a sharp line between the viewpoint of the actor and the observer. My description of the shunters aims at bringing the uncertainty of lived experience into the purview of my model. In the shunting yard, uncertainty has a profound impact on the meaning of skill.

The phenomenological view of skill, i.e. the shunters' view of what it entails to possess skill, and the structural view of skill, i.e. the aspects which emerge when we see the hidden principles behind the collective construction of skill, are both views which have to be considered in the light of ongoing praxis. Display of skill is a risktaking. I do not refer to the inherent risks of working in a shunting yard, but to the risk of destroying one's reputation and losing credibility in the eyes of the co-shunters.

---

[10] I am using the word 'structural' in a broad sense, including all scientific modelbuilding and systematizing straightjacketing of the world 'out there', which does not take openended temporality into consideration. 'Structural' anthropology is only one specific case of this broad category.

[11] The 'phenomenological' view of the gift is here Marcel Mauss' s famous study by that name. Cf. BOURDIEU, 1977, 4f.

The difference between skill and lack of skill depends on the future result. There may always be a new judgment, which retrospectively defines, or redefines, the act as one or the other, as failure or as success.[12] The time aspect may here indeed be considerable, since confidence may take years to build, but only seconds to ruin. Time, and the uncertainty of the future, is crucial in a practical theory of skill.

~~~

By giving an overview of the different chapters of the book I will give a more detailed picture of the main points of my argument, with a design to reveal and expose how technology, the organization of work and the social relations are intertwined. These are linked by the practice of work and by the way this practice is conceived of by the shunters themselves. This is therefore a book which constantly asks how shunters come to conceive and change their conceptions of shunting and shunting skills.

Chapter 2 is an introduction to the setting. The yard, the shunters and the reasons behind my presence in the yard are presented. My past as a shunter raises the question how a study of the kind I propose profits from, or even presupposes, that the researcher possesses the skills her (or him-) self.[13]

Chapter 3 describes the formal division of labour in the yard as well as informal alignments and dividing lines. Being rather detailed and thematic this chapter may be 'skimmed through' initially to give a general overview of the different tasks. It may thus serve as an inventory of the work terminology.

Working together may take many different forms. Chapter 4 looks at different kinds of team-work. I distinguish between forms of team-work which crystallize from the very organization of work; the division of labour, and forms which stem from preferences of individuals or groups. The latter I have called 'styles' of work. This chapter also examines what happens when team-work breaks down.

---

[12] In other words, there always is a first judgment, but never a final one.

[13] As Geertz so aptly writes: "The ethnographer does not, and, in my opinion, largely cannot, perceive what his informants perceive. What he perceives, and that uncertainly enough, is what they perceive 'with'– or 'by means of', or 'through'... or whatever the word should be." (GEERTZ 1983, 58.) I am not saying that I, by having been a shunter myself, thereby have perceived what the informants have perceived, but rather that I acquired an additional tool to grapple with the 'withs', and 'by means of' and 'throughs' of how people "(...)represented themselves to themselves and to one another." (Ib.) Timothy Jenkins argues when talking about fieldwork that one cannot have the role of buyer as well as of seller. (Cf. JENKINS, 443) While you cannot have them simultaneously, perhaps, you certainly can go from one to the other, and at every instance be a true seller or a true buyer, not the mix of the two, a 'beller'.

Chapter 5 describes an alternative route to the yard, compared to the 'bird's eye view' presented in Chapter 3. Chapter 5 allows us to enter the gates as beginners. We pass through the selection process, the test and the educational course, and we are then finally granted admission as apprentices in the yard.

Entry into the yard does not involve rites of passage, but depends on a willingness to show commitment to the work and the workers. I have distinguished between 'signs of commitment', shown by the beginner, and 'modes of acceptance' displayed by the seniors. Belonging is a matter of identifying 'us' and 'them', while simultaneously being an identification of the properties of 'real' work and how it should be performed. Chapter 6 gives us a view of how such perceptions of work and workers are moulded.

In chapter 7 we will have a closer look at skill and the acquisition of skill. We look at the skilled *('säker')* shunter, as well as the 'cowboy,' and the ignorant *'kabyl'*. A large part of the skills involved in shunting are, as a matter of fact, tacit and we will therefore study the implications of this for beginners. Here I will take a critical look at a theory presented by the philosopher Allan Janik and a group of researchers associated with the National Institute for Working Life in Stockholm. I will present an alternative, which takes into account the habitus of the learner. In this connection, I introduce the concepts of 'mimetic' and 'paraphrastic' modes of learning tacit skills. There is ample evidence of both types of learning in the yard and it is also possible to say something about their consequences.

Central to the conceptions of work is the idea of team-work. Team-work is here seen to consist of a hierarchical ladder of well-defined work roles, combined with a strong egalitarian ethos. It favours social action which is planned and routine-like, compromising and adjustable, safe and serious, while simultaneously encouraging instant and direct, idiosyncratic and personal, crazy and jocular. This chapter tries to show how this is made possible. The example of the card game, *plump*, which, unlike Geertz' Balinese cockfight is not only an enactment of relations that prevail, but which actually entails a change of those relations. As a 'microcosm' of the shunting yard the card table spells out the dialectic between structure and agency, the given forms and the possibility to change one's role and position with the 'cards at hand'.

Chapter 8 describes, in a chronological fashion, the events of the yard during the process of the reorganization that took place during my fieldwork. This chain of events broke up the old jog-trot way of work, revealing ideas about work which had otherwise remained tacit and invisible. Coming to the surface they now could be discussed and questioned. Groups became divided by lines which had been denied and concealed. Skill was no longer self-evident.

Chapter 9 problematizes the diachronic perspective. Changes in the concepts of space and time (as results of changing territoriality and organizational changes) are brought into focus here. While representing structural forms of change we can contrast them to change brought about through agency. In this chapter we are brought back to our initial note about the uncertain and open-ended character of the lived life, as opposed to models proposed, *post factum*, by the researcher. We can observe that the shunters adhere to different solutions and different strategies when facing the uncertainty of the future.

Chapter 10 offers a summary of how I have seen the relations between skill, workers and work in this particular shunting yard.

~~~

Despite the misgivings of my former colleague in the shunting yard, I have actually written a whole book about shunting. I hope that I have been able to show that connecting carriages also is a way of connecting people. Therefore this book deals with a rich and complex world which embraces much more than the 'simple' task of shunting.

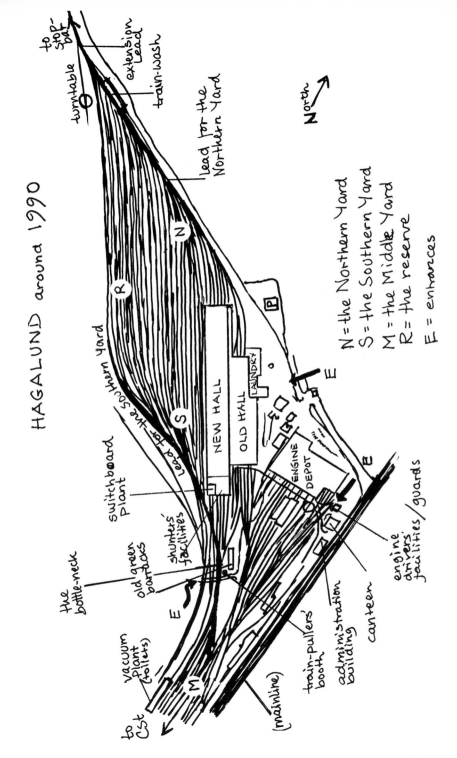

HAGALUND around 1990

to stop-bar
extension lead
train-wash
turntable
lead for the Northern Yard
North
N

N = the Northern Yard
S = the Southern Yard
M = the Middle Yard
R = the reserve
E = entrances

R
N
S
M
E
E
E

the southern yard
lead for the southern yard
switchboard plant
old green barracks
shunters' facilities
the bottle-neck
vacuum plant (toilets)
to Cst
(mainline)
train-pullers' booth
administration building
canteen
engine drivers' facilities/guards
ENGINE DEPOT
NEW HALL
OLD HALL
LAUNDRY
P

2. HAGALUND

Hagalund – A Part of SJ

SJ (pronounced 'ess-yee') stands for *Statens Järnvägar*.[1] The Swedish Government decided in 1854 that the State should construct and run the traffic on certain trunk lines (*'stambanor'*) in Sweden. These lines still today constitute the backbone of railway communication in Sweden.

Alhough two thirds of the Swedish railway system was built by private enterprises, the Swedish State procured a steadily increasing part of the private tracks, until a parliamentary resolution in 1939 finally nationalized the railways. In 1942 SJ could boast of the longest electrified railway in Europe, 2022 kms of track, connecting Trelleborg in the very South, with Riksgränsen on the Norwegian border in the North.[2]

In Sweden, SJ has become identical with the Swedish railways. As other institutions of the civil service, it has been subjected to criticism, often mixed with feelings of national pride. SJ is sometimes called *'hela folkets järnväg'* ('the railway of the people') and one demands – and insists that one has a right to demand – that Swedish trains should run on time.

SJ employees relate to SJ much in the same way as the public does. Criticism is mixed with pride and respect. It seems, however, that the latter part of this century has seen more of the criticism, while the earlier part was the period when one could still be proud of being employed by SJ. Senior employees remember with nostalgia when they were young and it 'gave you status' to work at SJ.[3] Although the pay was never high, compared to salaries in the private sector, state employment was seen as safe and reliable. One did not risk being laid off.

The criticism directed against SJ during the latter part of this century must be seen in relation to the intense competition that railway traffic has met from

---

[1] The Swedish State Railways. (Literally:'The State's Railways', not 'Swedish Rail', as often assumed.)

[2] Not much to boast of, perhaps, when one considers the state of the rest of Europe at that time, as well as the fact that this novelty coincided with Hitler's transits of war material through Sweden.

[3] SJ employees are civil servants and belong to the union of State Employees.

all sides. Cars, trucks, ships, and airplanes can offer flexibility, comfort, or speed that can be difficult to match. The advantage of trains is most visible in fast inter-city transport, where the combination of comfort, speed and flexibility may beat other more one-sided means of transport. Many of the deep-going changes that SJ has undergone during the last decades have aimed at improving its ability to compete in this respect.

In 1953 SJ had more than 73.000 employees, while the figures for 1995 show less than 25.000 employees. Rationalizations and modernization have made small stations, assistant engine drivers, linemen and several other categories of staff obsolete, and instead have introduced high speed trains (called 'X 2000') and computerized systems for train handling, service of rolling stock, booking and international communication. Taking the latest reorganization, the changes from 1988 to today into account, we can note that SJ now has reached an efficiency per employee, which puts it in the lead in Europe.[4]

The last reorganization, one of the goals of which was to make SJ self-financed by 1996, has led to greater economic independence for the various sub-areas. This has had an impact also on the tiny part of SJ we are to deal with here: the Yard Group in Hagalund. Hagalund is the Stockholm terminus for passenger trains. The trains are assembled by members of the Yard Group, which is one of several production groups at this terminus. The Yard Group, i.e. the shunters, is now 'selling' its services to other groups, while 'buying' engine drivers and material from the others. Saving costs in one area now means that money can be spent on other things, while earlier any savings you made would only disappear into the general account of Hagalund, and ultimately SJ. Now every service has a price. As one shunter put it: 'Earlier, if you wanted to clean the pits, you could just pull out a hose and do it. Now you have to **rent** the hose from the Hall and they will send you a bill.'

In the following we will primarily look at SJ from the point of view of the shunting yard. Ours is a frog's-eye view, where the different SJ departments tend to fade in the distance. In the yard, SJ is the term for people above, people who influence the daily work in various ways, but most of whom remain distant, invisible, or unknown. Hagalund is SJ, too, but in many ways Hagalund is felt to be a world of its own, sometimes forgotten, often underestimated and even despised by the rest of SJ. Hagalund has good

---

[4] Efficiency is here measured in 'traffic units' (=person per km + ton per km per employee). While the traffic units for Germany, GBR and Norway were about 400 in 1995, the number for Sweden was 1200. (Cf. Å95) Although one is tempted to relate this to the high work speed in Hagalund, I must stress that the shunters favoured speed and efficiency independently of, and long before, the last wave of rationalizations.

sides and bad sides; the former tend to be referred to as Hagalund, while the latter tend to be labelled SJ. 'Typical of SJ', the Hagalunders say about anything amiss. When they tell of something positive they proudly say: 'That's the way things have always been here in Hagalund'.

The Yard at Hagalund

The terminus called 'Hagalund' lies some ten kms North of Stockholm Central Station (Cst) and less than one km North of Solna (commuter-train) Station. From there it stretches along the main railway line going North. At the next commuter-train station, Ulriksdal, it bends and goes westward, parallel to the main road E 18. In the Southwest it neighbours the undeveloped and marshy areas around Råsta Lake. The part in the Northwest, where the yard converges into a single track and finally ends in a stop-bar, is called the Northern Yard (or the North), while the middle part, where the shunt yard proper ends in the turn-out tracks, is called the Southern Yard (or the South). The southernmost part, close to Solna, is mainly used for carriages on reserve, and, for reasons buried in the past, it is known as the Middle Yard.

The yard measures about a km and a half from one end to the other – i.e. from the stop-bar in the North to the southern tip of the Middle Yard – counting fortyfive tracks at its widest part. This may sound spacious, but lack of space is in fact a problem which Hagalund has struggled with as long as anyone can remember. The yard is shaped like a boomerang, which again means that almost every track is curved. One must keep in mind that straightness is the first and most essential requirement for a functionally sound shunting yard as every bend will cause carriages to obstruct the view and add to the hazards in shunting. Furthermore, the tracks are too few in number, sometimes making it difficult to find space to shunt carriages aside and leave them for a period of time. Engines of arriving trains also have problems when all tracks are filled with carriages, as they get trapped in the *cul-de-sac* in the North, finding no empty track for their return to the shed.

Not only are the tracks – extension tracks as well as sidings – considerably bent, but the yard itself is built on a lake bed and the ground is constantly subsiding. Despite perpetual efforts to lift and level the tracks they invariably sink back, creating new gradients and inclines. Shunters must therefore always keep in mind that, unless properly secured, carriages may suddenly and without warning come rolling back from their tracks.

Squeezed between the surrounding rocks and the main line, sinking into the ground by its own weight, Hagalund has, however, with pain and effort (like a Chinese lily foot) accustomed itself to its ungiving ecology. It triumphantly presents itself to visitors and strangers as a functioning impracticability. A maze of signals and tracks, it instills respect into visiting engine drivers, who, no doubt, have contributed to the nationwide reputation Hagalund enjoys as being a tough and inhospitable environment. The Hagalunders naturally complain about the problems that the environment inflicts on their work, but there is an undeniable sense of pride in the ability to cope with this aberrant yard. 'Hagalund is special!' they say, when they insist on doing things their own way, and refuse to accept criticism or advice from outsiders.

Despite its cramped conditions, Hagalund is the maintenance yard for all passenger trains arriving in Stockholm. Here, the engines are disconnected and the carriages cleaned and serviced. Beds are made, water tanks filled, repairs and regular check-ups carried out. The trains are then shunted, i.e. taken apart and put together into new trains. These are finally washed in a huge trainwash, connected to new engines at, brake-tested, and sent off to the Central Station to pick up new passengers and steam off to distant destinations.

The large service hall – called 'the New Hall', despite the fact that it was built some thirty years ago – dominates the yard. This is one of the busiest areas where trucks loaded with linen, mopeds carrying all kinds of equipment, cleaners pushing trolleys and shunters and other workers on mopeds and bicycles constantly move between the platforms.

The New Hall was previously home to the pay office, and the office taking care of sick leaves and dispatchment of free tickets for employees as well as an office for ordering work shoes. The managers of the different groups, and the top manager had their offices on the first floor. Many of these functions have now been moved to the administration building. The manager of the shunt group has moved to the shunters' new quarters at the end of the New Hall.

The all important Order Centre still lies in the New Hall. Like the spider in a web it consitutes the centre of internal telephone and radio communication and handles information about the progress of the different tasks in the train handling process. Announcements are made over the loud-speaker system, informing about changes of tracks and train departures.

The Old Hall lies side by side, connected to the New Hall. It is here that the repair and spare parts shops are housed, along with some offices and a lift which connects the halls to the separate laundry, where nearly all SJ laundry is cleaned.

14

Between the large halls and the main entrance gates, one has to pass the smaller engine depots and the new engine wash. The engine drivers have a small house next to the main entrance. A rack outside the door holds their black leather satchels, bulging with rule books, sandwiches, newspapers books, and all other things they need when passing a night at some distant station or when they are caught waiting for signals along the main line – or even at the entry to Hagalund.

The engine drivers' building also contains the little office of the guards. From here the adjoining main gate as well as two other gates are supervised and remotely controlled with the aid of cameras and a loud speaker system. As the 800 persons employed at Hagalund are not compelled to carry identification cards, the control is rather haphazard and lax. Card-operated gates are being installed, but they have not yet been effectuated.[5]

'The Villa' lies on a hill adjacent to the rocks that mould the yard into its boomerang shape. The Villa contains lecture rooms and an office for the local union clubs. Surrounded by bushes and apple trees it is a little odd oasis wedged between the dusty shunting yard and the thundering dual carriageway outside the gates. Office staff have occasionally arranged lunches in the garden, bringing new potatoes and homepickled herrings, made for the occasion.

On the other side of the large halls we have the shunting yard proper, where the trains line up on some twenty tracks with the carriages on reserve on the outmost ten. The tracks feed into the shunting leads in small bundles at each end of the yard . The forking is irregular and, due to the peculiar shape of the yard, also dissimilar from one end to the other, which all naturally adds to the confusion felt by new shunters and drivers.

The tracks are shunted from both ends; the teams working with Engines 1 and 4 pull in the North towards the extension track and the stop-bar, while the teams on Engines 2 and 3 pull out into the bottleneck in the South, interfering with the arrival and departure of trains and engines. Parallel to the extension track there is a track which passes through the automatic train wash, a plant with huge brushes and sprinkler systems, most aptly described as an overgrown car wash.

Besides their own quarters, the shunters rarely visit other indoor facilities apart from the New Hall and the canteen. They may occasionally have business at the pay office, or they pass through the Old Hall on their way to the canteen, but the laundry or the engine depots are very much *terra incognita* to them. This is how it should be, they feel. Keeping oneself to oneself

---

5 The present tense in this treatise refers to 1991, when I finished my fieldwork.

means that one does not interfere and is not interfered with. Sometimes, however, they do complain that they do not know people who have been working at Hagalund for decades. They recognize the faces, but that is about all.

The Shunters and the Yard

The environment at the yard includes gravel and diesel fumes, creosote-impregnated sleepers and buzzing high power electric lines. But you also have the sheltered haven of the Villa, where the garden in late spring is filled with the scent of blooming lilacs and apple-trees and where bees and butterflies search their way over the flowerbeds and the soft grass.

On such a warm day the garden is an intimate and soothing refuge from the vast macadam desert of the yard, where the converging lines of endless tracks trap the vision and lead it away into a distant mirage. While the garden is constructed according to a scale which seems inherently human, the yard has proportions which reduce humans into strange little orange upright ants, chased by enormous snakes of steel and commanded by thundering megaphone voices.

Such a picture may easily emerge to a Philistine eye, but well versed shunters have long ago acquired spectacles enabling them to read quite different meanings into the same landscape. True, every one of them would rather be free on such a fine day and perhaps spend it in a boat or in a summer cottage or in a garden resembling that of the Villa, but anyone making a comment to that effect will immediately be reminded of the much worse prospect of being 'locked up' in an office or a factory. The vast yard is a picture of freedom, of being on one's own, out of reach of managers and time study officers and what not. It is also an image of seeing far and being able to predict. A quick glimpse at the yard on arrival gives the shunter a hint of what the shift will be like – chaotic or calm – just as a look from a distance at an arriving train informs the shunter of additions and irregularities in its composition, predicting the tasks of the day. Vast open space means predictability and safety. Nothing can creep up silently and invisibly and take you by surprise. The contrast between the small and vulnerable human beings and the large iron vehicles does therefore not paint a threatening image; on the contrary, it represents one of authority and control.

Needless to say, shunters are not born shunters. Everyone has gone from a state of perplexity, bewilderment – even fear – to a feeling of command and familiarity. During the 1980s, when there was at least one group of

16

apprentices a year, the shunting community as a whole represented everything from beginner's confusion to the confidence of the veteran shunter; i.e. everything from 'students' to 'old heads'.[6] The skills were, however, not evenly distributed. A long employment stop in SJ twenty years earlier had given rise to a warped age pyramid.[7] Presented in a diagram it would vaguely resemble an hour-glass.

In the 1980s the 'bottom' of the hour-glass constituted a veritable swingdoor (to mix metaphors) where only a few people trickled in, while the majority seemed to have disappeared rather quickly. Of 87 persons who left the yard between 1982 and 1989, according to SJ data, 21 retired, 3 were granted sick pension, 5 died, 1 was fired, while the rest, resigning at their own request (altogether 56 persons) count 20-31 who worked for less than one year. (The uncertainty stems from the fact that, to my knowledge, some of these persons never set foot in the yard, but probably worked in some other part of the Hagalund complex, while being registered as shunters. Others turned 'about heel', so to speak, as soon as they sat foot in place as they left neither date of employment, nor date of resignation, in the computer record.) During the same period (1982-89) 26 persons were employed who were still in service 1989. This must be contrasted to the fact that the average length of employment of those who retired was 39 years and 9 months!

The shunting group, including the manager and indoor staff, consisted of 82 persons in July 1989, nine of whom were women (one, however, being on a long term leave and another one being the anthropologist).

The waist of the hour-glass divides the shunting group into what I will refer to as elder and younger shunters, but it could also be taken to represent other distinctions within the group. Among those 31 persons who were born in 1946 or earlier, only two have finished nine years of school or more. Among the 51 younger persons, born 1947 or later, at least 25 have completed further education, such as two or three years of high school, the rest having passed the obligatory 9-year comprehensive school.

The waist of the hour-glass is also, although less clearly, a regional boundary, dividing people from the country from people from the Stockholm area. One of the shunters told me that he (sometime in the 1970s) had found out that all the 24 provinces of Sweden were represented among them, each province being roughly proportionally represented. This 'miniature-Sweden' had only one lacuna: not one single shunter was a Stockholmer!

---

[6] Concerning the American expressions 'student' and 'old head', cf. GAMST, 1980, 30 ff.
[7] When an employment stop is declared no new employment contracts are made. The organization is slimmed down due to so called 'natural retirement', i.e. pensioning.

17

The typical elder shunter is thus a man from a small provincial town, often a railway junction. We have nicknames like 'Hoting', 'Krylbo' and 'Hallsbergs-Erik' as daily reminders of this. Other distinguishing marks of the typical elder shunter are that he has very short formal education and has worked in the railway company for decades.

The younger shunter may be a woman and/or a Stockholmer. S/he generally has somewhat longer education and finds the thought of staying in the yard for decades unlikely, unthinkable or even frightening. At the time when the eldest shunters were employed, the job was highly respected, not because shunting had high status, but because one was a State employee. 'The cake of the State is small but secure', is an old Swedish saying that senior shunters often repeat when they talk about their joining the company, often adding that this no longer seems to be true. 'Now the cake is merely small', they say with a sardonic smile.

Today, the transformation from an inexperienced 'student', often thinking of himself as being employed in the short term, to an experienced 'old head' happens by accident rather than design. Days turn into months, months into years and one day it seems odd to consider any other job. The shunter finds that he somehow 'got stuck' in the yard. The outdoor life, the 'freedom', the odd hours and the possibility to get a week off whenever one feels like it by trading a couple of shifts with the mates, or to take on a few shifts when surplus money is needed, has become something of a lifestyle. Office work, factory work, and all 'regular jobs' just seem to demand submission to clocks, to bosses and to a dull, predictable everyday routine which, from a yard point of view, resembles a prison. The shunters are trapped in the freedom of the job and have, somewhere along the line, become creations and creators of the world which centres around the yard, and which has been generated and kept alive by countless numbers of shunters before them. The lonely young men from the countryside have ended up as Stockholmers, but they have also become members of a group of self-proclaimed outsiders and individualists, who, to a man, endorse the values and embrace the ethos of the yard. The contradictions between freedom and commitment, between individualism and solidarity constitute perhaps the most basic paradoxes of the shunting world, paradoxes which all beginners have to learn to understand and cope with if they want to make this world their own.

The Anthropologist and the Yard

I came to the yard in 1982 not as a fieldworker, but as a person desperate for a job. I had been away from Scandinavia for five years and felt rather alien – a feeling enhanced by the fact that I had no income and no apartment. My husband and I lived on the dole, subtenanting rooms and flats and applying for every possible – and impossible – job in Stockholm. My husband finally got a job as a ticket-clerk in the underground, while I was getting more and more desperate and disillusioned. As I had graduated from the university, I would perhaps not have been considered for the shunting job either, but female applicants were explicitly welcome. I had underlined the words 'permanent job' in my application and this was what caught the employment officer's eye. (At least he commented approvingly, but somewhat surprised, on the phrase when I was called to his office.)

The need for a job can be assumed to be a common denominator for all beginners. However, the fact that it was October and that I possessed no winter clothes and was down to my last pair of shoes probably put me in a position a bit different from those who had just finished school, and who were living with their parents and wanted to make some money before doing their military service or going on to some further education. I further combined several significant minority properties of the shunting group. I was female, Finnish (there was one Finn, one Dane, one Norwegian and later one second generation Greek), I had higher education and an urban middle-class background, and I was older than the other beginners, a combination which made me stand out somewhat and caused some speculation. Rumour had it that my ticket-collecting husband was a professor (which he indeed is today) and that I was writing a book about the shunters (sic!).[8]

Positioned in this way I was definitely different from the 'normal' shunter – if ever there was one – but one aspect united me and the shunters as opposed to any participant observer who comes to do fieldwork for a predetermined period of time. My stay was openended and, lacking any other means of earning an income, I knew that I simply had to learn the job and survive the 'tough crew' I had been warned about, no matter what.[9]

---

[8] This was indeed a novel idea when it was presented to me as a question by one of the shunters. At that point my efforts to learn the job still exhausted me physically and mentally, and my only thought was to cling to this only chance I had to stay off the dole.
[9] I sometimes get the question whether I would have seen things differently had I been a man. I admit that I have not discussed 'gendered participation' or the consequences of being a female ethnographer with mainly male informants. This is a subject worth a treatise on its own. Until then I can only answer the question with a 'yes', while still refusing to see either male or

At a conference in Berlin on 'Taste, Strategies and the Logic of Practice' Pierre Bourdieu emphasized the need to distinguish between two modes of understanding, or two kinds of dispositions, represented by practice and 'the scholastic view' respectively. The latter, the scholastic point of view, is nurtured by the social conditions of academic life, which make possible, and indeed demand, a context-free outlook, a contemplation outside the bounds of practice. There is a given "...distance from the world and from the urgency of necessity."[10]

The scholar, then, is aiming at an understanding which constitutes a goal in itself. He takes a non practical view, not by removing himself, but by being removed in the first place from that practical urgency of the agents. Bourdieu takes as an example the notion of marriage rules, where the anthropologist tends to think of marriages in terms of kinship, while in practice a whole range of considerations – such as differences in material as well as symbolic wealth, differences in age, former economic and political relations concerning the partners – not only may have, but are bound to have guided the marriage strategies. The logic of practice evolves from the necessities of life, the practical interests and stakes, in kind removed from theoretical reflection, but sometimes even opposed to it. This is revealed when the model of the scholar mistakenly is seen as the prime mover of the agents themselves and the scholar reads actual marriages as somehow caused by the marriage 'rule'.[11]

Returning to the question of my relation to the shunters or, to use another collective term, 'the yard', my initial position was indeed one of practice rather than theoretical reflection. I did take notes, but this was more of a vocational tick than an ambition to conduct a study. My existential circumstances did effectively thrust me into the practical logic of things. I was not there in order to construct models, but to learn how to go about the social as well as professional life.

It is true that 'participant observation' always aims at a practical understanding, and it may seem preposterous to maintain that my two years at the yard in some qualitative way differed from the culture shock of ordinary fieldwork. After all, some shunters seem to have foreseen my eventual retreat back to the world of scholars and they indeed predicted my future with stunning accuracy and detail. In this respect they, ironically enough, took a

---

female views as isomorphic. (For a neat overview of some of the problems that have been discussed concerning gendered participation, cf. BACK, *passim*. and MOORE, H. 186 ff.)

[10] BOURDIEU, 1990b, 381.

[11] Cf. ib, 380 ff.

more scholarly point of view on the matter than I who, muddled by practice, was unable to see my own situation from a disinterested point of view. I was simply overwhelmed by the uncertainty of my situation. I was there to work and my field of vision was too limited to allow the academic world to appear at the horizon.

It is, however, exactly this uncertainty – and the 'urgency of necessity' to handle this uncertainty successfully – which came to imbue my approach to learning the job as well as getting by socially. I was not there just in order to learn: I had to learn to survive. As a result I let myself get absorbed in a way I cannot imagine I would have done, had I conceived of my presence as limited in time.

In 1988 I came back to the yard to prepare for fieldwork, which I conducted during 1989-91. During this time I made 22 longer, loosely structured interviews with shunters (and former shunters) and worked a few shifts in order to study the effects of the reorganization. But most of all: I listened, and talked, and listened – and played cards. If earlier I participated, I now observed.

My attempt in this treatise is, however, not to leave the logic of practice and see the yard exclusively from a scholarly point of view. I have tried to include the practical logic in my model-making and see strategies rather than rules, uncertainty rather than closed schemes, openendedness rather than closure. The reader will perhaps be disturbed by the paradoxes and contradictions that unfold in these pages, but they stem from the strategies of living, which unfold along the path of living-in-the-world, and are never intended to make neat models or maps for the scholarly gaze.

Above: Interior of the New Hall seen from engine cab.
Below: Train-puller on the engine side.

3. SHUNTING –
THE ORGANIZATION OF WORK

The Team

Team-work is a prerequisite for shunting, but the composition of the team may vary. It is often stated as an undisputed fact that a team, according to regulations, cannot be ordered to work with fewer than three members, but there is actually no such legislation in force. The management has, however, informally accepted that the shunters today refuse to go out into the yard if only two members of the team turn up.

It may be noted that as late as 1967 one of the engines was permanently manned by only two shunters according to the work schedule. It is also known that shunters at small stations often work in couples, but it is considered that the 'special circumstances' at Hagalund would make work in such small teams dangerous. In spite of this common definition that a 'full team' should consist of at least three shunters, the shunters may, in fact, work in reduced teams when the situation calls for it, e.g. late at night if the rest of the team has retired for the day and there is a last minute repair. Such incidents are surrounded by some secrecy as well as bragging, thereby stressing their irregular nature. The implicit message is that such exceptions by no means must be seen as precedents.

A team with three members is thus considered to be a 'full team' and it consists of a *växelledare* (shunt leader, Am.: engine foreman/ yard conductor), a *skjutspassare* (Am.: fieldman) and a *avhängare* or *avkopplare* (coupler, Am.: pin-puller[1]). An alternative nomenclature is *A-*, *B-* and *C-turen* (A-, B-, and C-member), respectively. Additional members will work as extra B-members, sharing the tasks informally between them.

The C-member is sometimes, very occasionally, teasingly called *koppelpojke* (coupling-boy), which is an elderly term that sounds corny and derogatory today – not only when applied to women.

---

[1] Frederick Gamst, personal communication. The American term 'pin-puller' seems odd in a Swedish context, as the coupling here consists of a hook and a link, like a clasp and eye. Thus, there is no 'pin' to be 'pulled'. For Am. terminology cf. 'Glossary' in GAMST, 1980, 137 ff.

23

'Shunt leader' is, on the other hand, a term that often is paraphrased as 'the one who is shunting'. This may be seen as a term that is easier to handle ('Who's shunting today?' as opposed to 'Who's the shunt leader today?'), but one can suspect that there also is a reluctance constantly to use the word 'leader'. Paradoxically enough the replacing term stresses, rather than suppresses, the leader aspect as it identifies the whole team with the shunt leader, eg.: '**He** is shunting Engine 2', instead of '**He leads** the team that is shunting Engine 2'. As we shall see the shunt leader is in many ways thought to personify his team. He influences and moulds it by his work-style and, when he speaks, it is often, although not always, assumed that his steady team members will hold similar opinions. The identification of the leader with the team is therefore widely acknowledged.

A work schedule based on a team-shift principle, i.e. shunters working in permanent teams, was not introduced until 1946. According to the minutes from the union club meeting, this reform had been discussed at least two years earlier as a means to achieve *'bättre ordning'*, 'a better order'[2], but it had been rejected as it was considered to be incompatible with the night-shifts. In 1946, when permanent teams were finally introduced, objections were still many. The minutes from the annual meeting lists several of them in detail:

"A lively debate followed and the contributions were many both for and against the proposal, for instance signalman A[...] uttered that at team-shifts it easily can be the attitude 'that one of the teams does so and so much' and the other one only 'so and so[much]'. N[...] continued the critique with what he himself had heard others say about 'I don't want that one and that one in my team etc.' Furthermore H[...] remarked upon the complaints to the stationmaster concerning the staff, that this is highly condemnable and creates feelings of dissatisfaction and uncomfortableness."[3]

According to the protocol the new order was 'nevertheless' accepted with eight votes against five and despite all the misgivings the new teams seem to have caught on rather quickly. One shunter describes the time of the fixed teams as something of a 'golden age', at least in retrospect, when telling of his entry to the shunting yard in the early 1950s:

"I was, in fact, so fortunate that I did not have to work [lit: 'go'] so long

---

[2] The expression is ambiguous and could also mean 'more orderly'.

[3] *"En livlig debatt följde och inläggen voro många både för och emot förslaget, bl.a. yttrade stk A[...] att vid lagturer lätt kan bli den inställningen 'att det ena laget gör så och så mycket', och det andra bara 'så och så'. N[...] fortsatte kritiken med vad han själv hört andra sägas om 'att den och den vill jag inte ha i mitt lag etc'. Vidare påtalade H[...] klagandet till stins ang. personalen, att detta är i hög grad förkastligt och skapar olust och misstämning."* Minutes from the local union club. (The titles of the railway staff are now obsolete and the translation of them somewhat uncertain.)

before I entered and was taken care of by a shunt team, which... well, the yardmaster, he became my father of sorts. Because it was like this, that we were five men and he who then was the foreman, he was around 50-55, and he who was shunting he was ten years younger [---] they stood, like, apart. Well, then there were those who tended to the kicks, two of them, they were a bit younger, and then the youngest was the coupler. [...] You were often at the home... invited to he who was foreman, at his birthdays, [...] the whole team. So, it was quite unbelievable, what a [...] social companionship. [...] Well, you could ask him [the foreman] about anything and he helped you and so on. So they really took care of you."[4]

The teams mentioned above seem to have included a *(lag)bas* (boss, yardmaster, foreman) as well as two B-members. Although there always has been a *bas* responsible for the cooperation of the shunting and related tasks in the yard, the *basar* (plural of *bas*, bosses) have not always been attached to specific teams, but have had a work schedule of their own. According to the informant above and comments in the union protocol this early spell of steady teams then included a *bas* who not only was seen as responsible for the order in the team, but who even might extend his fatherly duties outside the realm of the shunting yard.

In spite of its seeming success, the spell with large, steady teams did not last very long. While in 1956 it was stressed by the union that the *bas* should be responsible for the order of his team, there were already two years later complaints about the increasing responsibility falling on the shunt leaders, due to the fact that the *basar*, who were decreased in number, could no longer accompany the teams to the same extent as earlier. When a period of staff shortage followed in the 1960s the teams were reduced in number permanently.

In 1989 the three-member team was already a long tradition and, to the younger shunters, something that had 'always' been the case. It is against this background we have to see the belief that a team which did not have a leader, a *skjutspassare* and an *avhängare* was defective and somehow 'against the rules'.

~~~

---

[4] *Jag hade den turen, faktiskt, att jag behövde inte gå så länge förrän jag kom in och blev ju omhändertagen av ett växellag, som... ja, basen, det blev ju min pappa på nå´t vis.*
För det var ju så här att vi var fem man och då var han som då var arbetsledare, han var runt 50-55, och sen den som växlade han var tio år yngre [---] dom stod som i särklass. Ja, sen var det dom som passade skjuts, två stycken, dom var ju då lite yngre och så yngst var då avkopplare. [...]Man var ju mycket hemma hos... hembjuden till den som var bas när han hade födelsedagar, [...] hela växellaget. Så, det var ju otrolig, en så´n här [...] social samvaro. [---] Ja, man kunde fråga han [basen] om vad som helst och han hjälpte en och så där. Så dom tog verkligt hand om en." (From taped interview with senior shunter. INT 12)

Today the organization of the teams is back where it started in 1946. There are now, just as then, large teams, which include a *bas*, or *trafikmästare*, as well as two B-members, in addition to the shunt leader and the *avhängare*. In 1946 there were strong arguments against such steady teams on the grounds that comparisons of skills and personal favouritism would poison the ambiance.

Despite the strict hierarchy there was thus an egalitarian ethos, even if it primarily concerned persons on the same rung of the ladder. Vertically, the hierarchical ladder was held together by a paternalistic glue, a fact to which the quotation above bears witness. Senior shunters all refer to the extraordinary *sammanhållning* (approx.:sense of unity) of the old days. They tell of what a comfort this was to them as they in most cases felt very lonely in the capital, having left their families and friends behind in small villages or towns, often hundreds of miles away.

We must assume that there is a fair amount of glorification of the past, as some stories also tell of frightening yardmasters, 'whose words were law in the yard'. While the old shunters nevertheless stress that they could approach the *bas* with all kinds of personal problems, such intimacy, I dare say, is the exception rather than the rule today.

We must then conclude that while the organization of the teams in steady units very well may promote social relations between team members, it does not determine whether these relations prevail only in the context of work or whether they stretch out into the private lives of the team-members. It must be kept in mind that our stage, the shunting yard, is set against a much wider backdrop, which, however, will remain blurred when studied through our very closely focused lense.

The Tasks of the Team Members

The shunt leader

While the terms 'A-, B-, and C-member' signify the positions the different shunters have in the team hierarchy, the terms 'shunt leader', *'skjutspassare'* and *'avhängare'/ 'avkopplare'* are descriptive of their respective tasks, or rather, the terms describe the tasks that are considered to be the most significant ones for each team-member.

The shunting instructions, SJF 010.3 (vxi), define the duties of the shunt leader as follows:

"Shunt leaders shall ascertain that the trains are assembled according to regulations stated in SÄO § 40-43, in transport- and assembly plans etc. and additionally that traction contrivances are coupled correctly. He is in command during shunting and shall give necessary work instructions to other staff in the shunt team, [...]"[5]

The shunt leader is thus officially the leader of the team and the one who plans the work, on the basis of the work order of the day. His responsibility is to administer the tasks to the members of the team. The shunt leader might give his orders verbally, directly as commands, but just as often the communication is of an indirect or implicit kind.

Before going out into the yard the work orders are discussed and the leader, pointing at his papers, might e.g. say: 'They said that these coaches were urgent, so we should go up there first, but we could take this one along at the same time and then go directly over here.' This is a suggestion as well as an indirect order, as the other team members can accept it in silence, or argue for a solution they find preferable. By listening to comments that the shunt leader utters, seemingly to himself, while making notes on the sheets of the work orders, the different team members are able to figure out the required moves and plan their work accordingly. When finished, and when the proper trains have arrived or daylight is starting to show – or when everybody has finished his coffee – the shunt leader will turn to the B-member and e.g. ask him to disconnect the heating on 27 (i.e. track 27), and say: *'Lägger du 27'?* ('Will you line, i.e. turn the switches to, 27?') and then turn to the C-member and say: 'Could you fetch the engine and come to 27?.' This is the signal to break up from the coffee-room and to go out and start work.

At this point only odd and irregular jobs have been discussed, in addition perhaps to the first couple of tasks of the day. The rest of the work will be planned underway as information about possible changes of tracks and of the compositions of incoming trains – 'the raw material' – reach the boss and the shunt leader.

Once out in the yard the main task of the shunt leader is to initiate the signals to the engine driver and thereby also to take the responsibility for the movements. In everyday shunting at Hagalund you will find that the shunt leader is expected to be identical to the *signalgivare* (signaller). There are constant exceptions to this rule, but in these cases the tasks are often simple – such as fetching a loose coach on a sidetrack – or they are institutionalized parts of the tasks of the other team members, such as watching the rear of a train when backing into the Hall, and therefore they are not thought of in

---

[5] *"Växlingsledare skall se till att tåg sätts samman enl föreskrifterna i säo § 40-43, transport- och sammansättningsplaner etc samt att draginrättningarna är riktigt kopplade. Han har befälet vid växling och skall ge övrig personal i växlingslaget behövliga anvisningar för arbetet, [...]"* SJF 010.3. Säo (or SÄO as I will call it) stands for *'Säkerhetsordning'*, i.e. security regulations, the 'Rule Book'.

terms of a temporary take-over of the responsibilities of the *signalgivare*. Teachers of the SÄO-course are familiar with the tendency to conflate the two roles into one and they often ask the pupils during the annual repetition of the security regulations: 'Who is the *signalgivare?*', knowing that someone invariably will give the incorrect answer: 'The shunt leader.' The correct answer is, however, that anyone initiating a signal is a *signalgivare,* while the over-all responsibility lies with the shunt leader. The two tasks are not identical.

All important moves (eg. dangerous or non-routine moves) are then usually initiated by the shunt leader, but he has the right to delegate his tasks to whomever he sees fit. Evaluating the skills of the junior members of his team therefore becomes crucial in his decision to let them take over and act as *signalgivare.*

Before the engine driver is given the commands, by hand or lantern signals or lanterns, the shunt leader has first to ensure that no one *'är emellan'* (is standing between the coaches) when the train starts moving, secondly that someone is assigned the task to repeat signals and thirdly that someone is in the position to keep a watchful eye ahead to see that *'det ligger'* (the points are lined, i.e. that they are correctly positioned) and that the tracks are clear.

It is important to remember that shunting is done at all hours, all round the year, as this means that daylight and good visibility does not always prevail. The winters are long and dark and during that period not a single shift can be worked without signal lanterns.[6] During the dark hours every member in the team is obliged to carry a constantly lit *'palt'*, as the lanterns are called. They are operated with one hand, indeed one thumb, but they are still cumbersome and put aside as soon as conditions permit. The lanterns, as all other equipment, are not individual property, and they stand in a battery rack for loading when not in use. When the team goes out every member grabs a lantern that seems to be working fine, checking the strength of the light and the ease with which the red and green switches can be operated, knowing that his own safety and that of his team mates might depend on it. Due to the long distances between the shunt leader and B-turen the flickering light of a lantern down a distant track is often all the shunt leader can see of his B-member. When going between the buffers to connect the shunter always places the lantern on the coach-step next to him with the light shining in the direction of the engine driver to whom the steady non-swinging light signifies that

---

[6] On the Stockholm horizon the sun rises 8.41 and sets 14.44 on December 15th. The summers are on the other hand light and equivalent figures for June 15th are 3.34 and 22.02.

28

someone is still between the carriages.[7]

Constant vigilance is expected to be the hallmark of the shunt leader, but the various leaders feel and act very differently vis-à-vis this responsibility. The greatest burden lies on the shoulders of an inexperienced leader who has inexperienced members in his team, perhaps even a trainee, and an inexperienced driver on the footplate. Feelings are tense, advice and complaints abound, despair and exhaustion are round the corner.

The opposite would be an experienced shunt leader with a team that has been going steady for years, and a driver who has been at the footplate at Hagalund for an equally long period of time and knows the yard and the shunting like the back of his hand. In such a case the tasks of the shunt leader are, of course, formally unchanged, but in practice the feeling is much more relaxed. The members can judge what to do by themselves as well as they can rely on each other to act appropriately. The stage of advice, correction and criticism is long since passed. The shunt leader is not an expert who has to direct and delegate tasks, but rather a member of a team where tasks and duties could be cut in any one way. Responsibility is then a comparatively light burden to carry. Such a division of responsibility and tasks is indeed exactly the ideal which the new team organization presupposes as well as aspires to achieve.

The B-member

The functions of the other members of the team vary depending on whether the shunt leader is willing and inclined to (or indeed feels relaxed and safe to) delegate tasks to his juniors, as well as on whether the juniors show that they are apt and predisposed to take on such tasks. The B-member, can in many cases work more or less as a co-leader. One such experienced B-member was jokingly, but quite appropriately, called 'my right hand' by the shunt leader of his team. Alternatively he can be all but a beginner who often has not the faintest idea of what is going to happen next. The old hand works independently and will take initiatives of his own.[8] By looking at the composition of the train he will know how the shunt leader is likely to cut the train, and he may then conduct the coaches to tracks of his own choice, being prepared to stop the coaches regardless of how hard they are pushed ('kicked') by the shunting engine. It is said that a shunt leader should be able

---

[7] A steady lantern light means just the opposite in the US where it signifies 'safe to move'. Cf. NIEMANN, 44.

[8] In American railroad-argot 'beginner', or 'student', contrasts to 'old head' (a senior), but also to 'car hand' or 'rail' (experienced or skilled persons). Cf. GAMST, 1989, 70 ff and 1980, 137 ff.

to kick the coaches as hard as he likes – 'that's what we have B-members for'.

The alternative denotation for B-member is *skjutspassare* (litt:'push attendant'). The most important task of this member is to stop the coaches when they are kicked and shunted into various tracks (*'passa skjuts'*, litt: 'attend to pushes'), preventing them from crashing into coaches or cuts that already stand there, or, in case the track is empty, to run wild into uncertain destinies.

The coaches are stopped with heels, i.e. handbrakes, in Swedish *bromsskor* (litt: 'brake shoes').[9] The heels weigh several kgs and they are the most important tools of the B-member. By placing one or two of these on the tracks coaches are brought to a halt.

To know exactly where one quickly can find a heel is of paramount importance for the *skjutspassare*, as one never knows when the urgent need of a heel might arise. Planning his work the experienced B-member will pitch heels in strategic places all over 'his' part of the yard and in addition keep one heel handy at all times. Inexperienced B-members will all too often be caught empty-handed when a kicked coach suddenly approaches and have no choice but to helplessly watch it crash into other coaches ('make a hard joint') and possibly cause damage or a derailment.

Stopping coaches with the heels is not an uncomplicated task. Firstly one is to decide whether using a heel is called for at all. If the speed is considered moderate one prefers to 'go between' and connect the coaches at the very moment when the buffers clash, while if the speed is felt to be high one must brake the speed without pulling it to a halt. In this case the shunter has to make a correct estimation as to where to place the heel so that the coach will hit the heel, and, sliding on it, reach the cut of coaches it is to be connected to. The coaches should still clash with enough force to make coupling possible. If the coach does not reach the cut (i.e. when making a 'short joint') the engine has to back down the track and push the coaches together, which will be looked upon as an unnecessary move by the rest of the team. 'We had to back down on every track', is an excuse a team will present when blamed for finishing late. This is an implicit accusation towards the B-member, who might try to defend himself by blaming the shunt leader for shoving too softly, making the coaches stop half-way. Knowledge of the persons involved will decide for the audience which one of the two they should side with.

---

[9] Not to be confused with the English 'brake shoe', which is the part of the brakes which seizes the wheels. If frozen, stuck or applied too hard, the wheels may stop completely, creating great friction between the wheel and the rail. This gives quickly rise to 'flat spots' (*hjulplattor*)on the wheels, causing the train to 'walk' and hit the tracks as a hammer. Cf. GAMST, 1980, 39. The risk is that that the rail cracks and/or the train derails.

Opinions may be divided.

Estimating the braking distance for the kicked coach, as well as for the shoving engine, one has to consider several variables, such as weight, inclination, slope and weather conditions, such as moisture, snow and temperature. This is not done by mathematical calculation, but is learnt by experience. The skill so developed is tacit and is described as having the 'right feeling' for it.[10]

In addition to stopping kicked coaches and taking part in the manœuvring of the points, the B-member is responsible for connecting the heating systems of cuts and coaches to electric posts (*värmeposter*) at the end of the tracks. The posts carry a current of 1 000 volts and if live cables are pulled apart, or cut by the wheels of a train, the resulting short circuit causes a forceful electric arc and possible injury to persons or damage to material in the immediate vicinity.

If, on the other hand, the coaches are left unconnected there is a danger in wintertime that the watersystem freezes and cracks the tanks. When temperatures sink below −20° C the tanks might freeze in ten to fifteen minutes. The temperature might also drop quickly, particularly during evening shifts in the spring, and this irregularity makes it easy to forget to connect the heating – or to check that the heating is disconnected when a cut of coaches is pulled away. The sound of a torn cable is, however, such that cables rarely are forgotten twice during the same shift.

The B-member performs a variety of other tasks, too, which are not difficult in themselves, but which require that he can work one step ahead of the shunting, and to discern the status of the coaches to be coupled. He is to disconnect coaches in advance to make them *'färdiga att dra'*, ready to be pulled and shunted, and connect coaches that have been shunted down to a track and will be *'dragna för gott'*[11], connected for good, and thereby ready to go in a train. They also watch the crossings and operate the gates when backing into the Hall and close doors and windows before passing the train through the train wash.

~~~

While stopping kicked coaches is one of the most difficult, and above all one of the most dangerous tasks, many of the other tasks of the B-member are on the contrary rather trivial and can in principle be performed by a beginner. The

---

[10] We will return to the discussion of such tacit skills in Chapter 7.

[11] The word *dragna* (from the verb *dra*) here refers to the couplings, meaning that they are tight and well drawn, as opposed to *dra* in the expression *färdiga att dra*, which refers to the coaches and means literally 'ready to pull/ be pulled'. The ambiguity of the terms is another possible source of confusion for beginners.

difference between an experienced B-member and a new hand is, however, considerable. While the former can take over a large part of the work of the shunt leader, the latter can be more of a burden than an aid as he will need continuous instructions and his doings constant supervision. The skills of the B-member consist first and foremost of being able to read the process of work, to know what should be done and how the shunt leader is likely to proceed, in order to be prepared and ready to handle the tasks and to move to the right spot and turn up at the right moment – preferably also equipped with a brake heel. These skills presuppose a thorough knowledge of the work of the shunt leader, a knowledge which is tacit as well as often also passive. To know what a shunt leader should and is likely to do is not the same as being able to do it oneself. This fact comes as a painful revelation to many a B-member when the time comes to lead a shunt themselves.

The C-member

C-turen, the C-member, is also called *avhängare* ('unhooker') or *avkopplare* ('uncoupler') or, in rare cases as mentioned above, *koppelpojke* ('coupling-boy'). These terms sum up the position of the C-member in a nutshell. Despite, or because of, being the junior member of the team he is performing the bulk of the most arduous tasks; coupling and uncoupling cariiages.

It is true that the C-member for the most part works with couplings that have already been loosened and prepared for shunting. When finishing a train he can also leave the couplings halfdrawn, trusting that one of the B-members will finish the job when the train finally is brought down to a straight part of the tracks. It is, however, the constant jumping on and off the engine and the large number of couplings he has to perform in a shift that makes the job onerous and toilsome. The reason he may leave some of his tasks to be performed by his seniors is first and foremost that they are time-consuming. The team cannot be left at a standstill while the C-member is fighting with rusty or frozen couplings or with the impossible task of coupling coaches in a bend.

The saying goes that 'the place of the coupling-boy is on the engine' but the art of the C-member is to correctly combine and time jumping on and off the engine, keeping a sharp lookout forward, repeating signals and dashing in and out between the coaches to connect and disconnect.[12] The constant

---

[12] An old shunter claimed he had a long time ago counted the number of connections and disconnections he had performed during one shift making it more than two hundred. Today his sum seems exorbitant and unrealistic. Although I have not attempted to make any similar quantifications my guess would come up to a maximum of a hundred, of course amitting that I could be wrong.

movement, the heavy manual chores and the unremitting watchfulness gives the C-member little breathing space and time to rest while in the yard.

One of the rare occasions when the whole team may meet during work is when a train is finished and is backed down onto its track to be connected to the electric post. The B-member will be waiting at the post, cable in hand, and the C-member will jump off the rear coach when passing the post and the shunt leader, and sometimes the boss, will be there, too, in order to discuss or inform about the next task. These short encounters can be utilized for silent admonition of a co-shunter by letting him do the coupling. A C-member might just not make any sign of 'going between', but pointedly leave the task to a 'lazy' B-member, and vice versa. A boss or a shunt leader may go between, admitting he is aware that the shift indeed is a hard one, taking its toll primarily on the poor C-member. Or anyone may take on the task, just in order to be friendly and stress the team character of the work as opposed to keeping to a strict division of tasks. This little ritual may be accompanied by verbal comments, such as joking advice or critical comments. Although the task is a simple routine one, it has probably failed a few times only due to the fact that the shunter performing it feels uncomfortable in front of the critical audience.

As soon as the train is disconnected the engine will push off again, the C-member and the shunt leader standing on the foot plates, leaving the B-member(s) behind to vanish all but out of sight.

The C-member may often be within shouting distance of the shunt leader, but non-official handsignals showing one or several fingers in short sequences, such as 1,1,2,1, are nevertheless preferred as information or reminder of how many coaches the C-member should disconnect when the train stops. When the C-member is further off from the shunt leader he must repeat all signals to the driver and keep an eye on switches and obstacles on the tracks.

Being constantly on the move, and often working at a distance, the C-member has a legitimate reason to ask the leader 'what's up?' as he cannot be expected to find time to study the work order, known as *'lapparna'*, 'the slips'.[13] He will mostly keep his copy in his pocket. In rain or sleet when the sheets of paper become unreadable and threaten to dissolve completely or when some team-member simply has lost his copy they rely on the C-member for his slips, 'as you don't need them anyhow'.

There is indeed very little equipment available to the C-member. Apart from the signal lantern, the C-member may use a long metal bar,

---

[13] Am: 'switch list'. Cf. NIEMANN, 252.

koppelstång, used as a lever to uncouple the engine from the first coach. While adding to the safety, as it is operated while standing on the side of the tracks, it demands some technique on the part of the driver and the distrustful C-member might prefer to 'go between' anyway, especially in the cases where the rest of the team constitute an audience. Risk is preferred to a possible embarrassing failure.

~~~

The fact that the C-member is doing the heaviest work is suppressed. It is not legitimate to complain about fatigue during long and cold hours, so complaints will invariably reflect on the complainer, who is seen as lacking in technique, as making it unpleasant for everyone in the team ('we're all dead tired, but you have to take it with a sense of humour'), or as deeming himself unfit for the job. Endurance and perseverance are indispensable qualities for 'a shunter', and C-turen is only the first, 'easiest' step on the way. Only during particularly hectic shifts will the seniors silently admit that the lion's share of the labour falls on the C-member, and they may, especially when observed by the whole team, perform some simple task as a token of their empathy.

To be there, always visible for the driver, always at the right end of the cut, always ready to couple and uncouple any coach, always alert and prepared to tend to new orders, – the C-member is a true little boy scout, and the deletion of the word 'coupling-boy' from the vocabulary of Hagalund is just one more step to veil and deny this fact. Every shunter is 'free' and 'independent', and this includes naturally the C-member as well, doesn't it?

~~~

Summing up the organization of the shunting team proper, i.e. the three members who are considered essential and compulsory, we see that, formally, there is a strict division of tasks, which are considered functionally defined. One may be C-member one day and shunt leader the next, although, of course, for natural reasons the hierarchy tends to reflect seniority. One becomes a steady C-member no sooner than two years after enrolling, a B-member perhaps only several years later and a shunt leader after many years as a B-member. Earlier the advancement was still slower and it is said that as late as in the 1960s one could spend a decade as a C-member.

The view that tasks are functionally divided means that orders are seen as superfluous so that once everybody is informed about the next job they can, ideally, proceed with their tasks in silence, relying on everybody else to handle theirs. This division is based on a spatial distribution of the team which is indeed so effective that a conflict between team-members about who should perform a particular task seldom arises.

When such a situation actually occurs it lends itself to enhancing the significance of the assignment. Taking on a task 'belonging' to someone else will then convey a message to every spectator who has internalized the principle of the 'proper' allotment of tasks. An example of such a message is the silent acquiescence that the most arduous duties befall the C-member.

We have, however, also seen that depending on the skills and experience of the team-members, the strict division of tasks can be set aside to a high degree, and that the B-member may work as a co-leader. This co-leading is not officially recognized, but there may be a joking reference to the B-member as 'the right hand' of the shunt leader, or there may be comments like 'in this team nobody knows who is actually shunting'.

The standard way of talking thus enhances the importance of the shunt leader. He **is** the team, he **has** the engine, he **does** the shift, while the other members only 'are with him'.

The B-member's job is often seen as the most relaxed one in the team. It is said to be easy and not to entail any reponsibilities. The practice in the yard shows on the other hand that good B-members are crucial for the flow of work and it is the B-member who most often draws adverse comments and criticism. A B-member who misses a kick which causes a lot of damage will, no doubt, feel responsible and the shunt leader is most likely to ask him why he did not stop it. The statistics also show that this job is very dangerous.[14] This is, however, not recognized in everyday talk.

Finally, the task of the C-member is also underrated in everyday talk, and it is considered to be a completely mechanical duty requiring no knowledge, information or planning. The saying that 'the place of the coupling-boy is on the engine' is often thought to be an accurate description of all one needs to know to become a good C-member.

Nevertheless, as he is part of the shunting team, the free and independent qualities of shunting also rub off on the C-member, and the errand-boy – or coupling boy – character of the job is veiled and camouflaged.

At the Fringe of the Team

Bosses (tkm)

While the three-member team – the *växelledare*, the *skjutspassare* and the *avhängare* – work as an independent unit, planning their work and moving about much to their own (or at least the shunt leader's, liking) they are

---

[14] Tasks of the B-member recur among desciptions of fatal accidents. Cf, PERSSON, 12.

nevertheless dependent on many other workers.[15] Not counting the railway organization as a whole, or the different workshops in Hagalund that interfere in different ways with the shunting, the shunting team is working in close cooperation with at least two other important persons, the outdoor boss, *(lag)basen* or *trafikmästaren*, *tkm* for short (Am. terminology: 'yardmaster'[16]) and the *uppkopplare*, also called 'the knocker', *knackaren*.[17]

Before April 1989 these two were not considered part of the team proper as they worked their own shifts, which to a great extent were parallel in time to the shifts worked by the shunting teams, but which nevertheless were based on a different time-table or 'key', so that the constellation of persons was never the same from day to day. Bosses thus worked with all the different teams, until in 1989 they were made leaders of specific teams in the reformed work organization, as the bonus-system demanded that they reduce their number of shifts.

As we have seen above there is evidence of large teams with a similar composition during earlier periods, but it is rather futile to make any further comparisons between the large teams of the 1940s and the large teams of today, as it is impossible to reconstruct the tasks of the team members at that time in necessary detail.

Until 1989 the outdoor boss and the knocker thus worked independently of the teams, but still in close contact with them. We shall now continue to look at the state of affairs in this period immediately before the reorganization.

The yard is operationally divided into two main parts, the South and the North, each part having its own *trafikmästare,* or *tkm* for short (i.e. boss or yardmaster). The North is the operation area for Engines 1 and 4.[18] Engine 1 is worked by one team from 6.00 a.m. to 13.45, the second shift working this engine from 13.15 to 22.00 and the third one from 21.45 to 6.00. Engine 4 (also called 'the Hall engine', 'the wash engine' or 'the washing machine', as its main task is to pull the trains through the automatic train wash – often delivering them back to the Hall as the water on them could otherwise freeze in wintertime) is worked from 9.30 to 19.00. All these four teams have their own boss. Thus there are at times two teams and two bosses simultaneously,

---

[15] The 'freedom' of the shunters is, as we know by now, highly idealized. It is very much circumscribed by the tasks to be done – and the freedom of the C-member is very limited indeed.

[16] For terminology and descriptions of duties of railway staff in the US, cf. GAMST, 1978.

[17] Not to be confused with Am. 'car knocker', who is a "[c]arman who inspects and repairs cars". GAMST, 1980, 138. Note that *uppkopplare* is not the same as *avkopplare*.

[18] Engine 1, 2, 3 and 4 (distinguishing between morning, afternoon and night) are the names of shifts with a certain operational sphere. The actual machines as well as the crew vary. The shunt leader is said to 'have' Engine so-and-so, the others in the team are 'on' or 'with' it.

but the teams try to avoid getting in each others way as much as possible by working when the other team takes a break.

The South, including the Middle Yard (which we know is not in the middle but in the extreme South), is likewise attended to by two engines, Engine 2 and Engine 3. Engine 2 works only one shift, from 9.30 to 18.00, and so does Engine 3, between 6.30 and 12.30. Engine 3 is the only one to handle areas of the yard which are not electrified, and this engine is therefore not an ordinary small electric shunting engine but a diesel machine, usually a T26 model, but in some cases even an enormous T44.

The shift on Engine 3 always constitutes the first part of the so called *förmiddag-natt* (morning-night) shift combination. This means that after working from 6.30 to 12.30 one is free in the afternoon, but then resumes work on Engine 1 at 21.45, working till 6.00 next morning. As this same pattern holds for the bosses, the shunting team and the boss will work two successive shifts with each other on these occasions.

Although, theoretically, we have a rather even circulation of bosses among the teams there are instances where bosses are tied to particular teams. The first one is a regularity in the work schedule, the so called *fridagsnyckel* (lit. 'free-time key')'that distribute all employees in a number of groups, working different weekends. The *fridagsnyckel*, and the related *semesterlista* (holiday schedule), grouping employees in a similar way according to their holiday-weeks[19], have sometimes the effect that some shunters hardly meet for months, while others bump into each other daily for equally long periods. Due to this a boss will then work more often with some teams compared to other ones.

The second tie between bosses and teams stems from all the various irregularities that pop up in the work schedule due to sickness, holidays, paternal leave, leave of absence for studies, teaching or union commissions. In these cases the shunt leader is often called to stand in for the boss and the team members follow the ladder up one step, so that the B-member will do the shunting, the C-member the *skjutspassning,* and a new C-member will be recruited from the reserve list. Sometimes there is a move two steps up the ladder and the team will in one strike have a completely new composition, sometimes turning into a considerably more juvenile one. With the more experienced members absent, the atmosphere is tenser, perhaps, but it is also a time for the younger ones to demonstrate their competence and skill and to get used to their future tasks, under the auspices of the ordinary shunt leader, now

---

[19] There are four weeks of holiday, with a certain increase according to seniority. One week has to be scheduled 'off-season', i.e. not in June, July or August.

officiating as boss.

Without being an established member of the team, the boss is nevertheless intimately bound up with it in several ways. Through his portable radio the boss stands in contact with the *tkm* indoors as well as the *Ordercentralen* (the Order Centre) and the various repair shops – as well as with the other shunters on the fringe such as the knocker and the train-pullers. The boss, is in other words, responsible for the contacts between the shunting team and the immediate surroundings, keeping the team up to date with knowledge about delays, repairs, temporarily closed tracks, and trains which are being cleaned and must wait to be shunted, etc.

There are about one hundred different types of carriages, called *'littera'*, and this obviously creates difficulties in shunting. One has to find the right type of coach among the variety on reserve. One of the tasks of the boss is to find out the exact positions of the coaches along the tracks. Easily accessible coaches are naturally preferred by the shunting team, but these are for different reasons not always fit for use. The bed-making could be unfinished, or they could be reserved for a more important train, etc. In case no coach of the right *littera* is found, the boss has to know what *littera* can be used to replace it. It should, for example, have more seats or beds, rather than fewer, compared to the one it is to replace. The boss may therefore have to contact the indoor *tkm* or some foreman in the Hall to find out about the status of the coach. In this way he can plan ahead of the team and facilitate their work.

The big difference between the various bosses is in fact the degree to which they interfere in the planning and the work of the shunting team. Some bosses more or less disappear to tasks such as taking notes of the coaches on the reserve, helping the train-pullers operate the switches, or controlling the finished trains, appearing only occasionally from the darkness between the rows of carriages in order to offer the shunt leader some new piece of information. Other bosses insist on directing almost every move the shunt leader makes, either directly by telling him what to do next, or indirectly, by telling him that *'det ligger 22'* (the switches are lined for track 22), making the next move self-evident – or an already initiated move inevitable.

The circulation of bosses among the teams makes the team members familiar with the peculiarities of the different work styles. By looking at the day schedule, to see whom one is to work with, one will get a general impression about how things will be handled during that shift. It is no secret that some shunt leaders and bosses are particularly ill-suited to work together, both being unusually stubborn or particular about how the work should be done. They might, however, hold back their irritation as they know that the arrangement is only temporary and that they will have a more reasonable work mate the next day.

This is not to say that there are no outbreaks of temper, only that there is no legitimate channel for long term grudges. Sudden outbursts or angry remarks, forgiven and forgotten five minutes later, are seen to be typical of the general work-style in the yard. As soon as the team has a break all animosity should subside, and only jocular remarks – as well as good humoured responses to such teasing – should be used to describe and comment upon mistakes and close disasters in the yard. Acceptance of this easy-going style is seen as a prerequisite for staying long in the yard and the ambiance resulting from this conciliatory attitude is often cited as one of the main assets of the job.

It is then very much up to the boss to choose the degree of intimacy to the shunting team. The boss is in the last instance responsible for the work of the team under his supervision, but the weight of this responsibility, as felt by the boss, is of course dependent on the degree of skill that the boss ascribes to the team. If the boss has a team of freshmen at his hands he will be obliged to participate more vigilantly than when he is working with a team where maybe two of the members are experienced bosses themselves.

Not only is the constitution of each team different, but they are judged differently, too. A team that one boss feels he must keep a constant eye on is considered quite competent to manage on their own by another boss. The popular view is indeed that some bosses, regardless of the level of competence of the team, never relax in their duties, irritating the team by their constant interference, while others are impossible to get hold of even when they are needed.

At the end of the shift it is the duty of the boss to report *('lämna av')* to the indoor *tkm*. This is done orally and in a very informal way. The boss walks into the *tkm* office and sits down opposite the table and pulls out his, by now, rather tattered papers from his pocket. After an 'are you ready?' the outdoor boss runs through all the trains on the work order and comments whether they are completed, whether they have been left on a different track from the one suggested on the order, etc.

During the shift the outdoor boss has jotted down the necessary information on his papers, but failing that (due to lacunæ in his notes or finding that the weather conditions have made the figures difficult to decipher) he might be a bit uncertain as to the correct number of a coach or a track. This seldom causes irritation with the indoor boss today, but the shunters tell of earlier times when a now retired *tkm* would show much concern if the

39

reporting boss faltered and sounded uncertain. He would either send out the boss again to check the numbers properly or try to extract the necessary information from the knocker or the coach recorder. Even after obtaining all the information, he would finally bicycle down to the track himself to double check.

Despite the more lax attitude today, there is still – and this is true for the whole shunting group – a remarkable difference between the evaluation of mistakes made on a piece of paper and mistakes made during practical work. The former are quickly condemned and seen as signs of incompetence or stupidity, while the latter are met with smiles and jokes, only slowly adding to a judgment of a persons suitability and skills. A judgment which is also much more composite and holistic.

Something that always raise eyebrows, however, is when too many trains are incomplete or otherwise left unfinished, and have to be transferred to the work order of the next shift. This is never a popular thing with the team that has to take on the finishing hauls.

As team time-tables overlap, the boss, especially when the team has not been able to finish in time, is likely to find the on-going shift waiting for their slips when he has reported and retires to the coffee-room for a last cup before changing and going home.[20] When breaking the news that his team was not able to complete the trains on the slips he is likely to be met by shouts of protest: 'What, haven't you done train X?! What about train Y, then?' adding: '**We** had time to finish those trains yesterday', etc. This is said jokingly as everyone knows that only one delay in arrivals will cause a chain reaction and consequently make it impossible to complete all the trains on the slips. Even though this is common knowledge it is somewhat embarrassing to have to leave work unfinished, especially if this happens repeatedly with the same team.

When a team gets a reputation for not finishing their trains, or always being 'late' – which in most cases only means that they work until the stipulated end of the shift – the tone of mockery gets more serious. The boss will defend himself and the team more eagerly than only with a smile and, possibly, point out the delays of the day or earlier shortcomings in the work of the complaining team, or he may renounce his responsibility and blame the team – and thereby the shunt leader. After all it is not **his** team.

The responsibility for the work of the team lies formally with the boss, but we know that informally the shunt leader is just as likely to get the

---

[20] I have chosen to translate *'kafferummet'* as 'the coffee-room'. The American term would perhaps be 'shanty' .

blame, or the credit, for the results of the team. When the team has finished unusually early and doubts are aired about whether they have been 'cheating' (a way of reluctantly admitting that the team has worked fast) the shunt leader, as well as the boss, may say: 'But then we had such an excellent shunt leader/ boss in the team!' This is said jokingly, but as a joke it radically differs from the joke the C-member, echoing this phrase, might produce by saying: 'But then we had such an excellent C-member in the team!' – a pure joke, indeed!

It is thus informally acknowledged that the boss and the shunt leader are both responsible for the efficiency and the results of the team. As the actual distribution of tasks between them might differ to a great extent, the important thing is they should be able to cooperate in a smooth manner, sharing many of the tasks between them.

In case of trouble, individual workers might hold one or the other as the main cause of it all, but as it invariably can be pointed out that the particular person has had no problems when cooperating with **another** shunt leader, or **another** boss, such criticism tends to beat the air. One could then say that the boss (or the cooperation between boss and shunt leader) is more likely to be blamed for occasional shift delays, while repeated delays are likely to be blamed on the shunt leader.

Seeing the importance of the boss, it might be strange to find him under the heading 'at the fringe of the team'. The reason I believe that this is a proper title, however, is that when the team is working perfectly, the boss need not be around or even be informed about the moves until it is time for him to report. Within the team there can be no such detachment of coordination. A B-member may be at a loss, not knowing what is going on, but in this case he has no other tasks to fulfill. He is simply useless until he is informed. The boss, on the other hand, can, and often will, leave a functioning team in order to help and supervise knockers, train-pullers and coach recorders, to check equipment and the functioning of switches, the train wash, etc., or to work ahead and pave the way for later teams.

The overall responsibility of the boss concerns the results of the job in the yard, which includes shunting, but also train-pulling and other tasks, while the actual movements of the team is a responsibility falling on the shunt leader. When trains leave Hagalund with undrawn couplings the boss in question will be noticed, but he will turn to the shunt leader or a B-member and ask why they did not connect for good in train 92? The lack of penalties means that the formal responsibility has little bearing within the shunting community. The team will know 'who-dun-it', and there may be some joking remarks about it when they go out the next time: 'Don't forget to connect for

41

good!'

The boss is then responsible for trains leaving Hagalund, while the shunt leader can be said to breathe calmly as soon as the shift is over and there are no injuries or damages. One boss complained over the vagueness of the extended responsibility and told of an instance when another station had ordered a certain coach to be sent in a particular train. The boss found that the particular coach was not allowed to move at the speed of the train in question and called the Central Station (Cst) to inform them that he would send the coach in a later train. Regardless of this, he was told to send it down to Cst in the next train where 'it would be taken care of '. The boss said he directly suspected that the Cst would let the coach go in the fast train anyhow, so he checked the train picture later on the computer only to find his suspicions to be true. He felt he had been duped and said that he felt very uneasy as he guessed the blame would be laid at his door in case of an accident. 'This is what I hate about this job', he said, 'you don't know where your responsibility ends. You are likely to be blamed for things you haven't caused.'

Another shunter agreed and added: 'There are lots of people along the line who interfere with the coaches, but if anything happens they will always blame Hagalund, because of our old reputation for 'working fast'. And it is of course the boss who is responsible!'

Knockers

The proper name of the 'knockers' is *uppkopplare*, but this name is rarely used, except in the day schedules, probably because it is easily confused with *avkopplare*, i.e. the C-member. 'Knocker' is in addition a handy term as other words and expressions easily can be derived from the stem. 'To knock', is to do the job of the knocker, and to 'go on the knock' *(gå på knacken)* means that one is working on the steady list as a knocker. One can also ask whether a train is 'ready- knocked' *(färdigknackat)* or complain that it, or part of it, is 'un-knocked' *(oknackat)*. It is a matter of course that knocking results in a 'hole'. To say that someone has knocked three holes in a train therefore does not mean that any damage is done, only that the train has been prepared for an easy uncoupling in three places.

In other words, 'to knock' is to prepare the coaches so that they easily can be handled by the shunting team. It consists of loosening the coupling so it easily can be disconnected, as well as disconnecting the brake hose and the electric cable between the coaches where a cut is to be done.

The iron bridges, which provide passage between coaches inside the train, are to be raised and secured, otherwise they would be a great hazard to a shunter unhooking the cut. Entering into the dark between the coaches he can hit his head right into the bridge above him, or in case the bridges are not secured properly they can fall on top of his head.

When the engine is disconnected from the train, air is trapped in the brake system, which means that every single coach is braked and cannot be moved and shunted until it is 'aired', i.e. until a rod that operates the air valve is pulled.[21] This is also done by the knocker.

These are then the main tasks of the knocker. They are normally not difficult to perform, but in the winter the trains can be completely covered in ice and snow – especially those arriving from the Northern parts of the country – and only experience tells the knocker where to start digging and hacking. Frozen couplings can be helped by setting fire to newspapers wrapped around them, but electric cables and brake hoses must simply be kicked and beaten until they let go. Temperatures are milder in Stockholm than in the North, which means that trains covered in snow and ice sometimes will start thawing. The metal heats up more quickly than the ice, and the ice vault which has been created between the coaches may loosen while a knocker is working beneath. Such incidents are dangerous at worst, and at best quite annoying.

All trains that are pulled into the heated Hall on arrival thaw even more quickly, and although the knocker may be fortunate enough to find the snow and ice already fallen into the pit below, all connections will still be wet. Water will be pouring from the roofs, and the bridges will be covered in wet ice sludge. The pits are too deep to enable the knocker to reach the couplings, and he is therefore sometimes bound to hang from the coach in the most unlikely positions to grapple with the connections 'like a bloody octopus'. When dressed for extreme winter conditions knocking a train in the Hall means that one gets soaked through, and to return outdoors is extremely unpleasant. The shunters see this as the biggest drawback of this job and they also consider it a health hazard.

The inconveniences in wintertime mean that the knocker can be rather pressed for time. The demand is naturally that the knocking should be finished when the shunting team appears to start its work with a particular train. Meeting with the team is thus rather an indication of failure on the part on the knocker, while working in solitude, ahead of the team, is the normal state of affairs.

---

[21] The American term for this is to 'bleed a car'. Cf. NIEMANN, 247.

One important item of equipment of the knocker is a bicycle, or more common a moped, to enable him to move quickly between all the tracks and along the length of the trains to 'bleed' them. When the air is let out, you hear the consecutive 'psch'-sounds from every coach down the track as the knocker proceeds. It is often easier to hear where the knocker is, or has been, than to spot him.

On his moped he might also have a blow-torch to melt ice on the couplings and a metal tube that fits the handle of the coupling and which, by lenghtening it and adding to the lever power, gives the knocker a chance to unscrew rusty or frozen couplings.

He naturally has a copy of the slips to be able to decide where he has to knock the holes, and he also has a time-table of arrivals in order to be on the spot as quickly as possible. As trains do not always arrive on time, or even to the correct track, the knocker relies on his radio, calling the train-pullers to ask them if they 'have anything under way'.

To a certain extent, the knocker can thus plan his work in order to avoid shuttling to and fro between tracks that are far apart, but as the threat of being caught up by the team is always present he cannot leave trains unknocked for any length of time.

Checking the coaches on arrival, the knocker will notice any coaches that do not belong to the plan. He can immediately notify the boss on the radio and the boss will forward the news to the shunt leader who can then plan the shunting accordingly.

Out in the yard the knocker's contacts with his workmates are almost exclusively over the radio and a knocker working without one, which is sometimes the case due to personal preferences, will find his interaction with the others limited to a 'hello' to the engine driver and the train-puller when meeting the arriving trains, and an exchange of news with the boss when bumping into him.

The knocker is thus often pressed for time and he is the only shunter who, on his own accord, will turn up early for his shift. One knocker even had the habit of starting two hours ahead of a particular shift in order to find time to perform his tasks. Such adjustments happened completely inofficially. When training with this knocker, I was only told that he intended to start 'a bit earlier' the next morning. I therefore turned up at 7 o'clock instead of at 7.30, but found to my dismay that he had already finished the morning trains and was unwrapping his 'lunch' packet. Obviously, the all-important thing was planning and flexibility, not sticking to the work schedule.

As the lonely forerunner of the team, the knocker takes the hardest blows from weather and the change of seasons. Entering the coffee-room, however, he will learn of all the mistakes he has done and be reminded of his invisible shadows, the shunting team. They must stop to knock if a hole is missing or connect for good if there are unnecessary holes, and they are happy to let him know of every such instance – 'jokingly', of course.

Train-pullers

Of all the strange names for different kinds of shunters, *tågdragare* ('train-puller') is perhaps the most peculiar.[22] A journalist, who once interviewed one of the train-pullers, allegedly asked him what exactly a train-puller did. The train-puller replied, dead earnest: 'It's a very heavy job. You take a rope and attach it to the train and then you tie it around your waist and **pull** the train.'

There is an alternative term for train-puller which presents a more accurate description of the work; *tåglots* ('train-pilot'). While a sea or air pilot would find it a natural thing to present himself as a pilot, the train-pilot, as well as the knocker and the shunt leader, would not dream of using the term outside the work context. It was once found that an extra hand, who worked only during holidays (he was an art student) had entered *'tåglots'* as his occupation in the telephone directory.[23] His workmates' discovery of this led to roars of laughter. It was seen as a good joke. A boss added to the merriment by saying that he always stated his profession as 'drudge' *(gnetare)*.

In the context of work the terms *tågdragare* or *tåglots* have no such air of ridicule about them. They are simply descriptive and useful, not least on the radio, where the pilots call on each other with: *'Tågdragaren, kom!'* ('Train-puller, come!'). Just like the team-members and the knockers, the train-pullers could be considered to constitute a profession of their own, as they have a work schedule of their own.

Going on the 'steady list' as a train-puller, one no longer works in shunting proper, nor as a knocker, and the only variation comes from the shifts alternating between 'the engine curve' and the 'train-puller side'. These two tasks are still distinguished in the work schedule, but at least during the 1980s the train-pullers have not made a clear division between the two, but cooperate as if they all worked the whole area. Earlier the engine train-puller would not leave the engine curve in order to pilot trains, and the train-puller would not pilot engines.

---

[22] The Am. equivalent seems to be 'herder'. Cf. NIEMANN, 250.
[23] Swedish telephone directories list occupation as a distinguishing mark, in addition to addresses.

There is, however, one informal division of tasks and this concerns the night shifts. According to the work schedule there is one shift in the engine curve from 21.15 to 6.00 and another one on the train-pulling side from 21.15 to 7.00. The tradition is that both train-pullers work during the intensive hours when the last evening trains arrive. When the last train is in terminus around midnight, one of the train-pullers leaves and the other one takes care of the goods-train, the 'single engines' that leave early in the morning in order to fetch trains at other stations in Stockholm, and, finally, the engines that are to go in the morning trains. He will then arrange for their departures, sometimes helped out during these busy hours by a friendly boss, until he is released by the morning shift.

The informal rule, that the person assigned the shift in the engine curve is to stay while the other train-puller can go home, is so strong that it would indeed be impossible for the one assigned the 'slip-off' shift to stay on all night.[24]

The train-pullers guide the traffic to and from Hagalund. Trains arrive by two routes that flank the 'vacuum station' where toilet tanks are emptied. The outer route allows the trains to continue up to a road crossing and the inner one leads, well before its junction with the departure route, to a stop signal. This signal has to be switched to 'F' (forward) by the train-puller and the driver has, in addition, to await the hand signal 'forward' from the train-puller before he can proceed. The train-puller then checks the train number with the driver, jumps onto the engine and lets the driver proceed slowly towards the appropriate track, jumping off to turn the proper points as they move along.

Until 1985, all points were of the oldfashioned kind – a lever with a red and yellow sphere – which had to be thrown over manually. These were replaced by electric switches that were easily operated by stepping on a large button placed on the ground, or placed on a pole to be pressed by hand. The new points naturally save a lot of work, but they are slower to operate and they do not allow for an easy reading of the position of the points from a distance. Instead of reading the colours of the tops of the globes from a long distance, e.g. red-yellow-red, thereby being able to judge that the route is lined up, i.e. that these particular points are in the correct position for departure, one now has to stand quite close to, and at the correct angle, to actually observe the position of the tongues or switch blades.

---

[24] An incident in the yard once led to the 'discovery' by the management that the pilot responsible had left early and he was reprimanded for this. Ironically this happened to the most conscientious train-puller by far. Group pressure was, however, so strong that he, despite the official warning and despite his own strong feelings of obligation, had no choice but to pack off when the last train had arrived.

When all points on the route are lined, the driver can speed up to his goal, the electric post, and the train-puller should enter the footplate rather than hang on the outside of the engine. Hanging on the outside is always dangerous, but if the engine hits something at high speed (for example a forgotten brake heel), the train-puller may fly off and land on the tracks in front of the engine.

Entering the footplate is not all that simple, as the driver's seat stands so close to the wall behind it that the train-puller easily rubs grease and dirt from the overall onto the engine driver and the fixtures. The considerate train-puller will therefore cross the tracks and enter on the 'rear' side where, on the other hand, the ladder is high and steep and where he is not visible for the driver before he opens the door at the top. New drivers sometimes misunderstand the situation and believe that they are given a 'clear' (a highball) to proceed on their own and do not wait for the, momentarily, invisible train-puller, but speed up leaving him to the task of running madly, trying to catch up and jump onto the high ladder.

On hot summer's days the cooling breeze on the front of the engine is most welcome and all warnings/regulations about the necessity to stand inside the cab happily neglected. Female train-pullers, lightly dressed in shorts and a T-shirt, but still wearing greasy gloves and steel-enforced shoes, sweep by as bizarre caricatures of figure-heads on the engine fronts, proudly crossing a sea of steel, gravel and dust.

The train-puller is always obliged to ask the driver to show him 'the key', i.e. a handle which, when removed from its fitting, indicates that the electricity between the engine and the train is disconnected. When the driver has shown the key - it is not sufficient to give a verbal answer - the train-puller proceeds to disconnect the cable. When the brake hose is disconnected and air is let out of the main line, braking the whole train, the driver will reverse the engine in order to compress the buffers and facilitate the uncoupling of the engine.

As soon as the coupling is unhooked the train-puller knocks with the metallic end of the brake hose on the plow of the engine. This is the informal sign to the driver that he may drive away a few yards to give the train-puller more room to finish his work, i.e. to connect the train to the electric cable from the post next to the tracks. In the Hall, the engine blocks the way for trucks and pedestrians and the train-puller is eager to make the interruption of the flow of traffic as short as possible. (Not all drivers understand the audio-sign and the train-puller is then compelled to go out to show a 'slowly forward' signal to the driver.)

47

In the Hall, the front part of the engine is outside the great doors and there is only a narrow passage between the side of the engine and the doorframe. Correct signals, using the whole length of the arms, would not be visible under these circumstances and thus the train-puller has often developed idiosyncratic versions of the 'slowly forward' sign, much to the confusion to new drivers who do not know what to expect.

A young driver from another station admitted he had been nervous to come to the capital and Hagalund, with all its 'peculiarities'. He said, however, that he had been able to understand everything except one strange signal the train-puller had given him in the Hall. When he described the signal to me as 'the wheel' I realized that he meant the 'slowly forward' signal, shown by an old train-puller. The driver's description of the signal was a rather accurate one, but not until I explained it to him did he see that it only meant 'slowly forward', deformed by the cramped conditions in the Hall.[25]

When the engine is detached and the train is connected to the electric post, the task of the train-puller is to guide the engine to the engine-depot. Planning his work well the train-puller will return the engine along a track where the next train is going to arrive. In this manner he will leave the points behind him in the correct position and the arriving train can proceed without interruptions. This planning is often upset by factors that are beyond the control of the train-puller, such as a shunting team passing by, neglecting to line behind, or trains not arriving in the expected order. Sometimes, and this is the most upsetting scenario for the train-puller, he will find that another train-puller, working simultaneously, plans things in another way, and, deaf to all co-planning, insists on using routes that cut across and destroy lined tracks.

On the return the engine will first have to proceed onto the lead in the North in order to reach an empty track. If the shunting team is working on the lead, they expect the train-puller to urge 'his' driver to back down into the track as quickly as possible, and line behind.

Before reaching the depot, the engine has to pass the 'bottle-neck' once more, and thereby interfere with the shunting team in the South as well. The 'bottle-neck' is also frequented by engines on their way to fetch their trains before their journey, and by departing as well as arriving trains. Passing this

---

[25] These are two of very few instances of 'home made' signals at Hagalund. Signalling as a whole is done rather shyly and reluctantly, especially among youngsters, who repeatedly have to be told to improve their signals. We see again that cooperation at work ideally should be based on tacit understanding, rather than explicit orders. This can be compared to the elaborate sign system in the US, vividly described by Niemann. She writes: "An old head could practically order an anchovy pizza from a half mile away." Cf. NIEMANN, 4.

common section of the tracks therefore often requires a bit of nerve and experience on the part of the train-puller. Wavering or undecisive train-pullers will find that the shunting team or other train-pullers will take advantage of their hesitation, letting them wait.

Drivers of trains that have been delayed on the line, especially those delayed during their arrival at Hagalund, are seldom very jolly and their temper will often be turned against the train-puller, who is likely to be the first person they meet. There might be a bus or commuter train they want to catch and they put presssure on the train-puller to dart between other trains and engines. The train-puller, too, might be pressed for time, having rows of trains – with equally irritated drivers – waiting to be guided. What would, under calmer circumstances, be cooperation between the shunters and the train-puller, may during such hectic times turn into a silent, but fierce, conflict about the right of way.

During such a 'roundtrip', taking a train down to its track in the yard and guiding the engine to the depot, the train-puller covers a distance of about 2,5 km. The train-puller has to be attentive to announcements from the Order Centre on the loudspeakers. Trains that are ready to leave are announced: 'Train-puller, train 951 ready for departure.' Travelling in the cab, on the engine yard or when working to disconnect the engine from the train it may be impossible to hear the loudspeakers.

The trains are scheduled to leave Hagalund half an hour before they start their journey from the Central Station and the engines also have half an hour 'buffer-time' between leaving the depot and departing from Hagalund tugging their trains. The time-table gives the train-puller a fair picture of when the trains are expected to be announced, but delays or even too early announcements have to be counted on. Until the train is announced it may naturally not be sent off as it still may be under work, having a last minute repair or not yet having passed the brake-test.

The train-puller is often anxious that the trains leave in a particular order because he has lined the track for the next train or because he already has reported the trains to the Central Station on the *tastatur*, a signalling device. In order to change his report he will have to find a working telephone and call Cst. That of course means a detour and time lost as well as embarrassment, since he might give an impression of wavering control of the situation.

There are usually two or, during peak-hours, three train-pullers working at the same time. When the traffic is slow the train-puller might work on his own or, as during the early morning hour, be assisted by the boss.

The computerized switchboard plant made the train-pullers superfluous and

49

they have now all been transferred to other tasks. One part of their work, disconnecting the engines in the North, has been resurrected as a shift on its own, but it is not manned by any steady group of shunters.

~~~

Train-pullers are not considered to be proper shunters and even the name 'pilot' is considered to be too pretentious for their 'simple' task. Their position is seen to be inferior to the shunters, their work easier, but at the same time less independent due to the constant pressure of the clock.[26] One of the shifts is, significantly, called *'gubb-turen'* (old man's shift), and the other shifts, too, are seen as demanding very little skill and effort.

Persons whose eyesight or hearing has deteriorated, due to age or injury, are likely to be relocated to the train-pulling side, indicating that this is a job which can be performed safely even when such abilities are reduced. Such relocation normally means a dead-end to further promotion. Formally train-pullers with seniority can proceed to take up positions as indoor *tkm*, but by the time they have reached that point, they seem to have lost confidence in their understanding of the shunting and they tend to step back and refuse to leave 'the freedom and the open air'.

The 'freedom' of the train-puller must be seen to refer to the theoretical independence he has to work without orders from above, organizing the switches according to his own taste for planning. In practice this independence can only be enjoyed during relatively short periods of slack traffic. As soon as the yard gets busy the train-puller is squeezed by demands from drivers, shunting teams, co-pilots and the Order Centre – not to mention the clock.

The train-pullers can be seen as service-staff to the drivers, but may also be considered their charge-hands or conductors, as the drivers are obliged to obey their signs and may not initiate **any** move without permission from the train-pullers.

The shunting teams often consider the train-pullers to be a hindrance in their work, although the teams naturally depend on the train-pullers to obtain trains to shunt and to 'get rid of' trains, thereby clearing the yard and creating empty tracks, a necessity for every shunting team.

This dual dependency, between train-pullers on one hand and drivers and shunting teams on the other, is, due to the lowly status of the train-pulling job, often denied and suppressed. Furious drivers as well as pushy shunting

---

[26] I am not using the word 'tyranny', as Cottrell did in his famous article about railway workers. Cf. COTTRELL, 135. While ruled and dominated by the clock, the train-pullers have sufficient time margins at work, and no off-time obligations, not to be considered tyrannized by it.

teams may intimidate and control the train-puller, making him choose uncomfortable routes, push him into hasty decisions or to long, unnecessary waiting periods. Co-pilots may also take advantage of a weak and inexperienced comrade and lure him into doing an unproportionally large share of the work.

Depending on whether one wants to describe the train-puller as an independent planner and swift organizer with integrity, fantasy and guts, contributing in a substantial way to making the traffic flow smoothly according to the time-table, or whether one wants to see the train-puller as a drudge, bullied and humiliated by everybody, a slave to the clock, chased by drivers and shunting teams, is largely a matter of taste. Both extremes can be found and both can and do argue for their case.

I recall my sincere astonishment when a driver suddenly asked me: 'When are you going to quit this shit-job?' ('När tänker du sluta med det här skitjobbet?') The traffic was flowing nicely, the sun was shining, and I reckoned that I was acquiring a neat and even tan – and then this man comes up with such an absurd and insulting question. Seeing the driver sweat in his hot cab I proudly replied : 'And when are **you** going to quit that shit-job of yours?'

I must admit that during other weather and traffic conditions I probably would have given him a completely different answer.

Train-puller showing 'forward' to arriving train.

Indoor Staff

Trafikmästare (tkm)

The indoor bosses are in everyday language called by the same term as the outdoor bosses, *trafikmästare* or simply *tkm* (pronounced: teh-koh-em), but to distinguish the former ones from the latter the outdoor bosses are formally called *lagbas msa (lagbas med samordningsansvar;* team foreman with responsibility for coordination) while the indoor bosses simply are called *arbetsledningen* (management).[27]

Traditionally the appointment to indoor *tkm* constituted the last step on the promotion ladder of the shunters. After a long and faithful service in the yard, in sunshine as well as rain, sleet and snow, this promotion often meant a welcome comfort in the office for a number of years before retirement. As the body ages and ailments and infirmities lurk around the corner, the charms of outdoor work, the mobility, freedom and fresh air, weigh less and less against the disadvantages of it. This is not to say that the job of the *tkm* does not have its strains and frustrations, only that these are rather of a mental than a physical kind.

It may seem a radical change to leave the manual work outdoors for an office job, but many of the tasks of the indoor boss are already familiar to the outdoor boss, as e.g. keeping book of coaches in reserve, a register that is built on information provided by the outdoor boss.

The most visible and familiar task of the indoor boss, as seen from the point of view of the shunters, is the writing of the work orders, the 'slips'. The younger shunters in fact sometimes see it as the only task of the indoor boss and complain loudly if the xeroxes are not ready when they come to collect them before work.

The work-orders are constructed on the basis of the *sammansättningsplan* (composition plan), which the planning division at Hagalund makes for every new time-table. Earlier time-table shifts marked only winter and summer, now there is a new time-table several times a year. Shunters and bosses complain about never having time to learn the new time-table before it is changed again, forcing them to constantly carry and consult the slips and the composition plan.

The composition plan states the ordinary composition of every train arriving and departing from Hagalund. It lists the destination and starting point

---

[27] I will, however, use the terminology of the shunting community and talk about indoor *tkm* or indoor bosses, while reserving the term 'management' for the manager of the Yard Group (Barring) and other managers on levels identical or superior to him.

of every coach, the *littera* and order of the coaches in the train, their respective coach numbers and, most important, the number of the train they will be part of, on which day(s) of the week.

Using the composition plan the *tkm* gets the backbone of the work order for the shift. There will then be additional coaches, ordered by different stations, which have to be added to the basic composition. The work order describes the final composition of the trains and gives information as to how they are to be assembled by listing all the coaches in their correct order, starting in the South. Under the line of *littera* and coach numbers the shunters will find numbers referring to the trains where the coaches are to be found or to the tracks where they are stationed at the moment.

The trains that ordinarily provide some (or even all) of the required coaches for the new train are then found in the composition plan. The remaining coaches will be found on the reserve, in other trains or they may be released from the repair shop. The *tkm* has to put the jigsaw together and he should preferably choose coaches that are easily accessible for the shunting team.

Thus, the work-orders are a compound of information from several different sources. The composition plan, fax-messages, telephone-calls, mail, computer communication, and then additional information from coach recorders, *stinsexpeditionen* (approx: telegrapher) and from outdoor bosses have to be be ordered and transformed into slips which are easily interpretable and labour-saving.

At hectic moments it is easy to mislay a paper or get a number wrong. Such mistakes, when revealed after shunting but before departure, lead to additional work for the shunters. The slips being hand-written always reveal their originator, and the shunters will complain loudly to the responsible *tkm*, and to their co-workers, about his blunder. When mistakes pass unnoticed and the train departs with incorrect composition, there will most likely be angry phone calls to the *tkm* from stations further along the train route or from staff at the receiving end. 'We get the blame for everything that happens further along the route', one *tkm* complained. 'They phone and ask us about everything. Many times we do not have time to work, only answer all kinds of questions and complaints. Soon they'll be calling just to ask us what time it is!'

Outside office hours and during week-ends and holidays the *tkm* have the unpleasant task of finding replacements for shunters who are taken ill suddenly. To get a call on your day off, at six o'clock in the morning, asking whether you would be willing to do an extra shift is not always appreciated. It will be necessary for the *tkm* to use a lot of diplomacy and sometimes even promise a favourable exchange of shifts to the prospective stand-in. The task of allotting and trading shifts normally falls on *personalfördelaren* (the staff delegator) and the means by which the *tkm* has been able to solve a situation of crisis may not be looked upon with enthusiasm by the staff delegator at her return on Monday morning. She might find that shunters are missing, being given a leave as compensation for working Saturday and Sunday, and the work-schedules have to be planned all over again.

~~~

The *tkm*, then, deal with orders, requests, inquiries and information, finding replacements for coaches and personnel. Personal initiative is somewhat limited and may consist only of refusing to comply to requests that seem unreasonable, such as a request from the repair shop to have a coach shunted into the Hall for the single purpose of fixing a pedal in the toilet. On the whole the *tkm* can be said to plan and organize work to a rather limited extent, as their task mainly consists of compiling, translating and dividing different orders into trains, taking account of available rolling stock. It seems that the letters *msa (med samordningsansvar)* could be used for the indoor boss just as well as for the outdoor one.

The psychological touch in contacts with the shunting staff has already been mentioned in the extreme cases of finding stand-ins for unpopular shifts, but in everyday contacts with the teams and other shunters it is considered important to keep calm and collected.

Because of these intensive contacts between the *tkm* and other groups at Hagalund as well as with other stations, it is often claimed, particularly by the management and the *tkm*, that they are 'the face' of the shunting group. This has been stressed increasingly during the last decade and has led to discussions about whether competence and education is compatible with promotion according to seniority only. This is a subject I will return to later.

The indoor *tkm* are in an ambiguous position. They are members of the same union as the rest of the shunters and are considered to be shunters, expected to defend 'their group' against demands from other groups who try to load their work onto the shunters, or blame them for damages done miles away from the yard.

On the other hand it is considered that the *tkm* in the office forget what work is like in the yard and 'within two weeks' of office-work start to see things from a 'management point of view'. Indoor *tkm* easily get a reputation as unreliable persons who 'talk to the manager' and who – especially now that seniority no longer is the sole key to promotion – can mould and influence the manager's picture of the different shunters and teams. The *tkm*, as opposed to the manager, have all been in the yard for decades and have, everyone presumes, well formed opinions about their former co-shunters. Their views must therefore weigh heavily with the manager and a raised eyebrow or a heedless word from one of them could, the shunters presume, destroy a man's career.

Coach recorders

Coach recorders (*vagnupptagare,* lit. 'coach-up-takers') work in solitude, sitting in their room by their computer or hurrying across the yard on their bicycles with a little bag over their shoulders.[28] Their contacts to the shunting team are even more sporadic than those of the knockers and consist almost exclusively of inquiries to the shunt leader or the boss about the number of some coach that has been added to a train in the last minute.

The work of the coach-recorders consists of recording the coaches that go in a train. The composition plan indicates the *littera,* the types of coaches, that are to be used, but we know that in practice these may actually have to be replaced by other ones. Any change in this respect means that length, number of seats, the weight of the train, as well as the brake weight, may be altered and the new figures have to be noted and reported to the train personnel and the telegrapher.[29] It is, naturally, essential for the engine driver to get information about the the length as well as the brake power of the train.

The individual numbers of the coaches are noted and entered into the computer. By registering every journey the coach undertakes, it is possible to keep track of its mileage and take it out for maintenance at regular intervals. Coaches that the staff have reported as having serious damage or defects, which constitute a hazard to safety, will immediately be taken out of service. This information is also available in the report book of the coach, but the computer constitutes an extra security measure in this respect, making sure the coach is not reinstalled or left to go in a new train before it is repaired and reported 'healthy' by the repair shops concerned.

The new computer system has indeed had the effect that the work of the coach recorder has become increasingly redundant. Given the way things are organized today it is still necessary, but not very much imagination is needed to see that the information about coaches being used could be collected by the

---

[28] There are in all three coach-recorders, working a two-shift schedule.

[29] The telegraphers are not necessarily recruited from the shunting group (although there is a former shunter amongst them). Their office is next door to the coach recorders but there is very little interaction between them and the shunters. They definitely belong to another world and their job remains to a large part a mystery to the shunters. I will therefore not mention this group further.

shunting team. As soon as a coach is connected to a train, the team could enter the coach number into the computer, and this information could then easily be used throughout the internal SJ net.[30]

Today the coach recorder has to wait for a bunch of trains to be shunted, and when the team is finished he turns up with the computer print-outs to verify every coach and add the individual coach numbers to his list. He must also keep an eye on last minute changes and in case he misses one he will contact the boss, who also has taken down the coach number in order to report it to the indoor boss who will remove it from the reserve list.

Coach recording has never been a popular job among the shunters, because of its lonely character and not least because one shift starts at 3.30 in the morning, but it has been one of the 'safety valves' for persons who have been injured or otherwise become unfit for work in the yard. There are also a number of shunters who have tried the job for a shorter spell, only to return to shunting as they find that they become cut off from the everyday life of the rest of the shunters.

We saw that the knocker is a lonely fore-runner of the shunting team, constantly reminded of being followed and observed as his work is judged by the shunters who depend on his preparations. The coach-recorder is in contrast a lonely rear guard, chased by departure times. To miss a train does not cause irreparable damage, as all changes to the train will be noted by the boss of the shunting team. Even if it is embarrassing or time-consuming, a consultation with him can save the coach-recorder from even more embarrassing inquiries from the Central Station who are unable to submit the necessary specifications to the driver. Mistakes, such as entering the wrong coach number, is triumphantly spotted by Cst, who may ask if there really should be a sleeper in the one hour commuter train between Stockholm and Uppsala. Often these enquiries reach the coach-recorder through the indoor boss, who has been contacted initially, and then the information may spread to other shunters as well and enter into the gossip and general judging of the skills of the coach-recorder in question.

But it is only the exception that the coach-recorder will get feed-back on his work. Almost all his contacts during work are with the bosses. The meals and coffee-breaks are at odd hours with the shunters' and although they meet in the coffee-room the coach-recorder will seldom have time for a game of cards. When the shunters have a break it is all too often time to rush off on the bicycle and check the coach numbers of the finished trains.

---

[30] In fact, a couple of years after my fieldwork the coach-recording was removed.

Being a lonely job, unconnected to the task of shunting, functionally as well as spatially and temporally, and requiring little education, the job of the coach-recorder has low status. As a consequence, the coach recorder easily turns into a person who is a bit on the side, not partaking very actively in matters that occupy and stir the feelings in the rest of the shunting community. He may notice a lot of 'new faces', but does not come to learn their names before they leave – and they probably never realize what the man in that small office is working with, either.

Being an option for persons unfit for the yard the coach recorders are often old hands, who suffer from some ailment, and who find it difficult to find another job. The coach recorders are therefore often 'institutions', unquestioned and appreciated members of the shunting community, although their work actually would give one little ground to assume that this would be the case.

The staff delegator

The staff delegator, *personalfördelaren,* is not part of the Yard Group, in fact not even any of the production areas, but belongs to the office-staff. I will, however, talk about this person – in our case a woman – in this context as she works in very close contact with the shunters and must be considered one of the key persons at the workplace.

The shunters remember staff delegators from the past and their different 'eras' much more vividly than they recall former managers. Services rendered and injustices done by a staff delegator years ago can still be recounted with gratitude or anger, as the case may be, and comparisons are made to the merits or shortcomings of the present staff delegator.

One could simply define the task of the staff delegator as the obligation to make sure that the shifts of the daily work schedule are filled and that every employee in the group is assigned the amount of work hours and leisure time that the current labour agreements prescribe. The steady lists need not be taken into account as they are preprinted by a computer on a monthly schedule. To the worker the advantage of the steady list is that he can predict his shifts months in advance, if need be.

One of the shunters did exactly this when the bonus-reform was introduced. He constructed a work schedule for all members of his team for one year ahead and he also counted the exact amount of money, taking into account all hours of 'single' and 'double' overtime rates, all additional holiday pay, the total amount of the new bonus, etc., and finally came up with the exact sum the team would cost the company for the coming year. 'We are going to break the two-million line!', was his triumphant call and he would pull up his multicoloured schedule to be admired. He was mostly, however, met by smiles, head-shakes and mutters. 'Well, if you don't have anything else to do...'

Detailed information about the hours of work is then on offer for every one on a steady list, but very few use that possibility and the shunters mostly acquiesce in checking the schedule for a few weeks ahead, in addition to holidays, which, in case one wants to change with someone else, may have to be traded a long time ahead.

As the staff delegator works with a preprinted monthly schedule it is the VIK personnel, i.e. people on the reserve list, who have to be appointed to appropriate tasks. For the personnel working on the reserve list, also called 'skubben', days off (and holidays) are preprinted, but the rest of the days are blank to be filled by the staff delegator.[31] It seems simple enough to fill the shifts of the day schedule with names that the preprinted list lays down and then to distribute the names of the stand-ins, who should work on that particular day, on the other shifts. If there are too few staff to fill the remaining shifts these shifts will go on the 'gnetlista' (approx: drudger-list), i.e. be offered to volunteers for over-time, while if the staff are too many on a particular day, extra shifts will be constructed, such as training shifts, adding extra train-pullers for peak-hours, extra B-members for teams with a heavy workload or by ordering a couple of shunters to grease the switches.[32]

Greasing switches is a job that is disliked and of very low status. The greasers, equipped with brushes and buckets of black thick oil, are jokingly called 'the Rembrandts'. On the other hand the importance of this job is recognized, and during times when there is a shortage of staff there are often complaints that the switches are stiff as they have not been greased. (This does not mean that the person complaining would like to do it himself.) It is not a

---

[31] 'Skubben', or 'gå på skubben' (go on the ...) are etymologically unclear, as the verb 'skubba' can mean 'to run' as well as 'to run errands' and 'to play truant'. Cf. SO. I assume that it is the flexibility of the shifts, 'shifts running wild', which the railway argot refers to.

[32] The deputy list, or the VIK-list, is thus not a list of 'extras', called in to fill empty slots in the schedule. The VIK staff are permanently employed on a full time basis, just like the rest. They are only more 'mobile' in the sense that they, within the limits of their competence and, naturally abiding to the regulations concerning rest between shifts etc, may be moved to work where they are needed (NB only within the shunting group at Hagalund), jumping around the schedule doing shifts that do not follow a particular 'key'. One may compare this to the American system, which is entirely different in that a shunter may be called upon to work at short notice. While the rule in California was that the shunter was obliged to be within reach by phone, day and night, there are VIK- and other personnel at Hagalund who actually refuse to give their telephone number to the company, as they do not want to be 'disturbed' by staff delegators asking them to change shifts or to do an extra shift. For US comparison, cf. GAMST 1989, 258, n.3; NIEMANN, 18.

heavy job and it may be enjoyed for that purpose, the early retreat paying for the dullness and for the gleeful comments from the shunting team, who jokingly order the Rembrandts to grease particular, distant, switches trying to make sure they don't knock off all too early.

Other extra shifts are seldom disliked, but rather looked upon as light ones with the inbuilt right to knock off earlier, as soon as the the peak hour or the heaviest part of the job is done. This often goes for training shifts as well.

We have now touched upon two of the many factors that complicate the work of the staff delegator. The first one is that the supply of workers is constantly changing. There are the predictable changes due to holidays, but there are in addition others that may occur suddenly and rather unexpectedly. Disease obviously strikes outside all planning, but there are also a number of legal causes for leave. Some of them are compensated with full pay, others with partial or no pay, but they will all cause the same kind of trouble for the staff delegator who has to find a qualified person to do the job.

The other factor touched upon is the attraction different kinds of jobs have. We now enter the essential part of the job of the staff delegator. In order to fill empty slots in the work-schedule the staff delegator will have to negotiate with individual shunters and beg them to change shifts or to do extra work. According to one of the staff delegators the constant contacts and dealings with the workers is what makes this 'the most difficult job of all at Hagalund'. It is essential to know the abilities and skills of the shunters, their personalities and preferences, and naturally the assets and drawbacks of the different shifts, in the negotiations with the workers.

Staff delegators may easily come to see the shunters as 'knockers', 'train-pullers', or 'B-members', or as persons 'willing' or 'unwilling' to do extra shifts. When constructing the schedule for VIK personnel such labelling images easily bias the delegator to assign certain persons to certain tasks, as well as repeatedly ask some persons to fill in, while others hardly get an offer until the list of 'willing' persons has been exhausted. Women for example have at times, and by certain delegators, been repeatedly accorded shifts as train-pullers, until the injustice has become evident and the women have complained and demanded shifts in the shunting teams. One woman said that she sat down in the delegator's office and refused to leave until she was given shifts on the 'shunting side'.

The delegators often deny that such warped schedules depend on anything but co-incidence and chance, but complaining usually leads to a quick change. I was myself met with an array of explanations when complaining about being given nothing but train-pulling, but my shifts dramatically changed after the complaint. The explanations were firstly that it was just 'luck', but when faced with comparisons with other VIK staff from my own 'group' (i.e. persons who came to the yard at the same time as me and thus had the same training and seniority) the explanations took a defensive turn and the delegator said that I should consider myself lucky, as train-pulling was so much lighter and easier than shunting.

As the (at that time, male) delegator had no experience from the yard himself he obviously read the shunters' verdict of the job as being 'dull' as meaning an easy job with little to do, while we know that the shunters disliked it because they wanted to work with a team and not as service personnel to the drivers. We know that they consider shunting an independent job, disregarding the quite dependent role of the C-member.

The result of the view of train-pulling as 'easy' was, however, that the train-pullers had an unrepresentatively high number of female shunters (though only two in number). This resulted, paradoxically in a high number of female switch board operators (i.e. two), as mainly train-pullers were transferred to this new job.[33]

Considering the delegator's role in assigning staff for the day schedule we must conclude, however, that while prejudice, mistaken assumptions and old jog-trot ways of thinking obviously influence the assignment of jobs to different persons, there is on the other hand always the possibility for the shunter to bring out the monthly schedule and point out the injustice in black and white, just as one may try to influence the delegator with less confrontational means and display an interest or ask for certain types of jobs, etc. There is always room for negotiation – which may then cause the comrades to react and protest in their turn. Dealings with the delegator engages just about every aspect of one's negotiation abilities, from tricks and threats and 'first come, first served', to give-and-take and appeals to justice and fairness.

One of the shunters, philosophizing over the abilities of the ideal staff delegator, said that he must 'have psychology'. He then described how such a former staff delegator 'with psychology' had called the shunter to ask him to do an extra shift one early morning, ordering a taxi to pick him up when he agreed to work the shift. Such kind thoughts, the shunter said, made one

---

[33] The women had, of course, agreed to work as steady train-pullers. 'I don't mind it, I just wanted to work on a steady list' one of them explained. Men more rarely accept the offer of a steady job in train-pulling. NB, when empty slots appear on the steady list, the offer always goes to the next person in the line of seniority. In case that person prefers to stay as a VIK, the post will be offered to the next one, and so on. Seniority here is what Gamst refers to as 'competitive-status seniority'. Cf. GAMST 1985, 7.

compelled to comply with other requests. There was a moral obligation to return the favour and this made it worth while for the company to pay the taxi fare. It also created a general feeling of belonging to the company that meant a financial gain for SJ in that the shunters perhaps would do 'that little extra' which otherwise would be left undone.

It would be wrong to understand the give-and-take of the staff delegator as manipulative dealings that are made for the single purpose of gaining in the end. The position of the staff delegator is truly an ambiguous one since, on one hand, it has an inbuilt purpose to fill the work-schedule in the cheapest possible way, while, on the other hand, it constantly meets the demands and wishes of the shunters, which often go in the other direction. To look exclusively at gain would in the end make the job unpleasant and unbearable, as the contact with shunters is predominant.

The shunters very quickly read their skirmishes with the staff delegator as a result of a negligent, uncaring or hostile attitude that the company and/or the staff delegator hold towards the shunters, particularly towards him, while the staff delegator will more often read the situation as an outburst of anger in a heated discussion. As soon as the shunter calms down, he will 'realize' that his demands were unrealistic, against the rules, or unfair to his comrades as the case may be, all according to the benevolent reading of the staff delegator.

The staff delegator works then within the framework of certain rules and regulations, trying to take into account costs for the company as well as fairness and justice towards the shunters. Naturally, there are situations when there are no 'smidiga lösningar', flexible solutions (a favourite expression with the delegator), and sometimes mistakes are made, but the staff delegator will never plead grudges or ill-will towards the shunters.

One staff delegator described situations in which it may turn out to be impossible to avoid giving a series of bad shifts to a shunter. In such a case, he said, the staff delegator must prevent angry reactions by calling the shunter and say: "Unfortunately you have been given really, really nasty hours, but **could** you manage that?" This had a greater chance of succeeding, compared to the case where the shunter was left to find out for himself.

However, the inherent unpredictability is always at hand to ruin the most foresighted planning. One staff delegator described the nightmare side of the job with this fictive, but realistic, example:

"One has struggled and one has employed every means. One has said like this: 'Okay, you'll get a mark of honour when you retire **if only** you agree to work now! And one has continued like that, and finally, one has, on Friday, managed to get it filled up. One has filled **all** shifts. **But**, when the clock strikes four in the afternoon,

61

and one is supposed to finish at half past four, the telephone rings. And that is a person who is ill and who has an afternoon (shift) on Friday, a morning on Saturday, a day shift on Sunday and an afternoon on Monday.

Maybe one has been sitting and thinking at work that this was great!, now I have filled all the shifts and it feels really good. Now we'll do something nice when I get back home. We'll buy a grilled chicken, we'll take a bottle of wine... And I promise you that when that person has called, then the chicken goes into the fridge, the wine-bottle goes into the bar and nothing will become of the courtship in the sofa bed. [...]

That is something that can feel awful, I must admit. Then it is hard, because that is something you cannot influence."[34]

Making ends meet, matching shifts with available staff are problems that lie at the heart of the job. Periods with superfluous staff do arise and make the work much easier, but such periods will obviously not endure, as they are unprofitable to the company.[35] Soon the staff delegator will be back in the business of tempting and bribing the workers with easy shifts in order to fill every slot in the day schedule.

The staff delegators also complain that the job contains aspects that lie beyond the formal requirements. They refer to situations when it may be necessary to persuade the wife of a shunter that she 'lend her husband to SJ this week-end, too', or they refer to the personal problems and worries that shunters frequently confide in the staff delegator when asking for a day or even a week off (naturally to be made up for later). In the next sentence the delegator will, however, mention these aspects as some of the most interesting and stimulating ones the job offers; the personal contacts that bring out the 'amateur psychologist' in him.

~~~

We see that the staff delegator is a mediator between the company and the shunting community. The shunters do, occasionally, (in retrospect and only in

---

[34] "Då har man kämpat och man har försökt med alla medel. Man har sagt så här: 'Okej, du får ett hedersomnämnande när du går i pension bara du ställer upp här och jobbar!' Och så har man hållt på, på det där sättet, och till slut så har man, på fredag, lyckats få fullt. Man har alltså alla turer besatta. Men, när klockan blir fyra på eftermidda'n, och man ska sluta halv fem, så ringer det. Och då är det en person som är sjuk, som har eftermiddag på fredag, förmiddag på lördag, dagtur på söndag och eftermiddag på måndag.
Då kanske du har suttit på jobbet och så har du funderat på det här att vad skönt!, nu har jag fått fullt i turerna och nu känns det bra. Nu ska vi ta och ordna lite trevligt när man kommer hem. Nu ska vi köpa en grillad kyckling, vi tar en flaska vin... Och jag lovar dig att när den har ringt så åker kycklingen in i kylskåpet, och vinflaskan i barskåpet och herdestunden i utdragssoffan, den blir det ingenting utav. [...]
Det är nå't som kan va' jobbigt, det måste jag säga. Då känns det tungt, för det är ju sån't som man inte kan påverka." (INT 11)
[35] Staff have never been laid off, with the exception of a few of cases of flagrant absenteeism or criminality. The policy is rather not to employ new staff letting the normal turnover care for the necessary adjustment.

some cases) include the delegator as some kind of a member of their group, but otherwise they consider the delegator to be as close to a personification of the company as you can get. According to this view, the delegator is out to squeeze every drop out of the shunter, unless he is constantly on his guard, looking after his rights, discovering and exposing all injustice and partiality turned against him.

The delegators are remarkably fond of, even proud of, 'their group', the shunters, seeing themselves as lucky compared to the other delegators, who handle groups with severe problems of high personnel turn-over, absenteeism, or staff who refuse to cooperate with female superiors, etc. The shunters are said to react directly and furiously, but, again, never hang on to grudges. 'They can scream and shout, but half an hour later we are the best of friends again.'

The delegators get to know the shunters, and this knowledge spills easily over into creating the shunters differently in assigning them tasks that they become identified with. Yet the delegator claims to be concerned only with constructing a full schedule, utilizing the staff to the best, as well as trying to construct 'good' sequences of shifts for the individual shunters. The 'give-and-take' between delegator and individual shunters is constantly referred to when the delegators describe their job. This is, indeed, an explicit ambition.

The delegators are very seldom people with first hand experience in shunting and their perception of the abilities and skills of the shunters, as well as the nature of the different work tasks, therefore derive from the shunters themselves. The delegators are constantly absorbing the ideology of the shunters, through gossip, but also through everyday wheeling and dealing with them, and in assigning jobs, training shifts etc., the delegators thus turn the shunters' ideology into practice and into positions, thereby boomeranging the shunters' ideas about themselves and their job back into the practice of the yard.

The staff delegator is, no doubt, a very important person, constantly discussed and commented upon, examined and evaluated. It is no surprise to find that the 'coffee-table history' of the yard often pays more attention to staff delegators than to managers.

Conclusions

Among all the different jobs in the shunting yard, the shunt leader stands out as the prototype of a 'shunter'. Shunt leading may not be favoured as a task, as it is often stated that *skjutspassning* is the most varied, easy and interesting

63

task in the yard, but it is the shunt leader who sets the tone of work, who leads 'his' team and who has the greatest responsibility. He is the one who 'is shunting'.

Around this apex all other tasks shape themselves according to various degrees of importance and status. The freedom that the shunt leader is considered to enjoy rubs off onto the rest of the team, and C-membership is therefore preferred to train-pulling, not on the account of being physically lighter – which it oftentimes is – but because it is a 'free' job and part of shunting proper. It is team-work, as opposed to boring solitary work.

The knocker, despite being in a rather lonely job, also enjoys a higher status than the train-puller. This may be because the job is considered to be a good preparation for shunting – as you supposedly learn to read the slips in this occupation – and as there is a close affiliation to the shunting team. The team is directly dependent on the preparation of the trains made by the knocker. The dependence on the train-puller is not as directly visible and it is further down-played and ignored, while the 'inconvenience' of having train-pullers in the yard is often referred to.

Beside a difference between collective and individual tasks there is also a sharp demarcation line between indoor and outdoor work. The 'real shunter' works outdoors. Outdoors is a stage[36] with its own rules and its own way of thinking and a *tkm* who leaves outdoor work will sooner or later change and increasingly adapt an 'indoor' attitude and an 'indoor' point of view, putting loyalty to the company before the interests of the shunting team. 'Making us move carriages from one track to another just because it looks nicer on a sheet of paper', as one shunter put it.

The coach recorders have a past as shunters in the yard and even if their work has no practical connection to shunting they are nevertheless considered to be shunters of a kind, encompassed by the solidarity of the yard. They are outside the ordinary realm of work, being unfit, working mainly indoors and having a task which is seen as increasingly redundant.

The staff delegator is not part of the shunters' union. The delegator does not even belong to the same production area, but the importance of this job for the shunters means that the delegator, in retrospect, can be considered part of the Yard Group. In daily life the delegator is often seen as SJ personified.

---

[36] Needless to say, the use of the concept 'stage' (or 'region') is derived from Goffman. Cf. GOFFMAN, 1976, 109 ff. There are several stages in the yard; indoor and outdoor, of which the second one further has two stages; work and the coffee-room. Despite the fact that behaviour changes radically when moving from one of them to the other, it is nevertheless questionable whether one can talk about 'front' and 'back' stages. While relaxing from work matters in the coffee-room, one relaxes from the coffee-room jargon at work in the yard.

The role of the delegator is truly the most ambiguous one.

The homogeneity of this group, when inspected more closely, is thus divided by three easily visible demarcation lines. The first one divides outdoor and indoor staff. The indoor group often is suspected of having one foot in the SJ camp, but as this group consists exclusively of seniors and as these, furthermore, tend to be influential in the union, they nevertheless count some of the most highly esteemed protagonists of the shunting group among their members.

The second dividing line is established between team-workers and persons working in solitude. Shunting proper is identified with team-work, and this ideal labels the jobs outside the teams as menial, unpleasant and generally of lower status. Therefore, personnel holding such positions somehow also become secondary, peripheral or just not 'proper' shunters.

The third line separates the fit from the unfit, and thereby those whose career has come to a halt from those who are still advancing.

Solidarity and group feeling is considered to be a function of physical or mental proximity to the kernel group of the yard – the shunting teams, the shunters *per se*, who beat the yard in drudgery and toil, but who nevertheless enjoy the freedom of the yard and no longer can adapt to a 'normal' job in the society at large.

The gates of the yard surround an island of freedom, where the shunt leader is the executive leader, surrounded by superior bosses, who already are withdrawn from the field and sometimes mentally halfway over the fence to the 'managing side'. The shunt leader must therefore first and foremost depend and rely on his auxiliary troops, to whom we, in addition to the team and the knocker, may even count the outdoor boss.

As for the team primarily, but in the last instance for everybody who belongs to the shunting group, the functional differentiation of tasks and roles is overcast by an ideological identification with real, arduous, outdoor shunting, allowing **all** of them to consider themselves to work in a 'free and independent' job. This over-all ideology and identification with shunting makes the different categories of shunters unite for certain purposes and during certain times, while they under other circumstances and during other times tend to split up and bifurcate. One can all but discern the outlines of a segmentary system.[37] We will now go on to have a closer look at the

---

[37] As an anthropologist one is tempted to see such a system here (the classic examples being those of the Tiv of Nigeria and The Nuer of the Sudan). Although not based on lineages, the groups in the yard still unite and split according to a pattern of complementary opposition. Cf. SAHLINS, 50 ff.

conditions for unity and separation, solidarity and conflict.

Indoor *tkm* writing the slips.

4. MODES OF COOPERATION AND PLANNING

Cooperation and Planning among Train-Pullers

There are two tasks the beginner has been trained for when he starts to do shifts on his own *('gå egna turer')*. These are train-pulling and C-membership in a shunting team. As the tasks differ considerably, the beginner also finds himself in a different relation towards his co-workers when working as a train-puller as compared to a C-member.

As we have seen, all train-pullers formally work on an equal basis as soon as they work without a coach. Train-pulling shifts overlap – covering each other at breaks and at beginnings/ends – which means that the lonely character of the job is accentuated. When working in the yard there may be slack periods when two train-pullers have time to sit and chat, but a train-puller often eats his lunch alone and spends his breaks in an empty coffee-room. Only occasionally do the breaks co-incide with the breaks of the shunting teams, and the train-puller may then be asked to fill up the card team, but often he will have to leave the game in the middle as the trains line up outside the window. For these obvious reasons dutiful train-pullers are not, and cannot be, among the most eager card players.

The train-pullers, being formally on an equal footing, may informally have different influence over the work, according to whether they are on the steady list or whether they work as VIK. Deputies are often, with a few exceptions, beginners, but as even 'old foxes' in the yard may take on an extra shift the difference in influence is not dependent on seniority. The older persons, who have been working in a team for ages, do not know the informal routines such as when one should take the breaks, or even when to go home, and the steady train-pullers may, if they feel inclined, 'cheat' them into working longer hours. The same treatment may befall *'strulare'* and *'smitare'* ('muddlers' and 'truants'). A train-puller may announce to the co-workers his intentions to let a person who has been too invisible during the day stay on longer than usual. Such treatment is quite self-evident and in case the 'victim' finds out and protests the decision will be spelled out coldly, leaving no margin for discussion.

Such decisions on the part of a steady train-puller to decide when the extras may go home are legio, as the person working only occasionally as a train-puller will be uncertain of the routines as well as handicapped by not being able to refer to the day before, or the week before, when the train-puller proper left that very shift half an hour earlier.

Lacking a reciprocal relationship to the train-puller, the beginner, the old shunter from a team, or the *'strulare'*, who came one hour late and played cards for another hour, are in a weak bargaining position and cannot do anything but comply with the 'rules' as they are spelled out by the train-puller who works with this task every day.

The limit of the train-puller's influence, in terms of its time domain, is naturally the official time limits of the shift. To work down to the very last minute, unless there has been an extraordinary workload due to late trains, is close to humiliating. The person who has been obliged to do so will suspect that he has been taken advantage of by the ordinary train-pullers, but there is no way of establishing that this actually is the case, as his work experience is irregular and it therefore is impossible to judge the intensity of the workload.

We can here note that the workload is a relative concept when we talk about the area around the middle of a sliding scale going from nothing to do, to not keeping up with the time-table. To a beginner, or to a nervous or disorganized person, the situation may seem hectic – not to say chaotic – while the calmer or more experienced person might see it as a situation 'with flow' *('med flyt')*. One must note that the experienced person, often, but not necessarily, is identical with the calm one. There are calm beginners, who have no concept of the situation and who therefore cannot anticipate a rush, as well as there are experienced train-pullers, who worry that there will be delays even before any train can be spotted on the horizon, as they may fear that their younger co-workers will be unable to manage.

Shunters from teams, or those persons on *'skubben'* who mostly have been working on the shunting side, find themselves ignorant about other routines on the train-pulling side, too. They may, for example, have forgotten that some engines should 'turn' in the yard and go to new trains without first going to the depot, or they may have found out which of the engines 'turn', but may nevertheless be unable to find a place to park them in the interval. When asking the train-puller, who answers that the engine should be parked 'on the warp' *('på sniskan')*, the shunter again has to admit his ignorance. The train-puller has demonstrated that there are things endemic to the train-pulling side, too. The higher status of the shunting side does not transfer automatically into train-pulling.

The shunters are not completely without trumps up their sleeve, and there is one advantage they may have, especially over the younger train-pullers, stemming from their knowledge of the different trains and the approximate time-table of the shunting teams. This may come handy in the search for empty tracks.

Planning is the key to the train-pullers' work. It is possible to take things just as they come, but the ideal is to have a flexible plan in mind. When traffic is intense the possibilities of planning are severely reduced, and the demand for flexible solutions becomes greater. If one has turned the switches for a particular train, the shunting team in the South may turn up and the train-puller watches in dispair as the C-member runs in front of the shunting engine turning every switch in his way. There can also be engines coming out of the depot in the reverse of the intended order, and the train-puller has to walk across the whole yard to turn the switches according to a new plan.

These things can never be predicted with full accuracy, and the disappointed train-pullers exchange the eternal phrase: 'It's not worth planning. They always come in the wrong order when you've planned it all.' When it works, the train-puller will exclaim, preferably to less experienced train-pullers: *'Blås på! – Det ligger!'* ('Speed up! – The points are lined'), adding a jestingly triumphant: 'One must plan the work!'

The most irritating thing for a train-puller is not that the plans are ruined because engines or trains arrive in the 'wrong' order, i.e. another order than listed on the time-table, or that the shunting team comes steaming, turning every switch in sight. The shunters are often considerate and will comply when asked to 'line behind', i.e. to turn back the switches behind them. No, the worst enemy of a careful and clever plan is another train-puller who refuses to, or who seems to be unable to cooperate. A train-puller who sees nothing in the yard but his own engine and his own schemes is a source of considerable irritation and is an obvious danger to everyone else. Good planning can never substitute for vigilance and 'split-vision'.

From this follows that the train-pullers' plans are of two kinds. First you have the individual planning. This is the planning that a lonely train-puller can work out during slack periods, periods that we know are best suited for plans as the movements are then more predictable. There are also individual plans during busy periods when two or even three train-pullers are on the move, but such plans have to be communicated to and accepted by the co-workers. They seldom comprise more complicated planning than choice of

69

tracks for returning the engines. The track one chooses is preferably the one that next train arrives at, as the switches will then be lined, but one must be sure that no other train-puller is already on the track with the incoming train, on collision course with the engine.

The second kind of planning is the planning that is done between two or several train-pullers when they turn from co-work to division of labour. This is done either explicitly, as an agreement to work in a specific way, such as working different areas, or it is based on 'common knowledge', earlier agreements or on earlier forms of cooperation that have proven successful. This planning is to a great extent based on implicit understandings, tacit knowledge of 'the smart way of doing things'.

The greatest pleasure is when such division of labour works with the verbal communication cut down to a minimum. The train-pullers know how to divide their tasks in the most efficient way and they can rely on each other to wait for an engine, to pass on a second train, to jump off at strategic points and swap engines and trains. The radio is mostly silent and the traffic flows. The train-pullers constantly keep an eye on each other's moves. They read intentions from engines that slow down, from switches being turned and from body language read at long distances. The train-pullers work in almost complete understanding without discussions, changes of plans, backtracking and cries for help. One is tempted to quote the definition of full culturality presented by Ulf Hannerz: *"[...] bägge vet, och bägge vet att bägge vet"* ('both know, and both know that both know) as well as of trust: "I know, and I know that you know, and I know that you know that I know."[1] Here definitely both full culturality and trust lie at the basis of the cooperation.

The times when such division of labour works in a team-work manner are, however, all too easily destroyed in the train-pulling trade. The common goal is to create 'flow' in the traffic. The traffic consists of incoming and outgoing trains and engines as well as trains that are shunted. Except for the priority for outgoing trains there is no other priority that the train-pullers can agree on in case of conflicts.

Almost all moves the train-pullers make are observed by engine drivers who often complain about being delayed and grumble when there is some obstruction on the way. The train-puller feels the extra pressure particularly from the engine driver he is guiding at the moment and this is an incitement to see the 'flow' of the traffic as identical with the interests of that particular train or engine.

---

[1] HANNERZ, 1983, 162. For another possible variety cf. HANNERZ, 1992, 254.

The pressure of the engine drivers may even lead the train-pullers to make moves that are, or at least are thought of as, prohibited. Some of the more daring drivers, particularly a few of the older stock, refuse to change to operating from the other end of the engine, *'byta sida'* ('change sides') when changing direction of driving. They simply tell the train-puller to stand on the rear of the engine and watch out. 'We'll sneak up.' If the door to the rear cab is locked this could mean a very cold and dangerous journey across the yard, as some of these more daring drivers are also prone to speeding.

Hanging like a monkey outside the engine the train-puller is giving up comfort and safety in order to save time for the engine driver, but also for himself. He will naturally see it as a benefit for the 'flow', but he is tied to standing on the engine as a watchman and connot 'send on' the engine to someone else further up the tracks. He has to follow it all the way up himself as even the most daring driver would not back up the most busy track in Hagalund without a reliable train-puller working as his eyes and ears at the rear of the engine. In such cases the train-puller is then forced to break the division of labour between train-pullers.

The converging interests of the driver and his train-puller show that the cooperation between train-pullers, based as it is on the rather shaky notion of a 'flow', which, in this particular work, is easily upset by external factors, is a convergence of individual interests rather than a division of labour for a common goal. Everyone has, in the last instance, the responsibility for **his** train, **his** engine and may favour this instead of letting it stand back for the common good. Only as long as both parties gain on the cooperation will it be agreed upon. Cooperative justice entails that everybody should do his share of the work and, therefore, if one of the train-pullers manages to get round guiding trains by timing his exchanges well, there will sooner or later be someone who figures out the trick and tells the others to leave next train for that person. 'He shall not think he can avoid his share in this way.'

Persons who refer to the official division of working on the 'engine side' versus working as a train guide, a division that is stated on the daily work schedule, will find a compact resistance among the other train-pullers. 'We all work in the same way.' Some of the older train-pullers may resort to working solely on the engine side when there is heavy traffic, but it is only with some respect for their seniority, and by realizing that they are so stubborn that telling them to do otherwise would amount to nothing, that their behaviour is accepted. They are close to retirement and once they are gone no one will cling to such old-fashioned ideas.

The only time that two train-pullers can develop cooperation to its maximum, and divide the tasks between them, is during the late night shifts, when the shunters have left and there is only one team in the North pulling away the trains almost as soon as they arrive. Very few trains leave, few engines leave, and when the train-pullers have straightened out matters with the engine master and planned where to park the waiting engines, all that remains is to pull in the trains. The pullers are only two and, unless there are irregularities or obstructions, their work-speed becomes obvious. They should be able to pull every second train. There is no excuse to be slow and do less than one's share.

It is during such nights that the train-pullers come into full bloom, as it were. The morning shift can be met by an enthusiastic train-puller, who tells of last night as a wonder of cooperation and 'flow': 'You should have seen us last night! Bettan was pulling trains two at a time, sending up the engines to me. She really is a good worker! The trains did not even have to stop on the way in.'

It is during such shifts that train-pullers can develop their skills and create new and more efficient routines, routines that cannot be used during the day, but which can be recreated when the same persons meet again during a night shift. The persons who are prepared to change their routine towards more cooperative ways of working will then be preferred working partners. This normally has no significance as one does not have any influence over how the work schedule is construed, but in cases of changing shifts one may check who the co-workers are on the shift in question, and accept or reject the offer accordingly.

Train-pulling can be said to consist of individual tasks that are in conflict with each other in the respect that the more trains someone else pulls the fewer trains are there left for me. Good 'flow' is still a general gain for everyone involved, but the possibility to let someone else take care of a particular mess, an incoming train, or a few engines that have to be sent is still there.

One train-puller was nicknamed 'Flash', because it was considered that he had a well developed skill for avoiding work. When a train was spotted he would say: 'Oh, I forgot my pipe indoors!' and hurry away, leaving the train to be pulled by someone else. Or then he had forgotten his rain-coat, or his slips. Once, after two earlier excuses, he claimed that he had put on the wrong shoes by mistake. The other train-puller could no longer hold his tongue but exclaimed: 'You have been working here for twenty years and still you haven't learnt what shoes to wear!'

On the other hand, train-pulling is dependent on the time-table much more than shunting and therefore the amount, as well as the pace, of work within one shift is by and large determined by slack periods and 'rush hours'. Good 'flow' will only mean that there is less waiting as well as less desperate moves and cannot be seen as exclusively a function of good planning.

~~~

Train-pulling is often a lonely job. Cooperation is established only when individual interests converge and time admits ample room for planning. During busy periods the cooperation is rather limited and consists of keeping an eye on everybody else and showing consideration for co-workers.

Good flow is not necessarily the same for all parties involved. Drivers, who push shunters into seemingly elegant and quick solutions, may in fact disturb the flow for the train-pullers. Otherwise there is a tendency to identification between train-puller and driver, siding with 'their' engine against the shunting teams when fighting about tracks and moving space in the yard. Some train-pullers define indeed their job as a 'service job' – a thought very far from the thinking on the shunting side.

The need to subordinate and coordinate one's moves with the wishes and needs of 'outsiders' (the 'service'-part of the job), the constant time pressure as well as the lonely character of the job all combine to establish train-pulling's lower status when compared to shunting. One prefers to work for a team, rather than as a guide for 'stupid drivers'. This view of superiority is seldom, if ever, expressed as a disparaging remark about those who work as train-pullers. It is, at least seemingly, only stated in terms of personal preferences.

When temporarily working on the train-pulling side the shunters soon find that they have no opportunity to turn views of superiority into a position of authority. Due to their knowledge and experience, the train-pullers can use time as a corrective and as a means of domination. Slaves of the clock? Maybe, but sometimes time is on their side.

Team-Work among Shunters

'People working in the Hall think that this is an easy job. They don't see any work, they only see shunters riding up and down the tracks on an engine, doing nothing.'

The new manager was out in the yard during his introduction period and found two *skjutspassare* lazily leaning on an electric post chatting to each other. 'Those two', he said to me, 'what the hell are **they** doing?'

One of the most obvious contrasts between train-pulling and shunting is that the former can be accomplished by a single person. Shunting is team-work, demanding that several persons are available, standing by, but they are not necessarily busy at all times. Even with a team of three you may find intervals where two persons, unoccupied, and seemingly lazy, stand talking to each other. Ten minutes later these two persons are perhaps one too few, and someone has to make a rush, the engine is held up and has to wait, or there is some other kind of interruption.

Although the motto is: 'The engine should never stand still', shunting is nevertheless a job that has intensive moments alternating with moments of inactivity and waiting. This holds for every team member, although the slack periods may differ as they have different causes. There is often great differentiation in knowledge and skill between the members in a team and therefore the differentiation is one of space and distance as well as one of competence. Even if one member is standing in the right spot to do a certain task or to gather some crucial information he might not be able to accomplish what the situation demands.

The shunters, as opposed to the train-pullers, do not carry radios, and unless there is regular face-to-face contact between the shunt leader and the inexperienced shunter, the latter will soon become useless in the yard. One of the most pitiful sights in the yard is to see a desperate B-member, standing at the rear of a fast moving cut, trying to figure out what to do before vanishing out of sight, all the while the shunt leader trying to give him orders with exaggerated, Arsenio Hall-like hand signs.

The differences in skill and competence are, however, overshadowed by the hierarchical structure of the team. Every team-member is accorded specific tasks, and although there is some flexibility so that a shunt leader may couple carriages and the C-member may take care of signalling, the essential division of labour is never questioned as a whole.

One of the shunt leaders has the habit of standing ostentatiously at the side of the cut, waiting for the C-member to come and couple the carriages. Any sign of reproach from the C-member, or the B-member as the case may be, is met by a smile and a jestful: 'This is a task for the coupling boy. The shunt-leader should never go between!' This is highly idiosyncratic behaviour on the part of this particular shunt leader, but it is nevertheless quite common for shunt leaders to avoid going between, tacitly assuming that their responsibility for the signalling makes them obliged to stand within view of the driver.

The hierarchy and the division of labour in the team is then only exceptionally held up as a 'principle' to be adhered to blindly, and it is also significant that **when** this happens, it is done in a joking manner. The reason and legitimacy of the strict division of tasks is seen as exclusively functional. One has to know one's tasks, one has to be able to know what every person in the team is up to in order to minimize misunderstandings and thereby risks.

If we now look at the beginner doing his first shifts on his own, we can establish that the C-member already has learnt the technicalities of the tasks; how to couple and uncouple coaches, how to jump on and off and how the signal system works. What remains is the practical questions of **how** to position oneself in the right place; **when** to perform the tasks. All information comes from the shunt leader and a part of the skill is to find the strategies that allows the C-member to meet the shunt leader regularly. The C-member should learn to use every opportunity to get close to the shunt leader and keep his ears open.

Too many questions may be irritating and the C-member soon learns that a questioning look often is enough to get information about what the team is up to next. At a distance the shunt leader will communicate by holding up fingers in the air to signify the amount of carriages for every cut. By using miniature signs and body language he can also tell of future moves as long as he carefully distinguishes them from real signalling.[2]

The positions of the other team members, the switches being turned and the spot where the shunt leader jumps on or off are crucial pieces of information that the C-member will have to learn to decode.

In case the C-member stands on the engine without information, lacking the skill to guess and infer from what happens around him, he may find himself in the wrong place to disconnect the carriages, or miss his duties when the cut is backed down, just to find that he does not know where the next natural meeting-place with the shunt leader will be.

The whole workplace becomes an incomprehensible mumbo-jumbo and he stands all of a sudden alone in the yard, waiting for the engine, which keeps going up and down the tracks far away from him. Someone else might have taken his place and when the engine passes this more experienced person

---

[2] By stiffening the body or by making a sign in a jocular manner one has the possibility to 'quote' a sign in sign-language. Paradoxical as it may sound, the Arsenio Hall-like signalling is an example of enlarged miniature signs. A real sign is always done with relaxed body and a calm look. In signalling rigidity thus has less 'formal' value than laxity. The distinction is crucial as there must be no risk that the engine driver, or a beginner, mistakes it for the real sign. Therefore such 'quoted' signs cannot be used from the very start, but grow slowly out of the field of common understanding. In the beginning the C-member therefore has less information than the experienced 'coupling boy', although he needs it more desperately .

shouts reassuringly: 'We are just going to wash this!' or 'We are just going up to the reserve!' The C-member realizes that he will be unable to do anything for an uncertain period of time. Five minutes, half an hour? He has no idea. Stumbling through the gravel there is nothing else to do but to try to reach the reserve before the engine heads somewhere else, or to wait outside the wash, get onto the rear end of the wet train when it appears, get his gloves soaked – and feel stupid.

An experienced C-member often chooses to stay behind to let the others take care of a few moves. To the team it is quite natural that the C-member sometimes does not bother to follow the engine up and down the yard just in order to do a coupling or two, but leaves these tasks to the C-member. A beginner has too little know-how to venture to do the same. He does not know where he can catch up with the team again and might miss important duties as well, such as repeating the signals.

Omitting to repeat signals is different from omitting other tasks. the C-member might be negligent, ignorant about where to stand, mistaken about his duties, or just maladroit or lost. Whatever the reason it will be made clear to him that even if he neglects all his other tasks the repetition of signals cannot be overlooked. An omission is called a 'deadly sin' – and it is meant to be interpreted literally.

the C-member will always be reminded of his task. 'Go up and repeat', is the order as soon as a long train is going to be pulled. In many cases, though, the need for a 'repetitor' and switch-turner, is not foreseen and there will be problems, unless the C-member already stands on the engine. This is why it is preferred that the C-member give up a few of his tasks in order to stand 'lazily' on the watch on the engine.

Distance and visibility are factors that determine how many persons are needed in any phase of the work. Every bend on the tracks demands an extra link in the chain of signals, in order to instantly repeat a 'stop' or a 'slow'. Sometimes there are not enough team members to fill every gap, and the team has to resort to shouting to each other or one person will run back and forth like a shuttle in order not to miss a signal as well as to keep the next person in the chain assured that there is, at least, **close to** continuous contact. Sometimes the corners are so tight that the poor shuttler has to squeeze himself between the carriages, shout or stick out the lantern round the bend, trusting that the signal is visible to the next person in the signalling chain. Such intensive moments are short, potentially dangerous and relatively rare. Soon the persons in the chain of signals will scatter in order to prepare for other tasks, each one again adjusting his work territory to the other members of the team.[3]

Seen from a bird's eye view the team contracts and disperses as if the members were all attached to the engine by rubber bands, only to be scattered over and over again by some unknown centrifugal force. There are intense moments and slack periods, periods when people are running, and periods when people just stand and stare, waiting for a signal or a carriage to appear. To an outsider some of these slack moments can look like moments of relaxation and 'hanging around', but the shunters have the habit of looking careless and relaxed while they observe a number of things; the *littera* and the order of the carriages in a train, switches turned far up in the yard, movements by train-pullers and other staff, and, first and foremost, the shunting engine, its movements and whereabouts.

Longer slack periods are often spent sitting inside a carriage, on the footstep outside it, or simply on a rail. Such periods are dead time and not particularly popular. The team may be waiting for a late train, for the staff in the Hall to finish a train so that it can be pulled, or for an engine driver to turn up. 'There goes our coffee break', someone will mutter and the irritation is raised by a degree or two. When out working, the engine should be moving constantly.

The kicks should 'hang', the connections and disconnections should be performed with a certain rhythm. Everyone is keeping an eye on the engine and all extra periods of waiting and all superfluous movements are noticed. In case the team-members are young and inexperienced there is always the anxiety that they will do something wrong and dangerous, and although the responsibility lies on the shunt leader, everyone is aware of the beginner as the 'weak link' of the chain. It affects the work of everyone. It cannot be taken for granted that this person understands what he should do, even when being given explicit instructions, and the informal split of tasks according to where one is situated is hampered. This affects the flow.

With a minimum of knowledge, and as soon as he can show convincingly that he has a sound judgement and can be relied upon in all common situations, the C-member can work as a full member of the team, but he has nevertheless little positive impact on the 'flow' of the team. The main factor creating flow is the planning of the shunt leader, (and his cooperation with the *tkm* and the B-member), and the skill he shows in kicking carriages – and the

---

[3] I am using the definition of 'territoriality' versus 'space' according to Lyman and Scott. Cf. LYMAN & SCOTT, 236 ff. Goffman would perhaps talk about 'use space', one of the many types of territories he defines. Cf. GOFFMAN 1972, 58.

B-member in stopping them. If all the kicks 'reach' and the carriages 'hang' everywhere there is good 'flow' and extra trips going up and down the shunting route are avoided.

Style, Taste, and Opinions – Differences between Teams

> 'When I go out working with Pedersen he knows exactly, from reading the work schedule only, where I will start and what I am going to do. I only have to pull the train and I can start kicking down carriages. I can be sure that the tracks are lined. If I go out with someone else I constantly have to tell him what I will do. This is why I enjoy working with Pedersen. We always understand each other. We almost understand each other **too** well.'

The natural outcome of three persons working together day after day in a team is naturally that they learn to work together and develop their own routines. This is stressed by the shunters and it is considered that the understanding between the shunt leader and particularly the B-member often is of an almost telepathic kind.

New persons who are introduced to the team take up the particular way of working that prevails and they will then in many cases pass it on when they have reached a higher position in the team.

Persons who worked with 'Kansas' are for example said to have learnt to read the slips as well as to kick the carriages with such a force that they never stop short. To Kansas a kick was never too hard. Stories abound:

> Once a tremendous clash was heard, and shortly after Kansas appeared from between two carriages. He brushed some dust off his clothes and nodded towards a buffer that had fallen off in the clash. 'Remove this carriage for change of buffers!' was all he said before he walked away.

> A new team member had initiated a signal and Kansas corrected him harshly: 'Here **I** initiate the signals.' Moving along, the beginner, not daring to show 'slow' or 'stop', waited in vain for Kansas's signal and the cut crashed into another one. '...but **if** you initiate a signal you should terminate it, too,' Kansas said – and walked away.

Such stories are told to beginners as an explanation for prevailing differences. So and so was educated and thereby 'corrupted' *('förstörd')*[4] by Kansas, so he

---

[4] The word *'förstörd'* means 'destroyed' or 'ruined', but it does not always have the same disastrous ring to it in Swedish as in English. It is in fact often used as a descriptive term of someone being initiated and skilled, meaning that the person has lost the innocent view or mind

expects every kick to reach the cut, he can handle any 'smoker' ('*rykare*', i.e. a particularly hard kick) and he expects everyone to read the slips and figure out for himself what is going on. Often this may not actually be the case during work. Exaggerated expectations are induced as a side effect of, perhaps, a wish to tell a story or two about a 'Golden Oldie', rather than as a piece of useful advice to the beginner who is about to work with the former disciples of Kansas.

Due to the constant interchange of members in any team such idiosyncratic habits are bound to get polished and moulded more towards a common 'standard', but the memories of e.g. Kansas linger on and his examples are held up as yard sticks to others. If someone calls a moderate kick a 'smoker', the heirs of Kansas will laugh and say: 'A 'smoker', this!? You should have seen Kansas when...' The heirs of Kansas will not stop you from 'initiating' a signal, but if you show 'slow' too often they will perhaps tell you that it is better to give the shunting engine a miss once in a while than to constantly slow it down.

There are then three core-members in a team, and as they sometimes work together for years, they become an entity in the eyes of the rest. Particularly the leader and the *B-member* become a couple that are mentioned in the same breath, and although they may have little in common otherwise, they somehow adjust and grow together and often hold the same opinions.

If someone in the team does not play cards it affects the card-playing pattern of the whole team as a lack of players stops the game altogether. The team members may also arrive and leave together as one reason for joining a team has been that the members live in the same area and thus are able to co-drive to work. '*Bålsta-gänget*' ('The Bålsta Gang') was named as a consequence of such an arrangement. Those who commute on the trains also tend to travel together.

There is, then, ample opportunity for team-members to discuss matters of work. Going to work, working, spending breaks and going back home again in the company of the same persons means that the team-members share the same work experiences to a very high degree, as well as the fact that they formulate their thoughts, express their feelings and mould their views in each other's company, sometimes even after work hours.[5]

---

of the outsider. In the case above it signifies that the pupils of Kansas were accustomed to handling high speed and tough kicks.

[5] There is no institutionalized drinking or socializing in restaurants or pubs after work as the case is for example in Britain. (Cf. COCKBURN 1984, 18, 169) At times groups have formed around a particular waterhole down-town, but such groups have then dispersed, never constituting a continuous tradition.

The loyalty to the team became more pronounced during the reorganization period, when discussions were more frequent and opinions differed more sharply than before. In one of the discussions one quite young B-member was involved in an argument about standing on the ground versus standing on the engine while the leader of his team was momentarily absent; a fact that probably was the reason for the B-member to get himself involved at all, otherwise he might have left the argumentation to his much more knowledgeable and verbal superior.

Anyhow, the B-member was defending the new way of working, a way his team, too, had adopted. Another young shunter was telling him that this way of working only was a trap set by the employer in order to reduce the number of men in the team. The B-member denied this, but did not have any argument to back his views with.

The discussion then ended, but as it happened, it was brought up again when the shunt leader arrived. The shunt leader spoke up in defence of the new way of working, but when met with the argument that the new order was a way of luring the workers into more intensive work, eventually leading to a reduction in the team, the shunt leader – to everyone's surprise – immediately admitted that this was very likely the case. 'We'll probably lose a member in the team in the long run. There is no doubt about it that this is the point of the reform', he said 'but, I think that it is well worth it. I don't want to work in the old way anyhow.' To this his B-member immediately agreed, nodding and adding: 'Exactly.'

The team view was, no doubt, restored, and the B-member no longer had to deny the negative effect of the reform - negative from a 'union point of view'. It could be admitted. It was regrettable, but it was still 'worth it'. To this the other party had few arguments.

Thus teams often develop both a specific way of working as well as uniform opinions about work matters. The beginner who almost exclusively works as a VIK, is shuttled to and fro between all the various teams, getting a different taste of work every shift. If he ever had a uniform picture of 'the shunters' it is modfied little by little. The shunters appear increasingly as a colourful bunch of individuals with different styles, tastes and opinions. Simultaneously the beginners see themselves increasingly as part of the shunting collective, but there is no contradiction in this. The shunters are, according to their own picture, a collective of highly individualistic and 'weird' persons. One works according to the style of Hagalund, but as a person one is most likely to stay and thrive if one has a slightly odd personality. It is really considered that working at Hagalund presupposes that you are a bit 'crazy'. 'Those are the kind of people who always were attracted to this job.'

~~~

In sum, the team-work of the shunting team is more than cooperation. While the train-puller in principle can work on his own at any time, loosing only flow, and creating longer waiting periods for incoming trains, the shunter **cannot** work on his own. The only exception is the rare occasion when a shunter is sent to collect or deliver a single carriage. However, as soon as there are several carriages on the hook, the vision between driver and shunter is reduced, and several persons have to be involved.

Shunting proper is, naturally, not to move one carriage from here to there, but to split trains into smaller cuts and scatter these all over the yard – and assemble them into new trains. This requires that signals are repeated in bends, that carriages are stopped on the sidetracks, and that there is a leader who can coordinate the tasks.

If I may use a musical allegory I would say that train-pulling is like an assembly of recorders, all playing the same tune, while shunting is an orchestra, a collection of different instruments led by a conductor. It is not necessary for all players to play neither simultaneously nor continuously, what matters is that everyone is prepared to time his entrés, keep the rhythm – and play well.

When Team-Work Breaks down

As part of the reorganization new teams were formed. One of them consisted of a couple of old hands, one of whom, Örby, had consistently avoided working steady in teams. One could thus perhaps have predicted that Örby would have problems adapting to the regular working life of a steady team. As it happened he became the shunt leader in a team where the *tkm* was another strong personality of the shunting group; the Scarf.

The Scarf was also a man with firmly held opinions, and, like Örby, he made no secret of them. Diplomacy was not a concept familiar with the Scarf, and he never bothered with small talk, or greetings.

It has been almost impossible to find out exactly what brought Örby and the Scarf on a head-on collision course. The reasons varied from instance to instance, and all the various incidents seemed to have in common was that the contracting parties were unusually stubborn. The 'personal chemistry' (*personkemin*) did not work, was the general judgement, and this was also the view of one of the quarreling parties. 'I thought that after my holiday I could

81

come back and make a fresh start, that things would go more smoothly. But it did not take more than a shift before we were back to where we left,' Örby said, smiling at the thought.

The adjustment to the way of working did not take place as they had different views on almost every matter and as neither of them was prepared to give way. As they were in the positions of *tkm* and shunt leader, respectively, they differed from the usual socialization pattern, where the shunt leader teaches a B-member how to shunt, thereby moulding him to his own viewpoints in the process. These two were already both competent as *tkm* as well as shunt leaders.

The personalities, as well as a range of other commonly known biographical facts, made both parties in the wrangle well-established eccentrics, but as long as one of them worked as a VIK they could handle their disagreements. It was only when they were working together permanently that it ended in a disastrous relationship.

What is primarily of interest, however, is not the details of the wrangle, but rather what other things were revealed in the process. This case is the only case of disturbance within a team during the last ten years that has had an impact outside the team, in that it has been discussed and commented upon as an example. It seemed to concern everyone. It was constantly in the limelight.

One of the most important ingredients of the quarrel, as far as it is possible to discern, was the argument about the role of the shunt leader when driving the engine. Örby insisted on standing on the engine, and this irritated the Scarf, who wanted the shunt leader on the ground. The common reading of why the Scarf disapproved of Örby standing on the engine was that he was envious as he himself had not been educated as an engine operator (although he had declined this education when offered).

There were all opportunities for the other shunters to take sides in the argument on these grounds, saying that it was right to stand on the engine or it was wrong to stand on the engine. Although this was one of the important issues at the time, and the subject of many a heated discussion, the views of Örby and the Scarf were never brought into the arguments, and were never judged to be right or wrong from this point of view. The common verdict was instead that both parties were wrong **because they argued.** The wrangle **as such** was condemned, as well as their individual behaviour. A team should keep together, they should be able to compromise, to adjust, regardless of their views and regardless of their eccentricity. This did not mean that arguments or fights should be avoided at all costs, quite the contrary. Quarrels should be brought out straight away, but they should be resolved quickly and definitely, leaving no chafing grudges. Such quarrels could concern all kinds of work procedures, but not the team hierarchy.

Even in this case, where the disagreement coincided with a conflict which threatened to divide the shunters into two camps, everybody agreed that the different standpoint should not be allowed to enter the practices of everyday work. Work should go on, and arguing and fighting about roles at work should be resolved before or after going into the yard. 'It is horrible', one senior shunter said 'I have never seen the like of this during all my years here. One comrade is calling another one – well, almost an idiot!' Here he obviously did not refer to words uttered directly between two fighting-cocks in the yard, but to a fight being extended from the yard into the corridors and the coffee-room, and vice versa. Worse words than 'idiot' have been vociferated in the yard, and worse expressions may hail around the card-table, but these should never be transferred from one context into another, from one arena into another.

The fight ended when the manager finally found about the whole thing and separated the two combatants into different teams. 'This seems to have been going on for months', he complained, 'they just don't tell me about things like that.'

No Lingering Grudges

'This is not a workplace for the brooding type.'

'We shout and call each other names, but five minutes later it is all forgotten and we are friends just like before.'

'The new manager asked me if I knew 'a man called Strömqvist'. Well, I said, We worked together a little in the sixties, during the seventies, and during the eighties, and there have been a few shifts during the nineties as well. We had a disagreement in -76, but I think that it is more or less settled by now.'

The constant fighting in a team was seen as a disturbing factor at work, and not only that, it was considered dangerous. 'When you argue, that's when things start happening', one senior commented on the quarrel. On the other hand one will find that perhaps the most prevalent reason old shunters refer to when explaining why they have liked working at Hagalund is exactly that one never has to hold one's tongue. All disagreements are expressed immediately. You can tell someone off, or they could tell you off, and then it is all forgotten and over with.

One can question whether it is actually possible to imagine that the person being told off can, or even is expected to, forget the scolding. When talking to the shunters about being corrected or scolded, this seems to be far from the case. To tell someone off and then never to talk about it again is a way of restricting the outbreaks to the yard. Discussions, excuses, or sullen faces are not allowed.

Irritation and anger in the yard is seen as something spontaneous, deriving from the risk and danger that surrounds the shunters in their work. One does not mean to be unpleasant and angry, but one reacts instinctively for the benefit of everybody, for life and limb. It does not follow from this that the scolded party will forget the incident. Talking to shunters in private they can tell stories about 'the time I got a severe scolding', often in great detail, and often many years, even decades, after the incident occurred.

Vikman who has been working in the yard for about ten years told me, quite embarrassed, that he had been 'yelled at' once. He could remember the details of the incident very clearly and even added as extenuating circumstances that the severity of the outbreak partly was caused by the fact that the shunt leader who yelled at him was going through a difficult time as he was trying to give up smoking.

To be told off is thus something you don't forget. It is not unusual to ponder over the incident, and Vikman even tried to find extenuating circumstances for the scolding, not, however, denying he had done something stupid.

A multitude of minor reproaches, summons and reprimands are difficult to distinguish from orders and demands. An angry: *'Häng på där borta – och det är för gott!'* (Hook it over there – and it is for good!) is an order, but an order that perhaps had been unnecessary to a good B-member. Such common utterings can then be seen as simple orders or reprimands, depending on the ambition level of the person receiving them, or they can be seen as educational, reproachful or simply 'making sure', on behalf of the person uttering them. They may cause instant irritation, but are treated as if they were not given much afterthought.

The point is that while reproof and scoldings may be remembered for years, being referred to in stories and causing changes in relationships between persons, it is nevertheless **thought** that everything is deleted from the mind, forgotten, of no further significance. It is not legitimate to express intentions of 'paying back' for such incidents in the yard and it is seldom sucessful to read and explain the motives for other persons actions in terms of 'revenges'. When a shunter refers to a disagreement he had with someone in 1976, saying

84

that 'I think it is more or less settled by now', this is a joke which will only fall into good ground in the context of the shunting yard.[6]

Shunt leader showing 'coupling'.

---

[6] This jocular answer to a question from the manager draws a demarcation line between the shunters and the manager; the only person new enough to ask such a question. As a mild form for 'jocular aggression', as Pogrebin & Poole would call it, this joke points out the ignorance of the manager, as well as the social cohesion of the group. Cf. POGREBIN & POOLE, 189 ff.

Above: Rembrandts at work.
Below: Putting out a last minute brake heel.

5. THE CREATION OF GROUP FEELING – ENTRY TO THE SHUNTING YARD

Official Requirements

The selection of prospective shunters is determined by the fact that shunting work is classified as 'Security Service' (SeS). This category comprises a large number of SJ employees and the regulations list staff operating, handling, or coming into contact with rolling stock.

There are some general requirements for all staff in SeS, besides the knowledge of specified parts of the Security Regulations *(Säkerhetsordningen)*. These general requirements are stated in SÄM *(Säkerhetsmeddelande)* 7 as:

- Judged (through selective means) to be suitable
- Fulfilling medical requirements
- To have passed educational requirements
- To know[1] and to be willing to apply regulations
- Free from alcohol and narcotics while on duty
- To have passed further education

To these requirements a couple of reassuring remarks are added:

- A person who does not fulfil the requirements will be relocated
- In case you yourself feel that you do not fulfil the requirements you will get aid in your relocation[2]

One can naturally ponder on the difference between being relocated and being aided to relocation, but the unspoken message is that no one should fear losing one's job because of decreasing physical or mental abilities of any kind – or alcoholism or drug abuse, for that matter. One cannot be held responsible for

---

[1] The Swedish verb *'kunna'*, which is used here, means 'to know' as well as 'to be able to'. Here the first interpretation seems reasonable.

[2] SÄM 7.

illness. On the other hand, what one **is** responsible for is to put security first and notify one's superiors as soon as one is no longer able to accomplish one's tasks with the maximum of one's abilities. One is, then, not punished, but aided in finding another occupation, within the bounds of the company.

In spite of this, the thought of relocation often constitutes a threat to the employees as it is assumed that the job one is aided to find will be an inferior one in status. A standard joke in answer to the question how one succeeded in the annual exam of the Security Regulations is to say: 'Good-bye folks, I'm on my way to collect a broom.' The prospect of transfer is thus depicted as a one-way ticket to a gloomy future cleaning the pits in the New Hall.

There is, however, also another official requirement. In case of war SJ falls under military command and the staff in SeS will consequently have military obligations. This is a fact seldom mentioned except in the introductory course, but the term Security Service has a serious overtone that no doubt gets its strength from this very fact. Senior shunters sometimes tell of how during WW II they shunted explosives and other materials to secret armouries, thereby giving this otherwise very abstract and remote aspect of SeS a touch of reality.

War is indeed felt to be very distant and foreign to the daily toil in the yard, and although Swedish citizenship was still obligatory for staff in SeS twenty years ago, no one in the yard seems to give much thought to the position of non-Swedish citizens in SeS today. Being a foreigner myself I asked the teacher at the introductory course, as well as other shunters, what they thought would be the status of non-Swedish citizens in case of war, but I was met by faint smiles and shrugged shoulders. There is little, or no, knowledge among the shunters in general about what the military obligations comprise and one can only speculate what mistakes, breaches of regulations, disobeyance of orders, etc. would lead to in wartime.

Despite ignorance about the exact details of prospective military obligations the mere knowledge that shunting is classified as a job of such vital national importance creates an image of the shunters as standing up to specific requirements. 'We who are in Security Service...' is a phrase often accompanied complaints or demands concerning conditions of work.

Judged to be Suitable

If we look at the requirements for staff in SeS from the point of view of the shunting staff we have the initial selection process. This is when the applicants are filtered out by a recruiting officer. The procedure is quite normal as it consists of presenting *curriculum vitæ* and then an interview where prospective shunters are asked about their interests and their past working experiences.[3]

The employment procedure has changed during the last couple of years in connection with the Health Centre being separated from SJ and transferred to the National Health Service *(Statshälsan)*. This reorganization swept away the post of the employee counselor *(personalkonsulent)* who was formerly in charge of arranging the interviews and then handing the applicants over to the chairman of the union club. These two then 'made their observations independently of each other', as the club chairman put it, and by comparing notes they could dismiss persons 'who could not be considered'. Persons who for some reason seemed suspect could be checked further as to their former employment, and indeed one such man turned out to have a history of misbehaving and was as a consequence not employed. It seems, however, that such investigation was rather rare as this was the **only** incident the longtime union chairman could remember had resulted in rejection of the applicant.

Fluctuations in the labour market are of great importance for the number of persons showing an interest in the job, and this naturally makes a great difference to the work of the recruiting officer. In times of plenty the crucial question is how to pick those who seem to be promising, while during other times almost all effort will go into finding people at all.

Knowing that most newcomers vanish rather quickly the overall policy, when possible, has been to employ far more people than needed. The selection process under these circumstances is more a question of informing the applicants about the requirements of the job than of actively weeding out everyone who seems unsuitable. The employer might have thought that the applicant did not fit the crew, but if this person was stubborn enough to be willing to give it a try despite all warnings... well, why not? There had once

---

[3] At the time of my employment this interview marked the end of a 'Day of Introduction' during which most parts of Hagalund were shown under guidance by union representatives.

been an applicant who was a member of the Jehovah's Witnesses. Being shown around the premises by the club chairman he had the opportunity to observe the shunters playing cards. The chairman said:

"I warned him. I said : 'Go in and talk to the fellows in there and you'll hear what they say.' Well, the Norwegian was in there with that gang, playing cards. A hell of a noise it was, banging and shouting. When he had been in there and listened for a while and came out again I said to him: 'Can you consider listening to this every day?' No he couldn't, but he could consider trying to convert them. A dead loss, such work... 'My dear friend' I said, 'you'd better look for something else.' I told him honestly: 'You're welcome to work at SJ. Your merits are so good that you certainly can do that. But if you can't tolerate that particular jargon they have in there then you should not apply for this job, because in that case you'll create a hell for yourself."[4]

The company round the card table here incidentally included one of the most notorious card players whose roaring laughter has become legendary. The account does not tell us what words actually were uttered, but often it is the volume of the shouts and bursts of laughter, rather than actually foul or indecent language that could intimidate visitors. However, the sight of the merry card-players and the words of the club chairman must have been effective as the Witness eventually judged his prospects as a soul saver as rather poor, and transferred to calmer moorings within the company.

However limited the selective process was in practice, due to the small number of applicants, it was still in the hands of the local staff. As with the case of the Jehovah's Witness it was also possible to introduce the applicants to the 'setting' and give them an idea of the environment and style of interaction among the shunters. When this process later was removed to a distant office, *Regionala Personalkontoret*, (RPK), the regional personnel office, in Sundbyberg, the feeling was that there no longer was any control of how many, or what kind of applicants you were dealing with.

This spell of employing people centrally for the region only lasted for a few years, as the regional personnel office was split up as a part of the new organization of SJ (1988) and the central recruiting officers were dispersed to different stations willing to employ them. Hagalund, not being 'quick enough', according to one of the staff delegators, found itself left without a

---

[4] INT 8

share in the scramble supper and consequently appointed one of the local staff delegators to this job. This person described himself as an 'emergency solution' only and sighed that the task of recruiting staff to the whole station was too much to handle for one person alone. So far he had only been involved in recruiting one – the latest – bunch of shunters. This task had been simple as the initial twelve applicants had boiled down to the final three. Three persons had failed the medicals, and the six remaining ones had second thoughts when informed about the pay and the work hours.

'...the kind of people they send down here!'

From the point of view of the shunters the recruiting officer has an outsider's opinion of what it takes to work as a shunter, and over the years there has been criticism from the shunters about 'the kind of people they send down here'. This criticism is not in any way an official one, ie. it does not even reach up to the local union club, but it is just a grumbling in the corridors.

To the shunters, the fact that most of the newcomers leave the job rather quickly after, or even during, the introductory course, is proof that the selection process is too lax. Popular examples are often repeated which are considered to show the incompetence of the people responsible for recruiting staff. There you have the story about the man who turned out to be 'switch-blind', the one about the man who turned out to be crippled by atrophic legs, and the one about the man who was 'so short that he obviously thought that he could walk straight in between the coaches without bending under the buffers'. ('He almost got even shorter.')

Naturally, the truth of such stories cannot be verified. In the case of the examples above, the first is based on the assumption that there is a specific disability that the shunters call 'switch-blindness'. Persons who are switch-blind are not able to learn to see how a switch is lined. As a consequence such persons cannot work as shunters. The second story will, if recorded, be hidden in the secrecy of the medical files, while the third, which seemingly is critical of accepting people too short in stature to the shunting crew, really is a judgement of the mental aptitude of that person.[5] What you had was a person

---

[5] Switch-blindness as well as suffering from athropic legs was not stigmatized, but the fact that these persons were said to deny, hide and lie about their handicaps was seen not as brave and

who could, or would, not learn one of the basic unbendable rules; always to bend under the buffers.

There are numerous stories about persons who never stayed very long in the job and who displayed intelligence below normal, according to the general judgement of the steady shunters. The stories are told to exemplify 'all the nerds we have had to put up with', and it is often stressed that it is close to a miracle that no serious accidents have befallen these unfortunate figures. The blame is then, indirectly, put on the recruiting staff who are suspected of sifting out the more promising characters to other places while the shunters are given the task of taking care of what is left. 'They think that anyone can do this job.'

This view is not consistent with how the shunters look upon the service department, the staff of which is considered to be accepted without any selection whatsoever. Indeed, that is where some of the shunting apprentices should have been sent in the first place, according to these more suspicious and cynical readings. There are naturally shunters who recognize the difficulties facing the person who has to select staff to the shunting crew, as in times of low unemployment there may be very few candidates to choose from. It is further recognized that as no one has experience from shunting 'in the backyard at home', as eg. a car repair man might have, there is really no telling who can do the job without having a go at it. The ones who cannot cope with the work, or who don't fit the ambiance, will leave. 'That's the way it's always been.'

At times there has been a high turn-over among the beginners in contrast to the more experienced staff, who on the contrary have been remarkably stable. In the seven year period between 1982 and 1989, at the peak of the reorganization, there were twenty [+11] who were employed for less than a year. Six [+4] of these were women. The numbers in brackets refer to persons whose careers in the shunting trade were either too short to leave any dates at all in the registers or who were formally employed as shunters but quickly relocated to other tasks. This could be because they asked for it, because they showed some physical disability that was not detected in the the physical examination (such as perhaps switch-blindness), or because they did not pass the SÄO exam.

admirable but as foolish, unrealistic and potentially dangerous.

In 1988 the old complaints about 'the kind of people they send down here' started to dry up definitely as it was clear that external factors, ie. the at the time overheated labour market, was the main selective force. The three men that took part in the shunting course in November 1988 marked the end of the rope and all efforts to attract new people through extensive advertising in the evening papers proved ineffective. The result in terms of applicants was very meagre. Only one person was said to have shown interest, but learning how much she would be paid she found her present job as a market vendor more rewarding. The fact that it seemed virtually impossible to recruit new shunters worked as a catalyst for the events that were to follow during the spring of 1989.

Summing up, one could say that there was a swing from blaming the employers for not getting hold of people who could work and who were reasonably resistant to rain and wind, to blaming oneself for putting up with working conditions that everyone else seemed to shun and deem unbearable, given the pay offered. In discussions and comments one could feel the presence of questions like: Why doesn't anyone want to work here? Are we putting up with working conditions and wages that are completely outdated? Is the reason we are here that we are stupid, not enterprising enough or just trapped due to lack of other skills? The old saying: 'You have to be crazy to work here'[6] seemed to take on a new and far more negative meaning.

Some shunters pointed to the fact that the recruitment procedures were removed from the supervision of the shunters. It was said that there just as well could have been more than five (or one, the number varied) persons answering the advertisements. There were references to the former occasion of recruiting new staff when, it was said, there had been 70 applicants to the central office, while only three of them were referred to Hagalund.

There was obviously a certain discrepancy between the account the recruiting officer had given of the last successful recruitment of three beginners and the story that was told among the shunters. With some corrections of the figures the two accounts could be made to coincide, but it is important to notice that they stress different aspects and are used to illustrate two separate

---

[6] One of the most common notices on pinboards and walls in Swedish workplaces during the last decade or so must be the one saying: 'You don't have to be crazy to work here – but it helps!'

93

problems. The recruiting officer told of his experience in recruiting shunters – as opposed to eg. cleaners – and that he in that process never had faced the problem of assessing individual qualities. The initial (twelve) persons he had to judge boiled down to three 'automatically', without his intervention.

The shunter, on the other hand, was referring to the central office receiving a great number of applicants, but leaving in effect only three to Hagalund. Other stations were favoured, due to acts or omissions by people further up in the hierarchy. The point of this version of the story was then that there seemed to be people out there willing to work as shunters, but through procedures that were beyond the control of the shunters and local staff it was all made to look like the opposite. One could only suspect the motives behind it all...

There were thus suspicions of a rather unspecified kind towards people 'higher up' in SJ. It could be the local manager who wanted to save money, forcing the staff to accept a bonus-scheme with a harder work-schedule on the pretence that the over-time problem could not be solved by employing more staff. It could be the SJ bureaucracy and the other stations showing their anger, envy and stinginess towards the shunters at Hagalund once again. One could not tell. The only thing one **knew** was that the hours of legal over-time were running out and that Hagalund, and especially the shunters, had 'always' been disliked and maligned by all other groups. Wasn't it strange that the employment situation so beautifully fitted these facts?

So there were suspicions against the local managers as well as against other stations and SJ, seen as a whole and separate from the shunting group at Hagalund. The reasons for the hostility and envy that lay at the bottom of it all were lost in a distant past when the picture of the tough and unpleasant shunters had come into being. 'It's always been like that. Hagalund, and particularly the shunters, had a bad reputation already when I started here thirty years ago', the senior shunters would say.

In sum we can say that recruiting new staff is a serious and delicate matter. The shunters see the recruitment as an entry to the group, and the person, or persons, in charge of this are seen as gate-keepers of a kind.

The act of employing people means that new persons are admitted entrance to this rather closed world and the criteria you have when selecting newcomers is at the same time the definition of the group. Sending down people who have been unemployed during the time when work was abundant, or women who cannot work outdoors when it is raining because their make-up is ruined, is not only foolish, it is on the verge of insulting to the shunters. 'It's incredible that they send down people like that! What kind of people do they think can manage this job? Do they think this is some kind of a dump?' Comments abound.

Paradoxically enough, shunters acknowledge that is close to impossible to judge immediately who is going to be a talented, or even a decent, shunter, and who is not. There are well-known instances of persons who seemed very promising but failed later on. The fact that the inital selection is out of the hands and control of the shunters leads, however, to suspicions that the persons sent 'down' to the shunting yard do not constitute the best of the available stock. Whether such suspicions can be substantiated is not a point. Similar suspicions will crop up again and again as long as the common understanding is that Hagalund is disliked and despised and the shunters are downgraded, neglected and discriminated against.

Medical Requirements – The Beginners' Point of View

The second one of the criteria in SÄM 7, 'fulfilling medical requirements', is seen as a well-defined requirement. You either fail or pass. This view is held by the shunters as well as the recruiting officer. We saw earlier that the twelve applicants boiled down to nine because three persons failed the medical tests. What is it then that makes the examination at the Health Centre the crucial moment in the selection process?

While you can exaggerate your interest in the shunting job (and sports) and state that shift-work and out-door work suit you fine, that the pay is acceptable, etc., the possibility to 'cheat' at the auditory, lung, colour blindness and blood examinations seems nonexistent. The sophisticated apparatus used in the testing, all the apparently precise figures that are taken down in your file and finally the confrontation with the physician, dressed in the authoritative white coat, all places the applicant, stripped down to his shorts, in an inferior and vulnerable position.

The institutional framework of the medical examination suggests high demands, precise measures, absolute limits and clearcut categories. Discussion or negotiation seems out of the question. There are exact tests, which the doctor sums up, and then s/he spells out the verdict. The words of the physician are given a weight transforming marginal comments into judgements, and advice into decisions.

During my own tests the physician said that I was 'rather short', an utterance that, to me, immediately signalled a serious objection jeopardizing my employment. I was quite surprised to find later that there were several shunters working in the yard (men as well as women) who were actually shorter than me. This puzzled me and I mentioned the doctor's remark to shunters a couple of times. Beside pointing out that the persons who had trouble with their stature were the tall persons, who got back-trouble from the constant bending under buffers, they also asked me how I **managed to pass** anyway, which indicates that my initial reading of the remark was quite natural from the point of view of the applicant.

The medical is done by individual appointment and the applicant is therefore likely to face the nurse and physician after waiting all alone in the waiting room. The destiny of co-applicants who also took part in the interview at the Day of Introduction will then be uncertain. There is no one to compare notes with, so to speak, and the short meeting with the shunters may well have left an impression of a loud, tough and physically fit bunch of workers. The bulky overalls, the large gloves and steel-enforced boots add up to a picture of force, and the dirt and oil so visible on the sleeves, legs and backs of the orange overalls testify to the physical efforts that constitute – one assumes – the main part of the work.

Needless to say, the atmosphere of the Health Centre stands in sharp contrast to the noise and dirt among the shunters. Soft easy chairs in subdued colours, silent corridors, clean instruments and white coats are in every way the opposite to the shunters' coffee-room, but that is no more than anyone would expect. My point is that the initial knowledge one has of the shunting work as a dirty, heavy, and dangerous occupation is strengthened by the experience of going through the medical tests. Blowing into a machine, to test the lung capacity, sitting in a sound proof booth to listen to minute sounds in a couple of ear phones, taking blood tests without grasping exactly the purpose of them, being studied from all angles by the doctor; all this seems to contrast the idiosyncratic qualities of the lone applicant to an 'ideal shunter'.

This must indeed be seen as the moment when the shunters come to

96

constitute a distinct group, different from other workers at Hagalund, in the eyes of the applicant. The group is set apart by the threshold of physical requirements, a threshold that is invisible and unknown to the applicant, concealed in incomprehensible figures and measures, but at the same time assumed to be quite real, absolute and precise. The results are interpreted and mediated by the physician and there is no point in discussing the results. In case of failing one cannot go home, do some more homework and come back for a new test. One may instead be offered a job in the Hall,[7] with the cleaning or with the handling of linen, etc.

I am here discussing the setting in general terms. There are obviously great differences in how the applicants experience the situation. A tiny person, who feels that his/her physical abilities might be below 'normal' (i.e. compared to an average **man**), or below what the job presumably demands, will probably feel more intimidated and uncertain, and direct the mind to this threshold more than a physically fit young man who recently has undergone similar tests in the conscription to the army, and who might not give the procedure much thought. The height of the threshold thus varies significantly and thereby also the appreciation of the difference between the applicant and the shunters, as well as the difference between the shunters and other groups of workers.

The appreciation of this difference is later of great importance in the acquisition of skills. The view of what work demands, in relation to the conception and appreciation of one's own abilities to stand up to those demands, direct – as we shall see – the beginners towards different strategies of learning and coping.

Medical Requirements – The Medical Point of View

The staff at the Health Centre present a radically different picture of how the medical requirements are interpreted and applied. According to them there are very few medical indications that constitute an absolute obstacle for employment and this is a result of the development over the last twenty years towards more elastic rules. The physician considered this development to be caused partly by an increased knowledge about risks and diseases and partly

---

[7] 'The Hall' is used as a term for all staff working in the New and the Old Halls, as well as a term for the two buildings.

because there is generally an increased concern about justice towards the individual.

The earliest rules were concerned almost exclusively with the safety aspect from the point of view of the company rather than of the individual workers. Categorical judgements were used, ruling out the possibility to assess individual cases.[8] Today, according to the physician, there is a larger margin for considering every case on its own terms and judging the prospects from the medical profile of the individual.

That the test results are read within such a framework is, I claim, largely unknown to the shunters to be as well as to the old employees. It is well known that old and experienced shunters are likely to be granted exemption in the case of lesser defects, thus assuming that the criteria in themselves are definite and unshaken. Also the cases of 'carelessness' or 'incompetence' that they believe have been revealed stem from this view of the rules as set and unbent.

The indications that constitute an unsurmountable hindrance to the fledgling in shorts are really only colour blindness and various rather severe handicaps. A young man who insisted he wanted to become a shunter, although he had a prosthetic leg, was thus not employed. It is interesting to note that this case wasn't a clearcut one, in spite of the rather obvious handicap. The recruiting officer said that he noted at the interview that the man limped, but when questioned the man explained that he had recently injured his foot when mending his car. The recruiting officer felt that there was something strange about the explanation and asked the physician to check the foot of this applicant carefully. It was then found that the man had an artificial limb, but even so the physician hesitated about her verdict as the applicant stated that it would be no impediment at work. Only after again consulting the recruiting officer was it finally decided that the man could not be considered fit enough to work as a shunter.

Hearing and eyesight are not as strictly judged either formally (the limits are not stated in exact figures) or informally (ie. what the doctor judges to be a borderline case) as earlier and, as opposed to earlier, contact lenses can be accepted, provided the person has had them for a long time and is used to

---

[8] Cf.FAF, *passim.* ...

wearing them. New lenses, however that is defined, are still not accepted. The same can be said to apply to diseases like diabetes. An 'old' and meticulously treated diabetes can be accepted, while a 'newly' developed one cannot. Diseases of the heart and high blood pressure are also judged more mildly today. Some of the shunters had shown extremely high blood pressure in tests and were now receiving treatment for it, while still at work. Applicants with equally high blood pressures, however, would not have been accepted, according to the physician.

Citing these examples of preventive care the doctor stressed that the regular health controls benefit the shunters as much as they are quality checks for the benefit of the company and a means to reduce third party risk. The first one, the check of applicants, has still, despite its increasingly flexible criteria for what is to be considered 'normal' or 'healthy', strongly the character of a medical 'exam' as stated in SÄM 7, quoted above.

The Power of the Health Centre

The shunters do not without reservation share the view of the health control as a beneficial aid to discovering diseases and injuries at an early stage. Not only do they distrust that full secrecy is observed by the staff at the Health Centre, but they consider the quality of the care inferior and claim that they often see 'independent' doctors for second opinions.

It is important to stress that I am in no position to form an opinion about these claims, to decide what proportion of the shunters would subscribe to these opinions, which are 'opinions of the coffee-room', or, still less, to judge the merits of the Health Centre. I can only note that shunters in discussions with each other, and particularly when talking in the 'collective mode', cite stories about how they or some other shunter have had second opinions that completely differed from the alarming results they have received from the Health Centre. 'Up at the Health Centre they told me that I had a very high blood pressure, but I had tests done with modern equipment downtown and they told me I had the physique of a much younger man,' one of the shunters told everyone. Such stories are then quoted again and again, sometimes to comfort a work mate who has just received less than perfect test results, sometimes just in order to question the value of the free medical care being offered.

There can be no doubt that the suspicions against the Health Centre are given by structural factors. It is the institutional relationship between the Centre and the shunters, rather than the amount of actual complaints, which nourishes the distrust.[9] The physicians have the power to stop people from being employed and they have continuously the power to stop shunters from working or to have them transferred to other tasks. This fact cannot be denied although they themselves see their role as supportive, loyal and thoroughly helpful to the workers. It is only ironic that the workers consider the task of the doctor as a work to rule, an application of a standard to a high degree, while the doctor stresses the possibility and demand that all judgements be 'adapted to individual circumstances', while at the same time denying having 'power'.

The power of the doctor is considered obvious by the shunters and they seem almost to guard themselves against future possible rejection by declaring that the Health Centre is 'bought' by SJ and that the tests 'up there' are done with equipment that is deficient and outmoded. The doctor on the other hand considers the workers oldfashioned and admitted that certain tests were being done only because people expected that. Blood sedimentation rate *(sänkan)* was such 'cupboard food' *(skåpmat)*, ie. an oldfashioned test, which was done particularly to older people who considered it to belong to normal procedures. 'Otherwise they go down and say that the examination wasn't properly done!' the doctor exclaimed.

The fear of the doctor's power can in its extreme form lead to workers suffering from diseases and injuries for a long time. An old shunter wore out his knees completely, and not until shortly before his retirement was it found out that he was irreparably crippled. According to the files his knees had been normal ten years earlier. 'My God, why didn't you come earlier?!' the doctor

---

[9] Not only the shunters take a critical view of the Health Centre. In September 1989 the union clubs at Hagalund issued an article in their newsletter *Hagalundsbladet* about the Health Centre. This article contained some severe criticism particularly against one of the nurses, demanding her dismissal. Examples of hairraising treatment were decribed in the article. The shunters were eager to make sure I had a copy of the paper. Later, however, persons who had uttered critical remarks concerning the Health Centre indignantly told me that several of the stories in the article were faked. They claimed they had talked to the persons allegedly mistreated by the Centre, who denied everything, saying it all was 'a bunch of lies'. Things that had been stirred up for a moment went back to normal and the more general complaints of the kind I describe above again dominated the discussions.

exclaimed, but the shunter replied that he was afraid that he would have been relocated to a less attractive job. 'Had he only known me better...', the doctor sighed when telling me the story. This shunter was a man who despite his obvious pains performed his work to perfection, to the point of breaking informal rules of leaving early, much to the irritation of his co-workers.

As medical controls are carried out regularly, passing takes on a temporary character. The senior shunters' view of the medical tests are also different from those of the applicant, because the former have an increased knowledge about what the work itself demands, about the kinds of ailments that persons working there tend to bring upon themselves, and also about earlier cases of exemption being granted.

Nevertheless, the ever growing threat to be relocated because of failing health is a sword of Damocles to many shunters. One senior shunter had been told by the doctor at a health control that his hearing was so poor that it was questionable if he could be allowed to continue shunting as he could get run over by a train. 'I'd rather be run over by a train than do some lousy job (*skitjobb*) in the Hall', the shunter said he answered, to the doctor's surprise.

Not all shunters share this fear of being moved to some other job. There are persons who actively apply for removal, hoping the physician will help them by supplying the necessary certificate. One such applicant referred to a complaint in his knees, and wanted to work in the spare part shop, which he saw as a calm and comfortable workplace, but he was never granted this relocation before retiring.[10] To my knowledge, however, very few indeed were aspiring for such 'inferior' jobs in the Hall. Most of them wanted to stay with the shunting group or, if that proved impossible due to of the nature of their complaint, to work in a department that had a superior status, such as staff delegating or the pay office. Or they applied to become engine drivers.

In all such cases the role of the doctors at the Health Centre comes to the fore. Medical certificates from 'independent' doctors are felt not to have the same force as those issued by the Health Centre, the latter seen as being close to 'SJ attestations'. When relocation is refused it is often assumed that there is an inofficial agreement between doctors and employers, who are then collectively referred to with a contemptuous 'those up there'. Even then the

---

[10] Significantly enough he worked as a train-puller, i.e. as a 'loner', and not in a team with 'shunting proper'.

Health Centre is considered to be the decisive party. It is felt that the doctors have the power to arrange a long term sick leave, a sick pension or a transfer if they only want to, regardless of the opinions of the employer.

As opposed to 'concrete' diseases, diseases that often, but not always, have rather obvious symptoms and that are not stigmatized to the degree that they cannot be discussed openly with work-mates, there are naturally also more secret matters concerning health and wellbeing. Alcohol problems, drug problems or mental problems such as depressions and problems concerning relations at work are all such delicate matters. These are discussed among the shunters, but seldom or never when the concerned person is present, although close friends might confide in each other to a degree that naturally is difficult to assess. Anyone seeing the doctor in order to ventilate such questions will most probably do it in secret and not announce it in the coffee-room. I was told by a doctor that shunters indeed did consult the Health Centre for some minor complaint and that it then would turn out that the 'real' reason for the visit was that they felt they had been unfairly treated by workmates or by the company.

Distrusting the Health Centre is thus very much of a public attitude. In the private and in secret there seems to exist – although I cannot say to what extent – a fair amount of trust. At least the shunters know that the doctors know the 'devil' one is having problems with, and that they know the environment and the work. Being a centre of information the Centre is thought to be potentially harmful, but at the same time it seems that exactly because the staff have considerable local knowledge the Health Centre can be useful and a source of understanding and sympathy.

From the point of view of the newcomer it is obvious that the staff know a lot about the shunters and the shunting job. The doctor's loyal and appreciative attitude towards the shunters, as expressed when talking to the beginners (or to me), does not hint at any controversies or animosity towards the shunting group, something indeed several of the shunters take for granted.

'I seldom see the shunters as they are not the ones that come crying about every little complaint.'
'The shunters do what other people do in their leisure time in order to get fit; they pump iron.'
'The shunting job is much healthier than the repetitive tasks of cleaning and making beds.'
'Socially speaking it is a good job, especially for girls. But if you

can't take the language you'll quit rather quickly.'
Remarks like these, uttered by the doctor, describe a friendly attitude towards the shunters as well as they add to the overall picture of 'the shunters', as an outstanding and 'different' group – a group not anyone could join.

Educational Requirements – The Shunting Course

Even applicants who felt no particular uncertainty about passing the medical test or who never doubted they would be employed in the first place will come to notice that some of their co-applicants whom they met at the Day of Introduction are missing at the commencement of the shunting course. Persons who were eager to get the job and who seemed strong and healthy are no longer with the group. Rumour has it that they failed the medical. The threshold may be low, but it is precisely for this reason even more surprising to find that so many have stumbled.

The remaining candidates find themselves part of a group that from now on increasingly is being treated and referred to as future shunters. The group at this stage comprises 3-7 fledglings and even though any one group differs from the others due to the composition of its members, it is nonetheless safe to say that the group feeling, in case one develops at all during the four-week-course, does not stem from a common interest in either shunting or railways, nor do they any longer come from families of SJ employees.[11] It is clear from my interviews with the shunters that the absolute majority of them consider their reason for starting at SJ as more or less coincidental.

The course is to them a quiet, easy period which may be utterly boring at times, but which at least gives full pay and rarely ever counts with strict eight-hour days. It is something one has to enjoy or suffer, and only a glance at the program for the coming weeks tells the beginners that certain parts of it will require a considerable amount of patience. Security regulations (SÄO) have thrilled very few shunters, or shunters to be, over the years and the nickname *'Natti-Natti'*[12] of one of the former teachers signals the close to

---

[11] It is a well known fact that there are families where several members and from succeeding generations, have been SJ employees. Cf. NYSTRÖM, 125. The same has been the case in Britain and the US. Cf. McKENNA, 175 f., cf. GAMST, 1980, 30.

[12] Childrens language for 'good night'. The nickname is derived from an old comic sketch, known from TV, about a man who finds it hard to sleep in the sleeping berth in a train as he is

hopeless task of enlivening the security paragraphs to the students.

Several of the shunters state that the reason they applied to the job was that they detest indoor work, paperwork, or studying, and it is probably also among these one finds the persons who have reading and writing difficulties. These difficulties may not always be very pronounced, but there are those who even find it difficult to fill in a simple form, as the one for leave of absence.[13] To them the course must at first sight have seemed insurmountable, but to those who only dislike indoor work or studies it is mainly a question of trying to make the best of it and to look forward to the hours of practising in the yard. As it turns out, very little reading or writing is actually required as all important information is read out or discussed orally by the teachers.

As the shunters are in Security Service, the security regulations have to be repeated annually, during a one-day course including an examination (in 1990 extended to two days, as the test then was held at a distant locality). The repetitive character of the course, which is stressed to the students, adds to its importance at the same time as it points forward to the significance and particular character of the job. The shunters not only perform a dirty, heavy, and strenuous job, they are in SeS and confront risk and danger.

The course comprises several different parts and several teachers are also involved. The most important parts of the course are, naturally, the Security Regulations (SÄO) and the Shunting Instructions. Other parts are electricity instructions, types of carriages, dangerous goods and railway geography. The last one must be seen as a relic, although it no longer lists every station in the country, but only the larger stations and railway junctions. It is basically the *tkm* who must be able to judge where in the train a coach must go, a judgement that presupposes knowledge of the order of the stations. Compared to loading goods or shunting goods waggons, especially in the old days when stations were manifold, shunting passenger trains today requires very little knowledge of railway geography.

Dangerous goods are rarely handled at Hagalund, but security demands that all staff be prepared for circumstances that are out of the ordinary. This is also the case with some of the electricity instructions and instructions that concern

---

constantly disturbed by his fellow traveller. This disturbed person happens to have the same surname as *Natti-Natti*, who put the SÄO-pupils to sleep.

[13] During my spell in the pay office I also handled leaves of absence. Persons with writing difficulties could be found among the shunters as well as among other staff.

emergency situations that might occur on the mainline.

The final week of the course, recently added to the program, is a course that senior staff also have been taught from February 1990 onwards. Called *Teknisk Vagntjänst* (Technical Coach Service) it aims at giving the shunters an extended knowledge about the brake system, the electric system and the technical particularities of different types of bogies (Am. 'trucks'). The course also makes the shunters competent in performing the brake-test that every train leaving Hagalund must undergo. This test is performed by a special group of 'brake-testers' *(bromsprovare)* who do not belong to the shunting group, but to the service group in the Hall.[14]

Earlier the lectures were held exclusively in the two lecture rooms in the Old Hall, but ever since the shunters moved to the end of the New Hall they have used their new assembly room for courses taught by shunters. The new facilities have chairs with soft seats surrounding a large table, where the teacher will take a seat at the end of the table or at the corner closest to the overhead. Writing materials and texts, such as the Shunting Instructions, are laid out for the pupils in advance by the teacher. Students are used to such service and they always arrive empty-handed to the lectures. They scarcely use the pads for other purposes than scribbling down telephone-book graffiti anyhow. The formerly so generous distribution of pencils and erasers has been limited so that these now are recollected at the end of the course, accompanied by a smile and a comment about 'saving'.

The old lecture rooms were organized in a traditional way with rows of desks and the teacher's desk at the front, next to the humming overhead projector ready to show pale flickering patterns on the screen. 'SJ - The Transport Company of the Future' or 'A rolling carriage must not be coupled directly - IT MUST STAND STILL!' are examples of urgent messages delivered to the silent little group of students to meditate upon.

The transparencies are produced by some central authority like the Central Safety Committee*(Centrala Skyddskommittén)*, and although many of the courses they are aimed for probably will be small ones, with only a few pupils, the instructions to the teachers, the texts and the material as a whole seem to be constructed for teaching in front of a larger audience. 'Bid

---

[14] From the 1992-95 the shunters were responsible for the brake-tests.

welcome.' *('Hälsa välkommen.')* and 'If needed – direct the discussion in order to keep it within the topic concerned.' *('Om så behövs – styr diskussionen så att den hålls inom det aktuella sakområdet.')* are advice to the teachers that seem a bit above the mark in the ordinary teaching situation at Hagalund. To 'direct the discussion' assumes naturally that there is a discussion in the first place, but with three or four shy beginners this is not a thing that can be taken for granted. The slogans and the crudeness of the messages need to be accompanied by a rather more theatrical performance on the part of the teacher than almost anyone will put on in front of an audience of three pupils.

In this intimate sphere the teachers may catch the interest of the pupils by establishing a personal relationship with them in giving examples from his own working life, perhaps with a comic twist. While the material in front of the class is concerned with larger issues, such as national statistics about accidents or descriptions of situations 'in general' that all the time have to be modified in order to bear any relevance to the conditions at Hagalund - all written in a language that uses 'we' as a collective term for all SJ employees - the classroom situation calls for a more personal contact that aims at preparing the beginners for work at Hagalund, and this in its turn calls for more detailed and specific instructions that can be shown to be relevant to the students in the immediate future.

The teachers are not mainly pedagogues but shunters or planners, which does not necessarily mean that they are bad teachers, but rather that they differ in style and pedagogical ambition from, for example, the SJ teachers touring the company to instruct foremen. The greatest asset of the local instructors or teachers is in fact their long-time practical knowledge of the things they are set to teach and they assume, quite correctly, that they will earn more respect and interest among their pupils by a factual attitude, referring to concrete instances, than by fancy pedagogical tricks and a skilful performance with spectacular teaching aids.

The modifications of the general rules and instructions that the pupils meet when studying the SÄO or the Shunting Instructions soon give them an impression that Hagalund is 'special'. There may always be certain modifications when applying the Rule Book to local circumstances, and therefore every group of pupils at every station in the country may get the impression that their station is 'special' – I am in no position to make a comparison. But this matters little for the pupils at Hagalund who learn that Hagalund is an exception. Hagalund cannot be defined as a 'station' according to the Rule Book, it is simply 'Hagalund', and as the terminus of the capital it is the spider in the net, important and without comparison.

Slowly but quite noticeably the pupils start talking about Hagalund in contrast to SJ in general and seem almost to take pride in complaining about having to learn things that 'we will never have to concern ourselves with'. 'We are not going to work on the mainline. All those signals are things that we will never come into contact with.' There is a growing breach between the Instructions and the real world at Hagalund and the pupils start to 'side with' Hagalund, and to ponder about how things **really** are done out there in the yard. Whatever curiosity or interest the pupils showed in the course in the beginning is now cooling down and they are growing more and more restless. 'They want to go out and have a go at it,' commented a teacher when describing his repeated experience of this growing lack of interest of the pupils.

The end of the course is increasingly geared towards more practical instruction and the workdays are then getting shorter and at the same time more exciting. The time to step out on one's own into the yard is approaching, and the pupils are eager to learn how to couple carriages and jump on and off moving engines at the same time as they may be nervous about making their first clumsy attempts in front of their comrades and nervous about future work, in case they find some tasks difficult. To the amusement of the other students, many a beginner has struggled with connecting the stiff brake hoses which just refuse contact with each other. The first steps toward shunting 'in real life' show that the discrepancy between theory and practice is just as great as expected and that the saying of senior shunters that 'the only way to learn how to shunt is to shunt' is relevant from the very beginning.

The theoretical knowledge the beginners have absorbed during the course, has, however, to be tested before the beginners are out in the yard at the mercy of the Scandinavian climate. The exam is a written one, constructed according to the multiple choice principle, and it is hardly meant to be selective. The questions concern the most critical pieces of knowledge and there are no questions that can be considered to be merely floorers or posers. As a consequence, failures are rare and the reasons for not passing are rather that pupils drop out or are absent to such a high degree that they are not allowed to take the test at the end. It is considered more important to participate in the course than only to pass the test. By being present at the course one is, however passively, participating in an ongoing discussion about risk and a demonstration of **how to think** in security terms. The reasons that lie behind the rules are brought up and the rules themselves are then seen as articulations of the security thinking that the teachers want to convey, rather than being ends in themselves.

'To be willing to apply regulations' is no doubt an attitude that the teachers-*cum*-shunters hammer into the students during the obligatory course, not because they are required to do so, but because they are teaching from the perspective of their own experience. Their outlook is based on years of practical work and as the apprentices are to become future work mates, the teachers, as well as the pupils, constantly refer to 'the work out there', i.e. to practical rather than theoretical complications, to attitudes among the shunters rather than to models and ideals represented in texts and films, and to 'common good sense' (*'sunda förnuftet'*) rather than to subtle reasoning.

Legitimating the regulations by real examples taken from years of experience the teachers bring the apprentices closer to the 'thinking' at Hagalund and convey respect for security and risk. The Rule Book is seen as a product of 'planners' and *'höjdare'*, (slang for 'superiors') and as a symbol of SJ authority it is therefore held in certain contempt. However, the spirit of the regulations is given a 'human shape' during the course, and it is constantly stressed that among the shunters of Hagalund security is not a matter to be taken lightly. The reasons for doing things in a certain way are not that the Rule Book says so, but out of respect for your work mates and in order for the work to be organized in a 'sensible' (*förnuftig*) way. You may laugh at the Rule Book and joke about your ignorance of its contents, but this does not imply that you may work in a way so as to jeopardize the life and safety of your mates.[15]

---

[15] Gamst classifies different kinds of adherence and nonadherence to the rules, such as; absolute, perfunctory, and volitional adherence versus directed, uninformed, subordinated, insubordinate and agreed covert nonadherence. His material does, however, not translate easily into Swedish conditions, where e.g. the Rule Book (SÄO) is much less visible (shunters never being interrogated about its contents in daily work), and where disciplining action is very rare. I

The course is not intended to deliver such a message but the *habitus*, the predisposition, of the experienced shunters leads them to discuss and stress regulated procedures in terms of their uses and functions rather than stressing their character as regulations and rules that have to be followed without questioning. They regard the rules as means rather than ends and they constantly appeal to 'common sense' and ideals such as solidarity and comradely cooperation to support and legitimate existing rules.

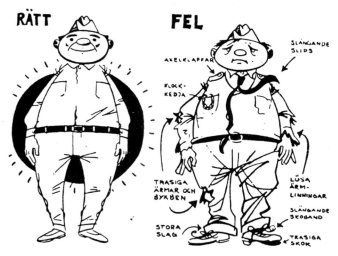

Dress: Right or wrong (from Shunting Instructions, SJF 010.3)

It is obvious that the students get their conception of shunting work not only from the curriculum of the course and from reading the instructions and listening to the teachers. During the breaks and before and after the course the students nowadays share the coffee-room with the shunters and are able to observe the interaction among the shunters. Even before the new quarters for the shunters were built and the students had no direct and regular interaction with the shunters, they could observe the latter pass the bottom of the stairs that lead to the lecture rooms. The shunters – perhaps dressed in hats that they

have therefore not found the categories directly applicable to my work. Cf. GAMST 1989, 75 ff.

had picked up in the yard, riding two on one bike, ridiculing the teacher by knocking on his helmet and asking whether he was afraid of wood-peckers, and generally creating quite a stir – did not match the picture of the 'correct shunter' which appeared in the shunting instructions. The students quickly understood that success in the yard probably was not achieved by slavish application of Rule Books and instructions.

There was another logic 'out there', a logic which might be just as demanding, but it was phrased in another language and it appealed to other loyalties than SÄO. People – the co-workers and mates – and their opinions mattered, not SJ views and SJ property.

Transition to the Yard – Getting Greasy

The setting in itself describes a great contrast between theory and practice. Indoor work turns into outdoor work. For the students this means a switch from sitting in temperate, comfortable facilities decorated in light colours and furnished with soft chairs into walking around a yard often littered with paper and garbage, as well as getting into close contact with dirty carriages, greasy buffers and couplings and, in the case of some foreign carriages, with unmentionable refuse from open toilets. Lighting is often scarce, temperatures vary and there is no shelter for rain and snow.

Accordingly the students will have to change their neat leisure clothes for the ungainly orange and blue protective clothing. Especially shorter persons might find it difficult to get outfits their size in stock and there is a lot of jocular comments when the overalls and jackets are tried on for the first time.[16] The students bring some old pair of gym shoes not to spoil the ones they wear in private until they receive the shoes they order from the general SJ store, a procedure that often takes months. Woollen caps are also private and are indeed one of the signs of identification in the yard when distance no longer allows faces to be discerned. Change of caps can cause joking comments about the confusion this supposedly has caused.

The gloves, clean when collected from the Hagalund store, will be rather

---

[16] This merriment, which between the lines can be read as making fun of the seniors – who do not find the beginners' outfits amusing – contrasts with the humiliation the miners, described by Vaught and Smith, have to undergo when acquiring new uniforms and equipment. Cf. VAUGHT & SMITH, 159 ff.

dark after only a couple of afternoons of practice in the yard and the overall is soon smeared with grease and dirt. Beginners are naturally less able in avoiding to dirty themselves and the older shunters like to point out greasy spots on the shoulders and laugh at black 'moustaches' that appear on the unwary apprentices. 'What on earth have you been doing?!' they happily exclaim and make the beginner embarrassed as all eyes will turn, and as more comments are automatically added by others.

The beginner, busy trying to perform the tasks correctly, is not yet sufficiently skilled to be able to think about cleanliness simultaneously, and as it seems pointless to change clothes as soon as they get greasy, the difference between grimy beginners and the older shunters is quite marked. The senior shunters are naturally often shunt leaders or *tkm,* which means that they seldom do the dirtiest jobs such as coupling and knocking. There are, however, exceptions to the rule that dirt and apprenticeship go together. Some persons never learn, or just never care, and the most notorious characters in this respect are remembered long after they have left the job as persons who managed to get black all over.[17]

There is one important distinction that must be noticed. To get dirty at work is a matter of amusement and one will get comments and perhaps even be told that it is high time to change clothes, but this is different from being filthy in private. Some persons who are very dirty at work are indeed meticulously cleanly persons, who leave work in shining light-coloured clothes, hair still wet after the shower and hands carefully cleaned from the black grease that only can be removed with special detergents.[18]

On the other hand, shunters who never shower before going home and who wear dirty clothes in private are a cause of embarrassment and are abused verbally when out of hearing. When joking comments sometimes are directed at them, glances are exchanged behind their back, and there is a general wish that the serious undertone will be noticed by the targets of the joking and make an impact.

Despite joking comments, the beginners are expected to get dirty while

---

[17] This is true of both sexes. Women, as a matter of fact, often belong to the dirtiest bunch.

[18] It is amusing to read what Frank McKenna writes about Britain already at the end of last century "Working on engines was a very dirty job, but *railwaymen were always noted for their cleanliness...*"(emphasis mine). Cf. McKENNA, 53.

working. Clean working clothes signify that they do not work but stand stupefied at the side, watching others work. (This may also cause joking comments.) The beginner is a victim of weather and circumstance. Unable to plan the work and take shelter accordingly in carriages and under roofs the beginner will be initiated by the harsh treatment of weather and wind.

To return wet, black and sweaty to the coffee-room is indeed the best answer to the standard question: *'Har du gjort rätt för dig i dag?'* (Approx.: Have you earned your pay today?)

Further Education – The Training Period

The last of the requirements listed in SÄM 7 for workers in SeS, apart from the permanent requirement to be sober while on duty, is that the worker pass 'further education'. In the case of the shunters this further education consists of the practical training in the yard, a training that I will call apprenticeship despite its rather short duration and its formal status as ordinary employment.

As soon as the students have passed the shunting exam, but not earlier, they are given a work schedule as VIK *(vikarie)*, i.e. they are put on the deputy list, but the ordinary shift number stated in the day schedule is complemented with the letters *övn (övning;* training) to signal that they will work as apprentices only and that there is another person appointed for that shift, too. This other person becomes the instructor or coach.

The coaches, on the other hand, only have a tiny cross in the schedules sihnifying that they are going to have an apprentice to take care of during that particular shift, and it is often not until the team members are on their way into the yard that someone will point out that 'oh, we have an apprentice today!' The new ones are, as mentioned earlier, generally quiet, but there has been at least one incident when the beginner was so shy that he never could bring himself to find out whom he was supposed to train with. The shunters all assumed that he was training with someone else and not until the young man had spent the whole morning in the coffee-room did it become clear for the shunters, who came in for lunch, that he should have been training with one of them, a person who was about to go home.

Such lack of enterprising spirit is definitely unacceptable and the future of that unfortunate lad seemed gloomy. He certainly needed a good excuse for this

112

lazy behaviour and much improvement in his willingness to work if he wanted a future among the shunters. This first day was a handicap of sorts for the immediate future. The story was quickly known to everyone[19] and no one was surprised when he quite soon left the shunting yard for good. This was considered natural as he 'didn't fit' and the story of his first day as a trainee was recounted again.

What people objected to was not that he had been lazying himself in the coffee-room, but rather the lack of go that seemed to say something about his personality. To sit for hours and wait for someone to take care of you is just not the spirit. You cannot work as a shunter if you cannot take the small initiative to ask around a bit to find out whom you are training with, was the general opinion of the shunters.

The ideal situation is that the staff delegator has organized the training period of the beginner in a continuous row of rather similar shifts with relatively few different coaches. The delegator informs the beginner in a reassuring way: 'Look here, I've put you up three mornings in a row with 35 Andersson and his team. They are very calm so you'll learn that in no time. Then you have the night here and after that I've given you a day off, which means you have a long period to recover and then you'll be back here with new powers to train four shifts with the train-pullers. That looks good, doesn't it?!' Thus encouraged, the beginner is likely to look forward to the first training shift with apprehension. But naturally not all delegators 'have psychology' and, especially earlier, the first training shift could turn out very differently.

Regardless of the preparations, physical as well as mental, and all possible encouragement many shunters remember their first training shift in the yard as something of an ordeal, and one can doubt whether anyone has ever stepped out into the yard for the first time without feeling at least a tiny bit nervous.

One of the senior shunters told the story of his first training shift, when he walked out to the box to learn train-pulling and announced to a man only a couple of years his senior that he was going to train with him that day. 'That's fine', said the trainer. 'Here are the slips. You just take these trains to the tracks that are stated and then you take the engines to the depot. I must

---

[19] According to Am. terminology the story entered the 'sandhouse', i.e. the gossip about 'rails', railroaders. Cf. GAMST, 1989, 72 f.

slip off now as I'm a bit busy. You see I must tend to my job at the airport. Bye, bye.' According to the informant his coach then rushed off and he was left all alone with this as the only clue. Trains started to appear and he tried to find their routes by walking down the yard in front of them, reading the number signs of the tracks. Then he had to ask the drivers how to uncouple the engines and where to take them. He had to back the trains a few times, but somehow he managed.

This happened more than twenty years ago. The attitude towards shunting work has changed since that. Shunters say that earlier, when there were no courses, it was considered that you just go out there and uncouple and start work almost immediately. But you were not allowed to come straight from the street and start to work as a shunter. Many of the older shunters had to work a couple of years in the goods shed before advancing to the shunting job. A very indirect form of training, if you like.

Today it is recognized that one has to learn a few things before it is safe to go out into the yard and consequently also the training with a coach is seen as more important. It is not considered that you learn much of the job as a trainee, but you get used to move about in the yard and get a fair idea of the distribution of tasks. To learn how to actually do the job you have to work on your own.

~~~

My first shifts have left me a with a vivid memory of confusion and despair. My doubts started actually the day before my first shift as the little group of prospective trainees walked around the yard, guided by our teacher. We happened to meet one of the old train-pullers and the teacher informed him, pointing at me, that he was going to have a trainee with him the next day. The train-puller looked at me from top to toe and said : 'Faugh!' This didn't feel very encouraging, and it was with considerable nervousness I followed him into the yard the next day.

Stumbling after the old train-puller in the gravel – trying to come to terms with my too large overall and giant's gloves – it seemed incomprehensible that one could make any sense of the jumbled tracks. The short man of very few words from the North, very aptly carrying the name Fjällman ('Mountainman'), walked across the yard turning the red and yellow points in a seemingly haphazard way.

'Why did you turn this one?' I asked.

'For the engine to 25', he answered.

He then proceeded to turn one point here, one there and I

114

persistently asked why they were turned.

'There are two engines leaving soon.' or 'This point should always be in this position.' were the kind of answers I got.

'How do I know?' I asked.

'You'll learn.' Fjällman said and continued his itinerary.

My desperation was rising from the initially already high level, but finally Fjällman pulled out a small folded paper with numbers printed on it from his pocket and held it close to his face with a finger following the lines.

'What's that?' I asked.

'It's the slips.' Fjällman announced and I found this extremely rewarding. Finally something concrete and written! Fjällman realized probably that he had overseen something in my training so he turned toward the *tkm* office, me still at his heals, and showed me with a minimum amount of words where one should collect the lists of departures and arrivals before going out into the yard.

When I at last had the key to the happenings in the yard in my hand it turned out that I had very little time to try to translate theory into practice. Engines and trains where pouring in from all over, it seemed. As soon as I thought I could foresee one move it turned out that I was mistaken and something else rushed by.

'What's that? Where is that one going?' I can still hear my stupefied questions, and the one syllable answers from Fjällman. Sometimes he didn't bother to answer my questions at all, but only repeated: 'You'll learn.' He then sent me home hours before the shift was to end. That was none too soon. I was exhausted!

It turned out that Fjällman was going to be my trainer during the following days, too, and for three short days (as I was sent home early) I struggled with learning the numbers of the tracks, trying to figure out how to predict the movements in the yard. As I more or less gave up asking questions our 'conversation' dried up. I felt that Fjällman was trying to keep things away from me. He would never tell me what I had to know.

The third shift was a night shift and when the last train had arrived we went indoors to take a break and eat our sandwiches and have some coffee. Fjällman was boiling the coffee the oldfashioned way in a pot as he refused to drink brewed coffee. Even that he had to do himself.

I assumed that we would spend the time in silence, as every time before, but all of a sudden Fjällman started to talk. He did not talk about work, but about his encounters with German soldiers on the Norwegian side of the border during the Nazi occupation and his close escapes on skis. He claimed to have been one of the first persons to ski slalom in Sweden and was still active on his slalom skis.

He talked about moose and wild game and fishing char and about life in his home in the North, a house which was situated miles from the nearest village and did not even have a road leading to it. He talked about the great opportunity of his life when a friend of his emigrated to Canada, asking Fjällman to join him. Fjällman did not dare to go and when the friend later made great success as the owner of a ski hotel Fjällman regretted this decision.

I probably listened with my mouth wide open, at least my surprise was of a magnitude that certainly could have led to such a behaviour. I had thought during these days that Fjällman objected to me, for whatever reason, but it turned out that his silence had nothing to do with me, as I in my self-absorbed state and nervousness had assumed. His thoughts had been elsewhere and he was working on routine, counting the days to when he was to retire – and, as he said, make a char-lure out of his golden medal he would receive for 'long and faithful service'. 'Char bite on gold,' he said.

After this night things started to run smoothly. I learned the ropes of the trade as I no longer was stiff with anxiety and no longer saw his silence as a means to hold back information from me.

We did actually get on rather well and years later, after he had retired, we met on the occasion of another retirement and I reminded him of his 'Faugh!' when he first was told that he was to train me. He had forgotten all about it and another visitor at the occasion, one of the old age pensioners, who happened to overhear us said :

'You probably objected to her because she was a woman.' Fjällman, in his slow manner of speaking, said:

'No, I don't think so. I guess I was worried about the responsibility.' Then he laughed and said: 'As a matter of fact you were my first trainee!'

This little story has ingredients that are very typical[20] , although they here are brought to unusual visibility due to the particular circumstances. There is the nervousness of the beginner, which concerns being accepted by the shunters as much as to do the job properly and the tendency to see the two as intimately connected.

There is the uneasiness about taking care of and being responsible for the trainee on the part of the coach. There are no other criteria for becoming a coach than having worked shifts on one's own. Anyone can then find that he

---

[20] I was amused to read Linda Niemann's description of her early experiences in the yard. "Since I was still learning the most basic moves, it was impossible to keep up with the pace. But how do you manage to learn? My strategy was to follow a crew member around like a baby duck, getting in the way. He then would yell at me and tell me what to do. So I'd learn something." NIEMANN, 6. Nobody yelled at me, but the baby duck image could have been used to decribe me, and many other beginners, just as well.

suddenly has an trainee to take care of. There is no pedagogy involved other than the shunter himself finds suitable and, looking back on their own training, they will find it difficult to recall what the yard looked like, seen with beginner's eyes.

There is no single formula or tradition of how to teach a beginner, which means that the pedagogy is almost wholly determined by mutual understanding, depending in its turn upon how the coach and the trainee get on with each other.

Only in my own experience the pedagogy of the coaches varied considerably. One of the women thought the whole thing was embarrassing and said she didn't know what to teach me and sent me home after a couple of hours, while one of the younger men (known for being somewhat lazy and immobile) let me do all the work, declaring that this was how it should be done; him supervising, me training actively. 'How will she otherwise learn?' he defended himself when the rest of the team jokingly reproached him for letting me, who was untrained both mentally and physically, work to exhaustion. Their comments let my coach know that the real reason for commanding me to do all the work was his innate laziness.

This man, however, stepped outside the ordinary concept of how one should learn the branching of the tracks by drawing me a map of the yard, where the different track groups in South and North were marked and where certain land signs were indicated to be used as points of reference. 'Track 22 is the one next to the clock, 32 through 35 branch twice into couples, 36 is alone and the first track of the reserve and these sidings are reached from this Englishman.[21] ' While he drew the map – which I again felt very happy about as it was 'something concrete' – the other shunters who observed this laughed at us and shook their heads. You don't learn tracks from a map, but from practice, they said. Why, I could never find out, because to me this piece of paper was a treasure that I used secretly until I knew my way around the yard. Even then I kept it in my pocket as a mascot until it finally disintegrated.

As it is said that you actually learn only when you finally work on your own, trainees are often sent home early with a little secretive wink and a few words like: 'You don't have to stay longer.' This is considered to be the

---

[21] An Englishman is a double switch; Am.: 'crossover'.

prerogative of the coach, but he may still be jokingly reproached for letting the beginner off too easily.

The beginner may also on his return the next day be reproached jokingly for 'slipping off' the day before, but this does not deny the fact that there is a lot of understanding at this stage that beginners have to be accustomed to the job slowly. Reproaches of this kind are 'coffee-room talk' and as soon as the beginner is alone with the team or talk to someone face-to-face the opposite is stressed. 'Work at your own pace.' 'Don't push yourself.' 'Don't do anything that you are not sure you manage.' There is thus a conflict between inducing the morale of 'doing one's share' and extending goodwill to a beginner.

To push someone and not let him get used to the work gradually would only risk losing him straight away. It would be outright dangerous, too. The beginners are watched all the time, partly because the coach, as well as everyone else in the vicinity, feel a bit uncertain about what he might do, but he is also watched because one wants to know what kind of a fellow he is. Unless he is extraordinarily clumsy the work itself is not very much to go on at this stage. It is rather the personality that one can assess. If the beginner complains, is reluctant to do anything or seems to think that he is superior to the job and the shunters, or if he does not talk at all, there will be doubts about his future in the yard. If, on the other hand, he takes the ardour with a sense of humour, shows some interest in the job, is willing to play cards and is communicative, the shunters will invest interest in him, learn his name and use it when talking about him, instead of using an impersonal term like 'one of the new ones' *('en av dom nya')*. He may even find that he has been vested a nick-name. This is no doubt a sign of transition from being an anonymous beginner to being a shunter with an identity and a position, however lowly it may be.

Working Your Own Shifts

When the training is considered finished the staff delegator will ask the apprentice to take shifts of his own. In case there is a shortage of staff the staff delegator may be more eager to convince the beginner that he will do alright. In cases of 'emergency', i.e. when there is no chance of filling the team without the aid of the beginner, the persuasion on the part of the staff delegator will be rather hard to resist. The delegator may describe the shift as a particularly easy one, the team one is to work with as the most perfect, pleasant and helpful one. The delegator may also promise a choice of shifts in the future or that the beginner may go back to training again after having worked this shift on his own.

The tone of the staff delegator during such a heavy bombardment of persuasion is never threatening or unpleasant, but joking and pleading. Some flattery is an ingredient in this joking cavalcade and, in case there is an audience of shunters in the office at the time, the staff delegator may throw out a question to another shunter, asking if the beginner isn't doing fine, and if they are not convinced that he will manage the shift without problems. Regardless of the actual skills of the beginner, the answer will naturally be 'yes, no problem'.

In his eagerness to fill the work schedule the staff delegator may throw out suggestions that the beginner takes as promises. In case they are not taken down in writing, i.e. the promised shifts are not marked in the work schedule straight away, there is a risk that the staff delegator will forget them, consider them as suggestions that did not catch on or that another staff delegator, not knowing anything about the discussions, will arrange the work schedule differently. Many disagreements between shunters and staff delegators ensue from such 'agreements' that are forgotten, misunderstood, never reported to deputizing delegators or, maybe, simply neglected. A more experienced shunter is wise enough to see to it that the promised day off or the promised shift is marked in the book straight away, but a beginner is in general less foreseeing and may find out too late what he should have done.

There are then shunters who claim that they have been 'tricked' into taking shifts on their own in order to 'help out' in a situation depicted as an emergency, only to find that when they try to go back to continue their training the staff delegator will point to the record in the book and ask why they should train, having already worked a shift on their own - and as far as the staff delegator knows it went alright, didn't it? The apprentice is naturally reluctant to say that the shift was a disaster, and will rather say that he has only had very few training shifts on that particular task. Here some flattery and the old saying among the shunters that 'you don't learn the job until you do your own shifts' will make the most hesitant beginner give in, and before

119

long he will be out there trying to cope with frozen couplings and switches, or finding himself on the wrong track with a string of trains behind him, irritated drivers hanging out of the windows and shunting teams taking advantage of every sign of hesitation and uncertainty.

~~~

To sum up one may say that apprenticeship in shunting is surrounded by lenience rather than harshness, and reassurance rather than mockery and bantering, but most of all it is a period of observation.

From the side of the company the beginner is, however, often seen to need a little push out of the comfortable position of the trainee. The speed of the advancement is often determined by the supply of staff, so that training may be extended during times of plenty, and cut down during periods of shortage. To the B-member or shunt leader positions training is necessary, and it can be a welcome opportunity to advance, but it can also be freightening and experienced as a premature step. Conflicts and accusations of being pushed ahead with too little training, or being held back by not being allowed to train, stem from these conditions.

For the beginner a slow approach – where the beginner 'gets used to things' – is favoured among the shunters. One may take one's time as long as it is not wasted. Given enough time even the daftest beginner will eventually learn.[22]

The generous attitude of the shunters is nevertheless conditional and depends on the beginner showing a positive attitude and willingness to learn. It is more dangerous to be over-ambitious, daring, and too inventive than to stand back and watch. But the look should be the one of a fairly interested viewer, not the one of someone who is happy to do as little as possible. Neither should it be a look *'von oben'*, but rather one which signals that the beginner **wants to** take part, some day, and **wants to** become one of the team. In this respect no sign is too small or insignificant, and no snort or complaint too silent or suppressed.

---

[22] This protected period of wait and see compares well to 'legitimate peripheral participation' as described by Lave & Wenger. Cf. LAVE & WENGER, *passim.*

6. THE PROCESS OF INCORPORATION – LEARNING ABOUT 'US' AND 'THEM'

The Group

We have followed the beginner from his first contacts with Hagalund, when he was selected for work in the yard, to the point where he works on his own as a shunter among the rest. From an unknown outsider he has transformed into a familiar member of the group; *bangårdsgruppen*, the shunting group.

This transition may seem simple enough, but as soon as we have looked at membership in the group, we have found that membership is far from a one-dimensional concept. In this chapter I will look at the ethnographic complications of establishing membership in the shunting group. What are the informal criteria for belonging to this group?[1]

As soon as we leave the formal definition of the shunting group, i.e. the organization's list of persons employed in MTÖ-B, we come up against the view of the shunting group as a mental image, a concept in the minds of people inside and outside this 'group'. It is, needless to say, this concept that is of interest to us, rather than the formal aspect of belonging. A quick glance at the list of persons on the pay roll tells us that we have persons in the shunting group who have not put their foot in the yard for years. Even if the ambition on the part of the employers is to make the persons formally employed identical with the persons working in and in connection to the yard, we cannot assume that 'the shunting group' as a concept used by the shunters is identical to either of these two 'groups' of people. We must look at practice and see what 'the group' means to people who use the word in the daily work.

The shunters often talk about 'us', 'the group' and about *stämningen i*

---

[1] I am here interested in the various ways the shunters define themselves as a 'group', but it should be obvious that we are dealing with a 'social group' with intimate face-to-face relations; a 'primary group' as Charles Cooley termed it already in 1909. Cf. COOLEY. The face-to-face character is significant. When one of the key characters in this group retired recently (1997) one of the shunters wondered how the group would fare without him. He found to his surprise that everything went on like before. 'We hardly even think about him. We are busy going about our own business', he said. Still, there is a kind of membership for life, as retired persons are always welcome back to visit. However, warnings against romantic assumptions concerning 'local communities' must be seen to extend also to our little group. Cf. COHEN 1992, 28 ff.

gruppen', the ambiance in the group. This last concept is undoubtedly most often on the lips of the shunters at times of change and unrest. Who belongs to the group is seldom discussed. Belonging is a matter of self-evidence. The new ones are 'the new ones', and as such their belonging is somewhat uncertain, but there are no attempts to keep them out, to make them feel alien or to set up fences that have to be overcome before they are accepted members of the group. In this respect the shunting group differs from many other work-shops where different kinds of obstacles make life more difficult for beginners, be it the argot, cruel jokes or some kind of initiation ritual.[2]

One cannot stress the gradual incorporation into the group too much. There are myriads of signs and signals that the beginner, as well as people talking about the beginner, unknowingly send out. Signals, which are interpreted not as coded messages, but which constitute parts of the process of 'getting to know' somebody. They are pieces of information that create familiarity and social contact, and they slowly paint the picture of a personality different from every other personality as well as of a shunter who knows what it is all about, who understands without further explanations, who can be talked to in the same way as one talks to every other shunter.

The process of incorporation is not only gradual, it is never complete. Beginners are only slowly learning 'facts' about work, about persons and events in the past, and the 'old heads' might find it difficult to keep up with the new events that quickly establish themselves as history and essential background knowledge if one is to understand the points of current jokes, mockery and horse-play. A longer holiday, sick leave or a spell working with tasks that do not allow breaks in the coffee-room when the teams have their breaks will quickly make a person lose touch.

Incorporation in the group is to a considerable extent dependent on individual qualities, social skills and attitudes, but there are nevertheless strong 'institutional' factors that create, as well as delimit, the space and the opportunities that every beginner faces. Here I will look at the most important factors that I think participate in the creation of group feeling in the work process.

---

[2] The literature on this seems to abound. Cf. e.g. ARVASTSON 1987, 77ff., COCKBURN 1984, 45 f, COLLINSON, 188, GARFINKEL, 420 ff and McCLELLAND, 193 ff., and MOORE W., 322ff. On the difference between jargon and argot, cf. GRAVES, 56 and MOORE W., **ib.** They define 'jargon' as words describing the technology of the work, while 'argot' is a collection of terms specific, and sometimes only known, to a group or a setting.

Shunters and Drivers – Separation and Servitude

As soon as the beginner works entire shifts, on his own, the 'geography' of work will create closeness to some and distance to other workers at Hagalund. The first category of employees, besides the shunters, that the beginner meets on a regular basis is the engine drivers. Before the introduction of remote controlled engines all shunting was completely dependent on the presence of an engine driver. The drivers of the shunting engine have their own schedules, their own facilities and in all very little verbal contact with the shunters.

The driver is in these cases but an automaton, a human substitute for a machine. He works according to signals and regulations and is not supposed to do any thinking or interpreting, he should only read and react to the established vocabulary of signals.[3]

Some shunt leaders do indeed have minimal contact with the engine drivers, but others have a more informal attitude and like a chat. There are, however, few chances to chat, except during breaks, but then the drivers often retire to their own quarters, or wait on the engine, while the shunters spend the break together in the coffee-room, canteen or cafeteria.

At night, especially during warm summer nights, waiting for a train to arrive creates an informal break which is spent in the yard, sitting on the rails or on a footstep. Then the engine driver and the shunters find a natural opportunity to chat as the above mentioned facilities will be closed or empty. Information is exchanged about accidents, about work conditions or the seniors reminisce about characters and events of the past.

Although such more intimate chats are rare, one finds that the senior shunters have a certain amount of knowledge of the old Hagalund drivers. They know them, perhaps not always by name or even nick-name (unless they have invented their own ones), but they know where they live, they know facts about their work life, and, above all, they know their style of driving, which is seen as an expression of their personalities.

The great generation shift that occurred among the drivers (from the 1970s onwards) has reduced them to a more anonymous mass of 'heads in the cab window', and although the shunters generally see the young new drivers as an

---

[3] The only signals in use in the yard are: 'Forward', 'Reverse', 'Slow', (and the combinations of 'Slow' with either of the two former ones), 'Kick', 'Stop', 'Coupling' and (very rarely) 'Throw the switch'. All signals are given by hand in clear daylight and by signal lanterns when visibility so demands. According to the rules, unclear, inarticulate or obscure signals should be interpreted as 'Stop'. The small number of signals contrasts with US conditions, as described by Gamst and Niemann. It may not be a coincidence that the argot (another class of signs) is much more restricted among Swedish shunters, as compared with the US, judging from Gamst's and Niemann's descriptions. Cf. GAMST 1980, NIEMANN, *passim.*

improvement to the old ones – many of whom were considered to think of themselves as being infinitely superior to the shunters – they nevertheless miss some of the old characters who did not drive solely according to signals, but who anticipated the moves and could kick coaches and 'give coupling' with enough speed and would drive fast where it should be fast and slow where it should be slow. These drivers were far from being automatons.

Naturally the younger drivers do not have a lot of routine and experience. They are uncertain about what is going on, why they have to stand still, or they may want to apologize for little mistakes they make, and as a consequence they turn to the only person available to talk to, the C-member, who stands on the foot-board right below the cab window. The C-member, often an age-mate and a beginner himself, is more likely to be sympathetic and understanding, while the senior shunters are more likely to snort: 'There was nothing wrong with the engine half an hour ago when the former driver was driving it!' when the driver complains that the brakes do not work properly.

As a result of the physical proximity between the C-member and the engine driver, the C-member is more likely to be a victim of irritation and anger on the part of the driver than are the other members of the team. One could suspect that the reverse was the case, that the driver would be the target of the C-member's frustration, but in reality it seems that the split goes between the team versus the driver and in case there is irritation toward the driver it is normally expressed by one of the senior members in the team.

It seems that the shunters expect the C-member to receive complaints, because it happens that the shunters inquire about an interaction between the driver and the C-member that they have observed from a distance. If it turns out to be a complaint directed to a beginner, the shunters will tell the driver to 'mind his own business', regardless of whether the complaint was justified or not. 'The driver shall drive on the signals ('gå på signalerna') and shut up,' is a common phrase.[4] Such little incidents mark that the C-member unambiguously belongs to the team. If there is scolding to be done it should be taken care of by the shunters. **They** – not the driver – are training the beginner.

To the beginner the situation signals that he belongs to the shunting team rather than to his physically closest mate; the driver. He answers to the shunters and it is their, and only their, evaluation of his work that matters.

It is soon clear to the beginner that drivers are a 'different species', and

---

[4] It is seldom necessary to say these things to the driver. The shunt leader will rather ask the driver if he has a complaint and that will be the end of the matter. Body language; a stiff look or a rigid back, will convay the message.

mixing is useless. A chat about the weather or some other neutral topic is alright, but the drivers are not part of the same ambiance, they speak a different language and the opportunities to establish deeper contact and understanding are next to non existent.   Drivers are socially superior, but inferior during work time in the yard. When driving the shunting engine they are not allowed to think, but at the same time they are required and encouraged to do so. This ambiguous position of the drivers is obviously embarrassing to drivers as well as to shunters. When the remote controlled engines appeared it became clear to everyone, even the ones that had not given it a thought before, that the drivers never appreciated shunting work. The drivers' union did not object to the shunters taking over the driving. It seems they thought they finally got rid of a lousy job – and the shunters were equally happy to work without them.

Train-Pullers and Drivers – A Short Encounter

The train-pullers are the shunters who have the most extended contact with the drivers, as every train they pull means at least a ten minute ride in the cab with the driver. The drivers are many. Some, such as the Hagalund drivers, are 'regulars' and may become very familiar to the train-pullers, while others maybe come to Hagalund only once a year. The former know the routines and the yard and also recognize all the train-pullers, while the 'outsiders' are uncertain about the most basic procedures and need a lot of information.

Sometimes the drivers express their uncertainty and explicitly ask for advice, but more senior – or shy – drivers can be reluctant to reveal their incompetence, especially if the train-puller is a 'young chick.' Before their driving has made it clear that they simply are disoriented, they may have caused a chain of misunderstandings with the shunters as well as the train-pullers.

The cooperation between the engine driver and the train-puller makes their interaction more intimate and the two often find that they side together against the shunting team. When they are locked in by a shunting team the driver and the train-puller can discuss the situation between them and decide what to do. The driver is also close enough to hear the conversation between the train-puller and the *tkm* on the radio for himself and thereby get information about the reasons for stops and hindrances which are not evident from the cab window.

When the driver and the train-pullers are far apart they have no means to communicate (except with hand signals) and the driver might think that it is negligence, inability or outright spite which causes the delay. Train-pullers, pressed for time, give priority to work and pull trains instead of taking time to inform drivers, who are left waiting with growing irritation or dispair.

On arrival at Hagalund drivers may have accumulated a lot of irritation from a long troublesome trip, only to pour everything over the first person they have the opportunity to talk to; the train-puller. Such often unpleasant events, when the driver seems to blame the train-puller for all past delays and accidents[5], makes it clear to the train-puller that their cooperation should remain a short encounter.

A rather innocent question like: 'Why is it always like this at Hagalund?' will soon put the train-puller in a defensive position. The question seems to imply that the train-pullers or the shunters are at fault, while it should be well known to everybody that Hagalund is crowded, cramped, unpractical and hard-worked. The train-pullers and the shunters think that they are doing a good job, despite all the difficulties. To them the proper question should be: 'How come you can avoid accidents and disaster in this mess?' The implicit blame that drivers seem to put on the train-pullers (who leave the trains waiting or pull them in the wrong order) and shunters (who block the tracks everywhere) helps to draw a visible line between 'us' and 'them', and on the 'them'-side are soon all drivers, including old Hagalund 'heads'.

The senior shunters, who worked in the 1960s and earlier, never doubted that there was a strict line between the drivers and the shunters. They still tell the story of one driver who visualized this by drawing a chalk line in the middle of the floor of the cab to delimit the area where the train-puller was allowed.

Another often repeated story tells of an angry train-puller, who, when refused access to the cab, walked in the middle of the tracks in front of the engine all the way from one end of the yard to the other and back. The driver had no choice but to drive slowly behind him, 'following him like a dog'.

All such stories are told to the beginners in order to illustrate that things have improved and that they should use their present access to the engine instead of hanging outside – a habit which is more dangerous, but which train-pullers nevertheless often resort to as it is easy and, during hot summer days, gives a welcome cool breeze.

To the senior shunters the access to the engine is still a reform 'in the right direction', but it does not make the train-pullers and the drivers equals. Differences in education, pay and status are too obvious. Therefore, when shunters and train-pullers state that they would **never** like to become drivers, ('Imagine sitting on that engine all alone, day after day!', 'You can see how

---

[5] Accidents, such as collisions with moose or cows are not unusual. Needless to say, the train-puller is not happy to stand on an engine with a moose smeared over the front.

frustrated they are when they come here. You're bound to get a heart attack in that job.') it cannot be considered a downgrading of driving and the drivers as much as marking the distance between 'them' – the drivers and 'us' – the shunters.

Those Below

Apart from the clear limit and the obvious contrast between the 'greasy' train-pullers and the 'clean', and occasionally even uniformed, drivers there are other categories of 'them' in the yard that contrast visibly with the shunting group.

These are the cleaners, the brake-testers, the repair-men, the people making the beds, filling the water-tanks, emptying the toilet tanks, and taking care of the sign-posting, and, up to the 1980s, the persons supplying the trains with glass decanters of drinking water.

It can be said of all these groups that they occasionally come into contact with the shunters, but as far as the beginners are concerned the contact is one of once in a while sharing the same physical space, such as the carriages, the roads, the platforms, the cafeteria or the canteen.

The tasks and responsibilities are strictly divided between the groups, creating a dependence, which, however, is undercommunicated and neglected. As work on a train loosely resembles an assembly line, in that certain tasks must be finished before others can be done, there is a strong dependency between the groups. If the train is not shunted the brakes cannot be tested, and it cannot be shunted as long as the *'fournering'*[6], the filling of water tanks, or repairs are taking place. Dependency implies an inbuilt antagonism in the work process and in case of delays the blame might travel 'down the line'. There is an age-old distrust, almost hostility, between the groups, the beginnings of which are lost in the distant past.

The beginners are nevertheless not slow in learning the jargon. Indeed, they often seem to overdo it a bit and blame 'the stupid drivers', 'the idiots in the Hall', etc. They may be met by mild reproach when they are obviously exaggerating or mistaken, but on the whole their agitated language is a sign of a committed attitude towards work and identification with the shunting group – and it is recognized as such.

---

[6] From *fournir* (Fr. for 'furnish'), i.e. providing the trains with all necessary equipment.

Those Above

Two of the most important and frequent contacts with other groups are those with OC and RepC, the Order Centre and the Repair Centre, but these seldom involve personal contact, only radio communication. The OC is a centre for information rather than orders and on the whole the contact between OC and the shunters and train-pullers is of a neutral and placid kind. On the contrary contacts with other groups often signify that there is a problem. 'The radio has been quiet' is an expression for when everything goes smoothly. The less contact the better.

Another important group, not least from the point of view of representing the superiors, is the collective of office staff. They occupy different positions, ranging from superior managers to rather humble office assistants, and the only thing uniting them is indoor, white collar work. Needless to say, they belong to a category far removed from the shunters. In the canteen they sit on the same side as the drivers, and as they work office hours they tend to appear at lunch-time, while you find shunters in the canteen at all hours, eating meals that do not match the hour; such as 'dinner' early in the morning.

The shunters, being fond of catchy descriptions, use terms like: 'stair-wearers' ('trappnötare') or 'paper-turners' ('pappers-vändare') for the ordinary white collar staff, while reserving 'small-popes' ('små-påvar'), for more superior staff and managers. Common denominators of such staff are that they do nothing, that thay make stupid decisions because they lack knowledge about how **real** work is done, and that they are vain and ingratiating, or they would not have been selected for the task in the first place. They are thought to be climbers who cannot work, but prefer the comfort and lazy life in a temperate office.

These rather extreme descriptions and judgements about the indoor staff, and about other groups as well, are frowned upon by other shunters. These are generally the ones who are more educated and who see shunting as a rather temporary arrangement as they aspire to higher education or other types of work, perhaps even office work. When talking in private they think that it is silly and oldfashioned to condemn persons who have other tasks, but they seldom, if ever, voice such views in the coffee-room. Their views are not valid currency on this particular arena.

As we know that the shunting group also includes persons who work exclusively indoors we are not surprised to find a distinction between 'them' and 'us' even here. It is considered that the *tkm* change their attitudes and sympathies when they turn to indoor work only. Their proximity and affiliation with the manager and other representatives for SJ makes them more like employers than employees. The fraternization with superior staff is seen as an ambition which almost automatically follows when the close all-day contact with the shunters is cut down to shorter spells of interaction when the final report is delivered or when the slips are collected.

On other occasions their status as white-collar staff is completely neglected. They have, after all, spent years in the yard and belong self-evidently to the 'shunters'. They are simply seniors who have reached the end of the line of promotion.

This demonstrates the constant fluidity of the demarcation-lines between groups of 'us' and 'them'; indoor/outdoor, shunters/other groups, Hagalund/the rest of SJ.[7]

Signs of Commitment

> Once is never. Twice is a habit.
> *En gång är ingen gång. Två gånger är en vana.*
> (Swedish saying)

Even though the beginners formally have the same status of employment, although not the same pay, as the old hands there is a vast gap between them.[8] The gap is one of position, influence, knowledge, not to say skill and experience, but also one of orientation towards the work and the workplace.

The old-timers are very conscious of their ties to the yard, ties that stem from the fact that shunting work has a very limited, close to non-existent, value on the labour-market outside SJ. As they say, it is not a 'trade' and as such the skills are not qualifications that can be transformed into a salary and a position in another workplace. The only exception is moving to another shunting yard, which almost exclusively means staying with SJ anyhow. But when leaving this particular yard one would leave not only the carriages, tracks and trains, work mates and the familiar surroundings behind, one would leave a large part of one's skills, as they are intimately connected to the physical environment, to the particular lay-out and conditions that prevail at Hagalund.

The longer shunters have been working at Hagalund the more they acknowledge their dependency as a fact. 'I don't know anything else but this

---

[7] Billy Ehn talks about the 'fluid limits of work', but his concept does not refer to conception of groups, but to aspects of interchanges at a multicultural workplace. Cf. EHN, *passim*.
[8] It is true that there is one formal difference concerning their employment as the principle for dismissal always must be that 'last to come is first to go'. During the period of my study the rates of unemployment were very low and the beginner was therefore a rare valuable rather than a rival for the jobs.

job.' 'I want my children to be educated for a real trade, not be like me and beat this yard.' Even if one may not on the whole object to it, one nevertheless finds that Hagalund is the place where one 'ended up', regardless of whether one actually applied to or actively chose it in the first place. 'Once you've been here seven years you're here for good.' This is how the saying goes.

'Fettered' to the yard the old hands are then at the other extreme compared to the beginners, who, no strings attached, have no other mental, social or educational investment in the yard and this particular workplace than what follows from a three or four week course (fully paid) and some rather vague expectations. 'I wanted a steady job.' 'I thought I might try it.' 'You must have a job, don't you.' 'I wanted an outdoor job.' 'I liked the shifts and the extensive free spells.' These are common phrases one gets from shunters who, in retrospect, express the reasons why they came to Hagalund.

The attitude of the beginners is then one of 'wait and see'. We remember that they keep a 'low profile', sitting quiet in the coffee-room, trying to make as little fuss around and about themselves as possible. They are listening, observing and behaving in a way that attracts a minimum of attention, but behind the silent façade they are busy working on 'blending in' – or deciding that they will not fit in. Their poker-faces make it difficult to tell. The beginners are naturally far from a homogeneous collection of people. The shunters, too, observe and wait.

The atmosphere of expectancy and suspense gradually wanes as little signs of commitment change the image of the beginner as a possible short-timer into a possible long-timer, or alternatively confirm the impression of him as someone who will leave any time. The change is slow and subtle, but the signs are like little arrows that point in one direction or the other. Among such signs you have first and foremost that the beginner turns up on time. To be late, or to be absent without early notice are bad signs indeed. Even to go on sick leave, and especially on one or two day leaves, seem to set little bells ringing. 'He's already sick', or 'The new one has 'phoned himself sick', someone will say with an insinuating voice. So far nothing more may be said, but it will be remembered if it happens again too soon.

A 'positive' sign would be that the person turns up, regardless of colds or minor ailments, trains for a few hours and then is sent home with a few encouraging remarks. A hang-over is also to be treated in the same way. To stay home the next day is out of the question. One drags oneself to the yard and gives everybody an opportunity to amuse at the sorry sight. The team can take pity on the suffering beginner and declare that he is a danger in the yard. 'Go home and come back in better shape tomorrow.' A repetition of such an incident is then unthinkable. 'Your brother turned 30 again?' would be the obvious comment and both the first incident as well as the second one would be judged improper.

The little signs may then not be very important in themselves, but if they all point in the same direction their collective force is quickly enhanced and what was seen as 'innocent' incidents are re-evaluated and re-interpreted **retrospectively**.

Another sign indicating that the beginners take an interest in the work and in the social life surrounding work is that they 'start talking'. They may ask questions about the work, and about work related matters. They may start to play cards, *'plump'*, or take part in story-telling. It is, however, rare that beginners are very successful story-tellers as most stories are expected to be work-connected or self-experienced. A beginner telling self-experienced stories might easily get the stamp of trying to stand out, to distinguish himself or to stress his background as opposed to his work identity. Beginners, as well as other persons such as the odd engine-driver who happens to frequent the coffee-room, are then often met with silence, with a mildly appreciative 'oh, really', or some such comment. To the shunters such self-experienced stories lack in work-connection and thereby in context. As a rule they simply do not make hits.

One last sign worth mentioning is the attitude of the beginner, something which naturally often is difficult to discern. If the beginner talks about earning a lot of money, projects, schools, mates that make a lot of money or if he 'acts like an intellectual' the prospects for his staying in the yard are seen as rather poor. Several of the senior shunters explained their staying at Hagalund as a possible outcome of their 'lack of ambitions'. They had not made 'a career'. Beginners who show too much ambition will not stay, as they soon will find out that the steps of promotion are few and only (after decades) lead to the position of *tkm*.

One of the youngsters was very aptly described as *'väldigt framåt'* (lit.: very forward); a very smart guy. 'He won't stay here long' was the inevitable remark that followed. This man later left and worked with a computer company for a while, but returned after some time, when finding out that his practical jokes were not appreciated there.[9] Despite his return there were still doubts

---

[9] He told of how he had dressed up as a knight – sword, helmet, etc. made out of cardboard boxes and computer sheets. Dressed in this way he had 'attacked' all offices shouting and waving his sword. 'Here that would have been appreciated, but those people only stared, without a smile, and when I reached the end of the corridor the manager came out of his office and yelled: 'What the hell are you doing?' The others must have informed him on the internal phone. I could not possibly work with people like that, so I came back here.'

whether he would stay as a shunter for any longer period.

The above mentioned signs are nothing but vague indications. There are several examples of severe misjudgments that are mentioned as counter examples every time speculations are made about the future prospects of a new group of beginners. 'Time will tell' is perhaps not the expression that is used to sum up the discussions, but it is nevertheless the most accurate one I can find to express the general attitude towards the silent beginner who does not stand out as a university student looking for a summer job, a misfit who shuns every kind of work and slips away in the middle of the shift, a social misfit who takes drugs and gets into fights, or a young man with high ambitions who tells everyone in so many ways that he is too good for this lousy job. All these have a clear prognosis, but in the majority of cases, the common cases, one never knows. The tiny girl who is never believed to last a whole night in -20° C, or the promising man with muscles 'like an oxen' may surprise everyone: the first one by her tenaciousness, the second one by his brittleness. The shunters have learnt from experience that such things never can be predicted.

Modes of Acceptance

While the beginners are assessed as to their individual character and abilities, and their prospective future at Hagalund is evaluated accordingly, the beginner's view of their seniors is remarkably different. To begin with, from their point of view every one is 'a shunter', and it is very difficult to judge their relative seniority except by relating to their age. This means that a beginner easily assumes that someone who is ten years older, but perhaps only six months his senior at shunting, has been working as a shunter for years. In a training situation the beginner probably overestimates the judgement and skills of such a 'senior'.

The seniority pattern, the individual destinies and the future prospects of the new work-mates are, naturally, of fairly little interest to the beginners. The natural focus of their attention is the work itself, how they cope and how they seem to be accepted by the regulars. Their problem is to learn names, get to know people, find out how they work and, of course, how to fit in in general. They meet a total situation, while the regulars meet one or a couple of 'new faces'.

The different styles and habits of the teams and of the trainers are among the most significant facts that stand out in the beginning as they radically affect the conditions of the training situation. There are rumours about a couple of teams, e.g. one team had a shunt leader who supposedly disliked women, but in most cases the individual experiences seem to differ and individual preferences make it impossible to judge whether the team one is working with is 'good'. While A liked his shift yesterday, his fellow student B might not like his shift with the same team today. The different ways of taking care of the beginner suit different tastes, and while one trainee finds it comfortable to take it easy and bide his time, another trainee appreciates to be given more responsibility and trust. Training is already a matter of fitting in.

While I have chosen to talk about signs of commitment, interpreted from the behaviour of the beginner, I find it more accurate to call the responses of the team and co-workers 'modes of acceptance'.[10] By this term I want to stress the various ways that the teams and co-workers accommodate the beginner. Talking and socializing, taking a 'soft' attitude to him when he tries his luck in 'plump', giving him responsibility at work, letting him off early, taking an interest in him by learning his name and spreading its use, initiating him into tricks of the trade as well as stories from the past; all these little things work towards gearing the beginner into a general feeling of being accepted and becoming one of the rest.

The reason I am talking of 'modes' instead of 'signs' in this case is that for the beginner there are no established signs, no particular traits to look for. Every person has to find out for himself, to create his own relationships and to be appreciated for his own abilities and properties. From the point of view of the shunters there is a common code, a map of 'good signs and bad signs' that indicate the degree of commitment the beginner has to his new job, although they admit that the signs not give the full picture. They may, however, be decisive as to whether the seniors will make social investments in the beginners.

To sum up, one can say that despite the great discrepancy between the beginner and the seniors, there is in reality no discernible difference between the beginner and the person who already has been working for six or eight months from the point of view of the senior shunters. A difference in skill, yes, but they may both, figuratively speaking, slap the seniors in the face by leaving the job all of a sudden, showing that they did not think it worth their while. The work life of the seniors is thereby denied value, and all the investments they have made in the form of helping, showing, being nice and appreciative turn out to have been made in vain. Too many such experiences,

---

[10]These signs are what Goffman called 'tie-signs', i.e. they contain evidence as opposed to communicate messages. Cf. GOFFMAN 1972, 324.

133

and the older ones start to say that they no longer 'can keep track of' the beginners, that there are all kinds of peculiar types 'streaming through' and that in the old days such a turn-over would have been unthinkable. That was when 'it had status' to work for the railways. 'But young people these days want something else – and I can't really blame them.'

Maybe the only commitment is the commitment of a worker who no longer has another place to go.

Apprenticeship – Passage without Rites

The last chapter was called 'Entry to the Shunting Yard' and one could as well associate this title to the passing of the gates surrounding the yard at Hagalund, as to the crossing of the boundary between the world of the shunters and the rest of the society that the neophyte undertakes in this chapter. The iron gates and the fences enclosing the yard are powerful images of separation, and consequently also of belonging, and it is indeed the metaphor of gate-keeping that Michael Coy uses in order to describe apprenticeship in *Apprenticeship: From Theory to Method and back again.*

"Potentially, if not actually, apprenticeship is a form of gate-keeping. It is the gate through which a few are permitted access to a craft and its skills and secrets. On one side of this gate is everyday social and economic life; on the other side of this gate is membership in the craft." [11]

Apprenticeship is a word that brings to mind shoemakers, bricklayers, and guilds, and a relationship between a master and a novice. A dictionary definition says that an apprentice is "one bound by indentures to serve an employer for a term of years in order to learn some trade or craft which the employer agrees to teach."[12] Such classic apprentices are still found in many trades all over the world, but Coy & al. pay less attention to the formal arrangements of the training and the relationship between master and novice and more to the entire context surrounding the situation where skill is passed on. The training may be formal or informal, structured or ungraded, short or long, but one is sure to find similarities regardless of whether one looks at future Tukolor weavers or East African blacksmiths, Hong Kong furniture

---

[11] COY 1989a, 10. Everyday life here seems to denote what is outside the gates. I talk about about everyday life in the yard, in order to distinguish what is seen as ordinary routine from extra-ordinary events upsetting that routine. Cf. discussion about 'everyday life' in GULLESTAD, *passim.*

[12] 'Indenture' refers to a contract or agreement under seal, the word stemming from the two documents that were cut, indented, at the edge to make them identical to each other. Cf. CCE.

carvers or US medical students, they argue.[13]

All apprenticeship implies a situation of 'not knowing how to' that is transformed into a situation of 'knowing how to'. Between these there is the gate distinguishing two social worlds, keeping the secrets of the trade on the right side of the border and making the neophyte undergo a complete transformation, adapting to a whole code of conduct as well as learning the skills of the trade. The conduct may concern the impression management of medical students who mask uncertainty, or ironworkers who conceal fear on the high steel or they may even imply playing along with attitudes of contempt and hostility in order to protect the craft monopoly. Secrets are kept behind the gate, or more importantly are **thought to** be kept behind the gate. As East African blacksmiths say: 'We don't know, but we pretend to know!'[14]

Passing the gate often includes an ordeal, which may consist of a test of skills or rather innocent pranks, but which also may take the shape of a longer process of humiliation and degradation, only slowly filling the measure that the apprentice has to take and eventually 'dish back' when he is thought to 'be ready'.[15]

Apprenticeship is, then, an introduction into a long-standing social relationship to the 'guild', the group of persons possessing the skills, as well as a creation of a new relationship to people outside that guild: those not initiated. This new relationship of practitioner and client is seen to be created by certain *rites de passage* of apprenticeship, where you identify rites of separation, transition and incorporation, as demarcating the pre-liminal, liminal and post-liminal stages, all according to the well-known scheme of van Gennep.[16]

The question is whether such a description serves any purpose for our understanding of the process of learning. In our example it is difficult, not to say misleading, to talk of rites at all in connection with the different phases of apprenticeship in the shunting yard. There are changing situations, changing conditions, changing roles, but where are the rites? During the course the beginners are 'separated' from the shunters, and when training with an older

---

[13] Cf. COOPER, COY 1989a, 1989 b, DILLEY, HAAS.

[14] Cf. COY 1989b 130 ff.

[15] There are numerous terms for degrading rituals, such as 'binging' or 'hazing'. They may consist of sending a beginner for 'a long stand' or to fetch cans of 'striped paint'. Cf. HAAS, 91 ff, COLLINSON, 189, GRAVES, 60. Slower processes of incorporation seem to relate to milder forms of degradation, such as 'joking down'. Cf. ZIJDERVELD, 297.

[16] Gennep's tripartite scheme has been used extensively by V. Turner. He uses a slightly different terminology, talking of 'aggregation' instead of 'incorporation', due to a different translation of the original *agrégation*. Cf. KIMBALL, VII, van GENNEP, 11, TURNER V., 80 ff.

shunter they could be described as being in a position of 'betwixt and between', as they do not yet belong to a team and they no longer are 'separated' in a class-room. Working on their own they are finally 'one of the shunters', but how are we to understand this process of transition?

We could read this in terms of the liminal phases offered by van Gennep, but I must say that this becomes a reading that is very forced and leads us to contemplate about the difference between rites, symbols, signification, and meaning. There is signification, because 'not knowing' and 'beginner' and 'new' and 'training' are terms that have significance and meaning, but there are no symbols connected to any rituals. There are rituals surrounding retirement (and death),[17] but there is no equivalence in connection with the beginners passing the test at the end of the course. There is no certificate, no emblem, nothing to mark the new 'status', except, perhaps, a handshake between teacher and pupils. The same holds for their entering the yard, or finishing their practical training. It may in fact only be the trainee and the staff delegator who know, or notice, that the beginner has finished training.

One actually gets the impression that events and everyday work as well as liminal situations are made to be as unritualised, as devoid of symbolic markers as possible. Leaving shunting after several years does not call for any special ceremony, either. At one occasion the person leaving his last shift tried to bid a slightly more formal farewell than the ordinary *'Ja, hej då!'* ('Bye, then!'), by saying *'Jag slutar nu, så hej då'*, ('I am leaving now. Bye, then!') only to be met by a few quick glances from the card table and the usual *'Hej då'*. (This all according to one informant who thought the reaction of the shunters quite amusing, but perhaps a bit **too** unfriendly.)

Having said that we are dealing with a practical training and a transition from beginner to senior that seems to be lacking the essential rituals of status elevation, of degradation in order to achieve a position of authority, of enactment of death and rebirth, we seem to have fallen outside the frame of rites of passage. This could be taken to mean that the transition process at this particular workplace is something else than apprenticeship. I think, however, that we should rather maintain the wide definition of apprenticeship which McCoy et al. propagate, and talk about apprenticeship without rites of passage, in the case of Hagalund.

It is interesting to note that, although devoid of ritualization, we find that there is conduct that **resembles** 'binging' and that **resembles** the ritualized humility and degradation that is forced upon initiates in rites of passage, but

---

[17] Some shunters actively avoid these rituals, too, by finding a way to sneak away from the last day at work.

we must stress here that although such conduct may be expected and seen as normal, there is nothing that outlaws the opposite.[18] Let me take a couple of examples.

The beginners are known as 'quiet' and it is thought to be 'natural' to be shy and withdrawn in the beginning. Still, there are examples of beginners who have been very open and talkative. This has not been frowned upon, but rather read as a positive sign. It is true that in these cases the persons are easily labelled 'too ambitious', and there is the fear that they will not stay but move on to more lucrative jobs, but this is regrettable. As long as their sociability does not express contempt for the job or ideas of superiority, the beginner may talk, be sociable and even cheeky. So, the beginner should show humility towards his seniors and accept their superior knowledge and skills, and he should not 'act as an intellectual', but there are no rituals that make this clear, no symbols that stand as constant reminders of the difference between the beginner and the rest, no 'binging' to bring them back to silence. The demand that one should not try to pass as better than one's mates, holds for seniors as well, and is part of the ideological stress on equality which prevails in the yard.

Without trying to present a functional explanation we can only remark that in a situation where the beginner has very little use of skills he has acquired previous to entering the yard, to the point of even having to learn how to walk and to jump without risking his life, there seems indeed to be little need to dramatize his ignorance in comparison to the skills of the old hands.

Binging, (for instance by delivering hard blows on the upper arm), hazing (in the form of misinforming or using jargon or argot unknown to the apprentice), or making the apprentice perform subservient tasks, have also vaguely resembling equivalents in the shunting yard. But, here again, the ritualized form is absent.[19] There is a lot of joking and kidding going on, and one can notice a difference in kidding between seniors and juniors, but the apprentices are not a legitimate target of kidding and cruel jokes. They are rather avoided when pranks and jokes are on the agenda and it is only when they have started to take part in the social life that they get their share. One must also notice that while binging presupposes that the binged person cannot answer back until he is 'initiated' into a higher status, the joking at Hagalund always assumes that the target of a joke has the right to give back, in equal currency or even with interest, also in the case of beginners.

There is, however, inequality built into much of the joking involving a

---

[18] Cf. the discussion of rites de passage in TRICE & BEYER, 110 f.

[19] The 'patterns' described by Wilbert Moore cannot be discerned. Cf. MOORE W., 326 ff.

senior and a junior shunter.[20] When the joke concerns matters of work, the junior person will find it difficult to pay back with accuracy, as the senior person easily gets the last word due to his superior knowledge and experience. Therefore one sometimes finds that a junior may react to verbal joking with physical retaliation, such as to throw a cup of water in the face of the senior or threaten to pour the contents of a coffee filter or some other garbage over him. This is not as elegant an answer as a senior person might, in case he is witty and verbally gifted, come up with, but it can nevertheless work as a final answer to the joking.

There is, then, a mild form of binging[21] and there are apprentices who show a submissive attitude, but there is neither a prescribed group of persons who 'must take' the jokes, nor any liminal rituals that describe when these things are expected to start or to end. There is slow progress, depending on the character of the individual. Either you show that you are prone to joking, and can 'take a joke', or you are 'stiff' and formal; you avoid joking and jokers avoid you.

There are limits, given by the formal hierarchy and thus easily observed, but they are not ritualized. To work one's own shifts is an important step, to become a shunt leader, or to become a *tkm* are important steps as well, and more significant ones to the co-workers than the first step into the yard, but perhaps the most important limit of them all is completely invisible. This is the limit that turns you into someone who is in it for good. Some shunters state that this happens after seven years, others say five – and the statistics point at an even earlier date, but this invisible and elusive limit is the one that makes a difference, as it is the one that changes your relationship to work. You are no longer free to leave, but you are someone who does not know anything else but 'beating the yard'. You no longer work **as** a shunter, you **become** a shunter.

The invisibility of this limit is connected with the fact that the possibility to get another job outside the yard changes considerably according to fluctuations in the job market.

'Being stuck' is not a question one might give much thought until a situation arises which suddenly reveals that one has few chances of alternative

---

[20] Sarcasms initiated by superiors in order to express authority relationships (as described by Seckman & Couch) can be observed, but it is a thing of the past to assume that such expressions would not be retaliated. Cf. SECKMAN & COUCH, 337 f.

[21] One shunt leade said his wife had enquired about all the bruises on his upper arms. "Well, if you have 'the Cap' as your B-member you just have to put up with it", he said smilingly. In this case it was one of the most respected seniors who accepted such a treatment from someone much younger and inferior in terms of position.

employment. It is thought that 'the work chooses its worker', but in the end the work does not only embrace the worker, it clasps him in an imprisoning grip. One has entered the yard – and there is no longer a way out.

Conclusions

We have seen the entry to the shunting yard from three different perspectives. First we have seen how the processes of selection and education construct meanings and mould the beginner's views of the shunters and the demands of the shunting job in opposition to other jobs and tasks. These views come to relate to and affect the beginner's appreciation of his/her own abilities and qualifications for shunting work.

Manual, outdoor, practical work is here contrasted to mental, indoor, theoretical tasks. 'Real' work is opposed to text-book regulations. How you do and how you fare in the context of the yard seems important, not discussing and defining rules for action in a class-room. Young men seem to focus upon being accepted by the future mates , while women stress the importance of managing the job. To put it simply; women want to command relations through the command of work, while men believe they will command work through the command of relations.

Secondly our study has concentrated upon how the apprentice is introduced to the organization of work and the ideological web surrounding this highly hierarchical structure. The egalitarian ethos, asserting that the stratified positions in the team are only differentiated due to technologically determined functions, constructs the shunting team as a cooperative unit, consisting of exchanging and interchangeable members of equal importance. Freedom and independence, which are thought to be among the main features of shunting work, thus comprise all members in the hierarchy, also those who are actually no more than 'coupling boys'.

The ideal picture of the shunting team as free, independent, egalitarian, cooperative, smoothly working, with a jargon which is 'raw but hearty,' thus comes to identify other tasks (such as train-pulling or coach recording) as inferior ones, or at least not 'proper' shunting.

Thirdly we have had a look at how the ideas about 'real' work, i.e. shunting, create a pattern of 'segmentary affiliation' within the yard as well as in contrast to the wider SJ organization. This affiliation is, however, rather a matter of verbal commitment than of coordinated action.

The beginner soon picks up the argot which distinguishes between 'us' and 'them', drawing on the ideology of what shunting is, as described earlier. Other groups are then constituted by the binary judgmental scheme where indoor contrasts to outdoor, manual to non-manual and execution to planning.

The use of such an argot is in itself, however, also seen as one of the important traits marking that the beginner is on his/her way to become 'one of us'. By complaining about and condemning other groups he/she shows a serious interest in accomplishing his/her work well. There is an emotional commitment to the group and therefore presumably an ambition to do one's equal share.

Membership is issued, not because one has proven identical to the rest, rather the contrary, but because one has shown willingness to adjust one's idiosyncratic ways and 'crazy' personality to the demands of team-work.

Membership is therefore built, not on passing a particular *limen* or test, but on the gradually increasing trust and confidence one manages to inspire over a period of time.

As shifts turn into years, the former beginner may come to the insight that the membership is a membership for life. However, his insight hardly comes as a sudden shock. As Bourdieu writes, the shunter may then already have 'chosen the necessary'[22] and be content with a free job, where 'at least you don't have to ask for permission to go to the toilet'.

Engine driver in cab.

<hr />

[22] Cf. BOURDIEU 1977, 44 ff.

7. COMMUNICATING THROUGH LEARNING – The arts of expressing, impressing, and oppressing

The *Säker* Shunter – Showing and Discerning Skill

'So you're with us today? Have you worked your own shifts before?' the shunt leader asked me with a slightly alarmed expression in his face. I answered in the affirmative, but a shunt leader of another team entered the exchange by saying: 'She's been with us. She is rather *säker*.'

We remember that shunting belongs to the positions within the company that are defined as 'Security Service' *(säkerhetstjänst)*, demanding that the holders 'should know and be willing to' apply the security regulations (SÄO). The skilled shunter can then be said to be formally defined by the requirements stated in SÄO (and SÄOK, the commentaries) and in the shunting instructions *(Växlingsinstruktioner)*, which are a complement to SÄO, specifying rules for shunting.

In the yard and in everyday work other, informal, requirements define the abilities and skills of the shunter and the shunter to be. These skills are not independent of the official demands. As I have indicated, ideas about what shunting entails are brought to the student during the selection process and the shunting course and the initial training period in the yard. The student is, however, increasingly exposed to the informal thoughts about work and about how to perform it. These thoughts include values that are not always made explicit, and they may be presented in so many indirect ways. Furthermore, many of the skills the apprentice is to learn are tacit, and thereby defy being formulated as explicit rules and regulations.[1]

---

[1] There is another dependency between formal and informal requirements. The employer has a whole range of informal demands, but these cannot be applied and brought out in the open unless masked and expressed in the form of existing rules and regulations – and often not without the cooperation of the union. Absenteeism and drunkenness are such vague notions. Shunters who formally have the same rate of absenteeism may then be treated quite differently depending on the assent of the union, i.e. in the last instance their employment depends on how well they are liked by the shunters – who influence the shop steward. Of two persons who were repeatedly late, or absent, one was fired after the shop steward had sworn 'I will get rid of

141

We are now going to look at this informal side of work, at the definition of the skilled shunter and thereby also skilful shunting, as it is comprehended in the yard, in the process of work.

Skilled shunters are said to be *säker*, a word that according to the dictionary means: 'secure', 'sure', 'positive' (about something), 'certain', 'assured', 'confident', 'cool', 'safe' and 'sound', but also 'firm' or 'steady' and 'judicious', when e.g. referring to style of walking and card playing respectively.[2] In fact, the dictionary definition lists so many of the aspects associated with the skilled shunter (style of walking and card playing included!) that the word *säker* almost seems to be tailored for this very purpose.

Embedded in its daily context in the yard the term *säker* takes on a variety of meanings, too. Although mainly referring to the confidence of the worker who knows what he is doing, there is no doubt that the safety aspect is implied as it seems almost impossible to keep these two aspects apart when talking about shunting. A *säker* shunter knows what he is doing, he does not hesitate, he is not nervous and unpredictable in his moves. He is a master of the situation and his calm, routine-like behaviour makes work smooth and safe for everybody in the team.[3]

While the skilled shunter is cool and secure, the beginner is on the contrary uncertain and nervous. Beginners do not necessarily cause problems to the team because they cannot perform the individual tasks properly, but because they need constant supervision as to their whereabouts and their doings. They are, and what is more, they have to be considered to be, unpredictable. They might make dangerous moves and without warning be in a place where they are not supposed to be. One extreme example was a beginner who suddenly went missing. The team searched for him, expecting the worst. It eventually turned out that he had gone home in the middle of work without telling anyone.

The fear a shunt leader has is, however, seldom that beginners go home – it was said about the man who went home that the team were rather content to find that they could work the rest of the shift without having to keep an eye on him – but rather that they stay and do too much. They attempt more than they can safely handle. They may for example go between the carriages all of a

---

him'. The other was given a second chance as he was 'different'. Talking around a bit with other shunters I got verdicts such as 'He is charming!', 'Socially he is a very nice guy', 'He is not cheeky.'

[2] Cf. S-E O.

[3] Bourdieu speaks of "... the ease which is the touchstone of excellence..." BOURDIEU, 1989, 66.

sudden and, the most frightening thought, without anyone noticing.[4] The engine may slow down to a halt because a switch is lined incorrectly, but to the beginner this suddenly appears as the right time to go between and uncouple a carriage he has been told is to be disconnected next. However, as no stop signal has been given the engine will set in motion as soon as the switch is lined and disaster is around the corner.

The *säker* shunter is then not primarily associated with official demands, formal status or even the security regulations. The day-to-day life seldom touches upon these matters, although they of course constitute the foundation upon which the execution of daily work is built. This is not to say that security regulations are never talked about. They are often referred to as a collective, SÄO, but it is understood that theory and practice are two different things. A common rhetorical phrase is: 'If we worked according to SÄO none of the trains would be finished in time.' It is well known that SÄO actually can be turned against the company as the threat of 'working to rule' is seen as a form of industrial action, a go-slow.[5]

The *säker* shunter works well in a team. Individual shunters can be referred to as good, 'half-good', bad, or even hopeless, but there is little agreement, and indeed no forum for shaping agreement, about who is good, or *säker*, as the skills always include qualities such as the ability to cooperate. A shunter who works well in one team may be considered a source of trouble in another, or even every other, team. Seniority and experience are possible criteria for being *säker*, but there are shunters who have been getting along for fifteen years who suddenly disagree about everything and are no longer able to work together in the same team, calling each other hazards.

Team-work in the yard entails that one can read and predict the moves of the others in the team. Body language plays no insignificant role in this. A person may well know what to do and manage to do it without trouble, but if he is seen to move on wobbly legs in a meandering and maladroit way, hesitate and change his path, and fumble and stumble on rails he will raise doubt in the others in the team about his capacity to work on his own and they will not let him work without surveillance. If it is found that there is no

---

[4] One fifth of the lethal accidents between 1976 and 1983 had no witnesses (Cf. PERSSON, 12), a fact which is accordant with the often expressed fear of having an accident in a lonely spot where no one will observe your predicament.

[5] Obviously this is not a local insight. McKenna writes about 19th century Britain: "Central policies contrasted with local methods. The *Rules and Regulations*, if carried out, simply meant the work would stumble into stoppage./.../The essential difference between railway work and the armed forces appeared when the railway workers realized that by carrying out their orders to the letter they would reduce the train services to a shambles. This 'working to rule' turns the concept of obligation upside-down." McKENNA, 30f.

need to worry, such odd behaviour may finally be excepted, but before this happens there is a strong tendency to see unstylish, jerky, or drooping behaviour as a sign of lack of control and potentially risky.[6]

There are persons who have been working for decades and still display a behaviour that seems odd in the eyes of outsiders. When passing Rolle, one of the senior *tkm* in the yard, one engine driver looked at him with pity and commented to me: 'So, they still let him beat the yard.' The seemingly aimless strutting walk made the driver think that Rolle was someone who was given minor tasks instead of letting him leave with a sick pension. When told that this man was a *tkm* the driver was astonished.[7] To the shunters, Rolle's comportment is well known as a personal style and even if they sometimes mock his ability to concentrate on his work, it is not the style of walking that causes doubts about his grasp of the situation or his skills in general.[8]

Muddle-headed behaviour is distinguished from nervousness. Persons with decades of experience can be considered nervous and unpredictable despite their controlled and, to the unfamiliar eye, self-assured comportment, and they may get the verdict *'koppelrädd'*, 'afraid of couplings'. This is a rather serious verdict as 'coupling-fright' is seen as a predicament that can hardly be cured. It is considered a personality trait, and persons afflicted should preferably not be working in the yard. If they do not leave of their own accord there is, however, nothing to be done about it and their predicament will not be mentioned to their face, but will, just like other individual traits, only become one more factor to be considered at work. When it comes to story-telling such handicaps are naturally useful and welcome motifs.

As moments of crisis are relatively scarce (particularly among those that C-members are expected to get involved in or have any responsibility to manage), so are the possibilities to build up, or severely damage, one's reputation. This means that a detached, cool and calm comportment in everyday situations is of great importance.

Experienced shunters know that cool behaviour is among the first things that the beginners try to imitate, and particularly men are considered to display

---

[6] Gísli Pálsson talks about 'getting one's sea legs' as a particular stage in learning how to move around a boat. Cf. PÁLSSON, 905. 'Getting one's yard legs' would be our parallel, and quite an accurate characterization of *säker* moving about in the yard.

[7] This is a kind of incident that meets amusement in the coffee-room. The point that people are not what they may seem, or what they want to be, goes well with the shunters. Ties, smart clothes and polished behaviour, all of which are considered to be superficial marks only, do not constitute a ticket to confidence, quite the contrary.

[8] In the fishing context Pálsson speaks of the skipper learning from the mate as well as the opposite. Cf. PÁLSSON, 917. I can think of very few examples of the former in the yard, although, of course, it cannot be ruled out. More obvious is that new styles are established, styles which newcomers later take on, while at the same time modifying them.

faked cool. However, experienced eyes are not fooled easily. Sometimes there is reason to hurry and 'any style goes' as long as the purpose is achieved. It may be to save an electric cable that someone has forgotten to disconnect from a post when a train is pulled away, it may be to make it in time to stop a fast kick, or to close a door that suddenly swings open in a moving train and risks getting smashed into the gates of the New Hall.

If you make it in the split second prior to an accident no one will comment the style, but if you on the other hand rush head over heels when no hurry is called for, reaching your goal with seconds or minutes to spare, your style will certainly be noticed and perhaps even commented upon.

Two examples highlight the distinction between cool that gets the verdict 'faked' and cool that is considered 'genuine'. After some time in the job B-members often show composure when kicked carriages approach. As 'kicks should hang' B-members avoid using brake heels as this may cause the carriage to stop short. The saying that there is no danger in going between carriages, despite their speed, as long as you do it on a straight part of the tracks, is then taken on literally, much to the disapproval of senior shunters. There might be a minimal risk that the buffers *gå omlott* (interlock), which is what the saying refers to in its full version, but there is naturally the risk of heavy *bakryck* (backlash), as well as a general danger as timing here requires excellent skill. The carriages, and particularly interior furnishing, may be damaged, too.

When told off by seniors, who shake their heads and enter the train to see if things have fallen on the floor in the restaurant carriage, the 'cool' B-member may answer with some snide remark, trying to 'cover up' his behaviour and make it look like he had been aware of the danger, but careless about the possible damage. 'It is only the damned *mas-tåg*, anyway.'[9]

Later in their career B-members learn to be more discriminating and appreciative of the different dangers that lurk when high speed is involved. The most remarkable change of attitude is known to take place when the B-members become shunt leaders and are responsible for the team. They are then jokingly reproached for the sudden carefulness they display, although the change is appreciated.

---

[9] *Mas-tåg* is a train going to/coming from Dalecarlia. (*Mas* or *dalmas* is a man from Dalecarlia. Although the word is not derogatory in itself, it is often used in a mocking and scornful way. Male persons from Dalecarlia will most likely count *'Masen'*, The Dalecarlian, among their nicknames.)

Standing in between.

A good example of justified haste and genuine cool was displayed by a young shunter who in the middle of a conversation with me and a couple of others in his team suddenly, and in no particularly elegant style, leaped to the rear of a train and pushed up the safety lid that locks the electric cable to the train. This happened in the middle of the night at a dark spot in the yard, but his observant eye, his 'split vision', had noticed that the cable was still connected when the train was being pulled from the other end. Thanks to his leap the cable slid out quietly and the train left without anyone but us noticing his feat. We could only admire his power of observation and his cool. Had he arrived half a second later he would possibly have had a bang, a luminous arc, if not an exploding electric post, very close to his face as the cable would have been torn apart or broken the post. This particular shunter was in fact often teased for being overambitious, doing things that did not belong to his job, and doing them even outside work hours, but in this case there were no teasing comments, only silence. I am probably not far from the truth if I guess that each of us onlookers wished we had grasped the situation a little ahead of him.

The *säker* shunter is thus someone who works calmly and often, but not always, with a style reflecting such calm and order. It is only in the rather rare

146

situations when the ordinary routine is upset that this calm style is put to the test. Faked calm, the pretence that 'it doesn't matter', or comments like 'the kicks must go all the way' (when they clash too hard), amount to nothing unless they can be matched with the purposeful cool of knowing instantly what to do in critical situations.

While calm, repetitive, routine-like work methods express masterly shunting, the verdict is finally passed on the basis of how a person acts and reacts in situations of stress, crisis and danger. The calm and cool may act confused and cause dangerous moves, while the muddle-head may act efficiently and calmly.

Stylish and calm comportment is a sign of being in control of the situation, but it is in the last instance the functionality of the reaction that counts. Faked control instantly opens a trap-door underneath the confidence in one's skill, while desperate moves may signal that one has judged the danger correctly and is prepared to do the utmost to save life and limb of the comrades in the yard. When disaster is close it only takes seconds to turn the safe and cool shunter into a stupid fool who seemingly could not care less if his mates were killed.

Imitation in the Training Class

When the beginners leave the classroom in order to learn how to handle and manipulate the material in the yard, they confront exercises quite unlike anything they might have tried before.

In preparation for the lesson the teacher has ordered a couple of carriages to be placed at comfortable coupling distance in a safe spot of the yard and he now shows every grip slowly, simultaneously commenting on what he is doing and why it is important to do the movements in this particular way and in this particular order. When lifting the coupling one should, for instance, hold the coupling bush *(koppel-tärningen)* with the palm of the hands and make sure that no finger or thumb grips around the iron into the loop *(bygeln)*, and when disconnecting the brake hoses, the vents on both the connected carriages should be closed simultaneously, while the hoses between engine and carriage demand that the engine vent should be closed first. Technical explanations are not elaborated on, as the students are not expected to have any deeper knowledge of the brake system, or whatever is at issue, anyhow.

After the demonstration the students are allowed to try, one by one, watched by the others. Every student will have to show that he or she knows how to perform every single task.

To imitate the movements as shown by the teacher causes few problems to the beginners. Someone might find it difficult to connect the stiff brake hoses, which just seem to strive in opposite directions, as were they propelled by magnetic repulsion. Others tend to read the switches incorrectly, or find it difficult to remember all things that must be done in coupling 'for good'[10], but on the whole, however, the training is not seen as demanding. No one admits afterwards that the practical part of the course was difficult,[11] and the trouble one had with the brake hoses is soon forgotten – at least by the person who had the difficulties. There is no particular hurry, and the teacher takes good time to ensure that every student has performed every task in a satisfactory fashion.

The coupling process is then trained in its entirety, and every student is told to 'connect', 'disconnect', 'couple for good' or 'uncouple'. After each exercise the comrades are asked to evaluate the tested student. Did the student perform the tasks correctly? Were the tasks done in the right order? Did he forget anything? Not until all students perform perfectly will the class be dismissed.

The practical training continues with similar exercises of all tasks. Different kinds of equipment are introduced, and finally coupling is trained with a moving engine. This is also when students are taught the technique that allows them to jump on and off moving vehicles at increasing speeds. Finally the student should manage to move the engine around the tracks by directing the driver with correct hand, or lantern, signals, while manipulating the switches adequately. The introduction of a moving engine causes excitement and some nervousness. For the first time the students now face danger, even if risks are minimized by the controlled situation and by the constant supervision of the instructor.

During these exercises it is understood that the driver will 'work to rule', allowing none of the normal interpretation of the situation that makes certain

---

[10] Coupling 'for good' implies a final coupling between carriages in a train, while a 'normal' coupling only means connecting two carriages loosely together, preventing them from rolling away. Coupling for good means that the coupling should be tight, the brake hose and the electric cable connected and secured and the unused coupling (both carriages have a coupling, of which only one is used) secured on a hook.

[11] At least not openly. One person, a female ex-shunter, said in an interview:"I remember the first time I went in between two coaches, what a bloody shock it was. [...] I was so dead frightened [...]. It lasted a few months, at least." When I asked whether she ever dared to say that she thought it was scary, she answered: "No, I bloody well didn't! (Laughter)"

signals seem superfluous and which therefore often are merely indicated or outright neglected. The training situation is a 'constructed' one and this is made obvious to the students. The driver will react by stopping short at signals that anxious students show too early or they will drive too far and block the switch if the signal is a bit too late, or they will even vanish into the distance when the student is busy lining a switch, oblivious of the necessary stop signal. The driver and teacher may smile mildly, but teasingly, at the students who just don't seem to get the timing right.

It now appears to the students that the practical training is not 'really real' either. The performance contains all a C-member has to know, but the situation does not resemble the one in the yard. This is supported by the so often repeated coffee-room saying that 'you don't learn the trade until you work your own shifts'. The students do not know how the informal interpreting and common understanding works in the day-to-day cooperation in the yard, but they assume intuitively, and quite correctly, that drivers do not work on such a literal basis 'out there'.

It is clear that the purpose of this method of training is not to tease the beginners, quite the contrary. By working to the letter in this way it is stressed that the shunters and the train-pullers are 'bosses' in the yard and that the drivers are at all times obliged to obey their signals, and work according to their planning. The beginner is in this respect, and within the limits of the yard, superior to drivers with thirty years' experience. This is a duty as well as a right and the beginners are trained to understand that their signals are, theoretically speaking, law in the yard.

To sum up we can say that the students find little difficulty in imitating and performing the tasks when these are presented as isolates during the practical part of the introductory course, devoid of the context of team-work. Soon, however, the students see the situation as constructed, artificial and as such different from what they assume prevails 'out there'. Such ideas, I claim, support and pave the way for the beginner to assert himself by applying the new skills with discrimination and by managing tasks in ways that do not slavishly reproduce the sterile and, in the mind of the assertive beginner, overcautious models offered to him by teachers representing the authorities that hover over the shunters in the yard: the company, the union and the senior shunters.

The assertive beginner meets certain difficulties, as we shall see. During the initial period in the yard, working as a trainee, his idiosyncratic ways of working take on a different meaning, as he is seen first and foremost as a possible danger to himself and his mates. Not until his movements in the yard are fully routinized does he appear as *säker*.

Initially there is then a conflict between the assertive and discriminate behaviour of the beginner and the demand for routines, identified as 'the way it is done' by the senior shunting crew. The solution of the conflict is a two-way adaptation. The beginner adopts established routines, while the shunters learn to 'read' the beginner, and distinguish safe idiosyncracies from unsafe ones, and nip the latter in the bud.

In short, while the practical training has the explicit goal of making sure every student knows how to perform various tasks that are seen to constitute the bulk of the obligations of the C-member, the training also has another, hidden, effect. By working slavishly according to the letter of the shunting instructions the students get an unintended message saying that the instructions are clumsy, ridiculous and impossible to apply in 'real work'. While such an assumption is correct in respect to how work is performed by the old hands, it nevertheless causes problems for the beginners, as negligent and deviant behaviour on their part is looked upon with suspicion and condemnation by the seniors. The beginners have no concept of the safe and 'correct' bending of the rules.

Cowboys and *Säker* Shunters

In old railway argot a beginner is called a *'kabyl'* [12] This denotation is today not known by everybody. It is in fact only among oldtimers and railway enthusiasts one can come across it, and then it will hardly be used without explanation. Although it is a dated term for a beginner I will here use 'kabyl', or 'kabyl behaviour', as key terms covering a wide variety of judging expressions in everyday language, i.e. everything from 'beginner' to the shaking of heads, scornful snorts and insinuating tones of voice. Kabyl in this sense is the epitome for all traits that are seen to signal ignorance, inexperience and freshmanship. The kabyl is the opposite to the *säker* shunter, but also to the 'cowboy', as we soon shall discover.

While unshakeable calm is what the majority of kabyls try to put on from day one in the yard, with variable success, this cover for uncertainty is distinguished from the cool that shunters with many months' experience put

---

[12] Pronounced with stress on the second syllable. Örjan Nyström reports that beginners in the shunting yard in Gothenburg used to be called *'späling'*. (Cf. NYSTRÖM, 134) There have certainly been many such appellations in the yards all over Sweden in former times. As there at the moment is no specific term in use at Hagalund I have chosen the now almost extinct term *'kabyl'* because of its history and because it has such a pleasant anthropological ring to it.

150

on. The latter is the foolhardy behaviour that stems from the newly acquired routine and the familiarity with what is going on in the yard. We might think of it as the initial feeling of mastery. When the shunter is trained as a B-member, i.e. when he has about two years of experience, this foolhardiness is considered to reach its peak. A senior shunter described this stage of the career as particularly dangerous, and the fact is that a considerable part of all fatal accidents indeed befall shunters with 2-3 years of experience.[13]

While the kabyl might gradually transform into a *'säker'* shunter without much ado, the newly aquired skills are then ever so often, although in varying degrees, displayed in what I will call cowboy behaviour. This term is, like kabyl, a loan that I rather insolently impose on what the shunters would describe in a variety of ways. It refers broadly to stylish and daring behaviour, which intends, more or less consciously, to impress viewers by signalling skill and know-how. Cowboy behaviour, polished by routine, transforms into a style, as posture and body movements are affected permanently.[14] Cowboy behaviour thus changes from being a coarse 'attitude' to being a 'natural' way of moving and working.[15]

It is obvious that one cannot give an exhaustive definition of 'cowboy behaviour', just as one cannot define 'smiling' or 'going for a walk'.[16] What we can do is to look at what the shunters see as daring, foolhardy, and irregular behaviour, but which is intended to give an impression of mastery.

---

[13] In 1976 to 1983 the victims in seven out of fifteen fatal accidents had a work experience of two or three years, while the remaining eight had worked 13 to 40 years, the average being almost thirty years. Cf. PERSSON, 12.

[14] The 'cowboy' metaphor has been used by other writers, such as Rosabeth M. Kanter, but although her use of it also implies a stress on individualism, we must end the comparison there. Cf. KANTER. Cowboyism in shunting is laid down in the physique just as much as in a mental attitude. It aims at a physical appearance that signals skill – skill which may or may not be there to back it up.

[15] The understanding of how work should be performed develops in and through the bodily techniques. 'Cool' is therefore to be regarded as symbolic capital embodied. Cf. e.g. BOURDIEU, 1989, 191 ff., 474. Marcel Mauss discussed such internalization of style already in the 1930's. Cf. MAUSS, *passim*. What could be seen as the other side of the coin is the exercise of power through control of the body, a line of thought naturally connected to Foucault. Cf. FOUCAULT, *passim*.

[16] Compare to Ryle's famous 'When is a wink a wink?' (Cf. RYLE, 480 f.) Concerning 'going for a walk' I feel compelled to illuminate the difficulties involved by telling an anecdote about a friend of mine, a senior Englishman, who once ventured to take a walk in a New Jersey suburb. He was stopped by the police, who had been alerted by local inhabitants. When he explained that he was only taking a walk the police decided to let him go, nevertheless warning him: 'Don't do it again!' Contextual factors, involving how one is dressed, where and when and at what speed one chooses to walk, are important for whether one can be said to be 'going for a walk'. Brenda Farnell advocates a form of script ("Labanotation") for recording movements. Cf. FARNELL, *passim*. Although this might be useful, it would nevertheless not account for the contextual, and in many cases even restrospective readings of movement that we are dealing with here.

We can then contrast it to behaviour which might seem analogous, but which is exempted from such labels, verdicts or judgements.

I have twice come across the very word 'cowboy' in connection to the shunters, and as these instances reflect different outsiders' views I will report them in some length. The shunters reject such a cowboy-image, but I will retain the concept as I think we, with some careful chiselling of the signifier and the signified, may talk about cowboy behaviour, or 'cowboyism', as something that occasionally can be observed in the yard. In other words, we shall look at how this cowboy behaviour differs from the view of shunters in general as a group of 'cowboys' and thereby modify the picture painted by the outside.

What is then the 'shunter-*cum*-cowboy' picture that has been presented by the outside? The first time I heard the shunters being compared to cowboys was when a rather shy reporter from one of the union (or SJ) magazines entered the train-puller's booth and started to interview the train-pullers with the question: 'Are you the cowboys of SJ?' This line was definitely not one to smooth the way for the rest of the interview, and as soon as he left the train-pullers snorted: 'Cowboys! Where did he get that from? What do they think we're doing?' If they were flattered or amused they certainly did not show it. The term was taken to be a 'typical' expression of the predjudiced view 'others' had of shunters; a bunch of brutes, insensitive to weather and pain, carelessly shoving carriages around the yard.

The second time the cowboy-image was presented was when I attended a SÄO repetition course in the company of three of the most senior and respected shunters; a *tkm* and two shunt leaders, one of them in addition being safety officer and a teacher at the introductory course. These senior shunters were shown a German video-film[17], where one can see a rather unlikely 'shunter', dressed in cowboy hat, fringed suede jacket and high-heel boots – with spurs – sneak around a marshalling yard, hitting his head against buffers, and jumping off a train at high speed. (There is also a sequence showing how such sequences are tricked when filmed, revealing that the actors land on piles of foam cushions, that the speed in reality is very slow, etc.) The overstated message of the film is that shunters are, or tend to be, ignorant of risk and

---

[17] The film was called *'Rangieren ohne Risiko'*. I was unable to attend when the film was shown, but on my request I was given the opportunity to watch it a couple of hours later, during a break. There is therefore no reason to believe that my presence and 'kabylishness' motivated the first showing.

danger, and that they act cool and tough just like little boys playing cowboys.[18]

In the particular showing that I refer to, the audience was the most unfortunate crowd possible. If ever there would be a referendum among the shunters to appoint the most trustworthy, conscientious, and skilled shunters, the men present at the course would without doubt have been among the strongest candidates. Besides representing, the three of them together, 108 years of experience they were shunters *sans peur et sans reproche*. [19]

After work: Waiting outside the trainpullers' booth for an empty train to the Central Station.

The showing of the 'cowboy' film at the SÄO course made it evident that the course was composed first and foremost with beginners in mind, but one can still see the showing as a warning to the seniors to keep an eye on the young and on emerging wild west fads. There was obviously some embarrassment on the part of the teacher as well as the 'students' because the

---

[18] The film is made for a German audience, but as it is imported to Sweden we may assume that this idea is seen to translate reasonably well into Swedish conditions.

[19] Pálsson and Durrenberger see the tendency to be impressed by the skills of the male informants as connected to a stress on individual skills and even 'a rigid distinction between individual and society and extraction and exchange'. (PÁLSSON & DURRENBERGER) I see their point, but I am not willing to see skill as a collective construct, as it were, *ex nihilo*.

film aroused my interest, and I was taking down notes about its contents. Perhaps they were alarmed by my new role as a researcher and thought that I was paying undue attention to this rather childish representation of the shunting trade. Did I think that this was a fair picture of how shunters imagined themselves; cowboys mounting and jumping off their steel horses!

Anyhow, the shunters soon, but in an apologetic and indirect way, made it clear to me that they thought the film was corny and they added that it was 'inapplicable to the conditions at Hagalund'. I very much shared the feeling of embarrassment mixed with indignation stemming from the possible insinuation that shunters at Hagalund would have anything to learn from such a film. The situation seemed absurd to me, all the more so when the shunters thought they had to tell me in this roundabout way that they did not take the message personally. To me it was evident; these people were daily risking their lives in the yard only to be told by the 'bosses', planners, educators, and indoor staff that they should stop playing cowboys!

This rather lengthy explanation to the background of the term makes it clear, I hope, that I am well aware of the derogatory associations the word might bring forth. I am nevertheless going to use it as there is no other word that conveniently would express the foolhardy behaviour I am about to discuss, and which I hope I can show is somewhat different from the behaviour of the inadvertently death-defying impostors of the educational reel.

Although cowboy behaviour is well known to the shunters, they do not talk about it as 'cowboyism'. Naturally, they do not see it as a 'cultural trait', but as recurring individual tendencies. They would use expressions like, 'he's a bit tough', 'he's quite a brute' *('han är rätt tuff', 'han är en riktig hårding')* but again many judgements are passed only with a tone of voice, combined with body language. 'He is a bit like that... [flinging the head back].'

Stories from the yard, as well as conversation in general, also encode such judgements in more or less implicit ways.[20] As is the case with other evaluations concerning work mates there is a reluctance to express opinions. There is joking and mockery, hints and snide remarks, but unless one is familiar with the actual goings on in the yard one might easily misread what there is to be read between the lines.

---

[20] A now retired shunter had the nick-name *'Stålis'*, (a short for *Stålmannen*, 'Steelman', i.e. the Swedish name for Superman), stemming from his tough work habits. There are indeed a couple of such persons, who stand out because they always kept their 'cowboy' habits and did not 'calm down' as part of the incorporation into the habits of the yard. We remember Arkansas as another example of this. His nick-name is no coincidence in the respect of the reference to the Wild West.

Our cowboy belongs to the junior half of the work force as the tough and foolhardy behaviour is something that is expected to, and indeed is seen to, wear off as young men learn 'the ways things are done here in Hagalund'. The wearing off is a result of 'getting into the team', a process of incorporation that the senior members handle, preferably in subtle and indirect ways. There should be no need for explicit correction, rules, or sanctions as it is a matter of internal adjustment to the working habits of the team. The lodestar in this respect is the omnipresent and all overriding principle saying that 'no one must get hurt'.

There is no doubt in my mind that the instruction film was felt to be offending to the senior shunters partly because this kind of correction is thought to be their task. They are setting the standard for their team, and the young shunters should learn their ways because they want to work with efficiency and care for the comrades in the team, not because they are advised, commanded, or forced to do so by the company.

Everybody starts, naturally, out as a kabyl, but time and experience might transform the most 'impossible' case into a good shunter. There is no way of telling the development in advance. We know that efforts to judge beginners are known to have failed.

Individual abilities are thus difficult to assess in beginners, but sex and age are seen as significant distinguishing traits. Men are in general considered to be more reluctant from the very start to do as they have been instructed.

'Men always want to do things in their own sweet way. They have to be broken in to the bridle, like horses. That is why women are much better in the beginning. They do things the way they have been taught from the start. They don't twist things around.' This explanation of the difference between the sexes was offered by one of the teachers.

Some of the beginners, particularly men, had to be taught not only how to do things, but they had further to be convinced that there was a reason for doing things a certain way. The various idiosyncratic procedures that they came up with were not the most rational ways of working, and in many cases outright dangerous, but this message was not easily conveyed to male kabyls.

There is a certain leniency towards the men's behaviour and performance during the initial period, stemming from a view of men and women as fundamentally different, as well as a benign attitude towards the shortcomings that the men later display, an attitude which could be called 'boys will be boys'.

The shortcomings, even if considered inherent to the sex, are nevertheless seen as a folly of their youth and it is thought that, given the right treatment

155

from their seniors, they eventually will conform to *'det som gäller här i Hagalund'*, (i.e.: what is the rule, what is accepted in Hagalund).

We can conclude that there is behaviour in the yard that can be said to be tough and foolhardy. By calling it 'cowboy behaviour' I do not want to bring to mind the fringed jacket buffoon although this caricature and our 'cowboy' do have a common denominator in a desire to look tough and cool.

We are well advised to think about cowboy behaviour as not primarily tied to certain individuals only, but as a type of behavior that almost every (in most cases male) shunter shows at some point in time. According to the shunters, much of the milder forms of behaviour I have called cowboyish is simply rather normal behaviour for young men ('boys will be boys'), and not something they necessarily find disturbing or dangerous. In cases of accidents they might, however, amongst themselves, bring up the 'careless' attitude of the culprit, even if the accident did not result from it.

It is said that 'either you work they way we work here in Hagalund or you leave'. The sacred rule is that you must not endanger life and limb of your comrades, and almost anything that breaks against the Hagalund routines can be interpreted as breaking against this rule. Incorporation does not involve compliance to a specific set of rules or norms, but a sensitivity to whatever the comrades in the team are up to. We must here pay attention to the two sides of the vague process of learning how to fit into the team and the accepted work methods. As cowboyism turns into style, and the beginner asserts his increasing skills the acceptability of deviation grows. What is unacceptable breaking of the informal rules in the beginner may be the fully accepted idiosyncratic style of an 'old head'.

There are characters who therefore never will be 'fully incorporated', but who still are respected as able shunters. These cases are considered to be odd personalities and their shunting make stories that resound decades after they have left the yard. We can state the case where such an oldtimer pulled away a train leaving a team-member between the carriages, who had to save his own life by quickly climbing up onto one carriage. In this case the culprit was not even told of his mistake, as the victim suspected him of failing to reform his ways anyway. Instead the situation was interpreted as a proof of the necessity always to be on guard for the unexpected to happen.[21]

These particular cases of non-conformism are interesting as they indicate that risk in these cases is redefined. These shunters, due to their long

---

[21] Blaming the victim; in this case himself. Mary Douglas writes:"Victim blaming facilitates internal social control; outsider blaming enhances loyalty." DOUGLAS 1986, 59. Blaming oneself is surely an internalization of social control.

experience (and it is crucial that they are thought never to have caused bodily harm), are working in a safe way because their long experience shows that 'they know what they are doing'. Carelessness or breach of skill is turned into a natural ingredience at work. What would be a deadly sin for an inexperienced shunt leader is then seen as 'something that can happen anytime, and which every shunter should be prepared to handle'. What should have been a slur upon the 'honour' of the senior shunt leader was here turned into a display of skill on the part of the relatively junior shunter.[22]

We begin to discern the complex, and truly dialectic, relationship between the process of incorporation and the range of movement of the social actor. The initial demand that beginners comply to certain informal rules and norms does not lead to a state of consensus, to an organic system of rule adherence. The senior shunters do indeed increasingly construct themselves as independent actors within the undefined, and undefinable, framework of 'what is accepted here in Hagalund'. They are shaping and creating idiosyncratic ways of working and behaving as well as they influence and dominate the stage where ideas, opinions and informal rules are formed and discussed.

I will now turn to look at the long and winding road that leads from the dependent apprentice to the skilled shunter. Writers such as Foucault and Bourdieu have explored the relationships between knowledge and power, domination, disicipline and the control of body – even style – and I will in the succeeding part develop the ideas concerning constructions of skill, knowledgeability, and style, by projecting them onto the screen of domination and hierarchy.

Learning the Ropes – Kabyls and Cowboys

> Out in the yard, observing team-work after the reorganization, I was asked about my opinion. As I had minutes previously observed one of the B-members couple a rather hard kick, instead of stopping it with a break heel, I answered, jokingly, that I would not dare to work with them any longer. The B-member in question looked surprised and asked me why that was. 'The way **you** go between!' I said, and the shunt leader said affirmingly: 'Yes, he is a bit tough, Ruben.'
> Young Ruben looked so astonished, as well as embarrassed, that I got the impression he never had been given such a verdict before. However, I was not sure whether his embarrassment was caused by

---

[22] One could also claim that the careless behaviour stemmed from the fact that the senior shunter **knew** that his team was skilled enough to handle such situations. With beginners he might have acted differently.

the fact that he never had thought of himself in those terms, or whether he felt he had been accused of 'playing cowboy'.

There is obviously more to learning than mere imitation. In training class every student has shown the ability to perform the individual tasks, but when students step into the yard on their own, the skills earlier acquired are quickly abolished and considered irrelevant, if not, as far as one can judge from the observer's point of view, childish and corny.

We have described cowboy behaviour as daring, foolhardy ways of working. It is a form that is always tending to the extreme. Either it is an overdimensioned waste of power, dressed in an air of ease, or it is a restricted, niggardly and close-fisted expenditure of power, signalling in both cases carelessness and nonchalance, indifference and aloofness.

The only thing the cowboy has in common with the kabyl is his reluctance to subjugate himself by conforming to what he sees as a given pattern. He is reluctant to imitate and copy the seniors when routine is concerned, but will immediately pick up odd tricks to solve new or difficult situations. To him the old jog-trot way is not necessarily the best one. The cowboy is always eager to invent new methods or to learn things that he need not know. He is more likely to know how to drive an engine and to trim a moped than how to handle the control board for the gates to the Hall. '(What the hell!) I just turn every switch until they open.'

In contrast to the kabyl, the cowboy is thus in many respects a skilled shunter, he 'knows how to go on'[23], but he is, just as the kabyl, reluctant to follow rules that are spelled out for him.

The kabyl has with some success managed the initial demands of performing individual tasks in a strict and artificial setting, the setting of the introductory course. He soon assumes that life in the yard will demand a different performance. Once out in the yard, facing up to the realities of working as a C-member, he is subject to the myth-making[24] surrounding the next step in his career, *skjutspassning,* the tasks of the B-member. *Skjutspassning* is, as we have seen, the most dangerous part of shunting, but

---

[23] This expression echoes Wittgenstein's discussion about how to understand 'the rule by which he proceeds'. Cf. WITTGENSTEIN, 38 ff. One is also reminded of Bourdieu's description of taste as the ability to discern among entirely new things what is 'good taste', as opposed to simply following rules. What I say is then that the cowboy has learnt to discern, rather than to follow rules. Cf. BOURDIEU, 1989, 169 ff.

[24] I am here using 'myth' in the sense Roland Barthes does when he talks about pictures, but also statements and expressions, which are considered truthful and self-evident. Cf. BARTHES, 109 ff.

also the one that is surrounded by the largest amount of informal demands and rules of thumb that admit, legitimate and encourage foolhardy behaviour.

> 'On straight tracks you can go between the hardest of kicks.'
> 'Kicks can't be too hard. We have B-members to stop them, don't we?'
> 'There is no danger in connecting a live electric cable – unless you do it slowly and juggle it around – and the weather is very humid, of course.'

Anyone who has connected a number of electric cables will know that they are quite tough and often require a bit of juggling around. (This is one of the few tasks that require a certain amount of strength in addition to technique.) Brake-heels 'jump' (fall off the rail), kicks clash into trains damaging the carriages or setting them in motion, backlashes hit the ribs or stomach of the coupler, and bridges jump their clinches and fall down on the head of the coupler. All such incidents are well-known as possible outcomes of hard kicks, but the B-member of two years' shunting experience feels confident exactly because he knows all this and thinks he can avoid the accidents. Most of his experience as a shunter has, however, been as a coupling boy, and his familiarity with the tasks of the B-member derive to a great extent from observation, and from listening to his mates discussing more or less successful kicks.

The uncertainty of the kabyl is rather soon varnished with a layer of calm and cool. As experience grows it is expected that the imitated cool will slowly grow into the steady behaviour and the skills of discrimination that the routine, sweat and ardour foster. Only an inexperienced shunter will take the expression 'You shall never run' literally. Such expressions are rules that make up a front, an image of how the work is conceived to be like. They are ideals, not rules to be obeyed. These catchy expressions cannot prescribe the correct procedure, as every situation differs in some respect and the shunter must use his skills of discrimination to know when to apply even the rules of thumb. Thus; if you have to run, you have to run, but a skilled shunter should be able to arrange work in a way that does not require running.[25]

Jargon, sayings, rules of thumb and stories about failures, stupidities and mistakes paint a distorted picture of the tasks, glorifying the daring power of action. The beginner is told of buffers that fall to the ground at Arkansas's kicks, of conference carriages cleared of their expensive equipment when being kicked, of collisions, derailments, walls torn down, and B-members

---

[25] On my photographs from the yard I find that I, inadvertently, have caught two experienced shunters in the act of running during one single shift.

desperately braking runaway carriages by running up to and entering them in order to work the tough, and often rather useless, handbrakes from inside the carriage.

These stories are accompanied by laughter and bragging about how many hundred thousand crowns of damages one has caused, implicitly conveying the message that 'accidents' are when persons come to harm, not the company property. Once the manager reminded Märsta-Johan that the team must comply with the rule that no carriages be kicked in the direction of the halls, as there had been a *tillbud* (narrow escape)[26] a couple of days earlier. *'Tillbud!'* Märsta-Johan claimed he answered. 'What I call a *tillbud* is when we drove into the wall of the Old Hall and they had a mason working on it for three months!'

All too easily these accounts make the kabyl adopt a careless face, not wanting to comply to the common recommendation that he should avoid doing tasks he feels uncertain about, or to show 'slow'-signals when he considers the speed to be too high.

When trying to apply his rather limited skills, his knowledge of the work process is too limited to allow for judgements that would pass as 'good working' in the yard. A strategy often resorted to is immobility and silence, which at least makes it possible for the team to read the comportment in several ways – 'calm and cool', hopefully being the preferred one – while questions and own initiatives more easily would make the reading unambiguous and reveal ignorance and 'stupidity'. Avoiding to 'overdo' is, however, often judged as reluctance to perform as instructed, or as creating own 'weird' ways of working.

Cowboys, young men with a couple of years' experience, do not face the same situation as the kabyls at all. They have already learned to work efficiently as C-members, they have trained as knockers and B-members and are now doing their first own shifts in these new roles, or they have even worked in these roles for some time. The cowboys have thereby created a style of working, a routine in the accomplishment of tasks and a rhythm in the interplay between bodily movements and the movements of the engines and carriages.

The decisive difference between the cowboy and the kabyl is, however, not always that the cowboy works with fluency and a good portion *'säkerhet'*.

---

[26] *Tillbud* has the double meaning of 1) a narrow escape, and 2) a slight accident that could have had much more serious consequences. This duality in meaning is often played on in stories from the yard. What the company see as a *tillbud* (narrow escape) is 'nothing' to the shunters. A *tillbud* to them is a slight accident, i.e. an accident that did not cause bodily harm, only damage to property.

The fluency, the discrimination, the way of talking and behaving has long ago led the shunt leader to relax and let the freshman work without constant supervision. Strengthened by the confidence, and encouraged by the increasing ability to foresee events in the yard, and therefore be located in the right spot at the right moment, the former kabyl can now widen the thoughts from the management of single tasks to partaking at an evaluation of the whole process. He lifts so to speak his eyes from the coupling to the flow in the yard. Acceleration and retardation, speed and halts are all judged as proper, slow, fast or lengthy by the cowboy, but he still does not have the ability to read, follow and predict the shunting procedures without effort. He must often consult the slips and get information from the shunt leader or the boss and even then he may be confused and at a loss – and slightly irritated when a kabyl asks him: 'What will we do now?'

The kabyl, lacking over-view and direction, contributes with odds and ends to the work process. To the shunters he is unpredictable, as they do not see any pattern in his innovations, and in his breaking of the rules. To seem 'dizzy as a goose', 'snurrig', is easily the outcome when the kabyl is trying to work on his own initiative. The cowboy has aquired a direction and it is rather easy to predict in **what way** he is likely to deviate from rules and norms. His increasing overall view of the work process has far reaching consequences for his work performance and indeed for the performance of the whole team. Considering the imaginary examples above we can conclude that the cowboy skills allows him to focus upon the flow ('flytet') of the cooperation in the yard. Flow, and the ability to increase the speed, take priority over individual considerations.

The kabyl has little grasp of how his work and choices in work procedures effect the flow and work of the team as his concentration is turned towards details of his own performance. In order to mark his 'cool' he might walk close, or even in the middle of, the tracks as there is no traffic in the yard, or he may, in case the engine stands still or moves very slowly, think it unnecessary to jump off in the way he has been taught during the course. He walks between buffers that are only a couple of meters apart – as there is no engine close by. He wants to mark that he has the ability to discriminate and that he is neither scared nor working to the letter. This is 'real work' and not the shunting course.

What the kabyl does not appreciate is that all these procedures are subject to very little thought and discrimination to senior shunters. They are part of the routine and belong to things done not because they are seen as necessary, safe or adequate in that particular situation, but because they are expected to be performed without thinking. It is indeed precisely the indiscriminate performance of these routines that constitute one of the attributes of the skilled shunter. 'It is impossible for me to walk in the middle of the tracks', they proudly say, 'it is engraved in my spinal marrow.'[27] Likewise they excuse their indiscriminate habit of repeating the signals 'slow' or 'stop' by asserting that their arms 'automatically go up in the air' when they see someone else show these signals. The kabyls often think it unnecessary and a bit embarrassing to repeat signals when someone else already does so, but with time they, too, will join the forest of arms, claiming they do it well-nigh unconsciously.

The comportment of the kabyl as well as the cowboy can be interpreted as a way to show 'cool' and powers of discrimination. The different outcome of this in the two cases stems from the different fields of vision the two have of the work and the over-all work process.

The kabyl makes decisions where no decisions are thought to be necessary, as they should be automatic and part of the routine way of completing the tasks. Kabyls hesitate, break self-evident work-procedures, and do things in 'weird' ways. This leads to a spiral of more intense supervision and more careful shunting, less flow, and eventually an increased number of moves and thereby even more decisionmaking.

The cowboy, making a point of handling the hardest of kicks and the highest speeds, challenges the shunt leader to trust him, but even if he in his behaviour signals courage and skill it is not sure he can convince the shunt leader of his skilfulness. A shunt leader will not send a 'rykare' (hard kick) to be handled by any cowboy, it is only when the B-member has shown that he 'knows what he is doing', that he has the necessary skills, that he instills enough confidence in the shunt leader to allow him to rather give a bit too much speed than a bit too little.[28]

While the shunt leader has to read the skill of the junior members in his team in order not to force them to do things they cannot handle, overcautious shunt leaders may, on the other hand, irritate the junior members when these find that they are not trusted and that their skills constantly are questioned. One shunt leader expressed the secret of shunt leading as 'having

---

[27] To work by *ryggmärgskänsla* ('a feeling in the spinal marrow') is a description of behaviour and reactions which have become reflexes.

[28] I am tempted to interpret some shunting as taking advantage of cowboys by giving them hard kicks and, as it were, make them prove their case. I have heard angry shunt leaders, after catching B-members to give the slip, swear to themselves that 'now he shall really attend to some kicks'. It is difficult to say whether such threats actually are put into practice. Mostly, I believe, it is more a positive declaration that the culprit will not be given an opportunity to keep himself invisible and avoid work again during that shift.

psychology'.[29] This, according to him, meant a slow transfer of responsibilities to the B-member. 'By making him feel important he takes more interest in the work and grows up to his responsibilities.'

The cowboy, making a show of his skills, is a possible danger in the yard, but his eagerness is, nevertheless, a sign of interest and a shunt leader may trust him, thinking that he will 'calm down' in due time and conform to 'the way things are done in Hagalund' when he feels he is trusted. Despite the condemnation of 'cowboyism' there are then incentives that work in the direction of 'letting it pass', of seeing it is a necessary folly of the young and eager, but also as a sign of interest and commitment.

We see that one of the social dimensions of cowboy manners is a summons to be considered skilful and able. As skilfulness almost exclusively cannot be shown by the end product – the finished train – but only in the way work actually is conducted, the body and the movements in the yard become signs of skill. Cowboyism entails an exaggerated signalling that might as well misfire and lead to suspicion, contempt or ridicule. When accepted it is as often because it is seen as a token of ambition as it is considered a sign of genuine skilfulness.

~~~

Summing up we can say that cowboyism is dependent on the combination of three factors. First, we have the impact of tacit knowledge. Much of the work cannot be formulated in formal rules, but have to be learnt by personal experience. Speed, weight, track curvature and gradient, and changes in friction due to humidity or snow must be judged from case to case. They are things that 'you just learn'. This 'open-endedness' facilitates a sliding from 'safe' to 'risky' without passing any clear thresholds or limits. Judging 'rather fast' from 'quite fast' and 'too fast' is a matter of long experience and a well trained eye.

Second, we realize that risks cannot be compared. Just as we, for instance, do not know what speed is risky, we cannot compare the risks involved in different work procedures.[30] The shunters have some obvious ground rules, such as always walking *'hinderfritt'* (Am. 'in the clear'), i.e. at a safe distance from the tracks, jumping off by stepping down in the direction of motion, not getting too close to the aerial conduit, *(kontaktledningen)* etc., but when we

---

[29] I.e. the same as holds for staff delegators. This word seems to refer to something similar to what Timothy Jenkins calls 'flair', i.e. an ability to avoid conflict and loss of trust. Cf. JENKINS, 441.

[30] I am not here talking about risk assessment in general, but about technical calculation of probabilities. Cf. DOUGLAS 1994, 44. When it comes to risk-perceiving the shunting community seems to lie somewhere in between Douglas's two forms of organization.

meet new techniques that do not break against such self-evident rules there is little agreement about how to judge the risks involved.[31]

Third, we have noted that skill can be signalled only by the style of working. The observation and assessment that the work-mates do of how one handles the equipment in different situations is therefore of utmost importance. One does not want to appear dizzy as a goose. The kabyl, as well as the cowboy, is therefore eager to show cool and smooth working. The risk of being exposed as someone who does not live up to the cool is always present, as the old hands are not very easily misled. The cowboy, skilled as he is to a certain degree, has a much greater potential than the kabyl to develop a convincing style, a style that combines a show of proper risk awareness with a show of careless and dramatically underpowered **or** overpowered moves.

Taken together these three factors; informal rules and tacit skills, the difficult risk assessment of new work methods and, finally, style being a salient signal of skill, prepare the way for the appearance of cowboy behaviour.

The skills we are dealing with are almost exclusively tacit ones. They cannot be taught, but come from experience acquired over a long period of time from a variety of situations. There is no other way to verify and pass the test of being skilful than to be accepted as such by senior shunters. The learning process of tacit knowledge is then as much a process of learning as a signalling of skilfulness and realizing it into an increasing capital of trust. To be exposed as an impostor and a fraud, a 'film cowboy', is therefore shameful and can be devastating. Cowboy behaviour must be backed by a matching degree of skill and discriminating powers.

There is a vivid debate concerning tacit knowledge.[32] On the basis of our understanding of the development from kabyl to cowboy, I think that we have reason to make a few comments that might add to our understanding of such knowledge. We will therefore proceed to a discussion of, as I see it, the two major problems involved in the learning of tacit knowledge; rule-following and imitation.

---

[31] The shunt leader who caught me in the act uncoupling with my hooked arm in the New Hall, did to my surprise not warn, scold or ridicule me (although I thought I had done something outrageous), but chuckled and said: *'Alla sätt är bra utom dom tråkiga'* ('All methods are good except the boring ones').

[32] Tim Ingold talks about skill (ot technique)as something tacit. Barry Smith about 'knowing 'how', while David Pye avoids these terms and introduces the term 'workmanship'. Cf, INGOLD 1990, 8, SMITH, *passim*, PYE, 22.

Tacit Knowledge and the Problem of Rule-Following

The philosopher Allan Janik states emphatically that there is nothing 'mystic' about tacit knowledge, and I find it easy to symphatize with that view. We are, as he points out, not referring to anything that compares to ESP (Extra Sensory Perception), some kind of esoteric knowledge or even 'intuition'.[33]

To state that we are dealing with knowledge that defies explicit expression is, however, not the same as saying that we lack the ability to talk about it, to talk about the acquisition of manual skills and about the 'logic' implied in the act of imitation and the understanding of analogical rules. Janik holds that tacit knowledge can only be discussed in terms of examples and case studies, and this could be assumed to be a consequence of the very subject we are dealing with.

In my discussion I want to expand on some of Janik's thoughts. It must be noted that Janik first and foremost wants to define the difference between tacit knowledge and artificial intelligence, while my questions not only refer to what tacit knowledge is *per se*, and if there are different kinds of tacit knowledge, but first and foremost how one learns skills that to a large extent depend on tacit knowledge. It is particularly Janik's ideas about 'imitation' and 'creativity' that I want to specify in terms of examples from the yard in Hagalund.

First of all I want to make it clear that tacit knowledge refers to knowledge that cannot be comprehensively expressed in words. Tacit knowledge is thus something different from knowledge that for some particular reason has not been put into words. It could concern things that are much more difficult, although perhaps not impossible, to describe than to exhibit.

Janik has classified the latter kind of knowledge into three types.[34] The first one is the 'guild type', i.e. knowledge that is kept as 'business secrets', the second one is the type (inherent in e.g. cooking or handicrafts) that has never been articulated, only passed on through apprenticeship, and the third type is broadly equivalent to what Bourdieu calls the *doxic* knowledge of everyday life, knowledge that is self-evident and normally invisible, until something happens that catches our attention and brings it into our vision.[35] The value of money, which is comparatively stable from day to day, until we

---

[33] Cf. JANIK 1988, 54.

[34] He somewhat surprisingly calls these 'tacit knowledge', immediately adding that they, strictly speaking, do not deserve this label. Cf. JANIK 1988, 54 ff.

[35] Cf. BOURDIEU, 1977,164, and 1989, 71.

have a situation of galloping inflation, would be one example of such self-evident knowledge, says Janik.[36]

I think that our knowledge of our mother tongue supplies us with examples that are even more striking. We learn our first language without reference to 'rules', but if we want to teach it we resort to defining our knowledge in terms of rules such as; 'third person singular, present tense, ends in an -s', 'the auxiliary verb is placed in front of the subject in questions', etc. In the case of language we have a whole science built around the effort to make explicit the rules that native speakers so effortlessly 'follow' and which they in normal conversation and everyday use of the language need not be aware of.[37] We know how to construct sentences, but we could not make that knowledge explicit without much thought and investigation into how we go about doing it.[38]

I prefer to collect all these three types under one umbrella, calling them 'silent knowledge', in order to avoid the rather clumsy distinction between strict and less strict, or real and less real (?) tacit knowledge. The name is quite appropriate also because we are dealing with knowledge, which **could** be brought out into the open by being given linguistic expression, but which, for whatever reason, is 'silent', or even 'silenced', for the time being.

Turning to tacit knowledge in the 'strict' sense of the word, again according to Janik, we similarly find two kinds. The first kind is the one that depends on experience and familiarity, such as the ability to recognize the smell of strawberries or coffee, or to recognize the sound of a clarinet and to be able to distinguish the same from the sound of an oboe. Our individual capacities in that vein are different, and can be developed, but there is no need to put the experiences into words in order to make someone else understand them. What is even more significant; we cannot, **even if we wanted to**, put this knowledge of ours into words. We cannot teach someone else the smell of strawberries by means of explanations. Everyone simply has to

---

[36] Cf. JANIK 1988, 54 ff.

[37] I am aware of the discussion concerning the issue of whether we can say that we actually 'follow rules' when we speak our mother tongue. (Cf. e.g. PYLYSHYN, *passim.*) By 'rule' I here refer to e.g. the automaticity with which we decline and conjugate new words according to given patterns. Take for instance the common tendency for Swedish- (and English-) speaking children to decline strong verbs as weak ones. These analogical applications occur without the speaker having any formal knowledge – knowing any 'rule' in that sense – about verbs, tenses, forms of declination, etc.

[38] Again we may say that we cannot inquire into the mental processes of how we go about 'making language', but this is not the point. We have a feeling for right and wrong in the language and it is the regularities of this 'ear' that we try to put into words, formulas, rules.

experience and learn for himself.[39] It is for this type of knowledge I will retain the term 'tacit knowledge'.

The second 'strict' sense in which we can talk about tacit knowledge assumes that we make a distinction between 'constitutive rules' as opposed to 'regulative' ones. Janik holds that the categorical separation between the two is the fundament on which the concept of tacit knowledge is built.[40] In fact he spends so much ammunition in establishing that constitutive rules are different from regulative ones that the more crucial question of the nature of the constitutive rules is, in my opinion, left in mid-air. Let me first continue with my reading of Janik's view.

Constitutive rules are the 'rule-following action which makes any behaviour at all possible', while regulative rules are explicit, discursive rules for the evaluation of certain courses of action. Here one might add that regulative rules probably also should be seen to comprehend rules that are not explicit, but that could be made so, should the need arise.

Janik's attention is, however, turned to the implicit, constitutive rules, which make it possible to perform particularly manual tasks, and perform them skilfully. By examples such as learning to dance, to play the piano or to compete in the high jump Janik depicts skills that are over and above the level of 'making mistakes'.[41] Once the technique is mastered we reach the point where a creative impetus is introduced. To learn how to play a sonata without making mistakes one starts with rules and routine, but in order to play the sonata masterly one has to create an interpretation, one has to go beyond the rules and add something. One has to be able to deal with the unexpected. This 'open-textured character' of rule-governed behaviour signifies creativity and a stretching of the rules, which Janik sees as the prerequisite for real expertise.[42]

There is, however, a problem concerning the basics of rule-following, Janik adds. He refers here to the initial learning of how to perform an activity. This is the part of rule-following that explains the term 'constitutive' rules, as it is in and through the very activity the rule is constituted. The initial learning is an analogical procedure, not a digital one, Janik explains. The student is following an example and it is only in that process that he learns the rule that is constitutive of that example. He learns what to see in the

---

[39] Cf. JANIK 1988, 56.

[40] Janik discusses constitutive and regulative rules at length in JANIK 1990.

[41] Nyíri talks about ´practical knowledge´; distinguishing between ´technical skills' (like cycling) and 'social skills´(like speaking or counting). Cf. NYÍRI, 19. It is obvious that talking is much more than conjugating verbs. Just to know when to say 'thank you' is a cultural art. There is all reason to agree with Nyíri.

[42] Cf. JANIK 1988, 56 f.

example as he learns it. Constitutive rules are thus 'open ended'. They are canonical as well as analogical as they combine imitation (initially) with creativity (ultimately).[43]

A rule in itself, as Wittgenstein already asserted, can never be applied without the knowledge of how and when to apply the rule. This demands a rule, which then requires a new rule, and so on.[44] Kjell Johannessen even speaks of Wittgenstein as "[...] obsessed with the fact that a rule does not dictate its own application."[45] This fact Janik takes as an indication that learning skills which imply tacit knowledge of the second kind, 'real' tacit knowledge, must be imitation; simply to watch and then attempt to do the same. I find this rather a question of how to use the word 'rule', as Janik describes imitation as an analogical process. Analogy, as far as I can understand, presupposes a 'rule', the rule which is judge of what is to be considered as similarity.

I do therefore hold that we should talk about rules, but be careful to state that we are not talking about rule-following in the sense that these rules describe some kind of manual or scheme that the agent consciously follows. The rules are rather lines in our unconscious that make us see similarity, possibility, equivalence, etc., and which silently and invisibly guide and order our cognition. Gilbert Ryle uses a suitable picture for this when he says: "The rules are the rails of [...] thinking, not extra termini of it."[46]

Janik states that in order to imitate one must know **what** to imitate.[47] Distinctions must be made, there is a process of selection involved. If this is so, then we surely must speak of rules as part of the initial learning process, too. We are, no doubt, caught in a seemingly infinite chain of rules and rule-applications. I think that the mystery cannot be solved, unless we simultaneously solve the mystery of human learning, of how it is possible for an infant (or an adult for that matter) to come to grips with the cacophonic multitude of stimuli that stream through the senses.[48] We truly have a

---

[43] The second sense of tacit knowledge, as well as the 'open-textured' character of developing skills pertaining to such knowledge echoes Gilbert Ryle. Cf. RYLE, 455 ff. Janik does not, however, refer to Ryle.

[44] Cf. JANIK 1988, 57, referring to Wittgenstein.

[45] JOHANNESSEN, 38.

[46] RYLE, 223. Also Scheler's 'being controlled by' laws (e.g. artistic laws) is a good example. Cf. SCHELER, 141 f.

[47] Bertil Rolf, following Polanyi, says that ' in order to see one has to understand'. This seems to be one of the few points where Janik and Rolf agree. Cf. ROLF, 153 f.

[48] This question has been the object of cognitive research for some decades (as different 'Gestalt'-theories). Whether one chooses to see the process as some kind of filter or as a case of parallel distribution, it is clear that longtime memory is decisive for picking out the dozen stimuli that reach the consciousness, out of the several millions that 'stream through' our brain

chicken and egg problem at our hands, because strictly speaking you cannot smile, nor understand a smile, before you understand what a smile is. Before that the smile is just a grin or an opening of the mouth. We only know that the infant in most cases manages to advance from the grin to the smile. The problem cannot be solved by erasing the word 'rule', as we still have to account for the mysterious process that makes us see the analogies, and gives the word 'imitation' its significance.[49]

The rule-like behaviour of a smiling child can be established scientifically before it is so identified in normal social interaction. The child imitates from the very first days of its life, which Janik most probably would stress, but the first imitations are so 'clumsy' that it takes scientific experiments to verify them **as** imitations. Opening the mouth is initially not read by lay observers, such as parents, as an imitation of a smile, because the 'rule' of smiling is not simply opening of the mouth. The child **improves** its ability to smile, but not necessarily by improving its imitation in the sense that a parrot 'imitates' a human voice. The improvement of the baby's imitation comes from learning to distinguish what 'makes' a smile, i.e. the meaning and the intention behind the movements it imitates.[50] The whole range of constitutive rules concerning 'smiling' in the cultural context is slowly acquired by the child. We have here the difference between a twitch and a wink, Ryle's example made famous by Geertz in 'Thick Description'. The closing of the eyelid cannot be called a wink before it is performed, and interpreted to be, in accordance with rules of meaning, the 'code' as Geertz clearly points out.[51] This is why the first 'smiles' of a baby do not count as such by its parents. They are 'grimaces', not smiles, because they do not comply to the social code. Only careful scientific observation can establish that there is a pattern of coincidence between the grimaces and the smiles of their parents, that the grimaces relate to the smiles. Although all constitutive rules for 'a smile' are

---

every second. (For a summary of these theories, cf. NØRRETRANDERS, 222 ff.) I can only conclude that there must be a cultural guiding device embedded in the selection process, or as Barry Smith writes: "...the subject may be said to choose the stimuli to which he will be sensitive." SMITH, 5.

[49] I call it 'mysterious' and refer to Elisabetta Visalberghi and Kathleen Gibson, who after ten years' studies claim that capuchin monkeys completely fail to imitate more complex new behaviour. We have 'something' that capuchin monkeys lack. Cf. VISALBERGHI, 142 ff. and GIBSON, 205 ff.

[50] The evolution of the infants' ability to imitate smiles and other facial expressions apparently proceeds in two distinct stages: From the very first days there is a first stage of 'primitive' imitation, which, as mentioned, is hard even to recognize as imitation without scientific experiments. This form of imitation decreases and disappears at about the third month. At about the ninth month a new form of more controlled imitation begins to appear. Cf. MEHLER & DUPOUX, 100 ff. The improvement that I talk about here applies to the latter stage.

[51] Cf. GEERTZ 1973, 6 f.

not being complied with, there is nevertheless a whole range of rules involved. Rules that concern timing, turn-taking, parts of the body that are concerned, etc.[52]

The need to talk about rules also concerning imitation becomes clear when we consider that imitation is not one thing but offers a variety of alternatives. I will distinguish two kinds of imitation, which I will return to in due course as alternative ways to learn the shunting trade. These I will call **mimetic** and **paraphrastic**, respectively.

The kind of imitation that the baby's smile represents, and which is so hard to recognize as imitation, has, despite this, a peculiar resemblance to what we see as slavish copying. In everyday usage, we tend to distinguish between imitation that is superficial and 'mindless' and imitation that seems to duplicate the meaning, 'the function', of the example. The former one is then the mimetic kind, while the second is the paraphrastic one. Let me again illustrate this with a picture.

There is a party game consisting of a charade that is performed to one person, and which this person then shall imitate in front of the rest of the party. The audience, and the person who performs the original charade, know what the charade is supposed to picture, while the imitating person, and succeeding him several other imitators, are kept ignorant of what the movements are supposed to express. The point of the game is of course that every imitation distorts the original charade. The amusement arises from seeing the movements of, for example, a careful glass-blower transformed into a trumpeter, an archeologist into a detective or a construction worker, and so on. Since the imitator does not know the 'key' to the charade he consequently does not know what the significant moves are. He does not know what to look for.

Sometimes the imitation is done 'blindly', it seems, i.e. the imitator has no idea whatsoever of what to illustrate. Even the most conscientious imitator will, however, sooner or later make a little mistake, revealing that he does not know what he is supposed to depict. (Even the slightest mistake causes amusement, as it will be a misleading clue for the last person in the chain, who is supposed to make a guess.)

---

[52] If one wants to argue that the cultural, or learnt, element in smiling is slight, one might instead consider how an infant learns to speak. It it obvious that neither regulative rules, nor imitation single-handedly could lead to language-skills. A baby who knows only twenty words can already communicate in an idiosyncratic and non-imitative way with its caregivers – who actually to a certain extent have to learn the **baby's** language. Imitation cannot be said to come before invention. It may be added that individual differences can be easily observed already in babbling infants. Cf. LOCKE, 201f.

When the imitator gets the wrong idea he may add the finger movements of, for example, a trumpeter, movements which had not been there in the first place. They are more or less unconsciously seen to have been there as the charade is interpreted as depicting a musician, not a glass-blower. The most boring charade is when the performer obviously has guessed correctly and knows what he is imitating. He is naturally not necessarily more accurate in the imitation, seen from an objective point of view, but the alterations of the movements do not cause the audience to laugh. The imitation is seen as 'correct'.

We can conclude that the 'correct' imitation not necessarily is that which is the technically most precise, but the one that stays within the range of metaphorical expressions of the body that are seen to belong to the model, or métier, in question. The smile of the child is not seen as a smile because it duplicates the smile of its parent – it may actually have a physical expression that is quite original – but because it uses the facial expression according to the 'rules of smiling'.

The most literal, technically and formally exact, imitation of the teacher of tacit skills may indeed seem 'sick' and even insulting. A piano player, or a dancer who imitates a great master is not a master, only an impostor who has not understood the art. The Moroccan singer who sings exactly like Bob Dylan is not a great singer, he is a fantastic impersonator – or a cheat.

When Janik talks about the learning process as, on the one hand, a development with the stages: imitation – drill – creation, and, on the other hand, a process where the teacher teaches the student all he knows, and the student only repeats what he has seen, we see that Janik conceives of the learning process as a transmission removed from the social world.[53] The student imitates a model. I claim that imitation is a matter of seeing an example in a particular way, and this cannot be done objectively. I will also

---

[53] It is not surprising that philosophers miss the social dimensions. More significant is that other researchers, who follow Janik's program, present learning and tacit knowledge as something which is construed in a social vacuum. Maja-Lisa Perby's recent work is an example of this. Here the intention is to give expression to the operators' view of process operation. Questions about rhetorics of work, how domination patterns influence the view of work, etc. are absent. Her 'emic' perspective is clearly stated when she demands respect for the craftsmen, "who have the supreme knowledge about the circumstances that sustain their craftsmanship." (translation mine) Cf. PERBY, 197. Her book gives a charming insight into the workers' view of what their work is about, but such an inquiry represents only one side of my objective, or as Anthony Cohen puts it: "(...)the anthropologist must go beyond the emic category – though taking full account of it..." Cf. COHEN 1979, 264.

claim that the process of imitation also implies a social relation and this further complicates the learning process.[54]

But first imitation seen as an example. I will see 'imitation' as a broad term encompassing the 'mindless' imitation as well as the directed, knowledgable one, the technically inaccurate as well as the pedantic mime. All imitation is anticipated by a rule, a selection process that concerns what, how and when to imitate. This is true of the smiling infant as well as of the dancer or the piano player.[55] In the whole process of imitation the rule is actually double sided. There is the rule of what to reproduce, as well as the rule of what is seen as reproduction. Imitation is a process of communication and as such it is dependent on the performer's cognition as well as the spectator's. This is why one cannot distinguish constitutive rules from regulative ones.[56] What counts as 'going for a walk' is not the same for me as for you, or an American police officer, as well as – and this is a different matter – what **you** do maybe counts as 'going for a walk' to an onlooker, while it would not be so considered did **I**, or an English gentleman, venture to do likewise.

And here we come to the point I am making. Imitation cannot be done without distinction and therefore the beginner in the shunting trade who is shown how to jump, how to connect cables and couplings, how to clear bridges and how to be on the right spot, and so on, is not a mindless imitator, like a parrot, but a person who has a whole range of preconceived ideas about what the work is 'all about', what appearance he will make and what attitude would be proper to take. There is also reason to assume that not two beginners will be seen as doing the same thing, that there is a possibility for the beginner to 'constitute' the task, to create an original and individual work expression. We will later see how this is done. How someone 'gets away with' doing a task in a new way, is a way (albeit a negative one) of expressing such a phenomenon in everyday terms.

~~~

Janik stresses the difference between constitutive and regulative (normative) rules, while I hold that although we can find contrastive examples of these

---

[54] Anthropological evidence shows a great cultural variety in teaching infants concerning the stress put on observation and imitation, instruction and guidance. There is even evidence to the effect that infants (6 to 36 months) are superior learners when given responsibility for their own learning. This supports my claim that learning tacit skills does not presuppose imitation and drill. Cf. ROGOFF, 120 ff.

[55] In the case of neonatals (up to three months) imitating smiles and other facial expressions the selection process is obviously not based on experience, but arguably on an innate 'body schema', which tells the child which facial movements correspond to the exemplar. Cf. MEHLER & DUPOUX, 101,103.

[56] As Giddens puts it: regulative rules and normative rules are two senses of rules, but they "[...] always intersect in the actual constitution of social practices." Cf. GIDDENS, 1979, 82 f.

two they nevertheless are not possible to distinguish from each other at all times. Analytically separated, they are still the two ends of a continuum. Furthermore, Janik does not want to talk about rules at all – although he does so – in the case of constitutive rules, as he fears that this brings to mind a picture of human beings as conscious rule-followers, behaving according to some kind of inner rule-book. Instead he recourses to a variety of terms; canonical and analogical learning, and following a model, a pattern or a logical grammar. To me all these are examples of regular, rule-like, behaviour. As Janik's terms stress, we cannot follow an example without knowing what to look for. There is a rule that unconsciously directs our mind. It may seem that Janik and I agree in principle and that our only disagreement is my stubbornly using the term 'rule', but I do think that I, by stressing the continuum between constitutive and regulative rules, end up with a view which sees culture as well as 'creativity' as far more fundamental than Janik, who assumes that we somehow can imitate and take over an example *in toto*. I claim that the interpretive element is always present, 'muddling' the model.

Even our most explicit and regulative system of rules, the judicial system, is completely dependent on constitutive rules. How negligent can you be before you can be sentenced for negligent driving? How much violence can you use in order to defend yourself before it is considered to be out of proportion with the initial assault *('Större våld än nöden kräver')*?

The question of how we are ever able to learn to see any patterns, any analogies, any logic, any grammar at all is still hidden in the mysteries of human cognition, and it is rather futile to speculate about it here. All we know is that such abilities do appear very early in life and that we cannot imagine what life would be like if we suddenly lost that capacity.

The fact that we are dealing with such deep-lying and fundamental capacities of human cognition makes our task very difficult when we ask how tacit skills are acquired. Janik paints a schematic picture with a chronological dimension going from imitation to drill and finally to creativity. Because of my view of analogy and rule-following I insist that these elements cannot be seen to follow chronologically, one after the other. In the beginning there is imitation **as well as** creativity. The process of **what** to see in the example we imitate assumes a creative process, (although the creativity may actually only be conditioned by previous experience). We are likely to see things differently. There are alternative routes.

The different ways we conceive of an example, is partly founded in our earlier experience, in our socio-cultural background, but partly conditioned by our innate ability for idiosyncracy ('creativity'). We could resort to the terminology of Pierre Bourdieu and say that we are endowed with different dispositions, different habitus, which give us different points of view, to put it crudely.[57] Without going into the depths of our cognition again we may say that among the different ways of perceiving what the example is an example of, we may distinguish two ways of performing in our imitation of the example. They are paraphrastic and mimetic learning respectively, and they refer to the degree of formal, superficial, or ideational and esoteric, closeness that the imitation has with the model. Shall I do as you do or shall I do as I believe you intend to do? How important is it that I look to the form as opposed to the 'content', the function and purpose of doing? They are, again, only two extremes of a continuum, but they will be crucial for our future discussion and we will look closer at the concepts in the chapter to come.

We must look at how the learning process, the 'creative imitation' works out in the yard, how the beginners understand that one should work, and how the performance of work is understood by the seniors. I will also show that the difference in the learning process between men and women stems from a gender specific habitus, gender specific perspectives. This will give an answer to why the women are so much better in the beginning, but leave at the stage when they are to become shunt leaders.

Submissive Imitation Versus Putting One's Foot Down

> O imitatores, servum pecus
> (Horace, Epist. I ;19, 19)

In order to see the significance of the different performances of male and female beginners in the yard we must dwell a bit on the question about how tacit knowledge is transferred. We want to look at a process of teaching and learning tacit skills, as opposed to learning and improving tacit skills through practice and training which is done all on one's own, without model or parallel. We are thus distinguishing the apprentice from the autodidact. There is a significant distinction between the two, due to the relationship between teacher, or mentor, and apprentice, a relationship that the autodidact naturally lacks.

We must first consider the constitutive rules, and the analogic learning process, which are the main features of learning tacit skills, according to

---

[57] Another appropriate term would be Ulf Hannerz's 'perspective'. Cf. HANNERZ, 64ff. I have used Bourdieu's term as it includes the notion of movements being dispositions, too, 'incsribed in the body'.

Janik, who stated that the presentation of a model simultaneously is an invitation to the student, or apprentice, to judge and discern what is relevant in the example. One has to learn to see a pattern. This is then the key for knowing 'how to go on', the creative and open character of the constitutive rules.

The process Janik describes, however, takes place in something like a social vacuum. The relationship between teacher and pupil is clear cut and uncomplicated by power relations. We have actors, absorbed by, nay, identified with their respective roles, entering and leaving a neutral stage, devoid of props. Janik's examples – learning to dance, to play the piano, to understand Chinese bronzes, etc. – represent learning situations that are distinguished by relatively sharp breaks with former experience. In these cases one can disregard the pupil's attitudes, understanding, knowledge and assumptions and regard the learning as a process starting from scratch, Janik seems to suggest. Although, as I have indicated, it would be wise to argue for the opposite case, i.e. that the student's ability to imitate in all these cases depends on his previous understanding of artistic expressions, styles and conventions, in the last instance the habitus, I will here leave this for the case that interests us at the moment; the shunting apprentice.

The beginner in the shunting trade is not familiar with the kind of work that he is about to train for, but this does not imply that he commences the training with a blank and open mind, ready to imitate. If nothing else, the shunting apprentice has an idea of how manual work should be performed, of what it entails to be a beginner – and a male or female one at that – at a workplace, how managers, work leaders and company officials relate to 'the common worker', and what 'making a fool of oneself,' or alternatively 'making a good impression', just might imply in this context.[58]

Regardless of whether the apprentice has a working class background, or not, he will have some idea of the comportment that is expected; how to act, how to speak, how to dress, and even how to move.[59] As we have assumed

---

[58] Barry Smith talks in a similar vein about the customs of training (e.g. in painting). He also stresses the importance of the social dimension in the relation between master and 'subject'. Cf. SMITH, 14.
The social dimension is also stressed by Collins, who sees tacit knowledge as a link between 'cultural skills' and 'manual skills', also admitting that there is an 'inexplicable component' 'which enables us to see the continuation of a series like 2, 4, 6, 8. – i.e. what I call a rule. Cf. COLLINS, 336 f.

[59] I am using the term 'working class' in the sense it is used in common speech. Here it is thus rather a question of familiarity with attitudes and styles that are considered to be 'working class', rather than belonging to a particular social stratum or category, defined by relations of production, income, or any other such formal criterion. E. P. Thompson propagates a view where class is seen as "...a very loosely defined body of people who share the same categories

above, such expectations are likewise directed towards the apprentice, as well as an understanding that being an apprentice entails such assumptions. There is an understanding that the apprentice is prone to be putting on an air, to play off.

The crux here is only that the unspoken rule, if we dare use the expression in such a common sense, is that the comportment of a worker should be self-assured, *'säker'*. You should give the impression that you know what you are talking about, and talk only about what you know. You should work and move with a relaxed, but determined, air – not 'loiter like the negroes in the Hall', as one shunter interpreted the careless walking style of some of the black workers at Hagalund. And, I must add, a beginner should not brag about former deeds and positions. What matters is the here and now. Former achievements are disregarded, the test is how you will fare in the yard.

With this in mind we see that even the limited knowledge of how to act cannot be practised by the beginner to any extent, as he simply does not know what to talk about, concerning the yard, and when trying to do so, he often finds that his comments are seen as questions and he is replied to in a way that expresses information, explanation, and correction, rather than recognition, mutual understanding and sympathy. As he does not know what to do, unless he is being told explicitly, it is very difficult to make his body signal a self-assured and relaxed attitude. In fact many beginners are almost painful to watch as they seem so clumsy, nonplussed and generally uncomfortable, while trying so hard to look unaffected and relaxed. The typical beginner is thus rather quiet, and tries to stay within hearing distance from the shunt leader or his trainer, following him across the yard, discreetly enough not to give the appearance of a baby duck (as Linda Niemann described herself).

Despite the obvious difficulties in keeping cool the beginners nevertheless, as we have seen earlier, avoid questions and movements that give their ignorance away. A beginner was told to 'knock' between two carriages, but was later found standing immobile next to the unknocked train. When asked why he had not knocked he did not reply, but turned and walked away, leaving the rest of the team to ponder on whether he did not hear or understand, whether he did not know how to proceed, or whether he just blatantly refused to comply.

Although this again is an extreme example, it nevertheless exposes how style and manners override the work process itself. Rather than asking and

---

of interests, social experiences, traditions and value system...". He deals with a matter of consciousness, and not a thing. It is such consciousness, I claim, that lays the foundation for shunting as a métier in society. Cf. THOMPSON, 85.

making a fool of himself he avoids the task altogether.[60] Assumptions about how to communicate mastery and dexterity, or just to avoid losing face in front of co-workers, mould the performance itself, even to the point of completely distorting the task or avoiding to perform it at all.

It is not only the poise in steps, the posture and movements in the yard that in this way are influenced by concepts about how to work. Even the elementary tasks, which so minutely have been shown and practiced during the course are distorted as they are no longer performed as showpieces, as entry tickets to the workplace, but performed in the context of the social relationships at work. To go on as if one still took part in the course, to keep to the imitation of a teacher, would be to subjugate oneself – hook, line and sinker – to the role of 'a coupling boy'.

As we noted earlier, no apprentice has been able to avoid training in how to jump on and off vehicles, and therefore they all know the basic rule that one must not jump with both feet together, but for some beginners it seems to be overambitious **always** to use the technique they have learned. When the speed is low they mistakenly assume that they just as well can jump off 'the ordinary way', signalling that they manage well and do not have to apply any special technique. They are then unaware that senior shunters no longer see this as conforming to the instruction book. To them, this technique is self-evident, and one of those things that you have to rub 'into the spinal marrow'. Jumping off should be automatic, not a matter of conscious thought. Jumping off in any other way than the routine-like one catches the eye and means that you are still a kabyl, you simply do not know how to do it.

Beginners may suspect that they are under special observation, but they hardly realize that different standards apply to them. A senior may jokingly, and very pointedly, jump off with both feet together, but a beginner doing the same is not likely to be seen as a joker. It is not certain he will be corrected, but he is observed and in case he makes other such mistakes he will soon be considered 'hopeless'.

---

[60] This is naturally a phenomenon that is understood to exist, but it is difficult to judge whether this is the case in any particular instance. Senior shunters consider it to have been more abundant in former times, when the hierarchy was stricter and there were no courses teaching the beginners to 'knock', for example. One of the bosses told of how he was instructed to ask for 'the key' when pulling trains. He complied without question and asked all drivers if they had 'the key', thinking, he said, that it was a rather stupid arrangement. Why should he remind oblivious drivers of their keys? Not until later did he come to understand that drivers were obliged to show that they had disconnected the electricity by showing the handle, 'the key', to the shunter. This was a sign that he safely could disconnect the electric cable between engine and train.

The unconventional ways the young men display are often the result of such double misreadings. The beginner wants to show that he can work without slavishly following the regulations, but he does not know the correct way of bending the rules. He is also in a position that hardly allows rule bending, 'correct' or not. He is expected to show that he can perform the tasks the standard way, or he will be considered a risk in the yard. The shunt leader and the trainer (in case he still has one) will feel responsible for him. They will not appreciate his 'jokes', his attempts to show himself off as 'cool' and daring, or make light of his idiosyncratic applications of 'tricks' he has observed in the yard. The obvious example here is the beginner who was said to try to stop a kicked carriage by putting pebbles from the gravel onto the rail, on the mistaken assumption that rolling stock could be stopped in this way, while the trick is used only to keep carriages from rolling back when the track is sloping gently, and only after they have been brought to a halt. Such mistakes stem from lack of judgement and skills of discrimination, and the beginner should therefore not resort to the tricks of the old-timers, nor experiment on his own. The seniors, the ones who are responsible for the beginner, demand that he keep to the range of tasks he has been taught.[61]

The fact that shunting is considered to consist largely of 'things you just learn' could be seen to contradict the assumption that beginners should keep to the restricted range of tasks that 'they have been taught'. We must remember that this thinking is founded in praxis. It is not a theoretical exposition. You should only do what you 'know how to do'. The question of **how** you know when you know does not enter the reasoning.

It may seem obvious that there is a strong demand that the beginner learns 'his place' in the team, that he accepts his position as a 'coupling boy' and an obedient C-member of the hierarchical team. Shunters, however, never refer to principles of obedience, or hierarchy, in serious discussions about problems with beginners. The idiomatic dress for such discussions can be summed up in the words 'risk', 'danger' and 'our responsibility'. A beginner working in an idiosyncratic manner is a danger to himself and others. His behaving and 'weird' ways of working may be dangerous in themselves, but hesitant, undecisive, contradictory or erroneous body signals may also cause someone else to panic, creating odd situations that may get out of hand. Therefore it is necessary not only to manage the tasks, and perform them correctly, but to

---

[61] Cf. GAMST 1989, *passim*, for a discussion about breaking different kinds of rules in a US context.

present a body language that clearly signals that one is doing, or going to do, the expected thing, at the expected moment, in the expected way.

The relationship between beginners and their seniors is thus in many ways conflicting and antithetical. While beginners seem to 'refuse' to duplicate what they have been taught, we see that there are several different incentives involved here. Beginners assume, and also observe, that regulations are broken against by seniors and that the course-book descriptions of how work is done 'out there' are inadequate. They have, however, not the discriminating powers to decide between do's and dont's, and they are in addition to that not judged according to the same criteria as the oldtimers. An old hand may bend rules, but beginners are not trusted to do so.

Beginners want to show strength, cool and skills of discrimination by idiosyncratic behaviour, but although such personal style is appreciated among seniors it is condemned as dangerous in beginners. Beginners have a 'gut reaction' against echoing the introductory course in their work. This gut reaction is based on ideas that are implicit, but nevertheless discernible in the reluctance to keep to what they have been taught. Imitation and slavish copying confirms the beginner's anonymity and turns him into a mindless robot, a 'coupling boy' moulded by the Rule Book, according to 'the company wishes,' or working as a slave, according to the wishes of his seniors in the team.[62]

There is an outspoken ideal saying that a shunter should be able to *'säga ifrån'*; state one's opinion, speak one's mind, put one's foot down. Beginners should not do things they are uncertain about. If the engine is moving too fast a beginner should have the guts to show 'slow' instead of keeping quiet, jump, and hope for the best.

To *säga ifrån* is considered to be an asset throughout the shunting career. A boss should *säga ifrån* to superiors and to other groups that make impossible demands. In addition to being ideology, to *säga ifrån* is also part of everyday rhetoric as well as praxis.[63] Within the team it is considered part of the general attitude that shunters *säger ifrån* (speak their mind) instead of bearing grudges, or swearing to pay back for wrongdoings. To *säga ifrån* is considered to clear the air and leave the anger in the yard. 'Five minutes later it

---

[62] One could say that there is a symbolic profit to be gained in self-presentation, the comportment of the body, but my point is that the beginners are allowed only small stakes. Investments that give the largest returns are out of their reach. Cf. Bourdieu's discussion of investments in self-presentation in BOURDIEU 1989, 200 ff.

[63] Anthony Cohen distinguishes between ideological, rhetorical and pragmatic dimensions of egalitarianism as 'we shall all be equals', 'we all are equals' and 'we behave as if we all were equals'. Cf. COHEN 1992, 33 ff. Apart from being applicable to the egalitarian ethos in the yard, such a triad is also applicable to the concept of *'säga ifrån'*.

is forgotten', is an often heard comment. 'When we go for the break it is like it never happened.' The irritation is brought about by circumstances at work, and it is there it should be solved. Anger is then considered in rational and functional terms. One must be angry and *säga ifrån*, as the situation so demands, but the anger should not be taken as a personal comment and as soon as the problem is solved and the situation is under control, the anger is erased and no hard feelings are allowed to crop up and depress the jolly atmosphere around the coffee table. This norm does not prevent longstanding animosities from brooding in the yard, but it describes an atmosphere that does not allow, legitimate or encourage retrospection concerning disagreements at work.

The balance between *säga ifrån* and being a trouble-maker, uninterested in learning and working as one is being told, is a dilemma for the beginner. One beginner who answered 'It is too much for the little brain' too often, was not considered to *säga ifrån*. The suspicion was that he, albeit jokingly, was trying to slip away from learning, and thereby from doing his duties. Resisting the subjugation of obedience and imitation, however jokingly it may be expressed, the beginner risks to be considered 'hopeless' and in need of additional supervision, or he needs to be 'broken to the rein'.

The accepted way to *säga ifrån* concerns situations where more skill or experience is needed, thus marking the difference between the beginner and the senior members in the team. Such situations are when the team has a driver prone to speeding, or when carriages are to be connected or disconnected over a pit in the Hall lacking a bridge to stand on. To *säga ifrån*, beginners seem to think, is a way to signal inferiority and lack of skill, while seniors who are good at *säga ifrån* are persons who take no nonsense, who are skilled and sure about how things should be done, and furthermore often direct their straightforward ability to *säga ifrån* towards other groups to keep them from pushing the shunters around.

The legitimate, and encouraged variety of *säga ifrån,* the one concerning work-speed, is ironically enough very seldom resorted to. It is felt that one has to keep up with the speed and not cause delays and trouble. One wants to show that one is not afraid. In case one is not much of an asset to the team, yet, at least one is not a fetter and a kill-joy. Again the kabyl is prone to accept what he feels is the run of things, regardless of what he has been taught during the course, and advised by the seniors in the yard.

Exceptions to this rule of conformity is found among the female kabyls. Several of them state that they thought things were going too fast, and they claim that in such cases they would show the 'slow'-signal of their own accord. The rate of occurrence being difficult to verify I can at least confirm that one of the women was described as doing this by a shunt leader. 'She is the only one who has the guts to show 'slow' when she thinks it goes too fast', he claimed. This was one of the things that made her, still according to this shunt leader, one of the most talented young shunters. 'One out of a hundred has her talent to read speed and to react without fear and hesitation', he said.

Also concerning other tasks the women claim they put their foot down. To connect in the Hall, and to go in between and couple hard kicks, are other such tasks that women declare they 'just won't do'. It may well be the case that men also avoid these tasks, but in that case they certainly also avoid talking about it. When the subject comes up they instead refer to these tasks as tricky, dangerous – under certain circumstances – objectionable as working positions, but they describe their own ways of handling the difficulties and their principles of deciding when to abstain from 'going between'. Such statements are not given in an apologetic, but rather in a programmatic, almost boasting, manner.

The rhetoric of work thus has a female tendency, which is to stress the danger and even if they do not take a moralistic attitude (e.g. condemning breaking of the rules), they declare that they consider it their privilege (as juniors) to refuse to participate. 'If they cannot wait for me to do it my way, they may as well do it themselves.' ('They' referring to the senior members of the team.)

Men condemn the organization of work that forces you to 'hang like a bloody octopus' between carriages when knocking in the Hall, or the general attitude of 'being in a hurry all the time', but they do not seem to resort to refusals or holding up the arm in a 'slow'-signal, forcing the driver to reduce the speed. Instead they stress their ability to cope, the tricks that save you in dangerous situations. **Others**, who feel uncertain, insecure, not up to it, have the right to, and should in fact, slow down the speed. They themselves do not have to resort to this.

It is worth noticing that the difference between refusals that are accepted and those which might stir up some irritation and grumpy remarks can be said to correspond with the attitude behind and the presentation of the refusal. By referring to 'rules' and principles one is likely to be considered unpleasant, and a potential stickler, while blaming oneself (e.g. saying that standing on the rails to couple is felt to be too tricky and that it can be done only if the team can wait for a bridge to be pulled to the spot) quickly is accepted as an excuse and brushed to the side without much ado. 'That's O.K., Pelle can do it.' One is accepted as lacking in skill, the only threat to the order of things being that this rare task must be done by someone else. One is not, however, threatening the Hagalund way of working, one is not questioning the accepted way of going about things, one is not refusing to blend in, one is only momentarily excusing oneself. This is the privilege of the beginner and also a not completely unwelcome sign that *'gammal är äldst'* (old people know best).[64]

The paradoxical outcome of this is that the women are seen to be better than the men, as they perform their tasks correctly, the way they have been taught, and dare to *säga ifrån* in the cases they feel uncertain and unaccustomed. To any shunt leader the irritating discovery that the C-member slows down the speed every now and then is nevertheless more welcome than the sight of a clumsy beginner throwing himself off the engine in desperate leaps that any moment may end in an accident.

The growing ground for all these readings is the extraordinary immunity that beginners enjoy, as compared to what we know about apprentices from the literature. Kabyls are seldom criticized, they are left untouched by the horseplay and mockery to a remarkable degree (the nick-name 'Cable-Tom' being an eye-catching exception), while the habit of leaving problems and conflicts in the yard when going for a break encompasses them, too.

The body language, the reading of movements and techniques, therefore becomes important in the yard. In this kind of team-work the behaviour of everybody in the team has an influence on the behaviour of the others, and with the risks at work ever looming in the background the slightest hesitation will be read to reveal a person as potentially dangerous.

The problem with showing skill and reading risk from body comportment is that this silent field nourishes misreadings, concealment, and deception as well as disclosure, revelation and silent understanding. A travesty of Ulf Hannerz may clarify some of the complications of this silent communication: 'You don't know that by the way you are showing that you know I can tell that you (perhaps!) don't know.'

But why should there be a difference between male and female kabyls? Why do the women seem to have a much less complicated way of communicating? Is there no roundabout way over pretence and disclosure, readings and misreadings in their case? We must have a closer look at female shunters, and how they fare in the meeting ground between work-roles and personal relationships, workplace and private life.

---

[64] This does not automatically imply that all seniors conform, only that if one wants to stick to such idiosyncracies these must be seen as such, as parts of an individual style, not as programmatic examples, which everyone should follow.

Relating the findings of this chapter in the light of what we have discussed earlier we see that we have certain problems. Contrary to what is the case in the philosophical model of how tacit knowledge is learnt we see that the apprentice in the yard combines the eagerness to learn with a reluctance to be taught. Shunting is not a métier with a status, it is a job that almost anyone can do. The selection process is, as we saw earlier, geared towards stressing physical qualities, ability to 'endure' the working conditions and 'take' the crude language, while the part of the introductory course which consists of reading and learning rules and regulations is seen as boring, obligatory, but hardly necessary and absolutely not prestigious. This view is expressed by students as well as oldtimers.

Shunting is physical work, but it is also technical. Surroundings more 'male' than what you have in a railway yard are hard to find: steel, rust, black oil, high voltage electricity, roaring engines, heavy and crude equipment, carriages that are to be distinguished by technical detail rather than design, an atmosphere devoid of colour – the only soft objects being the odd worker, dressed in dull blue or fiercely orange overalls. The hares in springtime, the plants – familiar also from shipyards and ballast heaps – the odd wild duck or pheasant with chickens that cross the rails in panic, are all guests or intruders that only accentuate the barren and desert-like surroundings.

Despite the novelty of the surroundings and the work itself, there is a conviction that the only way to learn is 'to go out and do it'. Common sense is at the bottom of it all. It is a common sense of a practical kind, a handiness and a general bodily malleability contrasting to the stiff clumsiness characterizing persons who *'aldrig har gjort ett handtag i hela sitt liv'* (lit.: 'never have made a grip in all their lives'), i.e. who have never done 'real' work, 'only' been to school or worked in an office. The contrast between indoor book learning and outdoor physical work is constantly referred to and it is obvious to the beginner that the CV in the yard is not written on a piece of paper, it is inscribed in your body movements.

There is no doubt that this rough 'go-out-and-do-it'-world is male,[65] but to the beginner it signals strength, cool and male attributes to a degree that is quite foreign to the old hands. If ever there were such glorified macho views of

---

[65] Concerning identification of heavy work and big machinery with 'male' work. Cf. COCKBURN, 1981, *passim*, COCKBURN & ORMROD, 40 ff., GUNNARSSON, 42 f., WAJCMAN, *passim* and WILLIS, 147ff.. Note that I am not talking about railways as symbolically encoded in the sense that technology here is designed with an enhancement of male values in mind. The symbolism draws its power from a wide cultural context, not from intentional design. About symbolic vs. functional encoding, cf. MACKAY & GILLESPIE, 692.

the shunting job they have long ago been scattered or overshadowed by the reality of monotonous routine and arduous toil.

It is the 'maleness' of the shunting yard, as well as the preconceived ideas of what it takes to handle this heavy rolling stock, that makes it necessary to distinguish between male and female kabyls. Even if they very consciously and pointedly are treated the same, their position and starting point are not identical.[66]

The male beginners enter a world of old hands, and while the youngsters are dependent on learning the job they are reluctant to silently take their place at the lower end of the line. They are, after all, strong young men, who need not care about the most economic ways to move and lift, to save their knee joints and backs. Let the seniors tend to their ailments, the young can take the strain – and after all – they are not going to stay in the job for life to become serfs on this barren turf!

For the young men the balance holds on the one hand a wish to be good at the job and to go with the stream, while on the other hand it holds a strong reluctance to become 'coupling boys'; apprentices risking being pushed around, dummies considered to be complying to the wishes of everybody senior to them. The stiff immobility, the 'weird' idiosyncratic movements and the uneven quality of the contribution in the yard of the male apprentices must be seen in this light.

The young females are never on the trail of becoming anonymous 'yardmen', silent little workers treading in the footsteps of their seniors. They are still something of pioneers (this term does sometimes crop up, especially in the speculations about finally getting an all-female team together), and may for instance find surprised outsiders stopping to watch them from the road-bridge above when they work.

Like the young men, the young women are opposed to the old men, who have families, children, and grandchildren and who, needless to say, were brought up in a world that was in many respects different from the one the youngsters know. The most noteworthy sign of that difference is that when the seniors started in the yard the presence of women was simply 'unthinkable'. To the young men the presence of women is natural. At least it does not entail questions of how to 'relate' to the women, or how they should be 'treated'.

---

[66] In Bourdieu's words: "Differences in dispositions, like differences in position (to which they are often linked), engender real differences in perception and appreciation." BOURDIEU 1981, 315.

During the introductory course the women are in minority. There might be one or two women in the group, but as the group holds only four to eight students their minority position is not on par with the situation in the yard, where most of the time they work with men only, and men who are not on their level of learning, but their seniors.

For the women it is obvious that there might be hidden objections against female shunters, particularly among the older men, and most of the women do legitimate their presence, in interviews or in discussions with workmates, by saying that one should be able to do the same job as 'everybody else', or that they personally have been told that they work 'like a man'.

A norm describing how 'a man' works is constantly looming in the background, but it is never made explicit. It is a self-evident concept and a conglomerate of how work has been done, how it is considered to be done, and how it should be done. It is an 'ideal type', based on traditions of male practice and male thinking about work.[67] The unspecified character of the concept 'to work like a man', is at the same time a retreat, as it is quite easy for any woman to find a specific man who is worse than her. 'At least I'm not as bad as **him**.'

Women enter the yard as individuals much more than the young men. They are noticed and are called by name much sooner than male beginners.[68] Their ambitions are not spurred by the feats of the most daring shunters, but by the fact that they can work as well as their mates from the introductory course. They might find some tasks difficult or frightening, but by stating that their legs or arms are too short to allow them to perform the tasks in the daring non-regulated fashion that is considered 'normal', they are excused.[69] As they admit to individual weaknesses and refuse to do risky moves that they feel uncertain about, the implicit message is that they feel comfortable with

---

[67] It is obvious that heavy machinery and processes developed to handle it are constructed with a male rather than a female 'standard body' in mind. Cf. COCKBURN, 1981. Cf. Niemann talks about 'male body mechanics'. Cf. NIEMANN, 37, GUNNARSSON, 28. However, my point is that it is the 'handling expectancy' which is genderized rather than the machinery being modelled on a male body. Too stiff or rusty couplings, too long a distance between the rails, etc. are not naturally male. What counts as 'too stiff,', 'too rusty', etc., to handle, i.e. what I call handling expectancy (regardless whether it is the person handling it or the task itself which is at fault,) constitutes a genderized classification of tasks.

[68] It is worth mentioning that Scandinavians rarely use names (neither family **nor** Christian names) when addressing each other. The example above thus refers not only to direct address, but also to when beginners are talked about, in third person. Before they are called by name they are referred to by decriptions, such as 'the new one with the cap', or 'the new guy from X' (name of the town he comes from).

[69] It must be noted that most shunters' arms and legs are too short for coupling coaches in the Hall without a bridge. They are not referring to some female quality, they are only stating what is obvious. Others take the risk and keep quiet.

the rest of the tasks. This is appreciated by the shunt leader who has the responsibility for life and limb. The flaw is then rather an asset. It takes guts to *säga ifrån*. Women admitting their weakness are then, due to the ever present danger in the yard, turning weakness into strength. Their work is more convincing and stable than the work of the male kabyls. Unfortunately this picture changes in less than a year, and the young men catch up and are even considered to surpass their female colleagues.

~~~

We have now seen that the relations of power and position reflect on the learning process as well as on how abilities and skills are read and appreciated. Style and manner cannot be separated from performance and execution. Learning does not commence in the yard. It is a process that brings several implicit pieces into interplay – assumptions, ideas and beliefs about what is to be taught, about what learning and imitation, as well as final mastery, entail. In our case we find ideas about manual, arduous labour, gender behaviour and a gender system, ideas about equality and submission, individualism and collectivity implemented and embedded in the definitions of handling equipment, skill and learning.

This should make it obvious that I cannot enter the discussion of how to define skill on the same terms as writers like Charles More, who distinguishes 'genuine skill' from 'socially constructed skill', or even Cynthia Cockburn, who distinguishes between 'skill residing in the man (sic) himself' and 'skill demanded by the job'.[70] Such a distinction, even if possible to impose on certain shunting skills, leaves out the important dimension of skill which turns it into a social lever.

We must therefore see skill as the perceived ability to master and cope with what is thought to be the correct task or the right thing to do. Quite regardless of whether speedy execution, technical elegance, or standardized rule-

---

[70] Cockburn distinguishes between "skill residing in the man himself", "skill demanded by the job" and "that which a group of workers or a trade union can successfully defend against the challenge of employers and of other groups of workers". Of these the first two are combined in More's 'genuine skill', while the outcome of the negotiation between workers and management is roughly equivalent to his 'socially constructed skill'. However, More stresses that the negotiation stems from a questioning of the reality of the skills, or their usefulness to industry. Rolf distinguishes between 'skill', 'know-how' and 'competence', seing skill as residing in man himself, and know-how as a performance (according to some rules) the success of which is judged by someone else than the performer. Competence, again, is the ability to change the rules that for what is considered good or bad performance. We can see that my concept of shunting skills contains 'skill' and 'know-how' as well as 'competence'. Cf. COCKBURN 1984, 113, MORE 16 ff. and ROLF, 116 ff.

following is to be considered skilful, there enters the element of coordination and cooperation, which builds on reading and understanding each other in a team. This means that we have a complex interplay of trust and expectations at our hands. In this chapter we have seen that identical execution may be evaluated quite differently, depending on who the executor is, as well as that it may be considered more skilled to **refrain** from doing some tasks than to accomplish them.

The Learning Process – Mimesis and Paraphrase

> "But when he sings of men, his whole appearance
> Conforms to man. What nature gives us not,
> The human soul aspires to imitate.[---]
> And Phrynicus, perhaps you have seen him, sir,
> How fair he was, and beautifully dressed;
> Therefore his plays were beautifully fair. For as the Worker so the
> Work will be."
> (Agathon in Aristophanes's play *Thesmoporiazusae*.)[71]

We are now going to look more closely at the concepts **mimesis** and **paraphrase** that were introduced in order to distinguish between different aspects of imitation in the learning process. We remember that imitation plays an important role in the process of acquiring manual skills and tacit knowledge, although it must be clear that imitation never can be a one-to-one process as it is always mediated by a specific (however preliminary) understanding – interpretation – of the exemplar, as well as the imitative act itself is coined by the pattern of movements inscribed in the body.

The concept *mimesis* traces its history back to ancient Greece, the earliest recorded occurrences stemming from the fifth century B.C. There is no need here to go further into the intricacies of the etymology of the word *mimesis* or other words related to it, suffice it to note that the history has offered a range of different metaphorical uses of the word as well as whole array of disagreements about its history and development.[72] For my purpose it may be considered a drawback that the word primarily seems to have referred to artistic

---

[71] Cf. ARISTOPHANES.

[72] There has been a discussion about the classical 'theory of imitation' and the etymology of the words belonging to the *mimeisthai-* group (words derived from the same stem as *mimos*, 'mime') around the middle of this century, triggered off by a dissertation by Hermann Koller in 1954. This background is aptly described and commented in Göran Sörbom's dissertation *Mimesis and Art*.

representation and imitation, but this is not exclusively the case. According to Sörbom, the concept quickly broadened its metaphorical range already in antiquity and was used for other imitation as well.[73]

Mimesis, as I see it in the yard, is an imitation that facilitates the melting in, as it means an escape from individual solutions and taking after a norm that is presented to the student. The model presented, the right way of performing the tasks, is nevertheless the doing of a person, and therefore there is always an individual trait present, as well as the imitation bears the individual mark of the person performing it.[74]

We remember from our discussion of the learning process that the student perceives 'an idea' of what the example is an example of, and has a host of pre-conceived ideas about the proper way to perform manual work, and about what properties are valued, such as display of strength, or a cool and unalarmed air. The act of close imitation of the model is mimetic, while a performance that disregards the model in favour of a purpose that the student thinks lies behind the example, I will call paraphrastic. The former looks to procedure, the second one to function. The former concentrates on how something is done, the second one on what is being accomplished, not ruling out alternative ways of accomplishing them.

In the process of imitation there are always mimetic as well as paraphrastic elements present, but I want to distinguish these two as contrasting types of imitation as that will help us to perceive and discuss the puzzling differences that men and women for example give evidence of when learning the trade.

Mimesis is a fragmented imitation that concentrates upon the individual tasks rather than the overall flow of work. It takes the given example as the ideal and the proven, safe and correct way to perform the task in question. Mimesis does not question the purposefulness of the procedure, nor is it flexible in adapting to circumstance. It assumes a narrow definition of the context. It is always safe to do it the way it is taught, in a situation which is as identical to the model as possible, is the assumption. The shunter asks the driver if he has got the key, not knowing why. The beginner has no alternative route in mind for the trains when a switch is broken, closing the ordinary route. The smallest deviation in the ordinary pattern leads to

---

[73] Cf. SÖRBOM, 37 ff.

[74] Bourdieu distinguishes between mimesis, an 'overall relation of identification', and imitation, a 'conscious effort to reproduce a model'. I think it is misleading to contrast the two, but I do agree that the processes of acquisition and reproduction of body schemes '**tend to** take place below the level of consciousness'. Cf. BOURDIEU 1990a, 73. Emphasis mine.)

confusion and paralysis of action. The stupefied beginner has then still a strongly mimetic attitude to work. He cannot do what he has been told and shown, and he dare not, and cannot even envisage, anything else to do. He will ask for help and hand over the problem to someone else.

Mimetic learning gives a competence which may work well in the flow of everyday work. Developed into a routine it gives the shunter a safe ground to stand on. It presumes that one is in a subordinate position, preferably working as a C-member. All decisions are made by someone else and the C-member is only coupling and uncoupling carriages, repeating the same arduous moves dozens and dozens of times during a shift. As a woman put it: 'The job can really be freed from intelligence!' Mimesis is a way of learning that minimizes individual traits; the beginner is almost turned into a robot. Not only does he, theoretically, work as every other beginner, he is subsumed into the hierarchy as a anonymous repetitor, unable to make decisions and question the work of his superiors. He is limited to a relation to the work which is routinelike at its best, and an eternal attempt to reduplicate the given norm at its worst.

Mimesis creates a worker who admits both submissiveness to his seniors, as well as a relation to the work which is distant. He has not appropriated the work, made himself master of the process, keeping himself ahead of it, working according to the needs and circumstances, inventing, creating, breaking the routines at his own will and according to his own judgement.[75] In comparison to the other students in his group he, however, stands out as exemplary. He is a good student and as such 'promising' (although the careful observers among the senior shunters know that this is not an indication that tells much about the future). He may ask questions, be inquisitive, in order to improve the performance, but he does not create trouble by questioning the way things should be done. He only wants to know the 'exact' procedure in order to learn it. If he wants to know why things are done, it is because he assumes that everything is done for a good reason. In many cases he does not even ask, as he is convinced that there is a good reason for doing so, anyway.

---

[75] Marcel Mauss talks about '*imitation prestigieuse*' which is found in the context of education, stressing the elements of authority and inequality: "*L'enfant, l'adulte, imite des actes qui ont réussi et qu'il a vu réussir par des personnes en qui il a confiance et qui ont autorité sur lui. L'acte s'impose du dehors, d'en haut, fût-il un acte exclusivement biologique, concernant son corps. L'individu emprunte la série des mouvements dont il est composé à l'acte exécuté devant lui ou avec lui par les autres.*
        C'est précisément dans cette notion de prestige de la personne qui fait l'acte ordonné, autorisé, prouvé, par rapport à l'individu imitateur, que se trouve tout l'élément social. *Dans l'acte imitateur qui suit se trouvent tout l'élément psychologique et l'élément biologique.*
        Mais le tout, l'ensemble est conditionné par les trois éléments indissolublement mêlés." (My emphasis) MAUSS , 369.

He wants to learn the trade, which seems to be there almost as a concrete entity, established by long experience, formed by thousands of toiling hands and bodies afore, a legitimate routine that functions because it is not questioned but performed punctually and methodically.

The paraphrastic way of learning the trade starts with the statement we met in a group of beginners: 'I bet this is not the way they do it in the yard.' Once out in the yard the paraphrastic attitude continues by considering the work procedures of the seniors as an oldfashioned, mouldy routine, void of thought. 'They cannot do anything in a new way. They just say: This is the way it always has been done', the students complain. The example shown to the beginners is seen as a sterile product, perhaps fit for certain situations, but often not applicable. The paraphrastic attitude is to try to grasp the purpose of the whole work process, taking advantage of whatever is at hand, doing not only what one is told, but everything that is not explicitly forbidden, and sometimes even that. To walk swiftly, handle things carelessly and with a good measure of superfluous muscular power, to react swiftly, and take up habits such as playing cards and expressing a negative attitude to bosses, the company, the 'lazy' people in the Hall, or whatever is currently on the agenda, is more important than learning the correct way to talk in the radio, or how to handle the signal system for the gates, etc.

To improvise and create a method on the spur of the moment is preferred to slavishly absorbing the wisdoms of the seniors. The contextual scope is always wide open and as a true *bricoleur* the paraphrastic student is ready to use all 'odds and ends' of work procedure for whatever purpose he finds fit.[76]

The paraphrastic attitude is thus turning the legitimate authority of the seniors on the head. The spectacular use of power displays a potential that day by day is slipping out of the grip of the seniors, who find the nights, the winters and the arduous tasks increasingly difficult to cope with, and who, after twenty years, suddenly start to ponder over the 'power' of the staff up at the Health Centre. Some work with exemption and several have filed claims to have their hearing troubles and other physical ailments classified as work injury.

The seniors claim that technique and routine are the secrets to success, and that only fools use physical strength and daring procedures. 'They will destroy

---

[76] Needless to say, the *bricoleur*-image was introduced by Lévi-Strauss in *The Savage Mind*. It describes a person, who creates by combining things that are at hand, rather than inventing from scratch. Cf. LÉVI-STRAUSS Chapt. 1 *passim*. There are shunters who seem to build their entire existence with objects they find. One shunter said he had four vacuum-cleaners he had found ('all in perfectly good condition'). He obviously did not need them all, but said that 'you never know, they might come in handy'.

their knees/ backs/ ears working like that!' To the young 'routine' is a bag with a mixed content where self-evident routine procedures mingle with old-fashioned, 'stone-age', shunting. The old shunters are considered as not only being fooled into accepting working conditions that no one in his right mind would accept if they were created today, but they are furthermore seen to defend them, refusing to change the tiniest routine as they immediately think they will lose their jobs. 'Everybody knows that shunting as a whole is a relic and should be replaced by automatic coupling, if only the European countries could agree on what couplings to use.' Such statements sometimes flicker by in discussions about shunting as an odd and outmoded job in the modern computerized world.

The contrasting attitude, compared to the seniors, that the paraphrastic beginners show has not one face, but several, and it often changes over time. Initially, as we have seen, there is stupefaction and/or superficial cool. One does not move, claiming, as it were, that there is no need to move. If the seniors think otherwise they may do it themselves. When moving there is no need to slavishly follow all petty instructions. It does not matter. This stiff and confused as well as confusing first stage transforms, however, into its opposite within a year or two.

When muscles and body respond to months of pumping railway iron there is an increasing demonstration of daring moves, waste of power and energetic foolhardiness. Simple routines are no longer objected to, they have now become self-evident. Experience has given the paraphrastic enterprise a form that is no longer haphazard and 'weird', but directed, displaying a logic that is well understood by the seniors. Routines are questioned, but the routines are not the petty ones of jumping off and connecting properly, but the routine readings of what is meant by 'slow speed', 'making sure', and 'safety margins'. The initial misjudgments are overcome and the uninitiated shunter's unwillingness to conform has become a well initiated unwillingness to conform. The young shunter is doing it in his own way, and there is some substance to his claim that he knows what he is doing. Chiselling out a path of his own he simultaneously transforms from being an anonymous beginner at the bottom of the hierarchy to a person with a will and personality which counts in the doings of the team. The paraphrase is the straightest road cowboy behaviour.

The contrast to the jog-trot of the seniors is still his mark. The resistance, the paraphrase he puts forward as his individual style, is inscribed in his physical appearance.[77] The way he walks, the way he handles the heavy materials of the yard and the stern but careless way he steps in between two carriages that are about to clash and deafen the ears for a moment, all this is evidence to himself and others that he is skilled and knows what he is doing.[78]

Statements like 'boys will be boys' and 'the young have always been impatient', sum up the attitude of the elders. They recognize the daring behaviour, but wait for it to wear off. Finally the youngsters will settle down and adapt to 'the way things are done here at Hagalund'. Time and the example of their seniors will work as water wears the rock.

One may see it as an irony that the paraphrastic beginner, now turned cowboy, strongly condemns the beginners who show the paraphrastic attitude of 'weird' behaviour and prefers those that display a mimetic one, such as women. But it is only natural that he should appreciate someone who obeys his advice and confirms his knowledge and skills. He is now someone who has a position, a style of working, and who only waits to take over after the old-timers and show that he can do it better... When asked about his own experiences from the first months in the yard he does not remember much. He was stupid and confused – although not as stupid as the beginners we have **now**. The seniors often seem to remember his career better:

> 'He was so lazy, he was the laziest beginner we ever had. I didn't think he would stay long. Look at him now! Not only is he one of the best shunters, he has soon completed his legal over-time ratio for the year and it is only March!'
> 'He was so hopeless. I always thought that it was because he was stupid. Now that he is given more responsibility he is working excellently. He is too smart, that is why he never bothered before. He thought it was beneath him.'

The excellence so mentioned is the excellence of someone who has appropriated the work process and made it his own. The mimetic skills often pass unobserved, and they are hardly ever met with superlatives and laudation. Someone is O.K., half-good, even *säker*, but there is a reservation added, in the tone of voice, if not explicitly. One may consider such a person a good member in the team, reliable and predictable, but still lacking in initiative and

---

[77] Ursula Scharma objects to a view which sees the body as 'a very passive receptacle forr cultural training.' I hpe it is clear that I see the body as a very active and – reactive – receptacle. Cf. SHARMA, 252.

[78] It is a personal victory for him, but, as male work tends to be identified with normal work, he contributes to raising the limits for handling expectancy. Cf. note 67, above.

the little 'extra' that makes work possible with a minimum of communication. The mimetic member works according to orders given, while the paraphrastic one either hardly works at all, or creates a lot of irritation caused by all unconventional things he is up to, or then he works with gusto, perhaps taking a few unnecessary risks, but always trying to keep himself a step ahead and do things before he has to be told to. He works in his own style, but he is still flexible as he possesses experience from a wide range of situations. Not accepting the model presented to him he has undergone some painful trials and errors, but he has also learned a few tricks on the side as his experiments and whims have advanced. If the crook is streetwise, he is certainly 'yardwise'.

The paraphrastic learner, just as the *bricoleur*, does not limit himself to what he has got in his (back)yard, he is constantly on the look out for new things to add. This holds for work methods as well as useful items. It looks like more than a coincidence that many shunters are scavengers in the yard and routinely take advantage of what the trains may bring along. This seems not only to be a trait of Hagalund. Linda Niemann writes about switchmen of the North American railroads:

> "Show me a switchman, and I'll show you someone who picks up junk. These guys would scavenge anything – wire, old clothes, hats, railroad spikes, other people's lunches, stray lumber, angle irons, tie plates, anything. On the job you switched out a lot of loading docks and passed a lot of backyards. It was a gold mine for scavengers. The crew would be talking in the engine, and suddenly a switchman would dart out the door and return hauling a cable or a hammer or a brown paper bag.
> 'Stop under the bridge on the way back, Joe; I want to put a few things in my truck."[79]

Not all shunters are scavengers, but the most extreme cases are – not surprisingly – also the ones that expose the most paraphrastic work methods, or methods of avoiding work. There are on the other hand shunters who must be seen as performing paraphrastic work, but who consider it beneath them to fall into the dirty habits of scavenging through the carriages. Women are, in general, not known as scavengers, although they may partake in company of others.

---

[79] NIEMANN, 211. This description could be from Hagalund, except that Hagalund shunters have to do with whatever incoming trains and their own yard offer. 'The Beaver' was the nickname of a particularly eager scavenger.

It is not, however, habits related to, and seemingly sprung out of the same attitude as the paraphrastic way of learning that is subject to my interest. I want to claim that although the learning process shows a sliding scale from mimesis to paraphrase it is for some reason more common that women resort to mimesis, turning the oft repeated movements and procedures into safe routines, while the young men start out with unconventional paraphrastic methods, correcting the basic procedures to what is accepted as safe and sound, but simultaneously resorting to more advanced idiosyncratic methods, 'cowboy' behaviour. The constant wish for and speculations about when it will be possible to put together a team with only women, must be seen as the intuitive longing for a situation where the women finally would be pushed into paraphrase.[80]

Skill and Risk

Skill, excellence in timing, as well as perfect cooperation, promote high work-speed. Such ever increasing flow is, however, a trend that is constantly inhibited by the practicalities of the ever-changing situations at work. Even if the majority of moves are routine, the routine also includes incessant vigilance and the constant seeing ahead. The immediate future is always present in the imagination as to what **may** turn up without warning.

Is there anything coming? Is a train-puller cutting through with an engine? Could there be a moped behind the corner or the carriage? Could anyone be in between? Was there a heel on the track? Is there a cable still connected? Has anyone thrown any of the switches behind my back?

Myriads of possibilities are internalized into the thinking of the shunters, being part of the 'backbone thinking' and as such hardly ever formulated into question like my examples above. The constant awareness of possibilities that may create trouble is naturally a high awareness of the ever present risks. In interviews, the shunters often say that 'it would be impossible to work if one

---

[80] Mass media today often describe the advantage that boys develop over girls as a function of their ability to 'grab what they want' (Sw. *'ta för sig'*). What this seems to refer to is, however, being pushful and assertive in general. I am referring to a tendency to take possession of the environment; things as well as social relations and work routines. There is a reluctance to submit oneself and a will to master the relations to people, procedures and things.
Gamst has a more detailed account of differences in 'enculturation' in the case of men and women railroaders. There are strong parallels to my findings, for instance women being more rule-obeying than men. Likewise Gamst found that women tend to quit sooner than men. However, the conditions which according to Gamst explain this situation are largely missing in the case of Hagalund: The women are not kept outside the comradeship or knowledge, they do not find that they are treated differently, etc., but all the same we find a similar end result: the women leave. This, I have argued, means that we must dig deeper into the conceptions of work.

thought about the risks all the time' and they even claim that they **never** think about the risks. I would quite to the contrary argue that thinking about the risks is so deeply incorporated in the way work is planned and performed that it has become a way of being and acting. It is in contrast to outsiders that the shunters see the difference most clearly. Outsiders cannot walk, move or drive safely and there are constantly complaints about the staff in the Hall and the risks they constantly create whatever they do or fail to do.

The vigilant eye is unavoidably also turned against co-shunters, especially younger and more inexperienced ones. The cool look of a youngster is always seen with a grain of suspense and distrust, as any extra-ordinary event may crack the cool surface and let out all sorts of unpredictable actions and emotional reactions.

All these, by now very familiar, ingredients of shunting work must be reiterated once more as we try to grasp the conglomerate of skill and risk, individualism and collectivism, hierarchy and egalitarian ideals.

To become a good shunter in the opinion of others is a long process because the real test, besides managing well as a shunt leader, is to manage situations that are out of the ordinary. By definition these are few and far between, and even then the situation and the actions on part of the persons involved are not easily defined in an unambiguous way. Mistakes made during routine operations are easily spotted, but when the extra-ordinary occurs there is no self-evident solution, and a smart and eloquent shunter may make even acts of panic seem justified.

There is, however, one particular arena where the conflicting game of skill and risk is conventionalized and clarified. This arena has disposed of everyday life with its ambiguous situations, its long spans of time, and its physical limitations and demands, and its ever redefined constitutive rules. In this arena, all that remains is the conflict between skill and risk, between planning and chance, and between collective spirit and individual gain, all in a frame set by confined space, limited time and regulative rules. This arena is the card table.

'Blackout' – Displaying Shunting Skills around a Card Table

Occupations which include long periods of waiting have often been associated with card-playing. Shunting is no exception, and being introduced to the yard the prospective beginners were told that the shunters wear out one deck of cards a week, on average.

Many kinds of card-games have been introduced to the yard over the years. One game has enjoyed popularity for some months only to be replaced by the next one. International fads, such as Canasta, which spread across the world in the 1950s with unprecedented speed, have not left the yard untouched. It is easy to understand the periodic change of games, offering variety and suiting different tastes.

The parade of games came to a halt, however, when *'Plump'* was introduced to the yard a couple of decades ago. *'Plump'* means '(ink-)blot' and this game did more or less blot out all alternative games. (Other games, such as 'Chicago' and 'Poker', have an insignificant position, being played only as alternatives when there is a lack of time or players.)

Plump can be described as a game in the large whist family, but the players do not work in partnerships. The closest equivalent I have found described in the card literature is a game called 'Blackout', alternatively 'Oh Hell!'.[81] These names could be applied to *plump* as well because the game includes a blotting out, or blacking out, of the scores of at least one member every round, which often leads to exclamations, screams and laughter. We remember that a prospective shunter, member of the Jehovah's Witnesses, changed his mind about becoming a shunter after witnessing the turmoil around the card-table.

It is necessary to give a description of the game because, as I will argue, the game could have been tailored explicitly for the shunting crew, as it balances elements of skill and risk, accentuating the very abilities and properties of the players that are seen as essential in shunting work.

The Rules of the Game

Plump is ideally played with five players, making a 'full team', but it is possible to play with four or even only three players. The players are first dealt ten cards each. In the case of five players, two cards of the pack remain. Of these two cards the top card is turned, indicating the trump-suit of the round. Now the bidding starts with the person sitting to the left of the dealer, moving clock-wise. All players state the amount of tricks they estimate they will take on the basis of their cards. A person responsible for the protocol will then add ten to the stated number and write down the bids in columns, one for each player. Every player is free to bid any number, from zero to the amount of cards they have on their hand (e.g., in the first round, ten), but the last to bid must choose a number of tricks so that the sum of all tricks bid does not equal the number of cards (in this case ten). It is therefore impossible for every

---

[81] About the card-games cf. HOLMSTRÖM, 23, 73.

person to get the amount of tricks they have 'asked for'. All persons who do not succeed to get the **exact** amount of tricks that they bid for will be blotted out of the protocol in that round; they get a *plump*. The others get the amount of points stated in the bidding, i.e. the number of tricks added to ten. (For instance, bidding three tricks will give 10+3=13 points, zero tricks gives 10+0=10 points, given that one can be as good as one's word. Otherwise one gets zero points, a *plump*.)

The game is thus constructed in a way that guarantees at least **one** loser every round. Often several persons get *plumps* and there is nothing that stops a round resulting in **every** person getting a *plump*, i.e. that every person loses! But there are many rounds to go!

The first round of ten cards is followed by a round of nine cards each, then eight and so on, reducing the number of cards until every person is to have only **one** card each. Here the game changes from bidding on the basis of one's card to a blind bidding. The bids are taken before the cards are dealt and the dealing is then done picture side up. When finally the trump-card is turned, winners and losers are instantly displayed. In the one-card round there is therefore no play, only bidding.

Having reached the round of one card the rounds start the second half of the game, now beginning with only one card each and working its way up to ten cards. When all rounds are finished, twenty in all, the points are summed up and all losers pay the winner the 'exorbitant' sum of five *öre* per point differing between him and the winner. (When five *öre* coins no longer were in use, uneven sums were raised by five *öre*.) The winner gains very rarely more than ten *kronor* in all (i.e. less than 2 US dollars).[82]

Some of the youngsters complain about the ridiculous sums of money involved, wanting a 'fee' of one crown per point, as this would make the game more exciting, but the seniors always proudly state that it is not the money but the honour that is at stake in *plump*. It is also of utmost importance that gambling debts should be paid, however tiny they are. Here again it is honour that matters. No one will brush away fifty *öre* that a player owes him and say that it does not matter. One may forget a hundred crown debt, but never a *plump* debt.[83] When receiving the money it is pocketed with

---

[82] After the introduction of the bonus the sums were raised by a hundred percent to ten *öre* per point (Ten *öre* coins now being obsolete demands that sums are evened to closest fifty *öre*). Moore writes that workers in general gamble about small amounts of money – as opposed to the army on pay-day. Cf. MOORE W., 328.

[83] This is the way it is considered to be. Naturally *plump* debts may be forgotten as well as there are persons who do not see the full implications of the honour being considered to be at stake in the game.

the contented and proud look of someone gaining a sum a hundred times larger.

Who Can Play?

Not every shunter is a card-player. Some have given it up, some have refused to start. It is a question of actively refusing as every beginner is coaxed into playing by more or less forceful methods. I was myself recruited during my first shifts in the yard by my trainer, who – after finding out that my initial refusal did not stem from a religious conviction – jokingly said: 'Today you are training with me, so you do what you are told! Sit down and pick up your cards!' Then my trainer, several years my junior, sat down behind me to 'back-play', i.e. to advise me during the game. 'Back-players' are common, but although they are considered to be advisors or co-players they hardly ever say anything to help the player they watch over the shoulder. They mainly scorn him and question his moves. However, in my case the back-player took it upon himself to advise me wisely, while simultaneously, teaching me the rules.

I was then, jokingly, given no choice, but was 'forced to play'. Later, working my own shifts without a supervisor, I could naturally have refrained from playing, but the game really caught me as it made me feel part of the team. It is also very hard to resist the enticing, begging, flattering and encouraging remarks, all of it in order to get a full team. This is the other side of it; to refuse to play means that a small team cannot get more than three players. This is not so much fun and there may not be game at all. In this situation, who wants to be a kill-joy?

The worst prospect is perhaps to sit next to a screaming card-table, trying to read or talk to someone, or to be reduced to a coffee-maker. This is the role that befalls a person, male or female, who does not participate in the game. The task is taken on grudgingly, and often it is outright refused (particularly women are very touchy about serving men and tell them off in harsh words), but this does not put the players off, they laugh and refer to yesterday when **they** were not playing and had to make the coffee, etc.

The card-players always occupy the same table, the table by the wall. This is because it offers the best seats, as two of the seats are too close to the back wall to allow back-players. In case there are two teams playing, the other table will also be occupied, but rarely, if ever, do the players resort to the non-smoking room. Many complain about the 'smoke-chamber', and some have stopped playing cards because they cannot stand the dense cloud, but no non-smoking card-table has been established that could compare to the institutionalized table next to the wall. Cards and smoking are the two sides of the same coin, it seems.

Between the two extremes, those who cannot conceive of a break without a card-game and those who never play, there is the majority of shunters who estimate how long a break they can take, knowing that a full game of *plump* takes 45 minutes, while simultaneously scanning the prospective team of players.

It is not uncommon for someone to scorn the team of players by exclaiming something like: 'Just look at this team! What a garbage-team *(sopgäng)*!' or 'Here they are, bidding zero with the trump ace on the hand!' Such remarks are considered to be jokes, but a closer look at the practice of playing reveals that the free and haphazard constitution of players into parties, which is assumed to prevail, covers a hierarchy of priorities as concerns team-mates. Some players are 'high-ranking' and find it easier to recruit a team, while others, lower in rank, will be met by evading excuses and uninterested rebuffs.

Talking about rank in the context of card-players must be seen as a very crude description of the esteem a favoured player enjoys. The following description of the game attempts to clarify the use I put it to here.

The ranking, just as is the case of ranking good shunters in the yard, depends on mainly two factors, and these are not easily identified. One of them is skill and the other one is the ability to create a cheerful and gamesome atmosphere around the card-table. As the card-game is a game of chance as well as a game of skill it is not easy to determine the proportions that in their turn determine the outcome.

The ability to create a joyful atmosphere further depends on a mix of timing, other persons present and the prevailing mood in general. One person cannot create a cheerful ambiance, but in a group one person can contribute in the interplay with others. To say that 'it is always fun when Allan is here' is therefore only partly true. The presence of Allan **often** contributes to a jolly atmosphere, true, but it is neither sufficient nor necessary for the creation of such an ambiance.

The well hidden fastidiousness gives rise to games of different dignity. It must be remembered that members of the same shunting team informally have first right to the card-table and that it is only when they do not sum up to a full card-team that auxiliary players may join the gang. As joining a shunting team as a steady member may already take the quality of the members as card-players into consideration, there is an initial process of selection that is also

199

invisible in the day-to-day formation of card-teams. Persons crazy about playing *plump* will not join a non-playing team or a team with lousy players. The common occurrence of VIK-personnel, however, means that beginners and bad players often mingle with the 'old card-hands' and enter games that are prestigeous and more serious than anyone would like to admit.

Playing the Game

When everybody has taken a seat, and the coffee is served and someone is coaxed into 'writing', the game begins. The one who 'writes' takes down the points on the special SJ forms for "Changes of Tracks', which are all but purpose-made for *plump*. Writing is not a very popular task, as it inevitably reveals if the writer fails to see who made his tricks and who didn't. For a beginner it is enough to try to manage his own cards and tricks and it is not easy to keep track of everybody else's in addition to that. Thus there are some persons who often end up as writers, some even proudly volunteering for the task.

Every round starts the bidding from the person next the one who bid last time, in order to even out the tough position of being the last bidder, who has the restriction upon him **not** to bid a number that will make the sum of tricks equal the number of cards on the hand. 'You may not bid two (or 'zero', or 'one', or 'three', etc. as the case may be)!' the writer announces. This is inevitably exactly what the poor player wanted to bid, of course, and he then has to estimate whether his cards are better for 'creeping' *(att krypa)* or whether he should take a chance and over-bid and bid three or even four or five – or all! Creeping, i.e. to waste the best cards as soon as there is a higher card – e.g. a trump – on the table, is not as honourable as bidding one trick **over** the forbidden number and try to win the extra trick by active and aggressive play, but it is nevertheless more common to decide to creep, or *'fegspela'* ('to play cowardly, 'chicken-play') as it also is called.

The highest bidder is also the one to start the play. This is an undeniable advantage when there are many cards to be played, but with few cards on hand it can be just as much of a disadvantage as the trumps are so much more dominant in the game when only few cards are dealt.

There is, partly as a consequence of the influence of the trumps, great variation in the opportunities to adjust the play to the number of tricks one has bid for. With ten cards in the hand the element of chance is rather small, and it is relatively easy to make zero, one, two or even three tricks with an average hand. Having very good cards may tempt someone to try to bid **all**

200

ten tricks, which, when successfully executed, amounts to 110 points (according to the principle of adding a 1 before the number of tricks), rendering the lucky player an almost unbeatable advantage.

With fewer and fewer cards in every round the element of luck and the difficulty of playing one's hand increases drastically. While there is – with ten cards in the hand, and five players in the team – only one card undealt (the one lying under the trump indicator), with three or two cards in the hand there are 36 and 41 cards left undealt, respectively. In these cases it is naturally impossible to predict which cards will be in play, and what trumps – if any – there are among the players. To get rid of a trump, even if it is a picture card, by playing it first is then a given success when there are ten cards in the hand, as every player must play a higher trump, if they have one. When there are only a few cards on the hand it may well be that two of trumps is the only trump between all players and it is impossible to force someone else to pick up the trick. There is, on the other hand, no guarantee that one may collect the trick with this low trump, either. The risk is evident to everyone, but the scornful remarks may still come forward. 'Bidding zero with a trump in the hand! Chicken-play!'

The single-card rounds are, as I said earlier, pure chance rounds. The bidding is either 'zero' all around the table, making the person whose card is the highest trump a loser, or then the first person bids 'one' (as he is the most likely person to win the only trick, as **his** card will become trump in case no one has the same suit as the trump indicator). In case the first person bids 'one', the last person to bid (given that everybody else bids 'zero', as they do in almost every case) **must** bid one, too (as one trick is at stake and the total sum of bids therefore must not be one). In this case there is more risk in the game, as up to **three** persons can get a *plump,* while the zero-bidding case makes **one and only one** person lose.

Zero-bidding in the two single-card rounds is seen as cowardly, too. The first person to bid is always coaxed: 'You'll take one, won't you?' and expressions of disappointed 'chicken-play!' abound, in case the first bidder says 'zero'. The last one to bid is on the contrary begging the first bidder to bid 'zero', pleading with him to be 'good to an old pal' and pointing at someone that they two should *'sätta dit'* (frame). In case the first bidder just laughs at these appeals and bids 'one', saying that it is the pleading person who needs a *plump,* this latter person wails and tells the writer to notify that he was 'forced' *('tvångsad')* to bid one. This is laughingly abided by adding a star (*) after the score in the protocol. This star has no value or importance for the game whatsoever, it is only a public gesture of pity, a sign that the *plump*

201

in this row was not duly earned, as there was no real play, only bad luck and evil scheming on the part of another player.

The demand of a star by yelling *'tvångsad, tvångsad'* may jokingly occur also when there are many cards on hand, but although it may be considered in case the play of two cards turned out to show an extraordinary bad luck (e.g. someone being forced to bid 'one' with two two's in the hand), it is mostly laughed off when the outcome is considered to be up to the skill of the player. A good player can choose how to play and adjust his tricks even when he is obliged to bid a number of tricks he would not ideally have chosen. Or so it is assumed.

Group Strategy or Egotistic Gain

While the obvious aim for every player is to avoid *plumps*, a secondary aim being to make as many tricks as possible, the game becomes boring and undynamic if all players stick to such an egoistic ambition. The protocol is open to all eyes around the table, and to other onlookers, and the black *plumps* tell at a quick glance, and from a long distance, the difference in position among the players. Someone may be 'unblotted' *('oplumpad')*, while someone else may be caught 'in a shoal' *('i ett stim')*, showing a long row of nasty black *plumps* down his line. When an unblotted person finally gets a *plump* the other players cheer and joyous remarks hail: 'Congratulations! You just won an egg-beater!' This standard remark refers to the movement of the pen when blotting out the points, while simultaneously referring to a typically disappointing and slightly ridiculous lottery-prize.[84]

The step from cheering when the person who is leading gets a *plump* to actually trying to enforce a *plump* upon him is short indeed. The rest of the players will quickly gang up to hurt the leader and bring him down. Especially someone who has been struck by a shoal, making it impossible for him to win the game, is supposed to sacrifice himself in order to make the leader *plump*. Group pressure is here difficult to resist and it is not very honourable to play for the sake of minimizing the cost of one's own losses instead of trying to nail the leader. Particularly when the leader is a person of high prestige – as a card player **or** as a shunter – the co-players will yell: 'Play hearts! He's got no hearts!' or 'Creep! Creep!' or 'You can't let **him**/ the

---

[84] It is obvious that the egg-beater acquires its derogatory and ludicrous qualities as a prize from its feminine connotations. Men supposedly do not need egg-beaters.

boss/ the shunt leader win!' When the joint effort has brought down the initial leader, the pack will cheer and immediately turn to attack the new leader.

Even without such assistance of the co-players there are often quick turns in the luck of the players. The middle part of the game is the one where plain chance can work havoc with the best of players and the surprising outcome of the rounds with few cards in the hand also give rise to tremendous bursts of laughter. I have on several occasions heard the screams of laughter from the card-players at a very long distance from the barracks (note that the barracks are well insulated with double-glazing, etc.). As mentioned earlier one of the shunters is known for his laughter at the card-table even among SJ employees at other stations.

Despite the unwritten obligation to bring down the leader to the level of everybody else, there is constantly a shameless boasting and promotion of oneself. When bringing home one's bid, 'fanfares' are tooted (for example the Popeye-theme), little jingles are sung and signs of victory are waved in the air. The Norwegian exclaims: *'Norge, du er best!'* ('Norway, you are the best!'), while joking insults hail over the other 'worthless' co-players: *'Släng er i väggen!'* (lit.: 'Throw yourselves into the wall!') The more inventive the remarks and insults are, the higher the spirits rise. The obviously ludicrous claim that the sudden and unexpected turns in the game are brought about by skill rather than by sheer luck takes all sense out of the insults and therefore everybody can join in the laughter. But in the back of the minds of the losers as well as the winners the thought will remain: maybe a portion of cunning skill played a decisive part in the success after all.

To the eye of an outsider the game gives the impression of combining conceit and shameless boasting with a democratic ideal, where everybody is, or should be, prepared to sacrifice himself for the good of his mates and the game. To have one person much ahead of the others is detrimental to the excitement as well as it is unfair, as there is always an element of luck involved and no one can remained 'unblotted' solely due to excellent play. To gang up on the leader is therefore only to help luck on its way and allow skill to come into play again.

To be too good is therefore almost an impossibility. The gain, pocketed with pride, is no more than a few crowns (some of which should be payed as a fee to the communal coffee-box, which also pays for new decks of cards), but there are other ways of establishing oneself as a good player.

One way is to play with an uncommitted face, reading the paper or talking to a non-player simultaneously, or just generally acting as if the game could be played without thought and almost asleep. This attitude is more common when the difference in skill between the players is quite obvious and someone who is already established as a good player agrees to play with beginners just in order to make a full team. It also assumes that the inattentive player leads the game before the act can be played to the full.

Another way to impress the public and create oneself as a good player is, as we have seen, to act with a good portion of self-confidence, seemingly directing and determining the course of the game, loudly commenting all moves. One does not simply play clubs, one declares with a voice that indicates that the outcome is planned and completely under control: 'And **now** we'll play some **clubs**!' It is an advantage to have a hold of the game at such a point, but in case the draw is a failure the comment may pass unnoticed, while in case it is a success the same player will rub it in by exclaiming: *'Den drog mask!'* (lit: 'This one pulled the worm', meaning it made the trick.) This godfatherlike manner can also be used in favour of the collective aim of bringing a leader on the fall. The outspoken and self-appointed expert player will determine when and whom to attack and will point at a strategy – naturally quite openly – that will fulfil the aim, often consisting of a bidding that will force the leader to bid a number of tricks he will find it difficult to get. To withstand all such public efforts by winning one's stipulated number of tricks anyhow will of course mean that the leader will describe his lead as the natural outcome of his skills, not as a result of a spell of luck. He will laugh at the efforts to gang up on him, scream with joy when the sworn enemy falls into their own traps, and exclaim: 'That's how it ends when you try dirty tricks on **me**!' Honest admirers, often back-players, might even add praise to his own boasting: 'I'm/he is playing like a god! Look at me/him, playing as if in trance!'

There is thus never a self-sacrifice so altruistic that it would not turn into the most exuberant boasting as soon as the luck turns. Playing in favour of the team and the good of the game can easily be combined with the purest of selfish motives, not only concerning winning the game at stake, but in order to establish oneself as someone **worth** beating at the card table.

The Yard and the Cards

It is hardly a coincidence that competence in *plump* echoes the abilities and skills that make a cool shunter. Of all card games that once made it to the coffee-room as passing fads, *plump* undoubtedly became the shunters' game *par excellence* as it acts as an instant testboard for abilities and properties which only slowly can be brought out for examination in the yard. The risks are simultaneously transformed from potential bodily harm, or death, in the yard to a handful of points, each worth five *öre* at the card table. The purely symbolic value became even more pointed as it stubbornly was held on to years after the five-*öre* coins became obsolete.

One of the properties of a good shunter that is equally important at the card table is daring cool. To be daring in *plump* involves among other things to bid for as many tricks as possible, that is to overbid rather than to '*fegspela*', play cowardly, and 'creep'. This is not a very lucrative enterprise, and the bravery consists of the fact that every additional trick only gains one point, while failure – to *plump* – means losing the lot, i.e. 10 to 15 points, or more. Daring play is therefore mainly a show and a way to dominate and take a more active part in the game, as the highest bidder opens the play, as well as the one to win the last trick also will be the one to start the play for the next trick. Winning many tricks thus means starting so many rounds as well and thereby deciding suit. In points it does not have a pay–off to match the risks involved.

To be too daring is naturally only stupid, and it is always risky to ask for many tricks with cards that are not considered to back up one's bid. 'Did you bid **five** with those cards!? Where are your trumps then?!' Especially a beginner will be seen as foolish rather than daring when bidding too high.

Being a beginner in the yard equals being a beginner at the *plump* table. Someone might be familiar with the game when arriving in the yard, but knowing how to play the game does not equal knowing how the game is played by the shunting crew. A beginner will therefore play a rather quiet and passive part in the game, keeping to modest bids, few comments and a low tone of voice. He will not initiate an attack on the current leader, and when lucky he will, instead of shouting triumphantly, rather mumble something about beginner's luck and that the game isn't over yet, and that he now got very tricky cards. This is all preventive to attacks, in case he is leading, and it is indeed unusual to gang up on a beginner. Just like in the yard, it is assumed that a beginner might manage one cold night or two, but it is the long run that counts. Nerves will pop up before the game is over, and the last rounds – when luck again plays a smaller part in the game and skill comes to the fore – will be too stressful for the beginner, making him earn his share of *plumps*.

One particular incident at the card table is quite enlightening concerning the silent and therefore also mostly invisible submission that a beginner in the yard – and at the card table – is expected to adhere to. This incident involved two extremes as far as experience goes, one being an extremely dominant player and an old hand in the yard, the other one being a rather

205

uncouth beginner and a novice at the card table. As it happened the novice had been dealt a very good hand of cards consisting of a nice suit of picture cards, but, however, lacking trumps. He had bid a rather high number of tricks, to the amazement of the other players, and he thus played the leading role, starting every round, and also successfully gaining his tricks in an uninterrupted flow. Meeting no resistance he collected his tricks in a high speed and with great confidence. His confidence was, however, false and he had not foreseen the possible advent of a low trump, thrown in without comment in the quick whirl of cards. Just when he was to collect the trick with a rather cock-sure face the senior player grabbed the cards just ahead of him, saying with restrained anger: 'Stop now! Can't you see it is trumped?! You're not the only one who bid for tricks, you know!' The earlier so eager and triumphant beginner sank back as a punctured balloon. His face all red he muttered something inaudible and stared down in his cards. The senior shunter *cum* player had revealed that the junior had got carried away when not meeting any resistance and had underestimated the other players, who were only waiting to pull out the trumps at the right moment.

The lesson was only too evident. The beginner *plumped* when the old hands started the **real** fight about the tricks. It was clear that a beginner should not develop a style of raking the table as if he had the play under control, but should concentrate on the cards and not take a gained trick until he was sure he actually had won it and assume no success until the last card was played. He should keep in mind that a gained trick might be a trick that the others **let** him take, not one that he had managed to steal from the rest.

The perfectly timed repercussion, the reprimand uttered with so much restrained anger and the embarrassed response of the poor novice all made the scene into one that any watching beginner would take care to avoid. Around the card table it was, of course, all seemingly in jest, but this was only the sugar that made the medicine go down. Mannerisms at the *plump* table, just as cowboy fads in the yard, cracked like empty shells as they did not grow out of complete control, given by skill and experience.

The lesson learnt at the card table is then a lesson for the yard as well. Even if there is no explicit recognition of this it is seen as self-evident that the card-table reveals personal traits, unexpected abilities as well as hidden flaws.

'Bernt, you write down the points! – Bernt is the brains in our team', Pelle, the boss, explained jokingly to the rest when sitting down at the table. Bernt had been considered a rather bad shunter, but at the time of this comment he had rather successfully started his own shifts as a shunt leader, and it was obvious that Pelle wanted to better his reputation by giving him approval publicly. The connection between the performance in the yard and the expectations at the card-table seemed only natural.

Relations in the yard and around the card-table do not only affect each other, they represent two important parts of establishing oneself in the Hagalund environment. They are distinct areas but still not isolated from each other and could rather be likened to different colours on a palette, colours that are blended in the final picture. The consequence is that cowardly, selfish, foolhardy, overly optimistic or controlled and well-planned cardplaying will be seen to have its equivalents in the behaviour in the shunting yard as well as work styles in the yard are seen to be reflected in behaviour around the card-table. Conflicts in the yard can, and do, therefore enter into cardplaying, but they will be disguised as one joke among many.

Only once have I observed a situation where an initially very jocular atmosphere was pushed further and further until it took absurd proportions and the spiteful intentions became visible. This case was when a card-team had been formed by some of the junior shunters, who were not working in a team, but were uncoupling engines or trainpulling. They had, quite out of the ordinary, managed to recruit one of the best shunters, a man not very much their senior in age, but well in experience, to their table as he also was a notorious card-player and this particular day he was neither working in his team, but was doing an extra shift as a knocker.

As the game proceeded the senior shunter soon got a considerable lead and the juniors decided to 'get him'. One of the juniors, the main protagonist, demanded that the others play only in order to *plump* the senior and he made such foolish moves that he *plumped* almost every round. The tactics succeeded to bring the leader down, but the exceedingly excited junior shouted louder and louder insults and continued to attack the now no longer leading senior, who tried to keep a stiff upper lip. He was by that time red all down his neck, and it was obvious that he regretted having bothered to play with this rather low-status bunch in the first place.

The merciless treatment continued, insults rained down on the poor senior who finally asked what he had done to deserve this. No answer came forward and what answer could have been produced?

To the initiated onlooker it was clear that the 'bad boys' finally had, so to speak, caught the 'nice boy' in a dark alley – and now they were giving it to him! There was no opportunity to challenge the colleague who was their superior, but still belonging to their age-group, in the yard. The card-table, belonging partly to the 'off-work' sphere, admitted, just like the dark alley, an arena where other laws prevailed. Under the cover of 'a jolly game' verbal abuse and ostracism could be practiced beyond all rules of decent behaviour normally observed towards a work-mate.

The card-table, seemingly an 'off-work' play-ground for equals, is – we must conclude – not only that. There is a clear connection between the doings in the yard and the play around the card-table. This connection is based on the view that personality traits which are crucial to good workmanship are also revealed when playing *plump*. *Plump* may indeed be seen as a catalyst bringing out hidden weaknesses, or strengths, into the open. 'Nerves' can be hidden for months in the yard, but will pop up quickly in a game of *plump*.

In fact, it seems that it is exactly the complete inutility and illusive isolation from the social world that create the catalytic properties of *plump*. Being only a game *plump* does not involve any outside considerations. The game – the rules and the cards – are the same to all players and it is only luck (in the short run) and skill (in the long run) that determine the outcome. One game, consisting of twenty rounds and 45 minutes, is a rather long run, while a year in the yard is still a rather short run.

The connection between establishing oneself as a cool shunter in the yard and a cool *plump*-player in the coffee-room becomes even more obvious as it is clear that persons who widen their work interests to comprehend union matters, safety regulations or ways to develop the work and the undertakings of the group, in most cases lose interest in the card-table and spend the breaks discussing matters that sometimes concern work, but which just as often touch other areas of life. It seems that the persons with wider interests no longer find the position in the yard all important and can relax without constantly defending their *nif* at the card-table.[85]

There are other reasons to stop playing, too. At the advent of new skilful players many old hands choose to withdraw from playing, claiming that they are 'fed up' with it and that they 'cannot understand how some can spend every break, every day at the card-table'. They themselves have 'other interests' and 'other things that occupy their minds'. They thereby deny the value of establishing oneself at the card-table as relevant altogether.

---

[85] *Nif*, the point of honour, (lit.: the nose) was introduced to the *lingua franca* of anthropology by Bourdieu, when he described the berber man of honour as the one who "...faces, outfaces, stands up to others, looks them in the eyes..." BOURDIEU, 1977, 15.
Around the card-table in Hagalund one is defending one's *nif*, not by winning, but by playing 'honourably' and bravely; adhering to the call for solidarity against the leader while simultaneously playing for oneself, bidding daringly but still within the limits of sense and 'good judgment'.

Conflicting interests seem to lead to withdrawal from playing. When there is no longer an agreement about what work in the yard should be like, the effect is that the card-game is seen as pointless. Thus the main opponents to the reorganization, which we shall learn more about in next chapter, refrained from playing cards for the period of the most intensive conflict.

We must conclude that it would be wrong to consider card-playing as a 'functional' institution, resolving conflicts, leading to integration or agreement in the yard. Far from it, it rather presupposes consonance and loses significance when there no longer is a basic agreement upon what matters at work and how work is to be conceived of in the yard.[86]

Conclusions

Learning the skills in the shunting yard is as much a physical as a mental process. The bodies of young beginners seem to swell before one's very eyes as the constant toil of coupling, uncoupling, mounting and dismounting coaches and engines, knocking frozen bridges and connecting reluctant hoses and cables exercises every muscle in the body. It seems like the shunter finally takes possession and control of the body, making use of limbs and joints that earlier seemed misplaced or superfluous. The undetermined movements of the earlier so awkward and uncouth youngsters are now replaced by increasingly deliberate and measured strides. During breaks, inactive hands no longer fidget uneasily, but rest calmly from work or drum impatiently on table-tops, waiting for action.

The body so appropriated; not only adapted to work, but starting to demand and crave action and movement, is the supreme tool to express a 'cowboy' style of work, as this includes an overpowered, almost aggressive, handling of heavy iron equipment. The action is not called for by the task. It is not demanded by co-workers, or even explicitly admired, but the youthful competition, the logic of the ardour and the swelling muscles of the newly shaped bodies evoke and call forth the excessive and unmuzzled display of power.

---

[86] Gambling, such as card-games, tombola, and naturally the Balinese cockfight have been viewed as metaphors, or expressive models of social life (cf. ARVASTSON 1985, LAVE & WENGER, GEERTZ 1973), although Geertz both states and denies that the cockfight should be seen as an 'expression' (cf. ib. 44, 446). In contrast to the Balinese case, I see the card game as an arena where social positions are affected and changed. I am not talking about a transfer of winners and losers from the card table to social life, but of a display and exposure of personal attributes which are seen as decisive also for shunting skills.

209

Cowboy behaviour is hardly specific to the yard. What makes it interesting is what is expresses in the yard, in the relation to evaluations of skill and risk, as well as the role it comes to play in age, seniority and gender relations.

Having established the two ways of learning and relating to work and work mates, we can conclude with some reflections on female and male beginners. As we know the women are considered to be better than the men in the beginning. After some months the men pick up and supersede the women.

Paraphrastic learning, compared to mimetic learning, results in late blooming of skill. Slowly, as a process of trial and error, the paraphrastic beginners accept the given way to perform tasks. While the correct performance of simple routines are incorporated in their repertoire they constantly turn their attention to new areas, new tasks. The direction of the 'inventiveness', to speak with the terms of Janik, now follows a logic that is simple to understand, and the initial 'weirdness' has taken the form of more predictable and comprehensible cowboy behaviour that counts irregularities ranging from the simple breaking of rules to mischief, pranks, or practical jokes. We are talking about behaviour which is predictable in kind, not as it appears in the progress of events.

The ease by which the women become accustomed to mimetic learning is not to be seen as a simple form of submission. As stated before, they do not enter the yard and the hierarchy on the same terms as the men do. They are consciously treated the same as their male peers, but there are expectations and readings that accord them a position of visibility. They are not anonymous, but interesting. They are not suspected of being there because they were unemployed, unable to find anything else. Their choice is seen as an active one, and they are assumed to hold, if not 'feminist' views, at least the view that women can manage a man's job. They are from the beginning considered to be something out of the ordinary.

Regardless of the explicit attitudes of treating everybody the same ('if you are here you must work as everybody else, it does not matter if you are a man or a woman'), and the assurance that women are not scrutinized and watched more carefully, the fact remains; women mean a little thrill and they are still the marked case. The men like to see that there is a woman – we still do not know what the opinion would be if there were *only* women – in the new class of beginners doing the introductory course and it is exactly this positive, welcoming and curious attitude that makes the women feel watched, but, no doubt, also appreciated.

The women do not arrive invisibly, nor do they imperceptibly turn into 'old hands'. Every step is still pioneering and they have to make a career for themselves. It is true that they are preceded by other women, but they are also told of the extraordinary qualities of their predecessors. Maybe these positive opinions are given in order to encourage the new women, maybe to show a positive attitude towards women in general, but they do of course set up an idealized picture in front of the shaky beginner. Not only does she know that she has to be as good as a man, she knows that this has been accomplished before her. She may doubt that her own abilities are in the same league as those of the 'great girls of ours'. At the same time she realizes that her failures will be failures ascribed to her sex. She is a representative of 'women' if she fails, but becomes a person – one of 'the great girls' – if she is successful, while a man fails as a 'freak' individual, but as a success he will be just an ordinary representative of his sex.

The female beginners, mimetically following the examples of their teachers and of the 'ordinary shunter', are much encouraged by their first efforts, as they soon prove to be 'good' students. They arrive in time, they develop routine and skills in answering back. They are well liked and defended against the assumed prejudice of the 'vicious' surroundings. All people who show signs of treating them differently will be 'handled'. Much sooner than the men, the women are being approved of and included in the group. They are on their way of working 'like a man' and they defend loudly and clearly the obligation that everybody in the yard must do the same job.[87]

The mimetic appropriation of work, the routine, the safe and correct way ot doing things, contrasts to the male appropriation. It is obvious that the show of strength and carelessness could be signs of such mastery, but it is equally obvious that the signified often is absent. It is a show, a display with no other signified than the sign itself, the sign of 'doing as I please is the only thing I please to do'.

In the best of cases the paraphrastic learning then leads to a genuine appropriation of work. It means learning all the possible ways of handling the material and the processes. It creates a preparedness for difficult conditions and original solutions in times of crises and danger. In the worst of cases the paraphrase is just a negative and eternally questioning attitude, with no skills to back it up. The careless and overpowered ways of working are to be

---

[87]Cockburn has a very different example from hot-metal composing in Britain. She quotes a worker who said:"But if I said to my mates I was working with a woman, they would feel , say, oh, he's doing a woman's job – because they can see that a woman **can** do it. They wouldn't think to say that she is the one who is doing a man's job." COCKBURN 1984, 180.

211

interpreted by the fellow shunters as one or the other. In the long run the 'blabbermouth' will expose himself, they trust. They know that in the long run it is the work that chooses the worker.

The women do not have equal access to the physical language of overpowered work routines. They simply do not have the superfluous muscular strength to make a show of throwing brake heels across the yard or holding couplings stretched in the air as if they were made of light plastic. The way women work, the way they move their bodies, differ from men, but shows of carelessness are also interpreted differently when performed by women. A remarkably strong man is strong as a bull, but a remarkably strong woman is strong as a man. Strength is a male game in which a woman always remains an impostor.

Even if the women lack the muscular power there are, indeed, other moments when daring 'cowboy' behaviour can be pulled off. How to handle kicks is one of the watersheds in this respect. To go between a 'fast' kick is not a matter of strength, but of courage. To judge when a kick is simply fast and when it is a dangerous *'rykare'*, which one should not go between, is on the other hand skill.

It is almost impossible to state with any certainty whether women more often are judged to be 'unskilled' and 'foolhardy', while men on the contrary tend to be judged to be showing skill and dexterity when performing similar tasks. Situations are never the same, and one may also take into account that the evaluation generally has a tendency to favour foolhardiness. Success is an argument which, here as everywhere else, is taken to legitimate foolhardy behaviour. If it worked out alright it was alright.

Significantly enough it is as trainpullers that women have shown paraphrastic attitudes to work. Here are no superiors, but everybody works for herself, in unison and cooperation with every other train-puller. The tendency to give women train-pulling shifts, as well as the fact that several women have accepted to 'go steady' in the curve has created an atmosphere where female dominance can be discerned from time to time. Here women have started to leave safe mimesis and turned to their own style and own work methods. Here the initiative passes over to the women, who set up the model. They suggest or announce new arrangements to the engine foreman, they come up with alternative routes and new solutions to problems. Men taking shifts in the curve shrink into mimesis and dare not do anything without consulting the 'steady' women.

Mimesis and paraphrase are thus not sex specific ways of relating to work. Paraphrastic methods pop up either in opposition to the established norm or when there is a gap in the hierarchy, so that the norm has no representative above you, only next to you. Time and increased skill may then turn mimesis into a new phase of appropriation of work and the paraphrastic female train-pullers step into the yard.

After a few years in the yard, as the young men reach the moment when they perform the tasks excellently, they surpass their seniors in the energy and the careless way in which they handle even the more arduous tasks. They make strength and fearlessness matter. The style, the jargon and the values that the young men express constitutes something of an oedipal revolt against the moderation and routinized practice of the seniors. The truth that 'one should never use strength, but technique' is swept away in the seemingly effortless waste of power. By paying lip service to exactly this rule the young men state that they are not using power, but technique! This is the ultimate challenge to the seniors. What is on display is not contempt for danger but technical skill and prowess!

By surpassing and overshadowing their seniors – who may shake their heads, smile and admit that 'Emil is a bit tough' – the young men appropriate and take possession of the work. They become shunters, they are no longer young men who work 'as well as' the senior shunters. They develop a style of their own. They may be difficult to work with, they may be seen as rather unorganized shunters, but they are not criticized for not knowing the ropes. Not everyone has the innate qualities that shunting demands, such as the ability to plan and see ahead, to keep several things in mind simultaneously, to possess 'split vision', or 'have psychology' in order to make the team work well together, etc., but everyone (with the exception of the incurable cases of 'coupling fright') has by now learnt to work (or mess up work!) with calm confidence or fortitude.

The style of work involves not only the display of dexterity in performing the work tasks, it is a style that is expressed in all other practices that surround the shunting work. The style of walking, the behaviour towards persons from the other work groups at Hagalund, the way forks and knives are carelessly thrown onto the tray in the canteen and the way of behaving and talking that one displays in the pay office or in contacts with the staff delegator and the managers, all these are generated from the same principle. The clash with the 'loitering' style of the 'negroes' in the hall, or the polished and reserved behaviour of the 'stair-wearers', the superior white collar staff, could not be more dramatic.

The ostentatious consumption of heavy meals, begging for second helpings at the canteen (asking the cook to add two more potatoes to make it

213

an even thirty) at tables for *'blåkläder'* (blue clothes), contrast in a similar way to the coffee and Danish pastry that engine drivers enjoy at the tables for *'gångkläder'* (walking clothes) at the other end of the canteen.

There is a homology between the different areas of practice that make up this style and it is seen as part of the personality. A similar homology is considered to exist between behaviour at work and behaviour at the card-table. The card-game exposes weakness as well as strength, 'nerves' and personal, petty greed as well as calm planning and generous solidarity. As long as the all-important aim is to establish oneself as a good shunter in the yard, the card-table is a good arena for showing *'nif'*. When other matters come to the fore, card-playing becomes just another pastime, and as such it gets boring after a while.

At the card table.

8. THE NEW ORGANIZATION

The Switchboard Plant

There had been rumours about a switchboard plant (a plant from which the switches in the yard could be controlled centrally by one or several operators) for at least three decades before construction work finally started. Scepticism about the realization of the plans was therefore widespread among the shunters until the very end, particularly among those who did not have first hand experience from meetings where the plans were discussed. Even the union representatives and the safety officer had been disillusioned at one stage or another, but they had enough information about the plans, as well as the obstacles, not to take such a nihilistic view as one of the old train-pullers who declared that the plans were just talk as it would prove impossible to make the necessary reconstructions in the yard. Hě claimed that the bottle-neck and the lack of alternative tracks would make it impossible to redirect the traffic during the necessary work-period. The planners had eventually realized the ensuing chaos and this was in fact what made the plans stay plans forever.

Construction work nevertheless commenced in 1987 and the switchboard plant was to be in operation by June 18, 1988 at 1pm. The switchboard plant was to be operated by two people, one taking care of the engine side and the train arrivals and departures, the other the shunting teams in the South. The Northern part of the yard was not to be connected, but would be operated manually, in the yard, as before.

Problems with the computer and the automatic switches in the plant were detected during tests, and two days before the stipulated date it was reported that the opening date was postponed until the 17th of September, at 1 pm.

Another notice, dated the 19th of September, corrected the opening date. Now the plans were to take the engine side into operation on October 8, while the whole signal area would be inaugurated on the 15th of the same month. The last paragraph on the notice was: "Keep you fingers crossed" ("*Håll tummarna*.").

The staff, it seems, failed to keep their fingers crossed, as the engine part of the yard was not in operation until October 14, and the rest of the Southern yard on the 26th. There had again been various technical problems, the whole plant was released (disconnected) when a train entered the New Hall underneath it.

The delay led to unforeseen complications as the nine operators appointed to the plant already received their new, much higher, salaries starting from September, while they were still working normally, as train-pullers and shunters, well into November. This was thought to be very unfair, as they thus got a higher pay for the old job. The raise in itself was questioned, too. It was seen as disproportionately high to the complexity of the task. And, finally, there were objections to the selection of the operators.

There was much speculation concerning the principles behind the selection. The only answer that ever came out of these discussions were that train-pullers (who became redundant as they were to be replaced by the switchboard plant), juniors and possibly women were favoured. The final selection was, however, not possible to understand as it was grounded in the 'ideas' of the former manager. He was considered to be a 'computer-expert' and was said to claim that he, by watching the sixteen persons invited to an introductory course, could 'see' who was suited to the job and who was not.

At least two persons quit shunting in anger over not being among the nine persons finally selected for the plant. One of them had asked the manager if he was not qualified enough for the switchboard plant. 'No, you aren't', the manager allegedly answered. This answer was seen as decisive for the resignation of the shunter and the common verdict was: 'This is no way to treat people!' The staff considered the shunter in question very clever and thought that it was beyond all doubt that the reason he was not selected to the switchboard plant was that he was such an excellent shunter that he could not be spared outdoors. They thought that it would have been proper for the manager to impart this to the shunter and by doing so perhaps prevent his resignation. As it were, the resignations came during a critical time and played a significant part in the events that were to follow.

Economic Reorganization

The preparations for the switchboard plant was the last contribution by the old manager before he retired. As it happened his retirement coincided with the start signal for the large reform program that aimed to transform SJ into a 'modern and competitive' company with a 'positive economic result' before the end of 1992.[1]

---

[1] Cf. P3,3.

VOB *(Vagntjänstområdet Hagalund, Bangårdsgruppen, Tjänsteställe 1492)*, i.e. the shunting group, was in November transformed into MTÖ–B *(Maskindivisionen, Trafikverkstadsområde Öst – Bangårdsgruppen)*. This change was not a nominal one only, but meant a profound reorganization as the group now was given economic independence, i.e. a budget of its own that was to be managed internally. In other words, what had been the National Railway Department was now to resemble an ordinary joint enterprise. Gains and losses no longer vanished into numbers in the general economy of the station, and finally the company as a whole, but were of consequence to the group. This new economic order presupposed a pricing system and the exchange of services between the different groups turned into selling and buying according to a price list based on production hours.

A price list announced the new order on the pin-board:

SHUNTING COSTS[2]

ENGINE TYPE Ue	189.00 HR
ENGINE OPERATOR	260.00 HR
SHUNTING -HEAD	260.00 HR
SHUNTING-B	260.00 HR
SHUNTING-C	260.00 HR
TKM/OUTDOOR	<u>260.00 HR</u>
	1.489.00 HR
	excl. switchboard plant
PRICE EXAMPLE	
CHANGE OF COACH TIME 30 MIN	744.50

The new system of invoicing changed the picture dramatically to the extent that a demand from the repair shop to shunt a coach into the Hall meant an economic gain to the shunting group – and an expense to the repair group – although it still naturally meant extra work for the shunting team. After the reorganization the repair shop would presumably hesitate to order coaches into the Hall for minor repairs, as this implied an additional cost, while the *tkm* would happily take on extra shunting work, selling the services of the

---

[2] All prices are stated in Swedish crowns (SEK). One may note that all shunters are estimated at a similar hourly wage. This reflects the relatively small difference in wages between different categories of shunters, and the constant mobility of persons with varying seniority within the hierarchy. Shunters otherwise get a monthly pay.

217

shunters at production cost.[3] This was therefore, in principle, a reversal of the earlier situation, where the repair shop gladly would demand coaches into the Hall in order to work under more comfortable conditions, while the role of the *tkm* would be to question and refuse 'unnecessary' requisitions.

Change of Managers

A new manager was appointed on the first of October 1988. This was a young man who had just finished an SJ course as a trainee in production management. He was considered an 'outsider' as he had neither worked in shunting nor at Hagalund. He was, however, a SJ man as he had been an engine mechanic in a provincial town for eight years. After that he had passed a management course at university level and then spent a year as a production management trainee at SJ. It is true that during the last six months of his trainee period he had been stationed at Hagalund, but as he had been working at the department of general planning his contacts with the shunting group had been close to nil.

The most surprising thing about this new manager was that he was young, only 31, and thus obviously recruited according to the new principles, which no longer favoured seniority. His youth and inexperience were not a pleasant surprise to everyone and comments like 'puppy' could occasionally be heard. More favourable commentators would say that they felt sorry for him, as it was not his fault, but SJ's, to have put such an ignorant person in that position.

The new manager immediately installed himself in a room adjoining the switchboard plant and the offices of the staff delegator and the *tkm*. Keeping his door wide open he was easily accessible to the shunters who would frequent the area in order to collect work orders, radios or signal lanterns, or just in order to check their working schedule. The former manager had had his office on the first floor in the New Hall. This was far out of the way for the shunters. There had to be a specific reason to enter this part of Hagalund, where the managers were fortified behind a reception desk in a corridor with a row of closed doors.

Even the title of the new manager was novel. It was now *produktionschef* (production manager), replacing the former *funktionschef* (function manager), although this was a change that escaped many of the shunters who simply changed from Antte (Antonsson, the old manager) to Barring (the name of the

---

[3] The production cost is calculated on the basis of wage hour for the team.

new manager), or 'this Berring-or-Borring-or-whatever-his-name-is', when talking about the manager.

An abrupt and definite break with the past, and one which did definitely not escape the shunters, was marked by the forms under which the old manager was succeeded. Instead of being appointed *produktionschef* in the new organization, the old manager was simply set aside to await his retirement only a few months later. Disappointed in not being promoted, he wrote a letter distributed to all staff at *bangårdsgruppen*. In this letter he described his feelings after being 'flushed', interpreting the general situation as troubled. The letter starts: "<u>1 October 1988</u> unrest prevails in the Hagalund camp. Many feel bad, very bad. A bitter after-taste!" [4]

Many shunters probably agreed to this description of the state of affairs in general, although several of them openly declared that they thought that Antte now, as one shunter put it, had been given 'a taste of his own medicine' (referring to what was seen as a clearly unfair selection of staff to the switchboard plant). Others – particularly persons slightly higher up in the hierarchy – were critical to such a treatment of a manager who had served the company for 47 years. 'This is no way to treat people!' was again the phrase of the day.

In general it can be said that there were no strong feelings for or against either of the managers, the old or the new. If there were such feelings they were at least not aired openly. The worries concerned more general and deep-going problems and it was felt that the situation could not be affected much by the actions or lack of actions from the manager.

Deepening Crisis

The change of management in the shunting group did not raise any expectations of improvement. It was, if anything, rather seen as an additional problem. What could such a young and unexperienced puppy achieve? The problems were in addition stemming from societal factors outside both the shunting group and Hagalund.

Jobs elsewhere were well paid and abundant, the youth of today better educated, the railway oldfashioned, and shunting dirty and cumbersome. Who could expect the youngsters to even consider starting to work as shunters? All this could not be changed by a new manager. To start with, wages had to be

---

[4]"<u>1 oktober 1988</u> råder oro i Hagalundslägret. Många mår dåligt, mycket dåligt. En bitter eftersmak!"

raised radically, but there seemed to be no such possibilities. The company would never agree to that, they would rather close down Hagalund! Even if they gave way to local wage increases – to ward of a situation of emergency – the union would never accept that one group of shunters were better payed than others.

The 'solidary wage politics' *(solidariska lönepolitiken)* that the central union had announced was a well known concept.[5] At times it even seemed that the union potentially was a bigger obstacle than the company. There was therefore talk about leaving the union, and rumours had it that several shunters already had done so. This was remarkable, but it was felt that the union fees were good for nothing. 'What does the union do for us? Soon we will have the lowest wages in Sweden!' Such opinions might have represented the most extreme ones, but they were nevertheless valid currency in the ongoing debate.

That there were few expectations attached to the new manager in such a chaotic situation was clearly confirmed by the first information meeting that Barring advertised. This first one – two were scheduled – was to be held on the 9th of November 1988 at 9.30, in the new conference room, just opposite the locker-rooms. At the appointed time the manager was waiting, skimming through a folder with transparencies, over-head projector lit and humming.

Only one person turned up at the information meeting – the anthropologist. The shunters claimed that 9.30 was a very unsuitable time for a meeting as the teams would be busy both in the South and the North. This was undoubtedly true, but the fact that no one expected the information to be important or new was another factor. I can confirm that their suspicions were correct to a large extent. I asked Barring about what he had intended to say at the meeting and we had a talk about his background and plans. Finally he lent me the transparencies to read.

The transparencies were standard SJ information. Facts about the recent development, plans for the future and the reorganization and slogans encouraging enhanced efforts.[6] Such information paralleled information presented to the public, stressing the aim to transform SJ into a modern company successfully competing with other forms of transportation. Apart

---

[5] Swedish labour market agreements and union policies have been centralized to a high degree. For a review in English, cf. GUSTAFSSON, *passim.*

[6] The efforts to enhance the collective company spirit have increased during the reorganization, but the group feeling of the shunters (at Hagalund, but also in the rest of SJ) has always been looked upon with some amazement. I felt that my study was seen by the managers as one which might provide the company with a 'key to success', a recipe to be used on more problematic groups. Christina Garsten describes the complete opposite; a company actively trying to introduce such a spirit from the top downwards, not sucking it up from the bottom. Cf. GARSTEN, 82 ff.

from arousing discontent because of the implied hints that the workers were not working hard enough, such information could be interpreted in very different ways by the shunters. A modern railway company, with fixed high-speed trains and automatic couplings, can seem incompatible with the oldfashioned manual shunting. Will such a development then mean that the shunters are threatened by redundancy? Or is there reason to rejoice at the prospect of the shunting becoming less arduous, dirty and uncomfortable?

What was good for Swedish society, e.g. low unemployment rates, was not good for the shunting group as the group was being deserted and the status of the job was lowered. Maybe the same might hold for SJ versus the shunters? What was good for SJ might not be good for the shunting group. The most rational handling of trains was perhaps one which eliminated shunting altogether? This uncertainty about how to interpret the information in terms of concrete consequences for 'me and you' was one reason why it generally was shunned and looked down upon.

Barring seemed slightly apologetic when handing me the transparencies with SJ information and murmured that he had planned to present only some of it as a general introduction. What he himself was more enthusiastic about were the local plans, the immediate future of the shunting group. This was a part of the information that certainly would have been of greater interest to the shunters, too, as it concerned them personally.

One of these local projects was already initiated; the radio-controlled engines. 25 persons had applied to be educated as operators for such engines and the goal was to have eight operators chartered before Christmas. The first course had four pupils and subsequent courses were to have two pupils each. The requirement was that the operator was educated as a shunt leader. The shunters seemed to be interested in taking on the driving and, perhaps surprisingly, so were the engine drivers. By taking over the driving themselves the shunters were said to save 30 engine drivers. The drivers were, according to the club chairman, not afraid of becoming redundant, only happy to get rid of the boring shunting shifts.

1024, the shunters' union club, had no objections to taking over the driving and the manager was very pleased with the local club, which was easy to deal with. He compared 1024 to the union in the repair shop which, according to him, only obstructed development. In that group management and union had failed to come to any agreements. Plans for a projected defrosting hall had been obstructed due to the union, and in the face of any other demand the union was very quick to announce go-slows or over-time blockades. The shunters, 1024, were reasonable. One could always discuss sensibly with them, Barring said.

The staff turn-over among the shunters was much lower than the one in the Hall, for example, where 48 out of 50 new employees left very quickly. The shunting group was in comparison a problem free group and the manager thought that the successful beginnings of this first project, the radio-controlled engines, made the future promising. The possibility of making the job more interesting by offering a change of tasks would make people more satisfied and less likely to leave.

As no shunter turned up at the information meeting, however, Barring quickly decided to cancel the scheduled second meeting the next day and he rushed off, looking not crushed but rather determined to skip such soft tactics. This was probably the last time the transparencies saw the projector light.

Acute Crisis

On November 16 (still 1988) an introductory course for newly employed started. The three pupils at this course turned out to be the last to be employed for years to come. For some years such courses had been arranged about twice a year counting 4-7 pupils at a time.

Not only was it difficult, not to say impossible, to recruit new shunters, but there was increasing restlessness among the senior shunters. Breaks were now often used for scrutinizing job advertisements in the stacks of newspapers that the knockers would bring up from the trains. The destinies of shunters who had quit the group were discussed, and it was reported from persons who had been in contact with them that they were earning 'much more' now and were very satisfied with their decision to leave SJ. Even shunters who had been working at Hagalund for more than twenty years started to talk about looking for employment elsewhere.

The uncertainty seemed to have a snowball effect. The more people who discussed the great expectations obviously awaiting them outside the SJ gates, the more hopeless and worthless did it seem to stay at Hagalund. Injustice in pay and promotion, an uncertain future – probably including rationalizations and cuts in shunting – more work for those who stayed on, more night shifts, finally even closure of Hagalund altogether, etc., such were the rumours and judgments that circulated. To an observer the picture of rats leaving – or trying to leave – a sinking ship could easily come into mind.

Although there was some enthusiasm about the radio-controlled engines there were complications as well. The plan seemed to be that the company was going to save a lot of money not only by replacing expensive engine drivers with cheap shunters, but that the operator of the engine later was going to be forced to work as shunt leader simultaneously. Two jobs in one! The shunters, naive as ever, would in the end find that they had been deceived.

Other savings were also planned. Two *tkm* outdoors and one indoors were to be abolished. This had been decided over the head of the union, causing much discontent. Also the 'extra B-members' were going to be withdrawn. One shunter angrily asked at a union meeting whether all the money the company was saving was going to cover the costs of the managers' salaries. It was known that the new general manager of SJ had a salary that was astronomical compared to the shunters'.

The comradeship was discussed, too, and there were many complaints about the lack of solidarity. No one seemed to care about his fellow worker any longer. Envy, meanness and bad feelings had replaced the former good ambiance. One shunter said that one no longer was interested in changing shifts with others. Others were given salary grades and appointments so they could just as well work their own uncomfortable shifts. Why was he to help them? The only reason he stayed on was because of the days off. 'That's not the way it should be', he said. Another shunter summed up his views: 'This is no bloody charity. I'm not going to help no bugger, because no bugger helps me!'

The first of January 1989 there were only 10-11 persons on the reserve list, most of whom could only work as C-members. The saving of three *tkm*-shifts did not help the situation much. Two *tkm* had retired, making it difficult to fill the vacancies anyhow. There was great need to train new *tkm* and shunt leaders, but as many shifts already had to be covered by over-time work it was not possible to put people on training shifts. The shunters were more than dissatisfied. The situation was becoming unbearable. There had been a spell of days when no one had recorded the coaches on reserve, which made it 'impossible' to shunt.

The most notorious *'gnetare'*, over-timers, were using the opportunity to make extra money, and even people who had refused to do over-time for decades found themselves talked into taking an extra shift in order to help out. The over-time quota, 200 hours per year, were therefore quickly filling up – and it was only early spring. The way things were going, there would be no over-time left when the summer holidays started to drain the staff even further. The union agreed to a dispensation, raising the quota to 230 hours/year, but it simultaneously announced that **no** further dispensations were going to be admitted.

The manager had observed the apparently never ending line of resignations with growing despair. One resignation per week was definitely not a rate that the shunting group could manage. Five large advertisements in the evening papers – in the sports pages, as these were thought to be read by the right kind of people – had resulted in only three telephone calls. However, when the prospective applicants heard what kind of pay they were offered they immediately lost interest. The situation called for a radical solution.

When the manager assumed his duties in October he already talked about the possibility of introducing some kind of a bonus for the staff, as money was saved through operating the radio-controlled engines. It was not easy to imagine how such a bonus could be shaped. The shunters talked about a possible bonus-system as if it were to be based on faultless shunting. Delays and damage to coaches or recruitment of extra staff would mean a reduction from a certain predetermined sum. A small yard in Stockholm, dealing only with goods, had such a system, but the conditions were radically different there. There were naturally jokes that the shunters, if such a system were to be introduced, would end up paying the company instead, but the more serious comments touched upon the impossible task of finding out whose fault it was that a train was late or a coach damaged. 'We have been accused of damaging coaches that were damaged on arrival' and 'If a coach is taken out for a last minute repair they still blame us for the delay', were some of these comments.

In January the rumours of the introduction of a bonus-system became more persistent and were verified by more authorized persons. It seemed that the bonus would not be of the 'no-wreckage' kind, but rather as a payment for extra work. A large colourful announcement on the pin-board called all shunting staff to an information meeting on February 1. Time: 18.30. Place: The Canteen. A list of all staff was attached and everyone was required to mark his/her name with a cross to indicate how many sandwiches and light beers were to be ordered. I added my name to the list.

The Information Meeting

The canteen was crowded when the meeting started. Some 60 shunters had filled the tables and I found no place close to the improvised 'podium' where the manager and a man from the planning section had seated themselves. The meeting started as all union meetings start, everyone helping himself to sandwiches, beer and coffee. Normally the treat is consumed in silence, but this time the sound-level indicated that discussions were going on at all tables. I do not think that the excitement I felt was of my own imagination.

Barring then opened the meeting by 'introducing' himself (sic) and the man from the planning department. He said that he wanted to 'develop the group', which was a term that he had used several times before. So far, he added, it had worked out beyond expectation and he mentioned the radio-controlled engines. However, the over-heated labour market had caused severe problems and he gave an account of the poor response to the advertisements. The labour agreements made it 'very difficult' to raise the wages. The only possibility to 'evade' the agreements was to introduce a bonus. The bonus that Barring suggested was going to give an extra income of up to 2.000 SEK per month. However, a warrant was needed 'for Cst' in order to justify that this group would earn more money than other shunters doing similar jobs. The counter-performance that he called for was an increased workload.

A voice in the crowd asked: 'What does the union say?' but Barring fended off the question quickly by saying that the union meeting next week would tell us that. He added that if everyone agreed here and now to his suggestion, the union would not have anything to say. 'Would they?' Even to the less observant participants it now became obvious that one person was absent; the shop steward. He had earlier mentioned that he did not intend to participate, saying: 'I'm already informed!'

Barring presented two possible future scenarios. The first one was accepting the bonus. If the meeting decided in favour of the bonus, the next step would be to construct new work schedules that would be scrutinized by the union representatives. Then a trial month would commence. If everything worked out during that month the arrangements would be made permanent. If, on the other hand, the meeting decided to vote against the bonus 'other measures' had to be taken. This was the other scenario.

The second scenario was a gloomy one, indeed. Choosing that one equalled choosing the road to liquidation. The radio-engines would be first to go. The second step would be to sell out the shunting to other stations and try to decrease the workload that way. One thing was sure: there was no possibility to continue as before. Something had to be done – immediately.

Barring distributed papers drafting the outline of the proposed reorganization:

ORGANIZATION PROPOSAL
MANAGER
FOREMEN [INDOOR TKM]
OCBG [STINSEX]
COACH RECORDER
SWITCHBOARD PLANT OPERATORS

THE NORTHERN YARD

Ue ENGINE 1   Ue ENGINE 2/3
(DAILY 00:00-24.OO)   (MON-FRI DAYSHIFT)
DRIVER/TEAM FOREMAN   DRIVER/TEAM FOREMAN
DRIVER/SHUNTER   DRIVER/SHUNTER
SHUNTER   SHUNTER
UP/UNCOUPLER   TKM   UP/UNCOUPLER

THE SOUTHERN YARD

T21 ENGINE 3
DAILY. DAY SHIFT
ENGINE DRIVER (TO BE HIRED)[7]
TEAM FOREMAN/TKM
SHUNT LEADER
SHUNTER
UP/UNCOUPLER

The only changes that were discernible according to this proposal concerned the outdoor staff. In the North the *tkm* would serve two teams, each of which had in addition a driver/team foreman (a term formerly unknown), a driver/shunter, a second shunter and finally a combined knocker and C-member (up/uncoupler).

One of the engines, Engine 1, was to run round the clock, while the other one, Engine 2, was doing a day-shift during week days only. In the South there was to be only one engine, a diesel one, on a day-shift. Engine 3, as this Southern engine was to be called, would replace the former Engines 2 and 3. It would require a hired driver, as there were no radio-controlled diesel engines as yet. The rest of this team would consist of a combined 'team foreman' and

---

[7] Ue engines are normal electric engines, now remote controlled and operated by shunters. T21 is a diesel engine, which requires an engine driver, to be hired from the engine depot.

tkm, a shunt leader, a shunter and a similar knocker-cum-C-member as in the teams in the North.

The new nomenclature in the teams suggested an altered distribution of tasks, and there were a few confused voices asking what the driver and the *tkm* were supposed to do. Barring answered that the driver would be responsible for the team, while the *tkm* would have 'cooperative' functions, just as before. He then swept away several similar questions concerning details by calling them *turlistetekniska* (work schedule technicalities). 'It would be to carry things too far to start discussing them here. The **important** thing is that all must be made to work.'

He then brought the matter to its point and asked: 'What do you think? Shall we give it a try or shall we flush it here and now?' There was a long silence. Then one of the younger shunters rose and said with a loud voice: 'I think we should go for it!' (*'Jag tycker vi kör!'*) He quickly added that he thought that there should be reinforcement in the winter. Barring said that there naturally would be reinforcement when needed. He then again directed the attention from details to a more general level saying that the goal was that **everyone should be able to do all the different tasks in the team**. Given the situation this had not been possible. But this was the ultimate goal. This brought the questions to a halt.

After a short interval someone asked when the trial month was to start. Barring replied without hesitation: 'On March 1.' A sough of astonishment swept the room.

Someone else asked who was going to work out the time schedules. Barring referred to the man from the planning department. There was laughter from a table where some of the oldtimers sat. One of them commented to his fellows at the table: 'The expert works out the schedules and we look at them!' Another one leaned forward: 'That's how it should be. The *turlistekommitté* (the union's schedule committee) shall **only** examine the schedule, nothing else.' They smiled contentedly, convinced that the suggestions **really** would be scrutinized. It seemed they thought that this would mean the end of the proposal.

Then the heated topic of the bonus was dropped and standard issues, which can be found in the union protocols all the way back to the founding of the union club in 1942, came on the agenda. These were questions about security, about the lack of working clocks and telephones, the need for more education, the lack of information and the bad cooperation between the shunting group, the engine shed and the repair shop. Barring commented the different problems involved and pointed at measures that had been taken towards solving them.

227

The meeting was thus closed with an air of almost amiable 'routine-complaints'. Barring and the man from the planning department left hastily after this, all but ritual, questioning, while some of the unusually large congregation of shunters stayed behind in small groups discussing the big news of the day.

During this informal discussion one of the shunters said that he did not trust Barring and that he suspected him to have something up his sleeve. Were there going to be more trains in the future, or were there going to be less trains due to more *spetsvändningar* (lit.: 'peak turns', meaning trains that turn immediately, without being shunted)?

The man who had raised his voice in favour of the bonus proposal said that the 2,000 crowns clearly was the decisive factor as far as he was concerned. Another shunter, one of the most eager over-timers, commented that he earned the same amount of money in two over-time shifts. 'Two-and-a-half', his comrade corrected, adding: 'Sure, but then I don't have to go down and work those shifts.'

Other comments blended in as an indirect defence of the bonus reform, still, however, carefully avoiding explicitly supporting it:

'I don't mind the extra work. If I come down here I might as well work. What's the point of sitting here doing nothing?'

'It has really been too lax the last months. Look at the breaks we've had!' Scepticism and reservation was necessary towards any proposal issued from above – and in this case in addition from an inexperienced outsider 'puppy'.

Summing up the meeting in terms of the public comments and points of view one can say that there was no opposition voiced against the bonus as such. There were questions, which most probably were intended as objections, but for the protocol they could be seen as unclear points only demanding clarification. The answers were at least not questioned further.

It can be noticed in passing that three women – out of the total of four in the yard at the time – voiced their opinions in the discussion. About half of the comments and questions concerning the reorganization were actually made by the women.

As opposed to the comments that were voiced publicly there were many comments that were passed between the shunters. Some were openly hostile, some were more sceptical, some indirectly supportive, but despite certain misgivings and a few sour faces, even one of the most notorious sceptics and complainers seemed to be in higher spirits than he had been for a long time. The long period of uncertainty when rumours abounded now seemed to have come to an end. There was a direction to move towards, even if the proposal had turned out to be more of an ultimatum than a suggestion. One did not have to agree with the reorganization, but at least something definite was happening.

Confronting the Indoor *Tkm*

One of the shunters on the union club board told me on our way to the information meeting that the question about introducing a bonus was a large decision that could not be taken in a trice. It had to be discussed by the union, locally and centrally, etc. However, one hour later it was decided to give the bonus system a try.

One week after the information meeting, the first week in February, there was a meeting of the foremen, i.e. the indoor *tkm* and Barring. Before the meeting Barring said, as I passed his office: 'You didn't think the bonus idea would work,[8] but now there will be a bonus and then I'll put life into the foremen!' I asked: 'What about the union?', but Barring dismissed the question and said that the union was 'OK'. 'I have talked to the shop steward and there's no problem.' The drastic cuts in the teams would not cause problems either, he assured me in reply to my question. The task of keeping watch on the tracks was going to be reduced and thus also the number of shunters. 'Forward there is no need to keep watch as the area is fenced, and backwards there is no need to repeat signals as the driver can now stand at the rear of the cut himself.'

My objections were obviously of no import to Barring. The thing that occupied his mind at the moment was the meeting that was about to start in a few minutes. Barring told me what I already knew, i.e. that he was going to withdraw the five *tkm*-positions and then only reannounce three of them. 'Now I'm going to give it to that bugger in there', he whispered to me with suppressed anger. 'I mustn't get angry. I mustn't get angry. I'll only tell him that **I** am in charge now.' He then collected himself and said in a normal tone of voice that it maybe was time to start the meeting and we crossed the corridor and entered the conference room.

There were three *tkm* at the meeting. On entering one of them demonstratively smoothed the table top where the coffee usually would stand and asked Barring jokingly where the coffee was. Barring explained seriously but apologetically that they would have to get their coffee later at the union's expense. There was a slight embarrassment as Barring answered the joke with

---

[8] I had raised doubts about a bonus system based on avoiding damage.

such a grave expression on his face. This had the effect of muffling the joking mood and there was a short silence before Barring started the meeting without any formalities.

The demands on the foremen had been raised constantly, he said, and this was why the foreman-meetings had been started. The old head-foreman-level had disappeared and now there would only be 'shift-foremen'. These new foremen would be in charge of staff and short-term planning. In the future it would be necessary for the foremen to be able to operate the switchboard plant and help out in emergencies.

A new computer-system would also be introduced, making it possible to localize each coach and check whether it was repaired, the tanks filled, etc. But such a system called for portable computers and could not be brought into action within the next two years. This was going to be a pilot project as far as SJ was concerned and therefore SJ would lend a hand. People would be coming to Hagalund to study the results. Barring stated all this as simple facts and there were no interruptions or visible reactions.

When he was finished one of the *tkm* spoke up. He protested against the increased duties, saying that one was pressed for time already today. 'Isn't that so?', he said and turned to his colleague next to him. Before anyone could answer Barring said: 'I'm talking about responsibility, not the daily work.' The *tkm* continued, taking an example from the week before when someone had taken ill on a Saturday and there were three shifts to be filled. 'If there is no staff, what shall we do then?' Barring said that the foremen were an elite, and that this was the reason they were foremen in the first place. Therefore it must be possible to demand more from them. The foremen have to *'ställa upp'* (approx.: play ball). This remark obviously irritated the *tkm* as he said in a voice that could not conceal his anger: *'Ställa upp!* I've been doing it for forty years, but what do I get for it?...' Barring cut him short by saying: '**I'm** in charge now! No more fuss about this! I'm not talking about peak loads or catastrophies, in which case there will be reinforcements. I'm talking about everyday work. The foremen will naturally get increased authorization, too.' 'What authorization? We already have it!', the irate *tkm* replied angrily.

There was then a long discussion of the future transformation of the tasks and work hours for the foremen, in which Barring's key phrase again was *'ställa upp'*. Also the other groups, such as the repair shop and the spare part store, were eagerly discussed. Their lack of organization and efficiency, their unwillingness to cooperate, and their lack of 'feeling' for their tasks was a subject which everyone could agree upon.

Barring summed up the discussion by saying that there seemed to a lack of insight concerning the fact that everyone was dependent on everyone else, and one of the *tkm* said that earlier every group had been protective of its own territory *(revirtänkande)*. Barring immediately stressed the importance of the newly initiated meetings of the foremen from the whole station in order to counteract that every group guarded their own interests instead of cooperating. 'The repair shop thinks that we are peevish, too. Everone thinks that no one else does anything,' he said.

The conclusive point was a discussion about the difficulty in recruiting new staff. This was the first question that Barring admitted he was unable to reply and he said it was one of great concern, too. 'The recruiting-officer is desperate.' Comparisons with the salaries of the shunters at the underground were unfavourable for SJ. In this connection someone mentioned graffiti, a word which immediately gave rise to a swarm of comments about 'The kind of society we live in'. 'The police are not even authorized to take the spray cans away from kids who destroy trains and stations with graffiti.' Everyone agreed that there was too much weakness on the part of the society. It was thought that the general trend was to 'coddle' delinquent youngsters too much.

This subject was one which everyone could agree upon and the meeting ended on a tone of consonance. All the *tkm* and Barring left the room chatting amiably about the society and where we were all heading. Compared to the problems of the wider society the problems of the shunting group already seemed smaller and easier to handle.

The shunting group was still a good group. One did not have to look further than to the other groups at Hagalund to find that they had larger problems recruiting competent staff – or recruiting staff at all. In addition, they were not very well organized, and above all, they were caught in oldfashioned thinking, unable to see beyond the limits of their own group. They could not grasp the totality and adjust and plan in accordance with the needs of the entire station.

It seemed that Barring had also succeeded in delivering the message that the outside world was the one to set the conditions for the changes. Staff had to be recruited or otherwise the shunting group would fall into the same hopelessness as the groups in the Hall. By being able to train more people for different tasks, and by even taking on new tasks, such as driving the engines themselves (there had been mention of driving diesel engines, too, in the future) the shunters would have smaller costs, and also less involvement and problems with the other groups. New drives had started to bridge the gaps between the foremen of the different groups and the greater understanding would also benefit the shunters. If the last instances of defending one's own turf could be extinguished from the shunting group, too, the workload would not be that much greater. Rationalization would on the contrary make the work more varied, more flexible, and thus more interesting.

An observer certainly got the impression that despite the resistance at the beginning of the meeting, the parties had reached an agreement about the roots of the problems and that in their concern for the future of the shunting group, everyone had, however reluctantly, agreed to the cuts demanded by the introduction of the bonus.

However, the congenial end of the meeting had been, if not an illusion, at least a consensus which was only skin deep. Feelings were momentarily calm, permitting normal intercourse, but no conciliation had occurred and none was forthcoming. Soon after this meeting the *tkm*, who seemingly had calmed down and consented to the changes to come, went on sick leave and never returned to the workplace before his retirement, two years later.

The Union Club Meeting

A couple of hours later the manager formally informed the union club about the bonus reorganisation. There were fourteen persons present at the start of the meeting and five more, delayed for reasons of work, were to enter later during the meeting. This represented only about a third of the club members and likewise about a third of the number present at the Information Meeting one week earlier. The majority has also been present at that meeting.

As usual, the place of the meeting was the canteen. There was not much news, but the discussion had an altogether different character from the large Information Meeting. The number of participants and the union framework induced an atmosphere of collectivity, however weak, and the contributions took the form of warnings and advice about what 'we' should do. The fact that the manager, Barring, was present in the beginning did not visibly change the tone or the subject of the discussion.

The bonus was now put into a somewhat longer term perspective and Barring was asked about the term of the bonus agreement. He reassured that the bonus was an agreement on par with the biannual time-tables and would, when signed, hold as long as the time-table it referred to. As the bonus was motivated by an extra work effort it was natural that the relation between time-table and work schedule would be the foundation of the bonus agreement.

One of the shunters predicted that the bonus would incite the other groups to look for compensation for their lack of bonus. 'In one year', he said, 'we will work 150% but all the others will have reached agreements about compensations and have the same wages as we do, without doing extra work. 'It's a damned big risk.' He said that the agreement therefore should contain a guarantee to safeguard the bonus against such strivings. Trying to clinch the argument about the possibility for other groups to get some kind of compensation, Barring answered that there was no way of finding money for pay rises unless there was an increased work achievement. If any other group wanted a bonus they would have to do similar savings as the shunters had done.

The shunter also summed up the view of the shunters about the bonus, as he conceived it. In his opinion all the young shunters were in favour of the bonus, while the seniors were negative. He stressed that it was important to let the positive attitude continue. If the bonus were to vanish the youngsters would simply leave.

He thus indirectly referred to the problems there had been finding young people willing to take up shunting. Right before this union meeting this man had mentioned that **he** had not been sitting next to the telephone when the alleged five – or three, the number varied – persons called to inquire about the shunting job. He said that there had been 70 applicants for similar jobs in the marshalling yard adjacent to Hagalund, and that they had taken the ones they found interesting and then only forwarded three persons to Hagalund. He therefore concluded that he had no way of knowing with 100 % certainty that the attempts to recruit new staff corresponded to the description being offered.

At the meeting he did not mention these surmises. On the contrary, he dwelt on the difficulties of recruiting new staff as a given fact and recommended the bonus-reform as a way to keep and perhaps attract more youngsters into the job. He no doubt judged the possibility of losing additional familiar young faces to be larger than the probability that new staff could be recruited, despite assurances to the contrary from management and union head. Although he took a stand for the bonus he nevertheless added: 'We'll sure have to toil...'

Contrary to what one could have expected the most heated feelings were aroused when the topic of the portable radios was brought up. The kind in use was considered useless. 'It is easier to win on Lotto than to reach *tkm* on the radio', the club chairman said. One shunter suggested using carrier-pigeons instead. A chorus of voices added: 'Distress! Terrible! Awful!' A *tkm* said sourly: 'They get extra money from the *tkm* now...'

To sum up one can say that there were no serious suggestions about turning down the bonus-schedule, only a comment about making sure the money was pension-founding and a warning against taking on extra work for monetary compensation as such compensations only meant a relative advantage that soon could be paralleled among the other groups in other agreements.

It seemed difficult to imagine what work would be like in the future and it also seemed difficult to object to the scheme as there were no possible alternatives. The conditions of the day were easier to comment and the issue of the portable radios obviously became a scape-goat for frustrated feelings and general, but undirected, discontent.

Anticipating the Bonus – Reactions among Staff

In retrospect it is easy to see the Information Meeting as a turning point. The staff here agreed to try the proposal from Barring, with the ultimate aim of accepting it in case it could be considered to 'work'. As we could see there were no discussions at the meeting about how the evaluation would be executed, or how a decision would be reached in case there were differing opinions about whether it 'worked' or not. At the union meeting I inquired about this, but was met with complete lack of understanding. 'We'll see if it works or not' was the curt answer from the chairman and, as far as I could judge from the the faces around me, this answer was thought to be proper and self-evident.

Later on I also tried to bring this subject up in other contexts, such as the small groups in the coffee-room, but the result was the same. It just did not seem to be thought of as a possibility that there could be disagreement about whether the new organization 'worked'. Despite all uncertainty, the differing opinions and even the animosity that had poisoned the atmosphere lately, it was assumed that the answer to the question would be obvious to everyone. It was considered to be a question of technicality, not opinion or evaluation.

If the Information Meeting turned out to be the start signal for the reorganization, this was far from evident at the time. It did have the effect of drawing the attention away from some other subjects. Matters concerning the staff in the switchboard plant and their salaries were pushed into the background. One of the shunters, who was suffering from an injury and was unable to work outdoors for a longer period of time, had been trained as an operator in the switchboard plant. This was accepted by the ordinary staff, although some operators grumbled about the switchboard plant being used as a 'dump'. When the injured shunter in addition was given shifts in the switchboard plant while some of the ordinary staff instead were given shifts outdoors, in the shunting, on their 'blank days'[9] the reaction was strong and complaints were made to the staff delegator. The switchboard plant was not to be turned into an 'infirmary'. These very upset reactions diminished at the prospect of the new bonus-schedule. The question was naturally how the demands for an 'increased workload' were going to affect the switchboard plant. In case of cuts in staff the 'blank days' would perhaps vanish and the problem with sick persons taking over would be solved by itself?

The opinions about the bonus varied and so did the ways in which they were expressed. Some persons discussed the bonus scheme as such, others details of it, while others only discussed it by indirect references: 'I've seen a B-memeber who refused to uncouple an engine next to him saying that it wasn't his job. That's not how it is supposed to be.' There was outright bullying, too. 'Well, you were one of those buggers who wanted the bonus!' one of the *tkm* allegedly said to a switchboard plant operator, who defended himself by saying that he could not know whether the suggestion was good or bad until he tried it.

Under the veil of passing as jokes a little exchange of opinions was made with the aid of a crash helmet that had been lying on the TV-set for a period of time. Some time after the Information Meeting someone had written 'Lars "Bonus" Marklund' on the front of the helmet.[10] It was easy to guess who the designer was, as there was one person, Bengt-Gunnar, who was known for such odd practical jokes. After a few days, however, the sign was replaced by a new one saying: 'Bengt-Gunnar "Supernumerary" Karlsson'. By writing only these three words in reply the writer could thus both point out who the anonymous culprit was as well as ascribe him a motive for his opposing the bonus reform.

The antagonists represented the young and the old, respectively. There was a clear hint of the otherwise suppressed opposition between the strength and ability of the young and the increasing infirmity of the old. To be 'supernumerary' was naturally not a fear that was realistic in the sense that the older ones ever would have to fear being laid off because of decreasing strength, but with growing age the risk of infirmity and different ailments, necessitating a move to some other task, was naturally increasing. The bonus, demanding a higher work-speed, favoured the young and demanded a pace of

---

[9] 'Blank days' in the schedules of the operators indicated shifts which were supernumerary, after all shifts in the plant had been filled. These blank days would then be filled with work in the yard, or some other task. Cf. Chapter 3: 'The staff delegator'.

[10] Lars Marklund was the name of the young shunter who stood up at the Information Meeting and said: 'I think we should go for it.'

work, which the older ones feared could not be kept up during a whole shunting career. Instead of enjoying increasing prestige along with increasing age, there was now the possibility that the seniors would have to face an existence as second rate shunters during the last years before retirement. It was therefore an existential fear of not being the kind of person who was sought after any longer that was activated by the expression 'supernumerary'.

Suddenly strength, speed and flexible 'go' had come into fashion. Reliability, routine, know-how and security were obviously not objected to, but these attributes seemed somehow to be oldfashioned and not quite enough. It could be assumed that the elder workers had a fear of not being able to live up to the new demands and this was cruelly exposed by the silent messenger, an old and safe, but nevertheless supernumerary, crash helmet.

New Schedules

One of the influential shunters, active in the union, explained to interested young listeners in the coffee-room that all these novel reforms and changes were in fact not new at all. In the 1960s there had been similar efforts at rationalization. History repeated itself. The attempts in the 1960s had finally disappeared into thin air as they turned out to be unrealistic and unsuitable for the circumstances. The shunting job was not the kind of work that could be rationalized as its volume was unpredictable and varied from day to day and as efforts to increase the work-speed inexorably led to a clash with considerations about safety.

The attempts to rationalize the shunting work during earlier decades, above all in the 1960s, constitutes one of the popular genres of stories about the past. One story often told is the one about a time and motion-study man who followed a team, dutifully recording the time needed to shunt the trains on the work-schedule. Not familiar with the shunting, however, he was not able to understand the work process as a whole and the team steamed off to the Middle Yard shunting carriages to and fro, finally returning with the same carriages they had left with. The time-study man never realized that the whole trip was done just in order to pull his leg and destroy his records. Another story tells of the time and motion-study man who came out into the yard in low shoes in the winter. After a quarter of an hour of (in two senses) bootless plodding through the snow he gave up the efforts to chase the team across the yard and retreated to the warmth of the Hall. It was said that he never appeared in the yard again.

These stories stress the unique character of the shunting job and the ignorance of the surrounding world – especially referring to 'experts' and planners – about the conditions prevailing in the shunting yard. Attempts from the 'outside' to intrude and tell the shunters about more efficient ways of doing things were doomed as futile. The moral of the stories is unambiguous in this respect.[11]

These stories were now given a rerun in the coffee-room and the above mentioned shunter concluded that the new 'bonus-whims' (*'bonusgrillerna'*) were not even worth fighting against. Being completely unrealistic they would collapse, wither away and vanish by themselves. The new manager wanted to make an impression, but he had no knowledge of the shunting practice and this was now the sad result. All the shunters had to do, however, was to go along and wait for time to tell. Regrettably, he said, there would probably have to be an accident before the management would abolish these whims and return things back to normal.

The body one could have expected to act against the bonus-proposal was naturally the union. The chairman of the union club summed up the situation, however, by saying that the choice they were facing was one 'between the plague and the black death' (*'mellan pest och digerdöden'*, sic.) . From this point of view there was not much action to be taken. One could only study the work schedule proposals very carefully and then push to make the most of them.

On February 14 the chairman was already going through the second proposal for work schedules. Sitting in the coffee-room with a red pencil and a determined look on his face he scanned the lists as if this was something he had been doing daily for years. His keen eyes wandered over the columns while he snorted every now and then and made little quick corrections in red. There was no doubt that everyone who watched him received an impression of routine and know-how. He had earlier stressed the general lack of knowledge in the union about the construction of a correct schedule-key and complained that even at the district level he was asked to do the job as the others did not feel competent enough for the task.

The expressive body-language of the chairman claimed as well as displayed his authority in this matter. Anyone who was dissatisfied or who had specific criticism towards the proposal could seemingly only lean over his shoulder

---

[11] The main objection did obviously not come from a fear that the shunters would have to work faster, as they normally suspect that the company will try to make them work slower. It is rather their conviction that they know the most sensible way of working, and that this was demonstrated. Productivity is here seen a natural side-effect of good and sensibly organized work. On standardization as a means for central control cf. PFAFFENBERGER 1992, 293 f.

and point out the deficiencies, but this unspoken challenge was not accepted and the chairman could work without interference from the shunters in the coffee-room. Now no one could claim not to have had a chance to influence the schedule. All evidence showed that the chairman enjoyed unwavering confidence from his club. They let him organize their work hours without as much as a glance over his shoulder.

The results of his corrections would first be presented at a club meeting and then they would be forwarded to Barring. As the chairman as well as the secretary of the club were going on vacation shortly afterwards, there could be no meeting until the beginning of March. The chairman planned it to be on the 2nd of March. However, Easter, with its peak traffic, was coming up and Barring suggested that the trial month should start on the 1st of April, instead of the 1st of March. April would constitute a more 'normal' month. This was accepted.

New Teams

Another preparation for the trial month was the formation of new teams. On February 21 sheets of paper were pinned to the board listing the names of the six newly appointed team leaders. These were all selected on the basis of seniority. In the space underneath the shunters were supposed to fill in their names according to taste. Some shunters took for granted that they were restricted by the free-day periods, i.e. that one had to choose a team leader who had the same free-days as oneself, but this requirement was not stated anywhere, only indicated by a date, signifying which Sunday-duty the *tkm* in question had at the moment. However, the teams were to be constructed from scratch and it would not matter which of the teams one chose, as the free-day groups would be adjusted accordingly.

The team-leaders were now the *tkm*, as opposed to the old teams where the eldest steady team-member was the shunt leader. Out of the nine *tkm* one had already transferred to the switchboard plant, so there were only two that were not to be team-leaders in the future. These two were, as mentioned, selected strictly according to date of employment. Those who did not qualify were employed 1959 and 1960 respectively, and they were now transferred to the reserve list. Reserve teams were also to be formed, but there was even greater uncertainty about the formation of these. There was only an empty space marked 'VIK-teams', but no leaders were appointed for these teams.

No names had been signed on the VIK-list on the 21st, and it was difficult to get a picture of how many shunters who actually had signed the main list

238

on this date, as at least one person, Pelle, quickly had filled the list beneath his name with the names of the persons he wanted. It turned out that his team eventually was given the composition he had wished for in such explicit terms. Later he nevertheless complained loudly, but jokingly, that he did not get any good-looking girls in his team...

The main teams, with one embarrassing exception, were quickly filled with aspiring shunters. As soon as there were four names under a *tkm* the shunters considered the team to be complete and they did not bother to add their names to the list. They did not seem to believe that they could surpass someone who had signed earlier and there was thus a silent agreement about something approximating 'first come first served'. It did not seem to worry anyone that this was rather unfair to persons who happened to be absent when the lists were pinned to the board. This was probably due to the fact that there was a certain correspondence to the earlier teams, as well as a self-censoring among the youngest shunters who assumed that their chances to get a place in the team in competition with senior mates were nil. Later, realizing that seniority counted, names were added under full teams. At this point the lists were, however, already quite a mess as they had become the target of jokes. Fictive names were added, and names were reorganized so that well known antagonists would end up in the same team, etc.

The new teams were constructed mainly by merging two old teams into one, but one team got members from three of the old teams and another team was a new construct with only one person from the old teams. It is remarkable that the team constructed in this way 'ex nihilo' was a team that had difficulties in recruiting members. For days the lonely name of the team-leader could be read on the board, in sharp contrast to the overfilled spaces under the names of the other team-leaders. There were few comments on this, it was felt to be embarrassing to have someone pointed out as 'unpopular' in this cruel way. When hinting at this in order to inquire about the reasons I got the same answer from several people. The *tkm* in question was 'nervous' and difficult to cooperate with. As soon as these reasons for not volunteering into that team had been stated the persons invariably added that they **personally** had no objections or grudges against the *tkm* and that he was a very nice fellow. But the fact remained.[12]

---

[12] Pálsson quotes a deck-hand saying:"A skipper may be good at catching fish, but he can be so boring that one is not willing to put up with him and work for him." (PÁLSSON, 913) In the yard we see this too, but we have conflicting loyalties here. One does not want to work for him, but neither does one want to ostracize him from the group.

There was a perceptibly increasing uneasiness about the way the 'vote' on the wall singled out one side of a personality, the work-bit, which then seemed to pass a judgement on the person as a whole. It is also significant that the person who finally broke the ice and signed on for this *tkm* was a man who on several occasions expressed strong opinions about unfairness and all kinds of behaviour that he did not consider cricket. He explained that he had no problems cooperating with this particular *tkm*, as he himself just ignored all symptoms of nervousness. 'I only announce to him that I'm going to do so and so – and that's it.'

After signing on for the 'empty' team he was immediately followed by two other persons. They came both from outside the teams, being former knockers who now were 'set loose' as the knocking group was dissolved, and one can therefore expect that they did not have as extensive experience of working with the *tkm* as former team members. But the team was now almost complete and the embarrassing situation solved and happily forgotten.

As a whole the selection for the teams was after all based on the date of employment. Only one former team member who easily could have qualified for the new teams chose to leave the teams in order to join the VIK-list. All in all four persons who wanted to join the new teams and who were members of the former teams were pushed out. Their dates of employment ranged from late 1984 to late 1987.

The new teams did not comprise one single woman, the only woman in the earlier teams had not signed for the new teams as she was resigning altogether, and judging by her date of employment she would not have made it anyway. One woman signed for the new teams from the VIK-list, but she did not qualify. The result was now that there were three women on reserve and one in the switchboard plant. As one of the women in outdoor work was pregnant[13] the future looked gloomy for the female cadres. One shunter told me in a stage-whisper in the corridor that he was dissatisfied with having to accept a certain man in his team instead of one of the women, who he thought was much better a shunter.

Complaints about the decreasing number of females were beginning to be heard more often. Old as well as young shunters started to talk about the times when there were more than one handful of women as the 'good old days'. Pelle, in his typical way, complained that there were no pretty girls left after

---

[13] This woman had a position in the switchboard plant, but chose to work outdoors in order to avoid being exposed to radiation from the monitors in the plant. As a means to escape electro-magnetic radiation this choice seems rather absurd – given the strong electro-magnetism in the yard, and especially in vicinity of the engines – but I never heard it being questioned, neither by management nor colleagues.

Anna resigned. It was pointed out that nothing was wrong with the looks of the remaining girls, but Pelle only snorted. No one with a small behind filled his criteria for being pretty, he claimed.

It was obvious that the atmosphere had grown gloomy and dull. The few remaining girls just seemed to vanish in the crowd. The happy comradeship and the joking was at an all time low. Even Pelle, the court fool, had given up most of his jokes and walked around dragging his feet, declaring in a loud voice that 'death will come as a relief!' Now it was just a matter of waiting for the increased workload and the 'bonus disaster'!

Turmoil and Confusion

Before the compositions of the teams were final there was a meeting with the aim of discussing the work schedules to be used during the trial month. As we know, the shop steward had already studied two proposals and he had made all the corrections he thought were needed. He declared that if **this** proposal was not accepted by Barring there would be no trial month and thereby the end of the bonus scheme. This certainly indicated that he had done the utmost to accommodate the demands of the management, but also – since Barring and other representatives of the management were absent – that his position was not one of accepting the bonus without a certain set of standards. To the shunters his declaration thus indicated that he had made some rather tough demands and that it was far from evident that they would be accepted. They were now obviously repelling force by force – although the shunters did not know exactly how...

To many of the more inexperienced shunters the proposal was not easy to read. As they had little knowledge of how to properly construct work schedules they were not likely to suggest changes. In addition, and this was true for all outdoor staff, young as well as old, the crucial point was not the lists in themselves as much as the reality that lay ahead. The amount of work they were going to face during the different shifts and the possibility to work according to the 'ideal model' that had been established could simply not be judged from reading the work schedules. The trial month would not even give the answer. The real test would not come until the summer holidays started or until there was a winter with heavy blizzards and traffic problems.

The meeting where the shunters were to discuss the schedules was of a completely unstructured character. The coffee-room was filled with people discussing with each other in small groups. People were coming and leaving, but there were constantly about fifteen to twenty persons in the room. There

241

was no formal opening of the meeting. No one was appointed chairperson and neither did anyone take on that role spontaneously. Questions were thrown out without being addressed to anyone in particular. Some seemed to be directed towards the shop steward, some towards 'those in power', but some were just cried out to all and sundry without specific address.

At least two persons called for proper procedures, but their wishes were drowned in the chorus of voices.

Some of the questions which could be heard concerned the lack of work descriptions as well as the lack of supplementary staff during peak hours. The shop steward answered that such shifts would in the future be put on *'gnet-listan'* (the list of over-time shifts, distributed on a first serve basis). As the question was posed by The Jacket, a notorious *'gnetare'*, the shop steward suggested with a grin that The Jacket could take on the shifts himself.

The 'meeting' continued in turmoil, small details and general questions being brought up pell-mell. One *tkm* was talking to a small group around him, one moment complaining that too little time was reserved for *tkm* to report while, in the next moment, stating that he suspected that the new team-order would give unpleasant and far-reaching consequences. The teams would be compared to each other and some of them would be considered B-teams.[14] Psychological pressure, accusations and animosity between the teams would destroy the good comradeship. He stated in the same breath that it was a matter for 'the young' to bring up to discussion.

As mentioned, there had been no agreement about how the evaluation of the trial month would proceed, but as the bonus reform was felt to be much more important than the regular changes between Winter and Summer time-tables, this additional common meeting had been announced. This was therefore an extraordinary opportunity to discuss the trial month. The rather tumultuous meeting was unprecedented, but could hardly be considered to give an opportunity for constructive discussion.

The reactions of the shunters was therefore rather predictable. A young proposer of a 5-shift system was upset that his scheme was not brought up.[15] He had been under the impression that the fact that he once had mentioned it to Barring meant that the planning department would be asked to work it out

---

[14] We remember the argument from the union minutes four decades earlier.

[15] A 5-shift system implies working four nights in a row, as well as having entire holidays off. The former was considered unpleasant and the latter meant that it would become difficult to exchange shifts. Those who were free during a whole holiday would presumably be reluctant to break their line of free days. The present system made it easy to get rid of the odd shifts during a long holiday by exchanging shifts with someone who already had a broken holiday. 5-shift systems had always been opposed by the union. Now it was proposed by a young shunter.

in detail to be brought up at this particular meeting. As I had been a witness to the interaction with Barring I was called to testify that Barring had 'promised to work it out'. This situation was very difficult for me as my memory did not agree with the proposer's (and as the last thing I wanted was to sound like a stern supporter of Barring). I said that I did not remember exactly what they had agreed on, but I felt that I was telling a lie.[16] However, the 5-shift proposal was never taken up to discussion and the proposer left very disconcerted to ask Barring why his proposal had been 'lost'. A couple of persons who, in more intimate discussions, had been positive to the 5-shift proposal were now conspicuously silent. The end of the matter was rather disappointing to the young man.

It had become obvious that the proposer and other possible supporters of the 5-shift plan had not even been able to turn the loose talk of the coffee-room into a formal proposal. They stumbled before they even came to the runway. Ignorant about the correct procedures and immensely gullible, they had taken for granted that the management would construct a work schedule for them on the basis of a simple question casually thrown at the manager. They also seemed more upset about the way their 'proposal' had been ignored than about the fact that they were not going to get a 5-shift schedule after all.

Another young shunter made comments referring to the treatment of the 5-shift proposal, although he addressed the union officials rather than the manager. He said that the whole meeting was a sham. There was no presentation of the different proposals, if there indeed were such. It was evident that the 'old buffers' were deciding everything between themselves, he said. These fierce attacks, although partly drowning in discussions carried on all around, were not commented upon by the shop steward, despite the fact that they were obviously directed partly at him. Finally the young shunter directed his harangues toward others, such as me, who at least seemed to listen.

The shop steward's reactions were not unusual. As a matter of fact his behaviour very often resembled what he displayed at this meeting. Apparently not hearing what was going on around him he went about with his own business, only suddenly to throw in a comment revealing that he had in fact been listening. Very selective about whom to discuss with, he managed to avoid unwanted confrontations, engaging himself only in discussions that suited him. This time, too, he avoided a quarrel and an escalation of upset

---

[16] When I later checked my notes, taken down immediately after the discussion between Barring and this shunter in the yard, I found that the notes agreed with my memory. Barring did not promise anything – although this naturally does not exclude the possibility that I misunderstood the discussion at the time.

feelings, and could perhaps be said to have won the round. He chose to talk to one of the *tkm* about details in the proposal, as this *tkm*, as opposed to the young shunters, was able to read the schedule and predict some of their consequences.

The accusations about gerontarchical rule were useless to confront. The youngsters had not even managed to get together an alternative proposal and the young shunter who accused the 'old buffers' of despotism was in fact only proving that his reputation as a leftist radical and trouble-maker was correct. Lacking serious alternatives altogether, there was only the shop steward's schedules to be discussed. This seemed very much to be the conclusion to be drawn from the way the shop steward and the other 'old buffers' reacted in response to the challenges posed by the youngsters.

Aftermath

One of the youngest shunters told me a few days later that the meeting was 'the worst thing he ever saw'. He had expected a proper presentation for the whole audience, and after that a general discussion. Now, he said, it had only been a private discussion between the shop steward and a *tkm* about some details and 'when one asked anything the chairman got angry'. He himself did not care for the the idea about a 5-shift schedule, as it would make it more difficult to spend time with his child, but as the present morning shift often finished work at 9.30-10, compared to the proposal of merging it with another shift which was busy until 12-12.30, the difference was in reality remarkable. It would become very tough to return in the evening to do the night shift, he thought.

Yet, a few days later, the issue of the increasing workload was brought up in the coffee-room when the 'leftist radical' entered in a state of anger. His rancour turned out to be directed toward the staff delegator, who had announced that Engine 4 had to work one man short with the comment: 'But that has been done before.' The young man found this comment upsetting and said repeatedly: 'Don't you hear what it sounds like?' in a insinuating voice.

Two middle-aged shunters, each of them with more than 15 years' experience, immediately came to the defense of the staff delegator. They said that it was not against the rules to work in a team of three and that there was nothing remarkable about it whatsoever. Then they started to talk in general terms about how the attitude to work had changed of late. It had become the order of the day to take two- or three-hour breaks, to see the *smit-tider* (early quits) as given and consider working until the end of the shift as something out of the normal. Things had gone too far, indeed!

It is fair to assume that not only the lack of support, but the siding of his mates with the employer, was what caused the junior to get even more upset. He attacked one of the elder workers saying: 'Would you manage working four hours, plus half an hour break, plus four hours again?' The calm and supercilious answer from his senior was: 'If I didn't I wouldn't be working here.' His mate agreed: 'Exactly!' The former then referred to the small shipyard he was working in during holidays, saying that **there** one worked from 7 to 4, 'on the dot!'.

These harsh words were then mitigated by an admission that in case engine drivers were having coffee for five hours – an example presented by the young shunter – while a shunter was driving the engine and the shunting team was working one man short, things were not as they were supposed to be. This supposed situation was obviously unfair, but the elder shunters did not answer their junior when he angrily commented that 'no one' was doing anything about it. 'If I criticize this they will only laugh at me. It has to be a *tkm* or a shunt leader who makes the objection.'

The elder shunters did not seem the least upset about the unjust situation described by the young shunter, but then just one minute earlier they had criticized shunters for taking extremely short shifts for granted nowadays. They might have felt that they would be throwing stones in a glass-house were they to take up the challenge to 'do something' about this situation. As it were they chose to read the story as an example, a figurative construct, and left it unclear whether they actually believed it to be true or not. If engine drivers had long breaks, while shunters were driving the engines, things were not organized correctly and fairly, but to connect this to a demand that teams should have four members, instead of the traditional three, did obviously not catch on.

These confrontations – in both of which the 'leftist radical' happened to be involved – can be read as clashes between different points of view. Arguments were delivered and the disagreements were obvious. Even more obvious was the dividing line between the opponents. The young versus the 'old buffers' in the first case, and the young versus the experienced middle-aged shunters in the second one. Looking closer at the two instances we can see that in the first discussion at the meeting about the time-schedules we had the club chairman and a senior *tkm* opposed to the youngsters – the proposer of the 5-shift, the so called leftist, and the most junior shunter.

Here the young shunters accused the old ones of 'deciding everything' over the heads of the young ones. The seniors obviously did not share this opinion. As a matter of fact the *tkm* in question had been perhaps the most bitter opponent to the bonus-scheme at the Information Meeting on February 1 and it was also he who went on sick leave shortly after this incidence, never to return. The club chairman had announced that he did not like the bonus-reform either, but saw no way to veto it. Indeed, it was due to the fact that the **young** shunters were thought to be accepting the scheme that it was kicked into being. It was the **old** shunters who had opposed the scheme, as they were more concerned about the workload than attracted by increased pay, but they felt that the only way to make the youngsters stay was to give in and accept the bonus.

In the exchange of opinions, however indirect it was, it seemed at the meeting that the roles were reversed. The young saw the 'old buffers' as those in power to decide, as part of the 'establishment', the company. By not taking up the challenge, the seniors indeed gave the impression that the issue at stake was their dominance and that the youngsters were only trouble-makers, who should be ignored as they did not play by the rules. They were not even able to formulate a proper proposal.

The second dispute, concerning the minimum number of team-members, also turned out to isolate the young shunter. When he found no sympathy for this initial complaint, he tried to take refuge in the apparently 'safer' issue of the increasing workload. But here, too, he found himself heavily opposed. When finally pleading for consensus by referring to injustice when comparing the work of the shunters to the engine drivers – the old common 'adversary' – it was agreed that if this indeed was the case, it certainly was unjust. This admission was, however, given in a matter-of-fact manner, lacking every trace of agitation or excitement, and it was made quite clear that the seniors were not going to support the agitated youngster in his disputes with the staff delegator, manager or whoever it may be.

In an interview earlier, one of these very same senior shunters had talked about the bonus-scheme and the devastating effects he considered it to have on the staff, and particularly the young. They would have to work still harder, although they already had the toughest tasks. The first years, working on the VIK-list, would develop into a deterrent. The shifts would be longer than for the team as the VIK-person would be forced to stay on and uncouple engines while the rest of the team were having a break, playing cards, etc. In the future it would be (even more) difficult to recruit new staff. The 'dog years' would get worse and extend higher up in the age-groups, even up to shunt leaders older than himself.

Judging from these statements, one would have expected him to agree with the young 'leftist' that the workload, if increased, was going to break the youngsters. Instead of recognizing that the youngster was playing his tune, he was on the contrary the one whose contemptuous comment made it clear that the young shunter had no reason to complain. If one could not manage full shifts one did not belong.

The issue was then not first and foremost that there was disagreement as to matter, but that the complaint was coming from the wrong person. The young were a threat to the older ones in that they had greater physical strength and an ability to work irregular hours more easily, and in addition they were more often unmarried and obviously not restricted by family obligations. They had thus no right to complain about the work.

There is reason to believe that the question of age coloured the argument to the extent that the factual content was distorted. Views that in another context would have been rejected were now forcefully put forward. This is of course not to say that one opinion is more 'real' or more 'true' than the other, only that the context brings out several sides of a matter. The opposition from a junior then brought out loyalty to the company, or was it the pride of the workman that gushed out?

The Trial Month

If ever there was an anti-climax the trial month surely was one. Work turned out to be more intense, just as expected, but it was not harder than it had been before the recent development, before 'sixty persons worked an eighty-man schedule' as it was often described. Some persons grumbled that it was wrong to test the new order on an 'easy' month. 'Just wait until the winter, when the snow comes. That will tell you how it works', they said, but no one paid much attention to such sour comments. The trend had turned, people were earning considerably more and there was no more talk about leaving. 'You know what you've got, but not what you might get' was again the saying when tempting job offers were found in the newspapers. After all, what other jobs offered the same freedom and independence?

The uproar and the envy which the reform had caused, at Hagalund as well as at other stations around the country (where it was said that the people at Hagalund were 'paid 100 crowns just for turning up at work') was rather a comforting assurance that they had a good thing going.[17] 'The other groups could earn more, too, if they had agreed to work more. They didn't, and now they are envious of us! It's their own fault to be led by those *'R-are'* in the Hall.'[18] Such comments came from all parts of *bangårdsgruppen*; shunters, staff delegator, *tkm*, active union members and, of course, the manager.

One commentator said that now the 'good atmosphere' and the 'excellent comradeship' was coming back again, and that there **really** had been **only one** person opposing the reform – the one who went on permanent sick-leave. This seemed actually to be a view which was accepted by the majority as a correct writing of history.

Conclusions

At times of rapid change it is hardly surprising that new judgments, strong emotions and groups holding different opinions burst forth, especially if we have a setting, which, like Hagalund, has been considered to be unchanged and even unchangeable. Anthony Giddens suggests that during 'violent and dramatic processes of change' one should "... examine how shifting institutional alignments condition, and are conditioned by, transformations of the settings in which social life is lived."[19] What one perhaps does not expect is quite as vivid a kaleidoscopic pattern of alignments as the one we observed among the shunters. Conflicts, emanating from quite unexpected directions (such as the 5-shift struggle, which seemed rather like a whim at first, but which quickly received symbolic value), carved out patterns which not only shifted from day to day, but even from one moment to the next.

In view of this, the remarkable outcome was that things went back to – what at least was considered – normal within a matter of weeks. Earlier conflicts were not only palliated but actually denied or, seemingly, forgotten.

What the chain of events revealed was an arena, or a setting, where new demarcation lines became visible and marked. Age, which had been downplayed, due to the egalitarian ethos, now came to play a significant role. The bonus was like an apple of discord thrown in 'to the strongest'. It

---

[17] The advisor to Barring and the shop steward said that their telephones were 'running hot' during the early summer as the bonus-agreement became known throughout the country.

[18] *R-are'* actually refers to a marxist group, which broke away from its maoist mother party in the 1970s, adding an R, standing for 'revolutionaries', to the original name. Here *'r-are'* stands for 'extreme leftist' in general.

[19] This comment comes from a critique of the work of Goffman, whose approach, Giddens says, seems 'irrelevant' to such dramatic processes of change, exactly because it lacks an analysis of the dialectics between the shifting institutional alignments and the transformations of the setting. Cf. GIDDENS 1987, 139.

demanded a harder pace of work, and would not be paid to those who took ill and thus were absent.

There was a conflict between the young, strong and able and the ageing, weakening and increasingly 'infirm'. The fact that the hardest work already befell the youngest, and that an increased workload would hit them hardest, complicated matters. This fact was, however, only admitted to me in an interview. It did not have value as currency in the ongoing debate. One sign of this was that one youngster protested in vain against the increased workload.

The paradoxical situation was therefore that the young, automatically, were seen to be those who were prepared to work more for more pay, their insatiable need for money always being assumed. The old were against the reform, it was said, but still we saw that the youngsters who did oppose the new schedule actually found no support among the seniors.

The seniors were actually sceptical, but as soon as the decision was taken to continue with the trial, the large majority of them changed attitude completely and did everything to administer and take back the initiative that they almost had lost for a moment. They were quickly back at the reins. There were some persons who did not manage this swift change of winds, and one of them left, while the other turned bitter and cynical, refusing to learn how to drive the remote controlled engines, thereby locking himself out of a position in the new teams.

In addition to a struggle between age-groups the bonus reform was a power struggle for the new manager to establish himself, owing to the fact that his position was not earned through seniority. The most stern opposition came from those just beneath him, the indoor *tkm*.

For the manager, 'the puppy', the events turned out to be a great success. (He later disclosed to me that he had decided to resign had the bonus scheme not been accepted.) As he said, his goal was to show the *tkm* – and the shunters – who was in charge. He did achieve this goal and there was no more talk about the 'poor kid' who had been put in a position he had no ability to understand or handle.

The most delicate position in the whole process was the one of the union club chairman. He conspicuously abstained from taking part in the Information Meeting and avoided all confrontations with the youngsters. First he opposed the whole reform ('the plague or the black death'), but very soon he defended it fiercely and told a young shunter who complained about the manager: 'You don't know what a good manager you have. The best one in all of SJ!'

To sum up we may say that the interaction order turned out to be more of a disorder than an order. Opinions and positions seemed to have no consistency from situation to situation, from minute to minute. There were simply too many demarcation lines, too many institutional alignments tossed about to enable anyone, it seemed, to conform to anything which could be seen as a pattern in the interaction. There were only instances of juxtapositions; one moment defending one's work role, the next one a union position, the third moment defending egalitarian ideas.

When the struggle was over – and the informal hierarchy re-established – the group consolidated itself by defending the group against the other groups, and the rest of the outside world. During the struggle there were attempts to smooth over too explicit conflicts by complaining about other groups at Hagalund, or the society at large, or even by discussing old and well-known union questions with a misdirected fervour (such as the issue of malfunctioning radios), but this had no unifying effect and seemed only to be a cosmetic to the conversation, an empty ritual, pleading to 'good old times'.

In other words; there was no correspondence between institutional alignments and interactional patterns. The first created oppositions and demarcation lines between indoor and outdoor work, between fit and unfit, old and young, superiors and subordinates, between 'proper shunters', working in the teams, and 'loners' at the fringe and finally between bachelors, who were 'over-timers' hungry for money and family men, who would choose time off rather than money.[20]

Interactional patterns would normally veil and mask, blur and deform these demarcation lines. Vague – 'gut-reaction-like' – egalitarian and democratic/anti-hierarchical ideals would be stressed in interaction. However, in this situation of crisis, the immanent demarcation lines (otherwise never revealed all at once) surfaced and became visible and obvious to all. As abstract categories they were not easily applicable on reality, as they cut in ways that crossed each other, and as – instead of making a neat easily handled pattern, as is the case when looking at the alignments one by one; such as old/young – there was a chaotic mix of categories, with inconsistencies and paradoxes, making individuals, as it were, 'sitting on the fence', switching alignments from moment to moment.

---

[20] It seems that the only obvious and expected demarcation line never to crop up was the one between the sexes. The women were actually never talked about in general terms, except for when it was asked why all women seemed to be leaving. For all other puposes they simply fell under the other categories.

250

It would therefore be difficult to speak of a dialectic conditioning between interactional patterns and institutional alignments. These two are mediated by another 'level' or instance, the one of ideology (and the habitus of the individuals), which allows for trading one alignment for another (such as status and seniority for joking and youthful comradeship). This 'ideological' (or whatever term we might want to use for it) level is the one that normally hides the paradoxical and inconsistent groupings of people, as moulded by formal rules and conditions, and makes it possible to ignore them and act as if they did not matter or exist. The extraordinary events of the reform brought them up, but it is difficult to see the interaction patterns as conditioned or conditioning them, without considering the intermediate level.

When the strife was over and the shunting group was criticised and attacked from all sides, the shunters were back again in the old position of being considered 'unruly' and favoured by the company (the lack of punch clocks was an old eyesore to the other groups). Things were in this respect also back to normal, and the shunters had again a clear answer to the misery of the other groups; they were afraid of work and had no ability to take part in constructive negotiations. They were a bunch of no-sayers and now they could as well sit there and watch the shunters get rich! Every complaint they had was met with: 'You are just envious because we earn a lot of money!' Self-esteem was back in the shunting group.

The rewriting of the history of the introduction of the bonus as one which was **actively** approved of by the shunters, and not one they were forced into, was facilitated by the restrained and reconciliatory attitude that dominated the different meetings. The lack of open conflict, and the care taken to make it appear that the parties parted as friends, made it easier to pretend that objections, condemnations and hostility had ever been present.

Here, then, the conflicting alignments sank back into invisibility under the horizon, and the ideologically established view of the shunters as a unified group – 'us' as opposed to 'them' – was back, stronger than it had been for a very long time. The reform did, however, cast a long shadow over the future, although it was not immediately realized. Seniority no longer ruled and the question of ability and competence had come to stay.

Train-puller jumping off.

9. SPACE, TIME, AND THE CHANGING PERSPECTIVES OF WORK

Regionalization – Changing Premises

The shunters were said to object to moving their quarters to the New Hall in 1967. The move was therefore never completed, and in 1982, when I first came into contact with Hagalund, the shunters used the locker rooms and washing facilities in the New Hall, while they still socialized in the old 'red barracks'.

The red barracks contained a large coffee-room and a smaller room, which was meant for non-smokers, but as the smaller room was very dark and grim it was often empty. The indoor *tkm*, and the coach recorder, had their office at the end of the barracks, and in order to reach it one had to pass through the tiny changing room that *tkm* and some seniors were using.[1] The introduction of women in the yard had as a consequence that the seniors would have young women pass through their changing room at all hours. It is difficult to assess the inconvenience this caused, as the women showed typical avoidance behaviour, never looking in the direction of the lockers.[2] There were occasional jokes ('Girls, come and have a look at Bertil's drawers!'), but mostly there seemed to be little disturbance created by this forced co-presence.

The symbolic value of the arrangements was of course larger, and the demand for new facilities could not be questioned. To have the seniors confined to a changing room without privacy was unquestionably improper and below any acceptable standards. The new, green, barracks were brought from another station, the newly closed *Södra Station* (Stockholm South Station), and reconstructed on a spot near the 'bottle-neck'. During the planning period blueprints were shown to the shunters, but they displayed

---

[1] This was not really a room but rather a hallway between the coffee-room and the office. As there were two doors to the barracks, one to the coffee-room, the other one to the office, it was possible to avoid this hallway by making a detour outside the building. This was, however, never practised.

[2] The glance as boundary offence is described by Goffman. Cf GOFFMAN 1972, 69 f.

little or no interest in the drawings. When the barracks finally were inspected the shunters were highly annoyed at the size of the coffee-room, which was considered far too small. The lack of a separate room for non-smokers was also criticized. There was a sign 'smokers | non-smokers' hanging in the middle of the room, with arrows pointing in opposite directions, but as someone remarked, the smoke did not seem to take any notice of it.

Moving to the new barracks in 1983 meant that the shunters finally would be under one roof, and that they would not have to share changing rooms with the other workers at Hagalund. There were now separate changing rooms and entries for women and *tkm*, as well as separate entries for the *tkm* office, the coffee-room and the changing rooms for the teams.

Although the *tkm* already earlier had been located separately, it was only in the new barracks that the separation of *tkm* from the other shunters caused scornful remarks and some joking. Earlier the separation had grown out of changing circumstances, now it was planned and thereby it acquired a different meaning.

As the *tkm* now reached their office and their own kitchen facilities directly from their locker room, they no longer had to congregate with the shunters during lunch-hour and other breaks. Sometimes they would come into the shunters' coffee-room for a game of cards, or in order to bring a message, or even just to keep in touch with the crowd, but as they had to go out of the barracks and enter by another door in order to reach the coffee-room they felt that they were alienated from the rest of the shunters and that the 'normal', more intimate, relationship to them had been upset. There were, of course, more or less serious comments (from the side of the *tkm*) saying that this was exactly what they had been longing for, but one can note that the one who said this with the most contemptuous vigour nevertheless was one of the most frequent guests at the card-table.

The planned switchboard plant had been hovering like a ghost in the minds of the shunters for decades, and now apparently these 'temporary' barracks were all they were left with, during their endless waiting. The shunters had been tossed from one temporary solution to another (as the first one deteriorated from old age), and typically enough the shunters had to make do with some second hand barracks with a tiny common room and overdimensioned facilities for the *tkm*. The marginal character of the shunting group was given visual expression. The fact that the barracks had spacious locker rooms and that they were nicer, newer and generally much more modern and convenient than the old locker rooms in the New Hall (particularly the male one was said to be smelly and appalling) was beside the point. Facilities for the shunters remained a patchwork, organized in a perfunctory manner.

When the switchboard plant finally became reality the shunters were moved again, now to what was said to become their permanent quarters. These premises were planned from scratch, as opposed to the earlier barracks, and they contained every function that was considered to be connected to the shunting enterprise. The whole complex was housed in an additional storey on the roof of the New Hall. The switchboard plant was built as a control tower, with tinted, outward slanting windows, offering a panorama-view over the yard. On the corner right above the 'bottle-neck' the operator could watch the important traffic in the yard, as a spider watching its net.

Several changes were instituted as the new organization was given its proper physical shape in the layout of the offices, the locker rooms and other necessary rooms and spaces. What was to be an economically self-reliant and self-sufficient group had now manifested itself in fortified privacy in their retreat above the yard where they could observe without being observed. The aerial conduits to the tracks in the Hall passed underneath the windows, which as a consequence were made impossible to open.[3] In the summer the heat could turn out to be almost unbearable, a rather ironic realization of how 'office-work' had been depicted earlier.

The entry to the facilities consisted of a long, shaky flight of stairs, made of metal grid, as well as another winding staircase and, in addition to that, a lift that was very slow – and extremely unreliable. All of a sudden the former intimate relationship to the yard was circumscribed, and although the view over the yard was excellent it rather resembled the view into – or rather out of – a large fish tank. Physical proximity to the yard was transformed into visual proximity. The transition between inside and outside was more cumbersome, and demanded more planning. One could not 'pop in' during a short break. Like a retired sea-captain who is confined to living vith a view over the sea, the shunters were during their breaks 'retired' viewers, overlooking the yard. The separation from the other workers of Hagalund had thus become institutionalized and permanented in physical terms. Quite appropriately, nostalgic memories of the 'good old times' in the old red barracks were now being expressed for the first time. 'It was much cosier down there. We were all close and together'.

---

[3] Aerial conduits are dangerous even if they are not touched, since the 16.000 volts can cause a flash-over if the safe distance around the conduits – one meter – is transgressed. Since the shunters' quarters are situated above the conduits, the risks of flash-overs are obvious in the case windows can be opened.

The manager's office was moved from the Hall, where the offices of the other managers were, and the new manager, Barring, was from the very start in close contact with his own group, the shunters.

The staff delegator had now also left the ground floor corridor at the opposite end of the New Hall, where the staff assigners had earlier been lodged in adjoining offices. S/he, too, was given an office in the shunters' 'fortress' in the midst of the group that s/he administered.

Why then was it thought that the shunters were 'all together' in the old barracks? The facilities there were naturally much more cramped, the shunters more numerous, but it was only in the purpose built lodgings that the shunters were assembled for the first time and could reach locker rooms and offices without having to leave the premises. It was in the new premises that the shunters were together for the first time under one roof. At least that was one of the aims of the plan.

I will argue that the new surroundings, despite the new unity, presented a new form of regionalization which separated groups and functions in a way that had not been done before. We must look briefly at the new floor on top of the New Hall.

Visible Spaces, Invisible Borders

The new premises are, just like an eagle's nest, not very accessible. When the lift is out of order one has to climb a flight of stairs that could enfeeble anyone with the slightest vertigo. This was naturally immediately recognized, and it has been a popular game to jump and make the aluminium staircase shake and swing in order to check the nerves of fellow shunters climbing the stairs. The stairs, and the malfunctioning lift, soon became targets for frequent complaints, and senior shunters especially found it humiliating to have to put up with these obstacles. As opposed to shunting work, climbing stairs cannot be done with technique instead of power. The stairs were thus an unpleasant test of physical fitness, and one of the senior shunters, who went on a diet and slimmed down remarkably, referred to the stairs as the incentive to his decision to try to lose weight. 'I couldn't walk up those stairs without losing my breath.'

Despite the seemingly cumbersome access to the new premises there was initially an almost constant trickle of visiting groups. They all had one thing in common; they came because of the new switchboard plant. They never spoke to or introduced themselves to the shunters, who consequently complained that they did not know 'what kind of people' they were.

The computerized plant suffered, as we remember, from a number of technical difficulties causing repeated delays of the inauguration of the plant. In the first months the plant altered between being partly in operation, and being brought to a standstill by a complete 'black out.

During break-downs it was assumed that the visitors were some kind of 'computer specialists', otherwise they were groups on 'study visits'. Sometimes, and often probably only depending on their way of dressing, the rumour depicted them as 'big shots', but they were all felt to be strangers that had one thing in common; they were sneaking around, probing and spying. They were somehow felt to be disturbing, although they hardly ever stopped to peep into the coffee-room as they hurriedly headed for the switchboard plant.

One may suspect that part of the irritation of the shunters originated in the fact that it was precisely the switchboard plant that attracted all this attention. Alas, even the SJ manager, Stig Larsson, came to admire it.

The outline of the premises also assigned the switchboard plant an air of importance. The new storey was laid out around a long windowless corridor, the middle part of which was lined with the *tkm* locker-rooms and rarely used facilities such as the conference and resting rooms, with a lonely dart-board cheering up the wall. This quiet middle part stood in contrast to both ends of the corridor, where all activities were concentrated.

One end of this dumb-bell pattern of activities held the shunters' locker rooms and the coffee-room. The locker rooms, however, were now divided and ordered according to status, so that one first had those belonging to the VIK-personnel, then the teams and the women and finally the *tkm*. The other end of the dumb-bell was composed of the offices of the staff delegator, the *tkm*, and the manager, and adjacent to these, the Argus-eyed and omnipotent switchboard plant. If the latter part contained the brains of the yard, the former was the heart and pulse of the social life of the labouring community – representing a true Cartesian split between body and mind.

The *tkm* office in the old red barracks had only an open counter to separate the *tkm* and coach recorders from 'the great unwashed'; the shunters who came to pick up the 'slips'. This separation became much more marked in the green barracks, where a sliding window crowned the counter and made it possible for the *tkm* inside to shut out sound, while still being able to see and be seen. (If one wanted to enter the office itself one had to enter by another door.) Contacts could thus be administered from inside the *tkm* office – and untimely or impolite demands from the outside could be ignored.

257

In the new premises the cake is sliced differently. The coach recorders are isolated in a separate office, which means that their contacts to the *tkm* have become more limited, sparse and formal. As a consequence they feel that the job has become even more isolated and boring. They definitely are no longer in the thick of the action.

The *tkm* still have a little glass window, where the slips are delivered to the shunters, but to the irritation of some *tkm*, shunters often come walking into the office anyway. To enter the shunters have to make a detour through the switchboard plant, but this does not put them off, quite the contrary. There is always an old mate in the plant and they like to drop in for a chat. From there the *tkm* office is only a couple of steps away.

There have been incidents when furious *tkm* chase out shunters from the office, but this is not accepted as normal or legitimate. The shunters firmly believe they have a right to enter the office without much ado, and they come in to use the copying machine in order to replace lost slips, to copy important information, or, usually at night, to manufacture funny posters and notices for the pin-boards.[4]

Across the corridor from the *tkm* office is the manager's office. The door is either locked or wide open. This room is not the property of the shunters and the inviting open door and the informal and relaxed attitude of the manager – feet on the desk shouting: 'Come in! I'm just reading the evening paper!' – cannot bridge the invisible barrier that divides his office from common grounds.

Entering the manager's office is not done without a particular purpose. One enters in order to lodge a complaint or venture a suggestion. One is also observed, and thereby **ascribed** a purpose by fellow shunters. Unless one enters with the purpose to complain, the entry can easily be read as an attempt to get into the manager's good books. Therefore the shunters prefer to stand on the threshold and speak in a loud voice to make it possible for others to hear and maybe even come to their support. Even complaining too frequently may lead to suspicion. It is thought unlikely that one can deliver complaints without involving criticism of fellow workers, directly or indirectly. Problems should preferably be solved without bringing them to the manager. In all the cases where this is not possible, the safest way to bring it to the attention of

---

[4] Ulf Mellström describes such 'Xerox-lore' at Microchips Inc. Cf. MELLSTRÖM, 92 ff. The very same example of 'engineering humour' which he cites (about theory and practice being connected so that nothing works and no-one knows why) can indeed be found on the pin-boards in the yard. Otherwise the pin-board lore favours pictorial material, such as photographs, drawings, collages or installations with funny captions rather than longer texts.

the manager is in 'the open', i.e. in the yard, in the corridor or in any other public place where there is an audience.

The manager's 'right hand', i.e. the *tkm* who was put to the task of introducing the new boss to the routines of the group, was unavoidably stained by the close contact to the manager. Although he himself expressed relief that he never had been forced into a situation where he had to report on his comrades in the yard, the shunters had their verdict ready. A general statement that there be 'informers running to the manager' suddenly got a clear target when one of the *tkm* made a spontaneous charade at the door to the coffee-room. When he was about to enter he stepped back, partly hiding by the door frame. Wit his eyes sternly fixed on the pinboard outside the door he rocked from side to side, so that he alternately appeared and disappeared behind the wall. 'Who does like this?' he asked. The laughter that ensued made it clear that everybody recognized the behaviour, and that the insinuation behind it was clear. 'Why does he do like this? What is so important on this board? These sports results!?' the *tkm* added triumphantly, disregarding that the questions were completely redundant. This very unexpected performance struck as lightning out of a blue sky, and it was over in a minute. There was nothing more to say. A few chuckles echoed as someone now and then recalled the event, but there was no discussion about the accuracy of the accusation of eaves-dropping, and the assumption of why it was done, on the part of the manager's 'right hand'. It was simply accepted as a fact.

Another instance of too close a contact was the junior shunter who had complained to the manager about the weight of the controller for the new remote controlled engines. The shunter had suggested attaching the heavy apparatus to a belt that would distribute the weight more evenly around the waist, thereby avoiding injuries. The manager had responded favourably, giving the shunter the commission to design such a belt in cooperation with one of the work shops. The shunter got rather carried away by this responsibility and not only completed the task enthusiastically, but started to promote the belt to other shunters when attending union courses and information opportunities throughout the country. Encouraged by his initiatives bearing fruit he got more and more involved in union matters, but soon found himself labelled as entering the manager's office too frequently. Disappointed and rather bitter he said during my interview that he was going to give things up. He felt he was suspected of having too much to do with the manager. 'I was too often in his office.' If he had to choose between un undisturbed relationship to his comrades and improving things in the yard, he did not hesitate to pick the former.

With all suspicions concerning too frequent contacts with the manager, one would think that the move of his office to their corridor would have meant a significant and disturbing change to the shunters. He could easily have been felt to be breathing down the shunters' necks, but his frequent passing outside the coffee-room door did not visibly hamper the ongoings inside. In case someone just had uttered a derogatory remark and was told that the manager just passed, he most likely would only shake his shoulders and say: 'So much the better that he hears the truth!'

It appears that the fear is not that the manager finds out 'a secret', whatever such secrets may be. 'He knows' is the laconic comment to anyone who shows anxiety over the manager 'finding out' something. It is not the revelation of disturbing truths that the collective fears, it is the thought of someone turning into a messenger, of separating himself from the comradeship. It does not necessarily entail that he is trying merely to get into the manager's good books, he might be quite naive and innocent, but the fact is that by fraternizing too much with 'the SJ side' one risks starting to see things from the company point of view. As soon as the *tkm* left outdoor work it was thought that they 'forgot what it was like out there' and started to see things from the indoor perspective that signified the company view. Even the club chairman was occasionally accused of having been fraternizing too much with the management. 'He is supposed to forward **our** opinions to them, but he seems only to try to forward **their** opinions to us!' one shunter exclaimed bitterly.

The only way to stay clear from gradually sliding over to the company side is to avoid unnecessary contact. The door to the manager's office can therefore stand wide open, the pale-blue plush chairs do not risk getting greasy stains.

The contrast between the manager's and the staff delegator's offices is remarkable. Although the staff delegator is also a representative of the company, SJ, there is no 'magic of contagion' that would inhibit the shunters from entering, be it on a matter of business or only to have a chat. Paradoxically, much more than the manager the delegator is a person who is in a position to hand out small favours that may be difficult to detect without continuous scrutiny of the work schedule. When detected, on the other hand, such favours can be complained about or used as a precedent for one's own case – one can 'raise hell' about it – while favours granted by the manager, say unfair promotion, is harder to fight today when 'individual capabilites' may be considered.

The discomfort caused by the evidently hierarchical relationship between the manager and the shunters is not present in the office of the staff delegator. Shunters have been seen to rush in or out of the office in anger, there has been screaming and shouting, and there has even been at least one spontaneous sit-in protest, where a woman refused to leave the office until the delegator gave her a row of shifts in the shunting teams instead of in the 'curve', i.e. as a train-puller.

The staff delegator was earlier situated on the ground floor at the end of the New Hall, half a kilometer away. It is undeniably much more comfortable for the shunters to pop into the office once it is in the same corridor as the locker rooms and the coffee-room, but the staff delegator is on the other hand now only a step away from the manager as well as the *tkm*, and this is considered to ease a line of contact that the shunters are not particularly fond of. The new spatial distribution is felt to establish a potential bastion for 'indoor thinking'.

The switchboard plant is planted in the midst of this hypothetical bee-hive and this undoubtedly affects the way it is perceived, and its potentials as an associate to outdoor versus indoor work. The problematics of the switchboard plant therefore demand a longer digression.

The Switchboard Plant – An Indoor or Outdoor Associate?

The switchboard plant lies at the end of the corridor, but it still has to be passed – by way of a U-turn – on the way to the *tkm* office. As the switchplant had no precedent, neither institutionally nor organizationally, the installation did not meet any particular feelings at all, at first, if we disregard the almost ritual forecasts, which predicted trouble and disaster in every novelty. The switchboard staff were busy learning the job as well as fighting technical problems, and there was some irritation over too many visitors and too many people peeping over one's shoulder all the time. All the staff longed for was that things would settle down and that they would get some peace and quiet. As it turned out they had to wait longer than they probably had anticipated.

As soon as it became clear that the persons selected for the operating jobs were not all qualified shunt leaders – which according to an earlier rumour would have been required – and as their salaries were not only considered too high but were also paid out months before the plant finally was inaugurated, tensions were building up among the remaining shunters. The operators themselves were not blamed for all this and no one (except the skilled young shunter, who left in anger as he was not selected for the operator job) actually claimed that **s/he her/himself** should have been elected. The shunters much rather talked in favour of somebody else, who they thought should have been elected, or they criticized 'the principle' behind the selection process in general. This did not prevent them from simultaneously observing and questioning the abilities of the novices, silently registering every mistake. The selected few would now have to live up to their high salaries, and demonstrate their (hidden) qualities to the world, it was thought.

Under this pressure the nut cracked in two, allegorically speaking. The operators responded in two ways to the critique, which was often hovering in the air, marked with silence and avoidance, rather than uttered explicitly in so many words. On one hand there was the unashamed enthusiasm for the new job. All chances to improve and enskill oneself should be utilized, and the knowledge and skills so acquired were cherished and kept almost as guild secrets, even to fellow operators. This was a golden chance to trade in the arduous outdoor work for a, maybe tedious, but still rather well paid job indoors, in the centrally heated as well as airconditioned comfort in an 'ergonomically correct' armchair.

On the other hand there was the anxious, guilty attitude, stemming from the thought that one had been selected on unfair terms, that one maybe was not very good at the job or simply that one was losing contact with the other shunters. The operator job was not seen as something permanent or final: 'I'll see if I'll cope with this for a longer stretch of time, maybe I'll go back into the yard again later', were the more reserved comments.

Every operator could probably have been caught uttering attitudes of both kinds, but there were some who rather pointedly mixed the two by putting on a cynical air. When asked how he liked the work in the plant one shunter answered: 'If I drop the pen on the floor I bend over and pick it up.' He was referring to the obvious fact that in the yard anyone could turn the wrong switch and cause disaster. In the plant there were security systems that eliminated such mistakes. The worst thing he could do in his comfortable chair was to drop the pen on the floor. And for this comfort his pay was raised three salary grades! The job was easy and boring and he said that he was in it only for the money. (But when the tape recorder was turned off at the end of the interview he added, concerning the cold instrumental attitude he had expressed: 'Maybe I'm not as 'tough' as it appears'...)

There were different strategies in the new and uncomfortable situation that had been created in the switchplant. Although there were a couple of cases that could be seen to adhere to one or the other of these strategies, a closer look at

262

them would reveal that they were never completely one-sided. It was as if even the strategy that seemingly was the most clearcut one always retained a back door open. Simply speaking, one did not put all the eggs in one basket.

I am not talking about a 'conscious' strategy, something planned in a teleological fashion, a case of maximizing the gains and/or minimizing the losses, but rather about strategies in the sense developed by Bourdieu, seeing them as growing out of or determined by the habitus.[5] The double-sided nature of the strategies, each of them standing with one foot in the other quarters, resembles what Bourdieu calls second-degree strategies, which are "[...] aimed at giving apparent satisfaction to the demands of the official rule, so combining the satisfactions of interest [pertaining to strategies directly oriented towards primary profit] with the prestige or respect which almost universally reward actions apparently motivated by respect for the rule." He adds: "There is nothing that groups demand more insistently and reward more generously than this conspicuous reverence for what they claim to revere."[6]

In the case of taking up work in the switchboard plant there were several 'collective, publicly avowable, legitimate interests', which both sides were trying to, if not exactly manipulate, at least persuade the collective judgement to accept as the official definitions of the situation, rather than the individual interests, which both sides, often secretly and in roundabout manner, ascribed to each other.

One of these publicly avowable interests was to show the world that the shunters were capable of operating the switchboard plant by themselves. This occupation is in many respects exactly the opposite of everything that shunting is seen to stand for. It is a white collar job, it is all indoors, being tied to a particular chair in front of monitors that are most easily read when the daylight is weak or absent, it is at least semi-skilled and learnt from texts and books more than from doing and 'finding out for oneself'. All commands depend on explicit codes and verbal communication over radio and telephone and many of the partners that stand in communication with each other have no idea of whom they are talking to, much less what they look like. This gives the job an impersonal and office-like character. The job is furthermore associated with the 'modern world', with computers and high-tech, i.e. the world that in so many ways is the opposite to the yard as well as the ultimate threat to it.

---

[5] Cf. BOURDIEU 1977, 72 f, 214 n.2.
[6] BOURDIEU 1990a, 109.

The visitors to the plant confirmed this picture of the operators as performing a new and advanced job. Here they were, having shed their greasy overalls for white shirts and ties, hacking away on the keyboards, staring at the networks of multi- coloured lines and flickering lights, alternaterly answering calls on the radio, on different telephones – and in between questions from visitors.

Shunters were thus not stupid illiterates, all muscle and no brains. The new technology was successfully handled by 'us, the shunters', and 'computer experts' were not needed for the operational acivities. There were such experts, led by a young woman, but they were all down in the basement, and were only there to install and maintain the computer. They could not actually work the systems and conduct movements in the yard. Only in combination with shunting was it possible to handle the computers.

The operators constituted then, as being part of 'us', a prestigious front of shunting. Their success or failure was a success or failure for the shunting group as a whole. To excel as an operator was to confirm and further the picture of the shunters as a competent and skilful work force.

The 'we'-aspect, the connection between the operators and the shunters in the yard because of their common origins, had, if we look at the other side of the coin, the potentially harmful effect of reducing the operators into some low status indoor workers, manual workers without manual tasks. They could be seen as operators who, much like telephone switchboard operators, only worked at the command of the 'customers', in this case the engine drivers and the teams out in the yard.

The interest in defining the switchboard plant as an advanced piece of technology, and the operators as (en-)skilled technicians, actively planning the movements in the yard as opposed to only taking orders, had its parallel in attempts to express the heightened prestige in forms of dress and in spatial strategies aimed at drawing a sharp line between indoor and outdoor staff.

In the old barracks the *tkm* and the coach recorders often wore blue SJ jackets over their 'civil' clothes, claiming that they otherwise got black from oil and dirt in the coffee-room and in their contacts with the shunters. In the new facilities *tkm* have in general resorted to their private clothes, while the coach recorders keep a jacket for outdoor wear as they go on their rounds to register carriage lables (tallies) in the yard.

The switchboard plant operators never wear SJ overalls or jackets. They have dark red plush chairs. The operators repeatedly complained that the chairs got stained when the shunters tested them for comfort, or leaned over their backs looking at the monitors.

264

The switchboard plant had a large area that was not being used, and the operators purchased a set of white plastic chairs and a table for their coffee-breaks. They also bought a couple of white pedestals for large green plants (one of which the shunters, however, abducted to their coffee-room) to screen the table off from the 'work part'.

The shunters' habit of strolling into the plant and sitting down in the wide window-sills, in the soft chairs and, now, also on the white garden chairs, was not easily broken. The operators grunted over oily gloves landing on their papers, and also about all kinds of funny comments pinned on the board, and even written on their work material. A diary they had lying in the plant where all break-downs and malfunctions in the plant should be annotated quickly had 'Karlsson has too high a salary' added onto the cover under the original title: 'FAULTS'.

The operators said that the police were dissatisfied with the security at the plant. Anyone had access to the plant and could manipulate switches from the key-boards. The operators claimed that there was going to be a locked door between the plant and the rest of the corridor, a door which could only be opened with an ID-card. Some said that they were longing for that door, not because they were afraid of intruders, but because this would keep 'everyone' (i.e. the shunters) from entering at all hours. Some said jokingly that it would keep the manager out, as the door to his office was just outside the door, but it was generally the 'stream' of people who messed things up and spread oil on the chairs who were not welcome. Only a physical obstacle between indoors and outdoors, a steel door with a lock that admitted 'staff only', could make it clear to the shunters that they did not belong.

To the shunters it was only obvious that the operators were reluctant to work in the yard. They had become 'fina' ('superior') and were now defending their privileged position. Naturally they could sometimes choose to work one or two good shifts in the yard for a change, but they would not dirty themselves on command. They had advanced to being 'indoor staff' and just as the engine driver in the past, who drew a line of chalk across the floor in the engine to mark the side where shunters were allowed, the operators were now trying to mark a line between themselves and the yard by closing this channel of exchange between the plant and the yard. All that was needed was the locked security door to the plant, and the operators would have managed to manipulate themselves into a truly fortified position.

The other publicly avowable interest that is easily identifiable is one that stands in sharp contrast with the first one. This second interest is to 'remain a shunter'. Just because one had left the yard and acquired a soft chair, one should not identify with managers, planners and white collar staff. The job as an operator was basically the same as the job the train-pullers had done, the only difference being that the operators were shielded from all the risks in the yard.

By down-playing the skills needed to operate the plant, by dressing in casual clothes instead of shirt and tie, and by defining the main task of the operators as a service to the shunters, this second interest crosses the strategy of the status enhancing efforts.

The clashing interests, both of which claimed to be in line with the interests of the group, led to quarrelling and acrimony between the operators as well as the shunters. The shunters were on one hand often contemptuous of the strategies that aimed at raising the status of the plant and the operators, but to groups external to the shunting group – contrasting themselves as a uniform group, *'bangårdsgruppen'* – they showed pride over the plant and the technological advancement it represented. The two interests can therefore be considered to be situationally defined. The enskilment interest being faced towards the outside world, the solidarity interest being dominant within the context of *'bangårdsgruppen'*.

The different interests were even reflected in different work policies in the plant. The desire to present the plant almost as a railway equivalent to an air-control tower made the contacts with engine drivers, the Central Station and other groups external to the shunters seem very important. The role of the operator was one who actively directed the traffic, found alternative solutions to blocked routes and who, because of long experience from work in the yard, knew the right strings to pull when something out of the ordinary turned up. These events were seen as important and significant. While it was true that almost everybody could learn how to operate the plant when things went smoothly it was these extraordinary events that constituted the skills of the trade – and legitimated the high salary, it was thought. Some of the people appointed to the plant did not have this background, true, but they could perhaps learn from the seniors.

The problem was that the other view, i.e. that it only took a couple of weeks to learn the job, threatened to turn the plant into a 'sick bay' *('sjukstuga')*. Shifts in the plant had been filled with shunters who were incapacitated from sprained or broken limbs, back trouble, or pregnancy, while steady operators were rescheduled to work in the yard, as they were experienced shunters. This led to an argument where one side defended 'the principle' of operators having prerogative to shifts in the plant, ('this is no sick bay'), while the other side thought it 'natural' that the staff be used in the most

266

efficient way, i.e. letting the physically disabled work in the plant instead of forcing them to go on sick leave. The first category stressed that they by no means objected to working outdoors – quite the contrary! – but the principle was that operators should fill the schedule before others were taken in.

As well as the publicly aired opinions about 'the principle' or 'too high salaries' there were then also strategies that were not aired and formulated openly. The opinion the operators had of the status of the plant was reflected in how they saw their work and how they solved problems in the plant. As we saw above, some operators stressed the external contacts. The plant was seen as a link in a large net of communication and the operators were eager to maintain and possibly enlarge this broad network. A friendly, 'chummy', tone was adopted in contacts with non-shunters as well as shunters in the yard, and regardless of the workload and 'mess' in the yard these operators tried always to keep the voice cheerful, and optimistic, signalling that everything was under control and that all problems would be solved speedily.

Towards the shunters the attitude was likewise cheerful and one made often a point of recognizing the voice of the caller from only: 'Ställverket, kom'!, ('The Plant, come!') by answering: 'Hej, Pelle! Jaså, du har tagit över där nu!' ('Hello, Pelle! So you have taken over there now!') This cheerfulness was, however, also expected to be responded with, if not equal cheerfulness and courtesy, at least due respect. When things went wrong and the shunters got annoyed, screaming on the radio, the operator could demonstrate the power of the position in the plant and let the rude shunters wait. 'If they get nasty I just give priority to someone else and they'll have to wait.'[7]

Such demonstrative use of the power by the operators was quite foreign to those operators who were trying to keep up the image of themselves as shunters of a kind. They saw their work as a service to the shunting teams, to which they themselves belonged. They had, of course, an obligation to let departing trains have priority, but otherwise they directed their attention to the service of the team rather than having 'chummy' relations with the switchboard plant at the Central Station, or with the engine drivers. Their future was with the shunters, and to get praise from the team was too important to be jeopardized by punishing measures, such as giving second priority to angry shunters.

Naturally these 'team-faithful' operators were no less eager to be accepted as selected for the job because of their qualities. They defended the 'flexible'

---

[7] It is common knowledge that complaints over the telephone easily turn into rudeness and insults. It is said that there are *tkm* who prefer to walk down to the workshops to complain or discuss a problem, in order to avoid that rude telephone jargon will distort the whole issue.

solution of letting in bad backs and sprained joints - 'we have our jobs nevertheless' - but in secret one of them aired the fears of perhaps being selected due to an ailment that the others did not know of, but which this person had referred to in an application for indoor service. The thought that the comrades in the plant would find out was all but pleasant.

The 'principle'-defending operators were likewise eager to counteract the accusations of considering themselves 'superior' by stressing the joys of outdoor work, or the irritation over the defects of the plant. The most unfortunate instance of this was when Karlsson picked the wrong moment for his complaint and the attempt to get sympathy from the shunters misfired.

This happened one day when the shunters had gathered to watch long-distance cross-country skiing on the TV-set in the coffee-room. A Norwegian skier was winning and 'the Norwegian' was cheering and shouting joking insults, making everybody laugh. Despite the bitter Swedish losses the ambiance was thus excited and jokes were exchanged.

In the aftermath of all this, unfortunately, Karlsson entered the coffee-room. He sighed and complained that the plant 'again' did not work as a switch had been blocked by snow. Signalling that he was a man of action, and that he did not fear outdoor work he announced that he had put on a jacket and gloves and gone out to clear and turn the switch manually himself.

Had the coffee-room not been full of already rather excited shunters, as it were only waiting to find a proper outlet for their frustration, this remark would most likely have been received with understanding nods and comments about the 'uselessness' of the plant. Now Karlsson's complaint met a storm of scorn and laughter.

'You don't say you went out into the yard!?'

'Did you remember how to turn a switch?'

'Poor Kalle, don't tell us you got oil on your hands!'

'Did you do that all on your own!'

'How did you manage the stairs?'

Karlsson was trying to pretend that they were only joking, but the complete unison of the reaction and the all too spiteful atmosphere made it clear that there was a clear message behind the jolliness. The shunters had suddenly a golden opportunity to air their opinion about the 'superior' plant operators and Karlsson could not find a way to answer back that would win the laughers over to his side. He was one of the indoor-staff, and when trying to peep out he only got the door flung straight back into his face.

A Tower of Control – Communication over a Distance

The two main factors that created the tensions around the plant were on one hand that the operators were to be isolated from the yard in the comforts of the 'control tower', and on the other hand the drastic increase in pay that accompanied that move. It was said that one of the *tkm* had been discussing the operating task with one of the shunters, saying that this obviously was a job for the youngsters. When informed about the salary grade of the job, however, he immediately added his own name to the list of applicants – and was later among those selected.

This first part of the story cannot be verified, but when we remember that the common view among the shunters was that they stayed in this job because they could not consider working indoors, and when we know that about sixty (out of around eighty) of them nevertheless applied to become operators, we must conclude that money was an important incentive.

Because so many had applied, the question of fairness in the selection of the nine operators came to the fore.

It was claimed that the salary was clearly out of proportion to the work, which was only a mechanized 'train-pullery' *('tågdrageri')*. Due to the automatic systems, it actually demanded less of the operators than of the train-pullers. Still, it was a good thing. One could not object to raised salaries. The high salaries did not affect the salaries in the yard negatively, and in the long run they might actually influence them positively. The manager had done them all a great favour by 'tricking' SJ into paying so much. The reason he managed to pull it off was that the superiors had a natural propensity to view indoor work as important and when in addition, lo and behold, **computers** were involved they were, without further inquiry, prepared to see this as skilled work. This was only evidence of what the shunters already knew about 'superiors' *('höjdare')*. They considered any desk job as more important than outdoor work. Now they had been deceived by their own illusions, and were tricked to pay outrageous wages for a simple task only because it was clean and 'modern'.[8]

The opposite view stressed that the operator was not only a transplanted train-puller. It was true that instead of moving across the yard to manipulate switches and disconnect engines, the operator was now tied to a chair. Despite the physical immobility the operator was not, however, incapacitated, quite

---

[8] Bryan Pfaffenberger discusses similar views about computers, large as well as personal ones. Cf. PFAFFENBERGER 1988, 42 f.

the contrary; the operator had control over the larger part of the yard. Radios, telephones and remote controlled switches meant that the operator was communicating with workers in the yard, with engine drivers, with the Order Centre as well as with staff outside the yard. The communication could be intense and hectic, but the distance and the remoteness from the scene of action meant that the operator could excercise his power over the movements and over the flow of information in a way that had been quite impossible for the train-puller. A new job had been created, a job that 'belonged to the future'. One can assume that one day automatic couplings would make the shunters obsolete, and the teams would be dismantled and replaced by some lone ranger, or more likely by the switchboard plant operators, who in any case would enlarge their dominions and develop their technological potential of control over engines, carriages, and trains.

The indoor/outdoor dichotomy in the plant represented not only a move from blue collar to white collar work, but a move from the manual traditions of the past to a computerized future. It also created a siding in the line of advancement that might open up to new and formerly unfrequented tracks past the dead end of the shunting trade.

While the plant initially was seen as a rational and safe way to turn switches, it turned out that several other aspects are involved. The technology is a medium for communication, but just as contact easily is established it can also easily be delayed. While the different means of contact, such as radio versus local or external telephone, already announces who the caller might be, it is possible at an early stage to give priority to one over the other. It is further also feasible to delay the execution of the demands of the caller. The caller has no insight into what is happening in the plant and can do nothing but wait for the switches to turn and the signals to permit movement on the desired tracks. In the case of a delay the computer could be to blame, other demands could already be on the list, other calls could keep the operator busy – in every individual case there is simply no telling from the view-point of the yard. The plant is a centre of communication and control as well as a remote and physically isolated place.

The paradox of this opportunity for control is, however, that it works only as long as it is not identified as such by the shunters. One might not be able to pinpoint exactly when the operator intentionally delays a movement, but over a longer period of time it becomes clear who is quick to execute orders and who tends to be busy and occupied by other things or blaming the computer. During the time of the 'infant maladies' of the switchboard plant it was quickly established among the shunters in the yard that the plant tended to break down when certain operators were at work and blames on faulty technology soon threatened to backfire on the operator.

As a long term strategy then, it seems impossible for the switch plant operators to excercise the opportunities of power and control over the work process that the medium of the plant extends to them. There remains with the shunters always the ability to obstruct the track by leaving a coach too close to a switch, thereby inhibiting moves in the vicinity. This is not to say that such measures are taken by the shunters, only that the switchboard plant is dependent on the shunters for its functioning, a fact well recognized by the shunters. One must not, however, forget that the means of control available to the switchboard plant operators often can be said to find support in the regulations, while the shunters must more often resort to breaking the rules in order to have an impact on the determination of the movements in the yard which are controlled by the switchboard plant.

The most fundamental impact of the switchboard plant on the work process of the shunters is the retarding effect it inevitably has on the speed of work and the stiff and less flexible planning it favours. Any change of mind will have to be accompanied by a change of earlier orders, thereby publicly revealing an earlier mistake or plain indecisiveness. There is a new formality in the work process as every move is brought to the ears and eyes of an audience behind the dark screens of the tower above and leaves a trace as a scribbling in the memory pads in this remote eagle's nest.

While the switchboard plant is a prerequisite for guiding arriving and departing trains, its utility for the shunting teams is not unquestioned. For long cuts and large movements it assures safe passage – the switches are lined – but for many small moves, especially when the switches do not concern other simultaneous moves in the yard, the switchboard plant only means that work is unnecessarily 'bureaucratic'. During slack periods, such as late at night, the shunters therefore often ask to 'take over locally'. They then operate the switches just as before the introduction of the plant, saving time and avoiding the detour over the computer. This is undoubtedly enjoyed by both parties.

Spatiality as Meaning

I will argue, on the basis of the explorations above, that the organization of spatiality offers a means to express, construct, re-form and generate relations of solidarity and equity as well as relations of distanciation, authority and domination. There is, however, no absolute determination in the organization

271

of spatiality. Spatial obstacles, in form of distance and physical obstruction, can be overcome by strong ideological and mental bonds, while closeness and open doors can be effectively 'closed' by invisible prohibitions and obstacles.

Invisible walls are far from new findings. All anthropologists are familiar with the long house practices of 'being out,' in e.g. the Amazonas, where a person turning the face to the wall is treated as absent. We do not have to go further than a crowded beach in Scandinavia to observe how strangers manage to remain unsociable and virtually 'unseen' to each other, despite their spending hours almost completely naked, just a couple of meters apart.

I want instead to draw attention to the particularities of the interplay between structure and action, and contrast areas of rigid order and institutionalization with areas that allow, or even seemingly invite, change and flux.

Hierarchical structures, structures of informal power and different ideological paradigms do not coincide with each other, and neither do any one of them conform fully with the spatial structuring of the workplace. The discrepancies and paradoxes that always and inevitably will occur therefore evoke different readings and kindle different strategies.

As the yard underwent a process of modernization during the period that this study touches upon (broadly speaking 1982 to 1992), the facilities of the shunters described a parallel development, being moved from the old red barracks over the temporary green barracks and finally to the brand new top floor on the roof of the New Hall. Both moves meant a move towards more convenient and modern installations and each move also implied a step towards a higher degree of planning and purpose fulfilment.

Needless to say, the planning was not the doing of the shunters, although the club chairman and the safety officer were involved in the evaluation of the blueprints. The planning had the explicit aim of gathering the shunting group under one roof. The green barracks already provided changing rooms and lockers to all shunters, and they had all (except one stubborn person) left the large common changing rooms in the New Hall. With the move to the top floor the shunting group was finally 'self sufficient' and set apart from the rest. This would supposedly enhance the group feeling and the solidarity within the group as well as diminish the distance and thereby the opposition between the management and the shunters.

The functionally based separation between different work groups at Hagalund did not end with this, however. We have seen that the different functions within the group were ascribed different locker rooms and different offices, a design which expressed the planners' view of shunting work.[9] We can e.g. see that VIK personnel is separated from the teams. From the yard point of view there is no obvious reason why this should be the case, rather the opposite. The teams now find it hard to know whether a VIK, replacing the ordinary member, has arrived or not as this member does not share the same locker room.

Looking at the whole row of lockers, descending from *tkm* (and women, who are placed next to the least 'dangerous' staff), to teams, and finally VIK, suggest clearly that VIK personnel are seen as fringe personnel and somehow inferior to the rest. This might reflect earlier times when 'extras' were brought in on week-ends from other stations nearby, but today the VIK are often senior shunters, employed full-time like everybody else, but enjoying the variation in work tasks. It is rather more uncommon for a team to lack VIK personnel than to have one or two VIKs in the team, due to holidays, changes of shifts, sickness, maternity or paternity leave, compensation in free time (instead of money) for over-time, etc.

When the *tkm* were given their own changing rooms in the green barracks there were already ironic remarks about segregating 'high status' personnel from 'the mob'. The former situation had in fact been the reverse as the *tkm* were obliged to undress more or less in public, the last years even with young women passing through their locker corner.

As all others had been changing in the large changing rooms, male and female, in the New Hall, everyone arrived to the barracks in work clothes, transformed to a shunter. This kept the 'civil' world at some distance as well as it made the barracks a world set apart. Arriving in civil clothes at the barracks one was as visible as a person in ordinary clothes entering an ice-hockey rink.

This chaotic representation of the hierarchy in the regionalization of the facilities in the yard led to incidents such as the one where a senior male shunter shared soap and shampoo with a junior female shunter in the shower, a situation that in the new facilities was ruled out completely, due to the well

---

[9] We have to include the shunters' representatives among the planners, too. The view is thus a construct removed from practice, being an official account of this practice. The relationship between account and practice is parallel to the one between regulative and constitutive rules. Concerning official accounts, cf. JENKINS, 436 ff., and for a longer discussion BOURDIEU, 1977, 33 ff. I am not using 'account' in exactly the same way as Garfinkel, but there could be a point in saying that the spacial plan is part of an 'account-making' (procedures for convincing others that they share a common factual world)of the formal organization of work. Cf. TURNER, J.,176 f, and HERITAGE, 248 f. When Ingold says that human beings construct the world "(...) by virtue of their own conceptions of the possibilities of being."(INGOLD; 1995, 63) I must add that here the construction is rather a backward looking one, it has no visions other than those given by an ageing hierarchy.

planned separation of young and old as well as male and female. It was no joke when a senior shunter commented that there really should not be separate changing rooms for men and women as 'we all look the same anyway', when he – aided by the anthropologist – was hanging new curtains in the male showers (the female showers being equipped with doors and locks...). He was simply sighing over the institutionalized order which, to him, seemed oldfashioned. It was probably his matter of fact tone of voice that made a senior *tkm*, who overheard the comment, abstain from the obvious – and otherwise inevitable – joking reply.

The planned layout was thus a hindrance for the individual to decide in matters of proximity and distance. By mingling more openly one could, as we have seen formerly, trade status and position for comradeship and youthfulness, a practical belonging to the juniors. Respect and obedience was exchanged for joking and easy sociability. The new order went against the grain of the spirit of the shunting community, not only because it made visible a hierarchy that was suppressed and denied in everyday life, but because it furthermore limited the personal choice of where one belonged. There had always been grumpy 'old bachelors' in the yard, who silently, but undeniably, insisted on formal rank, but there had also always been persons who opted for eternally belonging with the youngsters, showing indifference to matters of status and position by entering joking relationships with their juniors and by always retaining something of a flippant attitude to the job.[10]

The paradox is therefore that when the shunters finally, after so many decades, get their own modern, purposebuilt facilities, all under one roof, they find their everyday life transformed and organized in a way that goes against the grain of their understanding of their work and of themselves as a group.

Instead of slipping in and out of the coffee-room of a barracks next to passing trains and engines, making all the cups shake on the tables, one now enters a silent world far above the yard, fortressed behind security windows and stairs mountains high. The coffee-room, the beating heart of the yard, is no longer the centre confidently approached only by shunters in overalls. It is a room at the lower end of the corridor, next to the toilets and the changing rooms of the VIK, now separated to form a low rank category. The coffee-

---

[10] It is possible to see the novel phenomenon of entering the women's locker room to hang funny posters – or a collage torso – as a way of transgressing and denying an uncomfortable border. If the intention was to intimidate or shock, which I very much doubt, it certainly failed. The women thought it 'cool' (*'häftigt'*) and took active part in adding similar, if not even more obscene, pictures. The only nude pictures in the shunting facilities were those that the women tagged on their locker doors in the green barracks. The men never resumed such habits since the time Arkansas made his rounds tearing down all indecent pictures as a preparation for the entry of women in the yard.

room is passed by a stream of persons in civil dress, persons difficult to identify at a glance. Some are staff belonging to the offices down the corridor, but there are also staff from outside, such as 'big guns' *('höjdare')* visiting the manager, or groups on study visits, while some of the persons you get a glance of when they pass, are only shunters on their way to or from the changing rooms. This trickle creates discomfort, partly because there is the feeling that one is being watched by outsiders, but mainly because the coffee-room is turned into a room that people pass, not a room that attracts everybody in its vicinity, being the natural meeting point. People are passing on to something more important, it seems, the other end of the corridor, where the switchboard plant, the *tkm*, the staff delegator, and the manager reside. There are, in addition, now other coffee-rooms, too. One rival is enclosed by big green plants instead of cigarette smoke, and with computer games instead of card-playing, another one lies inside the *tkm* office, consisting of a tiny room with a minute table for two. There is no need to put up a sign saying that these are **not** for shunters.

The attempts to neglect and deny hierarchy as soon as one entered the facilities from the yard were now counteracted by the marked compartmentalization of space. The novel switchplant offered two strategies for its operators; one was the uncertain road towards prestigious and comfortable white collar work, enjoying the solitary breaks in fresh air amidst the plants, viewing the yard from a superior position, while the other was the stubborn sticking to the crowd, remaining, allegorically speaking, with one foot in the gravel of the yard by inhaling the smoke and enjoying the laughter around the card table in the shunters' coffee-room.

Despite the disintegrating effects of the outline of the new facilities, the intentions, i.e. to collect the whole group under one roof, are nevertheless acknowledged. The shunters are privileged enough to get their own modern lodgings. The oft repeated ambitions of the manager to 'develop the group' has here a physical and quite concrete manifestation, although it was completed before his arrival, and although the planning and the completion show flaws and defects. But what else can you expect from the planners, those indoor paper-turners with no idea about the demands of shunting work!

Organizationally the Yard Group is a distinct group, with its own economy, its own leadership, its own union (exceptions being the manager, of course, and the staff delegator), and now also its own quarters. Conceived in these terms it consists of a hardworking bunch of people in Hagalund; men and women who are not completely water-, storm-, and coldproof, but who are able to accept the awful conditions due to a sense of humour. They are restless outdoor people who see the summer as a wonderful compensation for the rest of the year, they see the comradeship between workmates as more important than a career and a high salary. They cannot conceive of themselves as working indoors (they get headache from sitting still) and they want to work with something real. Indoor work is corruptive as it makes people **think** they know, and **think** they do something. The phony character of their work makes them create images in order to convince the rest of the world of their importance. They dress fancy, talk phony, demanding 'good manners' and respect from inferiors. They become all surface while the content is diminished. Real people **do** instead of talk, their outward appearance and manners do not need any frills as a person will get the respect he deserves without asking for it. Good, honest and skilful workmates and superiors, who do not shun hard work, instill natural respect, even if their manners are not excessively polite.

This idealized picture of the good shunter, and at the same time the dividing line between indoor and outdoor work, breaks up as soon as we scrutinize the reality of the Yard Group. There is a general, and unquestioned, preference for the less physically demanding jobs, and for indoor jobs. As long as it is not obvious that one is avoiding hardship at the cost of someone else it is self-evident that one should not do more than absolutely necessary. The many applicants for the indoor job in the switchboard plant (around 75% of the entire work force) must be considered significant. At least it seems possible to compensate the outdoor advantages with a couple of pay grades.

What is the most significant evidence of a suppressed but very strong evaluation of indoor comforts is the whole construction of tasks in the hierarchy. It could be claimed that this construction is not undertaken by the shunting community and is not in keeping with their ideals, but it is on the other hand strongly defended. We can see that cases of controversial promotions to indoor jobs or to less physically demanding jobs are among those that have caused the most intense feelings of unfair treatment. (Here, too, a higher pay grade is often a strong incentive, but I do not believe that it can be seen as the sole explanation.)

To get away from the ardour of the yard is undeniably a privilege to look forward to as a crowning of the career, despite notable exceptions to this rule, where persons have refused promotion. The outdoor *tkm* is supposed to be helpful in lining the tracks, but there is considerable freedom to choose exactly how much the *tkm* should involve himself in manual labour. Shunt leaders also have a choice in this respect as they always can refer to the motto: 'A shunt leader should never go between.'

276

The splitting of outdoor tasks into executive/manual (B- and C-members, knockers) and commanding/communicative/ supervisory, as well as into team-work (shunters proper) and solitary tasks (train-pullers, knockers) represents as much hierarchical relations and conflicts of interest as the opposition between indoor and outdoor work, but these relations are not given expression and are covered by the rhetoric of 'the freedom of the team'. They are also veiled by stressing that train-pullers and shunters are complementary, and equally needed. 'Without the train-pullers the shunters would have no trains to work with.'

One line crossing the indoor/outdoor division, however, is often brought up and stressed: the line between on one hand the *tkm* and other seniors and on the other hand the younger shunters. Here the category of 'younger ones' is not coextensive with what I have earlier called youngsters, as it may include senior shunters, aged fifty or more. It is their 'social age' and mentality that counts. The 'younger ones' are persons who are flexible and can adjust to new ways, who have traded their hierarchical status for comradeship and joking acceptance.[11] In some respects the old and the new thinking that the two categories are thought to embrace parallel the orthodox union standpoint versus various standpoints with less principled and more practical outlook.

When the practical outlook dominates, the tendency is toward an even greater spread of interests. The difference between bachelors and family-fathers, between those who see the job as a temporary one and those who have no higher ambitions, and between those who prefer time over money and the reverse – all such personal tastes come to the fore and tend to split the opinion on almost every issue. We saw that the suggestion of a 'straight schedule' even popped up, to the despair and bewilderment of the union representative, while the younger shunters had no real objections to it, but judged it merely from their personal point of view.

Considering all these contradictions, one can ask whether there is any real foundation for regarding the shunters as a group with common interests, which they claim they are. They are organizationally dependent on each other as they belong to the same economic unit, but otherwise splits tend to cut through even the closest units, the shunting teams, as they naturally span the

---

[11] The trade implied here is not necessarily a transaction as it sometimes only implies that one chooses the necessary, while giving an air of an active choice. To 'trade' position for a joking relationship might therefore mean that the prestigious position was out of reach anyway. Cicourel takes up Collins's notion of encounters as marketplaces and writes: "The individual brings cultural (or conventional) and emotional resources to the encounter. Specific styles and and topics of conversation are said to reflect membership in different groups (...)" Here, too, it is more a matter of display than barter. Cf. CICOUREL, 59.

age difference from seniors to beginners. In the last instance it is 'every man for himself', or, as it was put so plainly: 'I'm not going to help no bugger, because no bugger helps me!'

The view, often repeated, that the shunters consist of a heterogeneous mix of weirdos, who have accidentally landed in the yard, seems to recognize this impossibility to find a concrete matter everybody in the group could agree upon. It may be that it is precisely this rejection of 'normality' and taking pride in the thought of themselves (or at least their comrades) as freaks, which in the last instance manages to bridge the gaps between the different shunters.

It is true that a couple of months indoors may make an old shunter get 'stupid indoor ideas', but were he to work outdoors again these would disappear as quickly as ice in the sun. There is unity in working in the yard and disagreement in the coffee-room. We know that there may be clashes in the work in the yard, too, resulting from pig-headed routines that clash in a particular team.

There is a paradox in the fact that shunting work is seen to choose its worker, thereby creating a common denominator among the shunters: not shunning hard work, having a sense of humour, etc., as well as it simultaneously seems to sift out 'odd' personalities, who create their personal ways of working and who are often quite obstinate about their own routines. While the common denominator is an outcome of practical work, of doing rather than discussing, the splits are formed in discussion. Inflexible, idiosyncratic shunting routines are formed in work, too, but the prerequisite for them is the relative isolation that is granted the teams due to their fixed composition and the time-schedules that practically prevent free movement of shunters between groups. The clashes are therefore exceptions rather than the rule.

The work-schedule has a profound influence in setting the shunters apart as a group of its own, while simultaneously creating divides within the group, enabling the development of different work-styles and routines. While the shunters stress the first effect, the second one is of little interest in the rhetoric describing 'us shunters' and is considered a practical oddity more than a specific quality defining shunting work.

We shall look briefly at the structuring of time in shunting. My argument is that by studying the aspect of time we can catch many facets of what Garfinkel has called the 'quiddity', or the 'just-whatness' of work[12] an expression which asks; just what does competent work consist of. Our case is,

---

12 Cf. discussion of this concept in HERITAGE, 262f.

of course, shunting. Conceptions of time set this occupation apart from other occupations which at the first glance would seem similar.

Clock Time, Social Time, and Working Time

'After working here I could never work in the industry.'
'Just imagine having time-clocks!'
'...and asking for permission to go to the toilet!'
(Shunters discussing the advantages of the yard)

The control of time in capitalist industrial social life has been discussed extensively, one of the earliest writers being Marx, who understood industrial time as commodified time. This understanding underlies more recent studies, which have widened the scope, but still kept the core largely intact.[13] As much of this discussion concerns the character of social time in modern societies, relating it to power, to global interaction and storage capacity of information, it has a bearing upon the shunting yard as a part of the modern industrialized world, but at the same time the theories involved concern society on a larger scale. There are common denominators to several of the writers, such as Anthony Giddens, E.P. Thompson, H.-W. Hohn, K. Heinemann and P. Ludes, which, no doubt, can be directly related to the world of the shunters, e.g. the claim that "[...] the capitalist work-discipline abstracts both work and time from their contextual meanings and imposes an independent metric dynamic."[14]

It is important to realize that these theories paint the picture of the complete jigsaw puzzle, while this study of the shunting yard describes the form and shape of one of the pieces. I am well aware of the profound meaning that clock time and other concepts of time have for the shunting world as part of the railroad system, the industrial world and modern society, but I will concentrate here on the specific aspects of time that distinguish the shunting yard from other parts of society. These aspects are often details that acquire their meaning precisely from this difference, i.e. from what you find, or what the shunters think you find, in other industries or in society at large, and I will therefore talk about the **secondary meanings** of time that are created by the shunting experience.

---

[13] For good summaries of the main contributions to this debate, cf. ADAM, 9 ff., GELL, *passim* and MUNN, *passim.*
[14] ADAM, 116.

Shunting entails shiftwork, but as the shifts overlap in several ways the overall picture of coming and going is not the one where one shift leaves and the other one takes over. The shift that is being replaced has probably already left when their replacement takes over, and as there may be another shift having a break simultaneously – with the addition of knockers, train-pullers, switchboard plant operators and *tkm* coming, going or having a break – it is virtually impossible to read the shift 'status' of all the persons that swarm around the coffee-room.

Although the yard is seen as a place where one always – day or night, work-day or holiday – can go to see friends, this does not imply that the yard, and consequently the coffee-room, are equally busy at all hours. There are peaks a couple of times in the morning, around lunchtime and in the afternoon, while there are slack hours at night. When the night shift is finished there may be only a *tkm* and a switchboard plant operator holding the fortress. It is, however, quite common that someone who lives far from the yard (which indeed most shunters do) does not care to go home for a few hours, but sleeps over in the resting room, in a locker room, or, more common, in a sleeping wagon in the yard. If one has been out on the town at night it may also seem safer to take the *'personalare'* (the 'personnel engine' commuting between Hagalund and the Central Station at night) to Hagalund and sober up on the premises, thereby gaining a few hours sleep as well as avoiding the risk of oversleeping. After inspecting their team-member in the morning, the team might decide to let the poor bloke sleep an hour extra, but at least they know where to find him and the uncertainty of waiting for a late-comer is avoided.

Despite the oscillation between busy and slack hours, Hagalund has the quality of always being there.[15] It may therefore function as a resort or refuge. The mates at Hagalund may poke fun at you for a week for your hang-over, but there is after all a forgiveness and understanding vis-à-vis the occasional lapse from good behaviour. There have been senior shunters wailing that they dare not go home to confront their wives. To take on an extra shift, or just to sleep over, may then come as a saviour from above.

Young bachelors from the countryside might find it more attractive to spend holidays working in Hagalund than to spend them in their lonely apartments. They may even prefer to stay on after finishing work to play cards

---

[15] When described as always-being-there', we see time and space connected in a representation of something reliable and secure. One shunter described Hagalund as his second home, and his work mates as a substitute for the family he lacked. A 'home' has normally a fixed, even if temporary, location, but it should perhaps above all be available and welcoming at all hours.

for an hour or two, but this is considered a sign of misery. 'Do you **live** here?' 'Don't you have anything else to do?' they will be asked. (Naturally with one exception, Örby, who demands that the others should explain why they come so early when they are in such a 'panic' to get back home again. He himself prefers to be half an hour late and not to hurry *('stressa')* on his way back home, sometimes staying on for an hour or two, talking or playing cards.)

The commodification of time, of which clock time is an evident expression[16], is fundamental to the division of time into working time and free time. This division is eternally subject to negotiation between employers and workers, but it also constitutes the warp of the fabric of meaning that I have called secondary.

The halting reversibility between time and money, referring to the fact that money in most cases can be turned into time (by e.g. the purchase of services), while time cannot necessarily be turned into money (as e.g. is the case with the unemployed) is indeed an interesting observation.[17] It is the emphatic denial of this imbalance that the shunters express by returning so urgently from work. Even if they are finished one hour early they put up an air of being equally pressed for time. 'Come on, you have time until one o'clock and it is only noon!' the card-players will try to entice a comrade to join the gang. The proud shunter will then ensure his mates that **his** time is money and that **he** has something very important to do. He is in fact already late... We remember the shunter who, when finding out that he had a trainee with him, immediately decided to leave. In his case time was perhaps money as he claimed that he had to attend to his second job at the airport, but even if some shunters hold second jobs, such as taxi-driving, which could turn an odd hour into money, it is obviously the case that for the most part, the time gained is of symbolic, not monetary, value.

Free time is time that you 'own'. Working time that you manage to 'steal' from the employer, albeit in the legal way of having finished work, is, as we have seen, the hallmark of the skilled shunter. *'Smittider'*, 'dodging time', is part of the character of shunting work and it is a strange kind of humiliation to have to work the shift until its very last minute. If this would be repeated every day one might as well work in an office! The minutes that are gained are somehow seen to be earned in exchange for the ardour, and for the silent agreement that shunters never will let the company down by going

---

[16] Cf. GIDDENS 1990, 133 f., and MUMFORD, 272.
[17] Cf. ADAM, 114 (from HOHN, 157).

home – regardless of whether the shift should be finished – if the situation is critical and trains have to be shunted immediately.[18] The shunters will be paid overtime, of course, so it is therefore not a question of repayment in time-for-time. While the employer sometimes tries to point out that the extra quarter of an hour that the shunter had to work the day before, and which he wants to get paid for, maybe should be regarded in relation to the amount of hours he has gained through his *smittider*, this is always sternly rejected. The two things are not, or **should not** be, considered to be connected.[19]

The reason why *smittider* do not enter the balance-sheet of give and take between the shunters and the company is that the time gained in a shift is paid for by keeping up a work-speed that is known as being high compared to other yards, and which since time immemorial has included transgressions of speed-limits and regulations. The company is of course well aware of the fact, but there is little they can do except forcing all staff to repeat the safety regulations every year. (As opposed to the earlier every three years.) The employer understands that the work-speed is a function of the skill and zest of work and that fighting it too eagerly would only back-fire in actions of discontent, such as go-slows, probably causing more danger than the enforced speed-limits would prevent. There is the additional recognition that the buffer of time created by the speedy shunters is of great value when there are problems in the traffic. After all, this is Hagalund, a yard that does not resemble anything else and which always has put particular demands on its workers.

One could say that in order for the trains to be on time there must be a certain amount of buffer time 'behind the stage', i.e. in the production of the trains. There are many links in the chain of preparing rolling stock that may cause trouble. One has to count on repairs, changes and alterations. Constructing a time-table that is too tight is sooner or later going to cause serious trouble, as one breakdown often causes a chain reaction. If incoming trains are late there may be a shortage of carriages of a certain type, delaying

---

[18] McKenna writes about the overburdened British railway worker at the turn of the century that "...he had a high loyalty – a loyalty to the job itself. No matter how irksome or onerous the task, it was tackled and completed." McKENNA, 57. It may actually be the case at Hagalund, too, that the loyalty is more a loyalty to the job and the comrades than to the company.

[19] Even here it is necessary to add that there is a difference between senior and junior shunters. A beginner might indeed be reminded of his *smittider*, even by shunters, in case he makes a fuss over working overtime. There are also persons who see overtime as partly their own fault, or who do not want to be considered over-particular. This latter 'generous' attitude undoubtedly stems from a recognition of the one-sided time-exchange, but it is very rare to hear it being expressed in such terms.

shunting, which causes other trains to be late and left on tracks which should have been emptied for other arriving trains.

Buffer time is thus no luxury, but a necessary part of organizing work. It is a safety margin, but it is simultaneously the hallmark of the good shunter. It is often taken for granted, but this is never allowed to be recognized even in informal conversation, and shunters who claim they have to leave earlier because thay have an appointment elsewhere will be told by the team that they have no right to take it for granted that they can leave before the end of the shift. One must always be prepared to work the whole shift and always see it as a special bonus and a reward for a good day's work.

Although never allowed to be taken for granted, but always taken for granted, *smittider* constitute an important part of the flexibility of work that makes shunting a 'free' occupation. The length and periodicity of shifts, and the length and frequency of breaks are all based on the laws of working time and on agreements between employers and unions. The negotiations behind these concern principles and official evaluations of the demands of the work involved, such as stipulations of how long time is needed for rest or for the intake of food or refreshments. The union chairman will not give up a single 'porridge wedge' in the schedule, on the assumption that such a short break is necessary and indispensable, while it is obvious to everyone that these short breaks are neglected and that the youngsters often have no idea what a 'porridge wedge' is, or even that there are such things on the official time-table.[20] The official schedule lives to a certain extent a life of its own, also being a kind of a buffer that is the last resort for the shunters in case the worst comes to the worst and all shifts would have to be worked full time.

Outside the workplace *smittider* have only a very limited secondary symbolic value. Time-tables being so odd anyway very few persons, except the immediate family, will ever notice the unscheduled early homecomings. What the surrounding world will notice is mostly the odd hours that the shunter works. Örby, who cultivated a look that was judged to be rather disorderly, was met one week-day morning at his local market-place by the comment: 'You who don't have anything to do...' To be seen walking around in the market during 'working hours' is thus often taken to mean that one is unemployed. The shunters often complain about neighbours and friends who

---

[20] A 'porridge-wedge' is a short break, marked in the schedule in form of a wedge, signifying that the break could be taken at any time during the shift. Usually you find porridge-wedges during the night shifts. The night shifts, which officially lasted until 6 o'clock in the morning, were mostly finished around one or two o'clock, without break. If the workload signalled a longer shift, the team could consider taking a break.

think that they have a very easy job, because they spend week-days at home. 'They don't realize that I was working while they slept!'

Shunters often stress the importance of the odd working hours. They enjoy making errands or going shopping with their wives during week-days, avoiding crowds, and they may be able to look after their children at home instead of sending them off to day-care, provided they fix their shifts a bit. When a young father complained about going home in the morning to look after his child after the night shift, a senior shunter announced that he managed such situations by playing 'at Alsatian'. This, he explained, consisted of him lying on the kitchen floor, after having pulled out the lowest drawers and having opened the cupboards for pots and pans. The toddler was then allowed to pull out and investigate all he could reach, while the 'Alsatian' shunter rested on his pillow on the floor, one ear in the air, opening an eye only when the noise seemed alarmingly reduced.

Although playing Alsatians cannot be said to be a significant trait among shunters it is one of many solutions to the odd situations that the discrepancies between the time-table of the shunters and the society at large present.[21] Another senior shunter, who lives far from his family, had the problem of distance added to the odd time-schedule. He told of one day when he phoned his wife and asked her to meet him at the railway station in his hometown. He then boarded a train in the yard and travelled more than 500 km (325 miles) just in order to have breakfast with her and chat for two hours. Then he returned to work his next shift.

Other habits, such as repairing the house at two o'clock in the morning, must be seen to result from being accustomed to using the night, as well as the day-time hours, for activities. Being the only alert and sober passenger on the last night-bus, or returning home on the commuter train early in the morning after finishing the night shift, looking into gloomy and somnolent faces, are everyday instances of going against the stream.

While the senior shunters consider it increasingly difficult to adjust to the night shifts, younger shunters often often enjoy working nights. The pay is good, and provided you can get some sleep in the day, it is as if you almost have a day off the following day. Winter nights can be bitterly cold, and autumn nights may surprise you if temperatures drop drastically, but early spring mornings and clear summer's nights, when it is light and the temperature is perfect for manual labour, have a magic that shunters talk

---

[21] The ability to improvise and manage child-care by slightly unorthodox methods, rather than to rely on public day-care is a typical shunter-*cum-bricoleur* thing to do.

lyrically about and which they think compensates for the drudgery of the long dark winter.

The periodicity of the seasons has a concrete influence on the social life in the yard as well. Holidays are naturally busy periods for the passenger traffic and nowadays often mean a shift in the train time-tables, upsetting the routine. The summer can be enlivening as well as irritating, but in any case it offers some variety. Extra staff may be employed, normally a couple of former shunters who have taken up higher studies. They are welcomed and accepted into the group without much ado, especially as the irregular encounters between shunters with different 'freeday-keys' sometimes result in the shunters being unaware that a person has been absent at all.[22]

Many shunters, especially the younger ones, appreciate the irregularity of the work schedules. One may work fourteen days in a row in order to have a longer period off, but the irrregularity has besides that a value of its own. 'Time flies' as all shifts are different, weathers and seasons change, work-mates change from day to day, in all combining and ranging the routine and repetition of the daily work processes into disparate periods of varied shifts. The pattern could be compared to a neck-lace of beads, where there is a variety of beads, no two beads being identical, all strung into a pattern that from a distance shows some regularity, but which at a closer look is irregular and full of surprises. Depending on the mood and attitude of the speaker it is therefore possible to stress **either** the flexibility and unpredictability **or** the monotony and uneventful jog-trot of the work.

'I could never work in a job where I knew exactly what I would be doing on Tuesday, April 2nd, one year, two years or ten years from now.' Such comments are heard from time to time, but often get a cynical reply: 'I can tell you. You'll be beating this yard!' – which of course may be answered by: 'How do you know that? I might have three weeks off and lie by a pool in Florida!'

The unpredictability that follows from shift work has, surprisingly enough, a corollary which is the exact opposite to unpredictability, i.e. planning. The multitude of shifts, in a day and in a year, gives the shunters the opportunity to trade their assigned shifts with each other. It is said that if you want to take a particular week off you can always fix it. You can work extra shifts for SJ and take the compensation in 'time', but if SJ is unwilling

---

[22] The anthropologist, known as 'the spy', was greeted with a 'are you here again today' after having moved to another city a year earlier. When replying that she had left her victims alone for a year and did not think that 'again' was an adequate complaint the shunter excused himself with how impossible it was to keep track of the time.

285

to enter such a trade, because of lack of staff, it is possible to change the shifts with one or several work-mates. If you are in trouble you might have to swap a good shift for a bad one, but the problem is more likely to find a 'buyer' for very unpopular shifts.[23]

The shift swapping is often clandestine, and it is seen as unnecessary to tell the staff delegator that although Carlsson is on the day-order as C-member on Engine 2, in reality Carlsson is out in the archipelago with his family, while Persson is down there coupling the carriages in the yard. Staff delegators have constantly fought this carelessness in reporting, as it is seen as essential – not least in case of accidents and for insurance matters – that the correct workers are listed in the books. The problem for the shunters is, however, that the discrepancy between the time-table and practice, which we have discussed earlier, makes it possible for them to accept working two shifts that partly overlap. They know that they in practice can manage both tasks, but this fact is naturally not possible to transpose into the official records. One person cannot work at two jobs, half a mile apart, simultaneously, even if it is only for half an hour. Such cases are then bound to be kept out of records.

Bargaining may also include favours, such as **me** working **your** night shift, while **you** are still in the books collecting the pay for inconvenient working hours*(obekväm arbetstid)*. Some staff delegators will agree to such a swap, and keep a double record – the pay record unaltered, but the day-schedule stating the name of the person actually working the shift. In case the staff delegator refuses such 'incorrect' book-keeping the shunters will prefer to swap without reporting it to the delegator.

The variety of shifts thus offers the opportunity to choose and swap, and even those who never bother to enter such exchanges say that they appreciate just knowing that there is such an option. It is part of the 'freedom' of shunting work. Some shunters are notorious swappers, collecting 'debts' as a buffer of security. 'People owe me more than twenty shifts', they may brag. Such debts do not collect interest, but as a matter of honour they should be repaid whenever the lender so requires. The lender is thus gaining power over the poor indebted, who may be called upon to work an unpopular and inconvenient shift on short notice. He has only himself to blame, unless the swap was called for by some unforeseen catastrophy, as a bit of planning would have made it possible to get a better deal and an immediate pay-off.

---

[23] Shifts are of unequal length, have different workloads and are differently paid, due to them being – wholly, partly or not at all – compensated for inconvenient working hours (of which there are two kinds).

286

There are some persons who do not manage to plan and come out as lenders, but who all too often ask someone to work for them, while they promise to pay it back 'later'. They risk their good reputation in the long run, because they inevitably end up in a position where they cannot pay back when asked to, and this news is spread by the lender with comments about the unreliability and uncomradely attitude of the indebted shunter. The worst sin concerning debts is when the indebted reveals that he never **had** the intention of paying back. He may have forgotten about the shift altogether and when reminded he says that he thought he already paid it back. Such excuses risk closing the door to future swapping.

Planned swapping can be a great advantage – as the case with the shunter who managed to avoid working Saturday afternoons for a decade because of *'Tipsextra'*, the live soccer game on TV – while swapping just because one wants to go out with the pals, instead of working the night shift, may create a bad habit of 'pay you back later', which quickly accumulates into a nasty debt.

We must conclude that there is in the shunting yard a recontextualization of time, resembling the concept of 'day work'*('dagsverke')*. Work is the measure of time more than time is a measure of work. Working time and leisure time are less separated, as they have a mutual dependency. Working time is organized to leave the most attractive leisure time intact. Indeed, the variety of leisure activities that regulate working time complement each other so that shifts do not stand up to a common standard of favourable shifts and unfavourable shifts. Circumstance and context are as important as clock-time. The official evaluation of time and work, such as double pay for nights and holidays ('red days') and a lower rate of extra money for certain hours, is accepted, but at the same time seen as slightly unfair. It is based on an ideal view of life that does not coincide with the interests and evaluations of all shunters. On the other hand the system of compensation has an air of being part of 'normal life', the way it is lived by others in society, and therefore it is not completely without reason, although for the shunters it is more like an arbitrary net of extra income that is cast over working life and which hits everybody rather evenly, unless one makes a point of 'picking out the raisins from the cake' as young *gnetare* do for all they are worth.

It is a danger to see shift swapping as a way to control the working time completely. There is much effort involved in the swapping, as one may have to get hold of the person assigned a certain shift, as not every shunter is qualified to take on shifts as *tkm*, shunt leader, knocker or even B-member, and as asking for a favour not only obliges one to pay back the shift, but also obliges one to respond favourably when asked for a similar favour. Shunters

287

are much more prone to *'ställa upp'*, to grant someone a favour than to ask for one. There are proud shunters who announce that they as a principle never swap shifts. 'I work my own shifts. I owe nobody and nobody owes me.' I think it is hard to find a more telling expression of the ideas of equality and independence phrased in the idiom of working time.

It is significant that the complementary interests of the shunters to a high degree stem from the wide age span in the yard. It is likewise no coincidence that Stockholmers have always constituted only a fraction of the shunting staff. The organization of shifts and holidays can be detrimental to social life, unless ones friends are shift workers too. 'My pals call me and suggest something for Friday night, but either I'm working that night or the next morning. They think I work constantly.' Young shunters who have arrived from other parts of the country have few, if any, friends in town and they go out with other shunters and often to water-holes where SJ people hang out. They find friends among other shift workers and are thereby not marked as 'odd'. To spend holidays, such as Christmas and Easter, in Stockholm is actually better if you work, as there is no family to go to. You earn a lot of money, take on shifts from those who have families and take a holiday somewhere in the Mediterranean instead, or you save days for the next holiday and go visit your parents and family during a longer spell.[24]

The saying of the shunters that the job picks its workers seems then to be true also as the time-schedule is concerned. Not everyone can adjust to shift work.

Increasing age, family and children put a new strain on the shunter, mentally as well as physically, but the drawbacks are always contrasted to the assets. Shunting is still seen as a 'free' job and even a shunter who **on principle** never swaps shifts will shudder at the thought of having to adjust to a eight-to-five job, to a time-clock or to a boss breathing down his neck. If things get into a mess he knows that there are mates who will *'ställa upp'* and that even SJ, personified in the staff delegator, is willing to trade with the honest shunter.

Meanings of Time

Summing up my findings concerning the meaning of time in the yard, particularly the aspects of time which can be assumed to distinguish this

---

[24] A senior shunter said about his first year with SJ in the 1940s: 'I had worked a lot and saved up days and went up to my home village. When I said that I had a whole month off my father did not believe me. He thought that I had been fired.'

workplace from most others, it gives me a certain thrill that the shunters in Hagalund stand out in sharp contrast to the railroaders of W.F. Cottrell's classic paper 'Of Time and the Railroader'. Far from being subject to the 'tyranny of the clock' the shunters are not very often pressed for time. In the winter they often wait an extra half hour before they go out to work in order to utilize the natural light and avoid the discomfort (and additional danger) of using hand lanterns, and some of them do not even wear a watch at work. The time pressure that exists is largely self-inflicted and a function, as well as an expression, of dexterity and skill. It is the employer (and the central union) who try to keep the speed of work **down**, while the shunters try to keep it at a maximum.[25]

It is obviously the piece-work character of the job (and the institutionalized habit of going home when finished), in combination with the broad margin between shunting a train and its departure that has given rise to the lax attitude towards clock-time and makes it possible to concentrate so intensively on the tasks at hand that it often comes as a surprise to find out what time it is.

Working time has the character of a necessary evil, and it should be obvious to everybody the one has 'better things to do' outside the gates. The shunter who came back after a fortnight's holiday asking for 'easy' shifts, as he claimed he had been working 18 hours a day – 'tax free' – obviously made the point that **his** time **was** money. The message is that one does not hurry back home from work in order to lie on the couch. There are things to be accomplished elsewhere. *Smittider*, i.e. those which do not imply doing a bunk on ones own, are not a sign of laziness but, quite the contrary, of a hectic life and efficiency at work. At the introduction of the bonus system one of the strongest arguments was 'once you are here you might as well work'.

To work all the overtime one is allowed to do in one year (200 hrs) in three or four months is not a sign of a deprived life style, but to stay and play cards after the rest of the team have left, or to clear the engine on the way up to the locker room is seen as abnormal. The comment : 'Do you live here?' also points to the view of time spent inside the gates of the yard as obligatory and forced. 'Money is the only reason I'm here!' one of the shunters shouted angrily behind my back as I discussed the conditions of shunting with another person. In my interview he stated other reasons, too, but publicly it is always

---

[25] Gamst reports from the US. that someone who is 'overly eager to switch more cars at faster speeds' is labelled 'scabby', 'wormy' or 'stoolie'. Cf. GAMST 1980, 109. Working fast is not ostracized in Hagalund, but doing extra tasks, outside working hours, would certainly be questioned. *'Gnetare'* is, however, the only common word which is sometimes used as a derogatory label for being overly eager in some respect.

a sound argument to deny all satisfaction other than the monetary compensation.

The only time this argument and line of thinking reveals some contradiction is when the question of union commitment comes up. The demand for unpaid work, and paperwork at that, seems worthless to the young people. The pay-off is questioned. Even the young bachelor who wanted to suggest a 'straight' work-schedule was abhorred at the idea of having to work it out himself, in **his free time**. He was not going to sacrifice **that** much even for what he saw as a radical improvement. Undoubtedly a large part of his refusal to work out the suggested schedule stemmed from the young man's feeling of incompetence. He simply had no idea how to work out such a schedule. But rather than admitting it he sulked and said he 'had no time' to spend an evening on something like that. Even if one should leave an hour early from work every day there is still 'no time' to spare.

The time one gains by slipping off early is time 'won' at the expense of the employer. There are limits to how much one can gain. The shortest shift I ever worked during my time as a shunter was a morning shift at Engine 3 when the team spent twenty minutes in the yard. After such a short shift there is no question of going home, the team must stay on, in case something turns up. There is then card-playing for a couple of hours, until the next team is about to arrive and can take over any such emergencies.

It is not possible to shorten work by collapsing the whole shift into one spell in the yard (except for Engine 3, which works mainly in the non-electrified parts of the yard) as there is nothing to do before the proper trains have arrived. When the workload is extremely small, or trains are late, it means a lot of useless waiting around, and, consequently, irritation. There is always some sanguine person who enjoys the opportunity to play cards and who could not care less, 'as long as I'm paid', but long before the shifts have shrunk into the ridiculous length of twenty minutes the conscientious shunter has apprehensions about whether he has performed a day's work, whether he has *'gjort rätt för sig'* (earned his pay) as the saying goes.

Slipping off is thus not really getting paid for nothing. The pay is earned by the good day's work one has performed. One has fulfilled all duties that were required by the employer and one has **also** fulfilled all possible demands of earning one's pay. The time gained is a function of the extra effort one has put into the task, planning it with elegance, not stopping for every legal coffee-break and keeping up a speed of work that only years of practice admit. Slipping off is **skill** transformed into time, and thereby a matter that the employer has little to say about. 'The manager does not know how to shunt!'

290

Were there demands that the employees stay until the very last minute of the shift, the shunters would resort to playing it according to the rules, which implies working in a way that is safe for a beginner. Denying twenty years of experience one would lose all pride in the work and work in a robot-like fashion according to the instructions and clock-time. One would resort to sell time for money, without the intervening consideration for a good day's work and the swapping of skill for time, and in one blow it would no longer matter if the day schedule had been completed or not, or whether trains were on time. A go-slow would not be a retaliation for the introduction of the time-clock, it would be the natural outcome when skill no longer was allowed to be exchanged for time.

Asking whether one has 'earned ones pay' is the way the seniors instill the idea of the fair exchange. The exchange has three partners: the employer, the comrades and ego, and it has three determining ingredients: the concept of 'a good day's work', the influence of skill and flow, and finally the demands of work itself.

While time use normally has seen to be the interest of management, and efforts to intensify work have been objected to by the workers, we here see a tendency for the opposite.[26] The management and the union are constantly trying to slow down the pace by enforcing new speed limits for different areas and different work tasks. These limitations have an impact, but they are not seen as threats. They may slow down work but as long as the piece-work character of shunting remains, the ground rules for 'a good day's work' will be same. The real threat has always been the time clock, not time scarcity, or intensified time use.[27]

It is now time to look at time in its aspect of skill and flow.

Timing and Flow

Industrial time is commodified and standardized into clock-time, which is free of context and possible to divide into different lengths, which again cut and order social life into parts and sequences. The secondary meaning of time is then, in the shunting yard, the way this cutting of time is managed and the

---

[26] Cf. STARKEY, 100 f.

[27] The shunting yard goes against many general assumptions about work. For one, stricter supervision in the yard would lead to a **slower** pace of work and would infere with flow, the execution of skill. One former manager said to me: 'I know how they work [i.e. fast], but I don't interfere. Do you think I'm lax?') Cf. STARKEY, 112 f, for comparison with work conflict at British Rail, where skill is seen (by the union) to be threatened by intensification of work (demanded by the BR Board).

way pieces and lengths of time are exchanged and the significance they have for the shunters.

Cottrell described the reality of the 1930s in the United States as a system resembling the assembly line, where the speed and punctuality of operation affected every aspect of the lives of the railroaders. The whole personality is transformed as they are constantly vigilant on the movements of the second hand of their watch – this 'sword of Damocles to the railroader'.[28]

We have seen that very little of this vigilance is present in the work of the shunters in Hagalund. The shunters feel that they manage time, that they are free, as opposed to factory workers. The view of Cottrell was indeed revised almost twenty years ago by L.S.Kemnitzer who wanted to extend the time aspect to include "[...] the ability to integrate time, distance, and subjective estimates about weight, slope and speed in making decisions about the movements of cars and engines in switching."[29] This time-sense he called *switching time*, and it is not difficult to understand why he saw it as fundamental as regards matters of competence and safety. I have decided not to use the term *switching time*, not because I prefer to talk about shunting instead of switching, but because I find it pointing in the wrong direction. The time-sense Kemnitzer talks about I find to be close to a sense of timing, a skill needed to play with a ball or to exercise skipping-rope.

The skills of timing are indeed so fundamental to our moving about in the world that we for the most part do not notice the skills involved. The reader may be familiar with the peculiar sense of timing that we suddenly become aware of if we use the same elevator daily and become accustomed to its specific way of coming to a halt. Without visibly moving a muscle in our body we are prepared for the particular gravitational effects of the slowing down so that, if the elevator **fails** to stop at the floor we expected when moving downwards, we sense a feeling of suddenly falling although the elevator just moves with unaltered speed. Timing is then mostly expressed in movement, adjusting the body to external objects or phenomena, but it can also be an inner preparation **for** movement, such as balance and alertness that is brought in accordance with external stimuli. Timing is the ability to *'hänga med'* (lit.: 'to hang on', i.e. to keep up) physically as well as mentally.

In the case of timing in a shunting yard, body movements must be brought into harmony with movements of different kinds. Jumping off an

---

[28] Cf. COTTRELL, 190.
[29] KEMNITZER, 1977, 27.

engine at high speed is an art which differs radically from the art of signalling when carriages are being kicked.

In the first example there is coordination of body with speed and distance, while the second example includes a whole series of effects where several factors vary from one shift to another, and sometimes even within the same shift. Kicking a carriage or several carriages means that the signaller must estimate the speed the particular cut of cars needs in order to reach its destination. This can only be done by judging the cut with your eyes. Apart from the weight, distance, grade and curvature, the weather (rain, snow, wind and temperature) has a strong influence on the movement, too. Presumably the signaller signals 'stop' to the driver when he estimates that the cut has acquired sufficient speed. This is not the whole truth, as there is timing involved in the way a driver drives the engine, too.

I have on several occasions witnessed how a shunt leader has been surprised at the sudden 'odd' behaviour of the engine. A closer look has revealed that the driver has been replaced by another one. The skills of driving differ considerably from person to person, and the shunt leader has to adapt to this in his estimation of when he should signal. The whole chain of variables makes it difficult for even the most talented and experienced shunt leader to execute a perfect kick every time and there are the occasional 'rykare' (very hard kicks), or alternatively loose kicks that have to be given a second push or be backed further down the track.

According to the view of the shunters, as we know, drivers should function as automatons and react swiftly and unquestioningly on all signals given to them. In the ideal case the chain of timing is reduced so that it is seemingly the **engine** that reacts on the signalling. The human factor in driving is ideally reduced to nil. There is no hesitation due to misunderstandings, as there should be no understanding, only blind obedience.

It is interesting to note, however, that despite this common view of how drivers should perform in their work, there is, parallel to this, the practical understanding that a driver who actually drives completely according to signals is a bad driver. This stems from the fact that there are very few signals, and therefore the same signals are used in a variety of contexts. When carriages are coupled the shunt leader shows 'slow', and 'stop', but there is no way to signal the process **in terms of timing** to the driver, in order to make the clash perfect for the shunter standing in between ready to couple. The driver must know and judge for himself.[30]

We can therefore conclude that the feeling of control over the engine that the shunt leader aspires to is seen to be achieved when the driver and the shunt leader have the same view of shunting. It is also the old Hagalund drivers that are generally considered to be the best drivers.

There is thus a systematic misrecognition of the interplay between shunters and drivers. Officially drivers are good when they 'drive on the signals' ('kör på signalerna') and bad when they do not, while it can be shown that good drivers in effect are those who know the work procedures and use their own judgement and experience. When a shunt leader mutters: 'Here one does not even have to show signals', it may be an appreciative comment, but it is simultaneously a warning that any mistake by the driver will be judged severely. In the yard it is and **should be** the shunter who issues the commands.

It is therefore in terms of dominance that we must read the misrecognized cooperation between shunter and driver and the downgrading of the driver to a mere automaton. The work-relation is considered to be a chain of timing, although the execution can be simultaneous with the order. If the execution pre-empts the order repeatedly there will soon be irritation on the part of the shunt leader, and the driver will be called back to order. The hierarchical order of the yard is not to be questioned.

There is an example, which beautifully highlights my argument and leads us up to a different kind of cooperation; 'flow'. This is when the remote-controlled engines came into work and the shunters took over the driving themselves.

In the case where the driver was manoeuvering the engine from a position on the ground he was simultaneously shunt leader **and** driver, thereby collapsing the two roles into one and reducing the chain of timing as he was in command over the engine himself.

In the other case, when the driver insisted on standing on the engine, there had to be a separate signaller on the ground and the process of driving was in effect exactly the same as before the introduction of the remote control. Here, however, the shunters were known to drive on their own accord and the signaller could abstain from showing signals. This order of things was now

---

[30] The shunters have noticed that inexperienced drivers seem to be more 'careful' when they see a woman go in between. They stop so that the buffers meet without clashing, thereby making it impossible to reach the hook. In the following attempts of backing, and halting, the drivers often create dangerous situations as they push the loose coach away at increasing speed, while the c-member runs in between, desperately trying to , literally, make ends meet.

quickly accepted, as the driver was 'one of us'. The shunters were happy to skip 'unnecessary' signals and treating the driver as an automaton. The shunt leader/driver cooperation was brought out into full bloom, and the engine was worked with an energy and skill that from afar made it evident that it was driven by a shunter. Occasionally it was driven with higher speed, but most of all there was a difference in tempo, there was more energy in the driving as well as a shortened reaction time. The chain of timing was reduced whenever the driver could see what was going on, relying on signals only as a safety measure when the sight was reduced or the plans uncertain. (Orders were also often given in the form of descriptions of what was going to be dealt with during the next hour or so, rather than in the form of a list of only a few moves ahead.)

We have here reached the next sense of time in our exposition, a time-sense which I want to distinguish from 'timing' and which I have called the 'flow' of work, *'flyt'*.[31] The flow of work is a function of good planning and cooperation, but it also entails skilfulness and timing. Timing and flow are thus not mutually exclusive, as timing is one of the ingredients and a necessary prerequisite of flow.

Although timing is an individual skill and flow is created in cooperation, it is important to stress that timing nevertheless has profound social implications. It is a personal expression which, just like a person's handwriting, simultaneously is an important instrument of communication. While writing a beautiful hand seldom constitutes a matter of life and death (an exception maybe being a doctor's prescription), correct timing in the shunting yard has an air of compulsion that draws its legitimacy from the unspoken, but always present horrors of what otherwise could be. Correct timing is a personal style and elegance as well as a sign of competence and safety, while bad timing is not only bad style, it is presumptive danger.

Good timing comes from routine and experience, therefore it is also a sign of skill and control. Timing has the dual quality of being a personal statement, a routine-like manner, an individual style, while at the same time, precisely because of its character as a personal label, it acts as a means of communication. In order to create flow in a team it is imperative to know

---

[31] 'Flow', as a psychological term signifying well-being through concentration, has become known through a number of articles and books by Mihaly Csikszentmihalyi and his research team. This term, referring to an 'optimal experience' of the individual, stands for something different from the term 'flow'; when co-operation at work is going smoothly. There is still a relation between the two as 'flow' at work may be a sufficient condition for, and is likely to induce, such an optimal experience in the individual; psychological 'flow'. Cf. CSIKSZENTMIHALYI, *passim.*, EDELMAN, 160)

what everyone is doing, as well as it is indispensable to know what everyone is capable of doing. The end of calm routine, such as hesitation, delay, jerkiness or any behaviour that is 'out of style' is then a signal to the others that there might be a hitch somewhere and that there is reason to be on the look-out. Good flow means increased work speed, but the vigilant eye is constantly watching for the weakest links in the chain so as not to push the most inexperienced team-members into situations they cannot handle.

Apart from timing, good flow requires planning, foresight and the ability that the shunters call 'split vision' (using the English term). It is not only the other members of the team that have to be kept under the eye, but all other unpredictable and sometimes highly dangerous moves initiated by train-pullers, knockers, other shunting teams, repairers (shooting out of the repair shop with their light rail motor tractor), service staff from the hall (walking or driving mopeds) or even outsiders on business to the yard, who carelessly venture over the tracks on foot, in cars or lorries. This overall vision and simultaneous planning is not only the task of one member of the team, e.g. the shunt leader. Every member of the team has to partake in creating flow by adjusting his being and doing to the work process and to everybody else's activity in the yard.

When asking the shunters 'what makes a perfect shunter?' the answer often includes the ability always to be in the right spot at the right moment. Several informants mentioned one particular shunter who had an almost supernatural ability to turn up when he was needed. This excellent workmanship is not timing but part of good flow. Just as a good soccer player probably has a good sense of handling a ball, his being in the right spot at the right moment is an ability that partly is an individual skill, but which to a degree also is dependent on the division of work and the strategy and tactics of the team. Referring back to the shunter we must realize that being in the right place at the right time is a variable depending on the expected role of the shunter in a team. There is a social, organizational element in the creation of flow that is judgmental in respect to what is seen as 'right' and 'wrong' positioning.

In the everyday work context the social element is often forgotten, and the right positioning is seen as self-evident. The roles in the team are given and the expectations as to where everyone should be at any time is not questioned. 'Everyone is doing his duty'. It is only when the organization of the team is undergoing change that the issue comes to the fore and 'the right spot' suddenly may be somewhere else.

The conclusion to be drawn from this is that, while timing is a skill independent of the social organization, as it describes the tacit skill of estimating the combination of force, weight, speed and friction, the creation of flow may be the result of different kinds of cooperation. Train-pullers create flow, and so do shunters in the traditional as well as in the reorganized teams. Flow is the outcome of successful cooperation, no matter what the organization looks like. Flow is what team-work always aims at; it is the indication of a successful team.

The traditional shunting teams are hierarchically organized, and in these, flow is created by planning the work according to a routinized pattern, so that every member easily can identify the tasks that befall him. The overall principle can be compared to the assembly line, where the distribution of tasks is clear and the dividing lines kept firm and undisturbed. There can be flow without every member having an understanding of the overall process. Cooperation is mechanic. The constant need for orders and directives tends to move the members of the team in irregular pulsating shuttles, between the shunt leader and their respective positions in the yard. There is a centre and a periphery on the ground, just as there is a hierarchical order of positions.

The reorganized shunting teams have a blurred division of labour and work according to the principle 'the bystander performs the task'. In this case flow is the outcome of a successful coordination of tasks that could be described as organic. Every shunter must be able to predict what has to be done and move to the right place at the right moment, always keeping in mind the positions of the others in the team so as not to intersect in one area while leaving gaps in other parts of the work field. This egalitarian way of working disregards the position one is formally ascribed and presupposes that every member has the ability to read and understand the work process and the doings in the yard. The shuttle between positions in the yard and the shunt leader is replaced by constant movement within particular areas of the yard; describing a pattern much like a jigsaw puzzle. The ideal is to use radio communication between the members, keeping everybody informed. Driving the engine by remote control is combined with shunt leading, but this position is ideally passed between all members of the team.

Both timing **and** flow are important factors concerning competence and safety, and it is obvious that the two are intimately linked through the skill of the individual shunter. There is, however, one big difference. Faulty timing may effect team-work negatively, but irritating as this may be there are seldom moral implications in bad timing. Having bad judgment or a cowboy attitude is criticized and condemned. One is told off, instructed or, most commonly, met with a telling silence. The expectation is nevertheless that the persons will eventually learn. Correct timing is learnt and cowboy fads vanish as the shunter learns 'how things are done here in Hagalund'.

Obstructing good flow can momentarily be done by bad timing and lack of skill, but there are other factors that may cause irritation and upset the rhythm of work. A fundamentally different conception about how the work should be done or organized, the inability to adjust to cooperation in a team, or trying to avoid work by sneaking away, all have the symptom that the person constantly is found in the wrong place at the wrong time, creating distrust and insecurity. Shying away from work, or refusing to adjust to the others are signs that the person is not fit to be a shunter. Having a different conception of work is not necessarily wrong, but in the hierarchical team one should work according to the style of the shunt leader and hold one's tongue. To start an argument is in itself condemned, because quarrels within a team mean that 'things start to happen'. Permanent members of a team have chosen to work with the particular shunt leader and should accept his style, while temporary members are only guests in the team and can comfort themselves that they only have to suffer a few days.

Being in the right place at the right time is thus a sign of agreement and collective spirit. One is throwing one's stone to the pile, creating good flow and gaining time off for everyone, not only for oneself. This is what I prefer to call 'switching time' – or 'shunting time' – as it is the hallmark and pride of a good shunting team.

Timing is a necessary, but not a sufficient prerequisite for flow. Timing is a personal skill, while flow is created in social interaction. When we talk about skill we include timing **as well as** the ability to partake in the creation of flow. This duality, the personal versus the social aspects of skill are recognized by the shunters themselves, but the emphasis on one or the other depends on the particular situation. When things were calm in the yard it was common to stress the team spirit and the group feeling as a prerequisite for good shunting, while during the time of organizational crisis it was every man for himself and skill was seen as pertaining to the individual, as something one could pack and take among the rest of one's luggage. Looking for a job elsewhere a senior shunter said he thought he would be able to work in another workplace just as well, because **he** had always been able to cooperate.

Here we find the key to the paradoxical co-existence of the rhetorical 'the way things are done here at Hagalund' and the well established styles that different teams develop over time. I think we can say that 'the Hagalund way

298

of working' is not a mere fiction, there is a common denominator, partly in the actual work methods, but also in that it signifies an agreement to disagree. As far as work styles go it works as a *lingua franca*, providing that the interaction is temporary. As long as visits over team borders were short encounters one could adjust and make things work, but when the teams were reshuffled it became evident that there were different views of what shunting work was all about and how it should be done.

It is noteworthy that we are not distinguishing between socially dependent versus socially independent skills.[32] Timing and shunting time (flow) are both socially embedded and evaluated. Timing is part of body language, while flow is part of a wider communicative process, where a whole range of aspects are involved. There we have not only views on equality, democracy and delegation at work, work procedures, functionality of hierarchic role allocation, etc, but rather how these are to be formed in practice. While timing is inscribed in the body, and to a low degree formed and reformed by conscious consideration, flow is a product of an interplay between conscious choices and the outlook on work and life in general. This is why work styles can be transformed temporarily into a *lingua franca*, but also why one in the long run, cannot partake in a workstyle, which goes against the grain of one's learning and views, that is one's conception of what good work should be like.

Changing Times – Changing Skills

'The Hagalund way of working', just as 'good manners' or 'good taste', are established ways of seeing, doing and judging, which cannot be exhaustively described – because they refer to a compound of constitutive, not regulative, rules.[33] The change brought about by the turn-over of shunters who carry individual as well as 'generational' styles, being brought up in different teams during different periods, is a change which only slowly transforms the Hagalund way of working.

This slow change, brought about by the combination of individuals in the social context of the yard, the coffee-room talk and the card-table, all presenting their views and doings, their sympathies and antipathies, is

---

[32] Bertil Rolf distinguished these two by calling the former 'skill' and the latter 'know-how'. Cf. Chapter 7: The learning process...

[33] Confusing the two is equal to confusing 'rules of etiquette' with good manners. The strict application of rules of etiquette, i.e. one which does not consider circumstances and context, easily neglects good manners. (The extreme case being to point out other people's failure to comply to such rules.) Rules, which are intended to bring about comfortable intercourse, may therefore bring about the exact opposite; embarrassment, unease and disagreeable social interaction.

contrasted by the abrupt change that was brought about by the sudden reorganization of the work routines and introduction of new technology. The rules of the game were changed in one sweep, and things which had been taken for granted and become self-evident were no longer in force. What was to be was uncertain, and in addition the mere fact that things were changing created feelings of mistrust.

The situation brought a variety of different ideals, opinions and preferences into the open. Different strategies and modes of action could be discerned – including the decision to leave the yard altogether. In many cases it was also difficult to identify who were for versus against the reform, as conversations and discussions often concerned only parts of the reform, and those who were for some novelties were against other ones. As we have seen, opinions could shift only depending on situation and context.

There seemed to be diversity concerning every single issue. Opinions seemed to go in all directions and, apart from some rather predictable negative responses from persons who generally were against all novelties, there seemed to be very little order and structure in the different lines.

Some shunt leaders were reluctant to delegate tasks to the junior members of the team as they claimed that the leader was still formally responsible and would be hauled over the coals in case someone else failed. The new order therefore contained unforeseeable risks. The one who had the responsibility should also be the one to give orders, and the others in the team had to obey while working within the safe range of tasks that they were trained for and appointed to do. To step outside these routines would sooner or later prove fatal, figuratively speaking, but possibly even literally so.

Risk, however, was also the main ingredient in the rhetoric supporting the change. The chain of repeating signals had become obsolete over night and it was now possible to control the engine while standing next to the coupler and actually watch his manœuvres from a short distance.

The rhetoric of risk was used vigorously by both sides – accusations were not direct but consisted of utterances thrown out around the card table or in the coffee-room without specific address. Every shunter knew, of course, the directions of the attacks, but any person who was not a shunt leader was at a loss to judge the quality of the arguments and choose between them. To the younger shunters the 'responsibility' of the shunt leaders was something that the seniors always came up with in order to enhance their own status and importance. The youngsters did not feel that someone else was responsible for them. They judged themselves equally responsible for their own safety, as well as for the safety of all other team-mates.[34]

There were other distinctions, too. Some shunters went for all the education they could get and happily opted for learning how to drive the new remote controlled engines. Others refused such education. Some teams adjusted to the new way of working that the remote control allowed for, given that the driver adopted his position of driving on the ground, while some teams went on working the old way with the driver standing on the engine. Some drivers, contrary to the wishes of their team, refused to leave the platform, forcing the team to work very much in the old way, with a C-member repeating signals.

Some saw driving as an impediment to their health, as driving on the ground meant carrying a heavy, and in wintertime cold-conducting, apparatus while constantly pressing one button with a finger when the engine was in motion. Others saw this as a minor problem, referring to the newly constructed weight-distributing belt for the remote controller. Among those driving on the engine the dividing line went between those who enjoyed the comfort of the platform, being protected from vicious weather, and those who found it no great advantage to stand in a heated cab hanging the head out in the cold.

Some considered themselves too old to learn how to drive. Some thought that the youngsters should not drive until they had a lot of experience as shunt leaders. The bosses should not drive, some said. One team thought on the other hand that **they** represented the ideal, as their boss, their shunt leader as well as their B-member, knew how to drive.

One consideration, which quickly seemed to get the upper hand once a shunter had started the training to drive the remote controlled engine, was that driving was fun. Driving in itself was seen as stimulating because it added to the variety of work-tasks, and – a view held primarily by those driving on the ground – because it offered a way to control the movements in the yard from ring-side, instead of having to rely on the constant insecurity of the line of signalling. The increased flexibility was thus considered a way to improve safety as well as mental health conditions.

All these considerations offered a variety of standpoints, but it seemed likely that persons known as stern union advocates would go against the reform, while the more individualistically minded persons would welcome the collapse of the yard hierarchy and enjoy the variation of roles and tasks and be

---

[34] As we remember, the young shunters were heavily affected by the new reponsibilities when they started to work as shunt leaders. Some of them transformed their behaviour in quite stunning ways.

tempted by the individual rewards in the offing. That this was not the case depended on the strong suspicion that those to be rewarded and promoted in the new organization would not necessarily be the skilled ones, but rather those who were mainstream and who had 'good contacts' to the manager. The odd and individualistic persons were indeed those who often went against the grain and who were not afraid to tell the manager one truth or two.

Some saw the new teams as a desk product, constructed by someone (understood as the manager) who had never set his foot in the yard. 'Anyone who had worked in the yard' could see that the knocker could not work the same hours as the team, as he had to prepare the trains ahead of them. Even earlier the knocker used to start his work before the official hour, voluntarily, in order to get the work done in time.

The idea that the tasks should be performed by the 'closest' team-member, instead of being allotted to a specific member as belonging to his duties, was seen as another 'nice idea' which in reality would lead to confusion and lack of responsibility. It was certainly dangerous! Others saw this as the only sensible way of working, realized at last. One such person exclaimed: "To have a B-member stand next to a task, refusing to do it because 'it's not my job'! Now, this is not the way it should be, is it?"

Some saw the negative side of the new teams being that beginners would find it even harder than before to learn the job, as the work assumed that everyone knew what was going on in the yard and could predict the moves. The principle, and the ideal, was that everybody in the team was trained as a shunt leader. But others found that fear exaggerated. The team could adjust and take care of a beginner, they argued. Maybe it would take a bit longer, but once the beginner got the hang of it, he would find the work more rewarding, and perhaps stay.

Some objected to the new order as it meant a reduction of teams, making the remaining teams work so much harder. The morning-night shift connection worked only because the morning shift had been a very light one. Now it would be a full shift, which would be impossibly tough, it was argued. Others scorned this view, saying that they rather worked than sat around when they came down to the yard. The extra bonus of 100 crowns per shift was indeed worth the extra effort.

The indoor bosses objected to the abolition of the night shift. That meant a loss of money as well as lack of control of what happened during the night. The night was the only time to sort things out in peace and quiet. They also doubted whether the 100 crowns would influence the pension (which many of them were about to receive soon) at all.

Then there were some who saw the reform as inevitable, just as the manager had described it. If it did not work, the yard was threatened by closure. Some saw the reform as the result of a conscious choice on the part of the shunters. 'Look at the communists in the Hall! There were offered a bonus, too, but refused to accept it. Now they constantly refer to how much we earn!' The shunters prided themselves of being 'sensible'. Things could be discussed. They were not mindless no-sayers, like the 'communists'. Also the fact that other SJ-staff in the country had reacted and protested against what they saw as a hundred-crown 'attention-fee' was proof that this was something to be envied.

Some did not object as much to the reorganization as to the way in which it was introduced. The trial month did not end in a democratic vote or even a proper meeting. The new time-schedules had already been signed by the union chairman long before the meeting. This was scandalous – a treatment which did not agree with the shunters' view of themselves as sensible and open-minded. The way things were brought about seemed to imply that the shunters were not trusted after all. Maybe the manager had something up his sleeve?

Some took a view of the whole reorganization in broader terms, seeing the drawbacks clearly – such as the goal being ultimately to reduce the number of team-members – but still defending the new order as it put the shunters in a good light considering future development. As the other groups at Hagalund were in serious trouble concerning overturn of staff and deadlock in staff-management relations, they could be persuaded or even obliged to sell out tasks to the shunters, who would again get more variety in their job and gain control over a larger part of the organization.

A shunter, who had initially severe criticism and many arguments against the change, found the new way of working so superior that he wondered how he had been able to work in the old way for two decades! He was looking forward to a situation where the strengthened shunting group would be able to secure the employment – and possibly even lead to new recruitment. He got involved in further education of the group and was trying to enhance the interest for matters outside the traditional work-tasks.

Another shunter enjoyed driving so much that he refused, even in the face of physical threats, to step down from the engine, thereby conserving the old way of working. This shunter claimed that driving was a good opportunity to advance, and he planned to leave shunting for engine driving if, as he suspected, the worst would come to the worst.

As different as these two shunters were in their conception of the situation and in their outlook and planning for the future, they were, however, both

303

united in one thing; they had turned towards a way of thinking that included non-yard considerations and that represented a denial of the shunting team as the all important stage for performing skill. Their rhetoric and argumentation brought in the outside world, and the yard was made a part of a greater whole. By enlarging the scope to matters outside the yard, they crossed the borders to careers – if still only halfway, and partly only mentally – to areas which had been considered to be closed to shunters. These were areas in which not only bravery or cautiousness, solidarity or selfishness were at stake. Book learning, technical curiosity and knowledge were equally important.[35]

These standpoints held that driving the remote controlled engines was only a step towards becoming an engine driver, and that an understanding of the technical systems of carriages was a logical development from shunting them. Such standpoints saw the reorganization as a possible beginning to something new, more varied and 'modern'.

To these shunters the question of how one fared in the game of prestige and position within the narrow scope of the shunting yard was no longer all-important and it is therefore no surprise to learn that they gave up playing *plump*. 'I've lost interest in it. I really don't see how some people can go on being excited over it,' one of them said.

Evaluating Shunting Skills

To the large majority of shunters the outside world seemed still distant, at least distant enough to make it unnecessary to take any precautions or specific steps to adjust to it. Accommodating the new way of working, the new teams, engine-driving, etc. was enough to preoccupy one's mind.

There was nevertheless one element, brought in from the outside world, which was felt to have deep going consequences. This was the new grounds for promotion of indoor *tkm*, where 'suitability' *(lämplighet)* was to be considered.

As opposed to earlier it now mattered what the manager thought of your skills. Judging 'suitability' differs undoubtedly from judging skill. Not only are outdoor skills very different from the abilities that are appreciated in indoor work, but the evaluation of shunting was always approached from a practical and a theoretical point of view. The first one is the shunters' view, seeing skill as the creation of flow, and consisting largely of tacit, cooperative

---

[35] One of them remarked that he simply could not understand that shunters in general never had bothered to find out about the carriages they constantly handled. 'How can shunters move among these things and never inquire about all the different handles and signs?' he asked.

abilites. The second one is the management, but also the union, point of view. Due to the fact that the theoretical view of work by necessity must be explicit, oral or written, and preferably formalized in regulative rules and regulations, it tends to see work in terms of fragmented tasks, and skill as the performance of a prescribed way of carrying out these tasks. The evaluation thus concerns something radically different from the evaluation of skill in the yard.

There is another complication in the discrepancy between outdoor and indoor evaluations of shunting work, namely that tacit skills – particularly those where the end result does not distinguish between beginners and oldtimers – cannot easily be observed by someone who does not possess the skills in question. The judge, i.e. primarily the manager, has no experience of practical shunting, and he has consequently no other way to form an opinion about the skills of the shunters than to rely on information and formed opinions given to him primarily by *tkm*, but also by the rest of the shunters.

It is not surprising that the shunters become suspicious about persons entering the manager's office and that they themselves hesitate to enter in a way that could be read as clandestine or secretive. The threshold to the manager's office is the obvious gateway for all information, which, it is presumed, will lay the foundation for promotion in the future.

The indoor *tkm* tend to judge the teams, and thereby their leaders, by the work-speed, saying that it is obvious that some teams always finish later than others, regardless of work-load. They also mention a clear difference in the accuracy of the figures and statements given by the outdoor bosses, when they come to report at the end of the shift. There is, however, an obvious problem in equaling time-saving with skill as increased work-speed has an immediate effect on the safety. Time is connected to skill, but also to risk-taking. The accuracy of the figures in the work reports may indicate that the team is badly organized, or that the outdoor boss is careless. However, as an indicator of individual abilities or skills it must be seen as a rather poor indicator.

The drawbacks of any promotion system which takes individual competence and skill into consideration become all the more acute when the skills are tacit (and, as in the case of shunting, manual and based on team-work). The problem of management is, however, less a question of getting information about the skills of the staff than to legitimate their choice of promotion. We can perceive the clash between aquisition of a favourable or even prominent position in the eyes of the work-mates and the new system of promotion.[36]

A slightly ironic point is that the new way of working easily can be fitted to the ideals important to the shunting crew, while it is more difficult to see how the new skills developed in this system, such as shared responsibility and more complex cooperation, will fit with the new order of promotion. One could see it as a tendency for greater autonomy for the shunters combined with greater influence for the management. The former due to the large teams and the latter due to the advancement system, which allows ability to override seniority.[37]

The SJ solution to the promotion dilemma was that formal training and education should be favoured.[38] Courses should matter. We remember that when the three indoor *tkm* posts were reappointed, the appointees were those who earlier had attended SJ courses in leadership. The choice was felt to be deeply unjust, by the shunters as well as by those who were not appointed. Also in the lower end of the team hierarchy the stress on formal training made its way as juniors were trained to become shunt leaders after only two years in the yard. This was not considered enough by the seniors, who did not doubt that the youngsters would manage to learn to shunt in the way of giving signals and finding out in which order things should be done. Anyone could be taught to shunt, but no one could aquire 'the feeling of the spinal marrow' – the gut feeling – in a couple of years. Situations, tasks and weather varied too much to allow such a beginner to have experienced more than a fraction of the 'out of the ordinary' events.

The formal education of new shunt leaders was not opposed – despite doubts about whether it could turn out skilful shunt leaders – as the new organization of the teams led to a demand for equal skills among **all** team

---

[36] The clash between the position given by the formal hierarchy and the informal position of esteem, stemming from skill and authority, will paradoxically be strengthened. The egalitarian principle – promotion according to date of employment – mediated earlier between the classificatory system and the incongruent real life since it eventually granted everybody the same formal rights. Thus the classification could be considered merely functional, creating a hierarchy without necessarily establishing positions. One could compare this to other classificatory systems, such as age hierarchies, or age groups, which also must confront the clash between the schematic classification and the 'unfortunate tendency of real events not to occur normatively', as Alfred Gell puts it. Cf. GELL, 53.

[37] Stephen Wood discusses such development at length. Cf. WOOD, *passim.*

[38] Another solution, which the new EGS-group seems to point towards, would be some kind of Japanese system with 'quality-circles', *Kaizen*, where new foremen could be recruited. Advancement along both of these lines, however, will presumably favour qualities other than those which make a difference in the yard, verbal skills being one example. About Japanese 'quality-circles' cf. WICKENS, 46.

members.[39] In the teams therefore the new requirements were seen as leading to a more democratic order and one in which experienced team-members were allowed to use tacit skills to a higher degree than they had been before. 'This is shunting at its best!' ('*Det här är växling av den högre skolan!*'), one of the shunters exclaimed happily.

To educate the youngsters was also seen as a way to make them stay in the yard. Growing responsibility often led to a change of personality and it made the job so much more interesting it was thought – the puzzling exception being the women, of course.

It was not, then, education as such that was opposed or disliked. What was questioned was the validity of the knowledge and skills so acquired. Training to become a shunt leader was to a high degree a practical training, while 'Technical Coach Service' was largely a theoretical one. Both of these were conducted by shunters and they were seen as necessary and useful, respectively. Neither of them led to a higher paid job, but were rather complementary, making it possible to vary the work-tasks.

The traditional union-education courses were not subject to criticism either. The standard joking comments, by participants as well as by others, depicted such courses as a way to avoid work, but the courses as such were not seen as a threat. The courses that **did** constitute a threat were those that all of a sudden, and retrospectively at that, had been elevated in importance and now were adduced as qualifiers for the tkm office. Also the 'work-leader'-course (to which I was denied access after the first session), was questioned, as was also the three-day course that was said to be decisive for who were going to be selected to the jobs in the switchboard plant, and who were not. These were all courses that raised a considerable amount of emotions.

It is easy to understand objections to courses, earlier considered completely optional and voluntary, suddenly being used as instruments to sift out *tkm* from offices they had held for years. It is also natural to question that the three-day course, which was said to constitute a crucial test to some operators, was seen as unnecessary for others, who just learned the job in the switchboard plant by training on the spot. These were seen to be cases of injustice and badly disguised covers for insidious and despotic behaviour on the part of the managers.

The reason why these cases were seen as deeply unjust was not so much the way the proceedings had been handled, the formalities or the retrospective

---

[39] There was some grumbling about the seniority principle not being followed, but as mentioned earlier such injustice could stem from pure technicalities considering time-schedules and/or unwillingness on the part of the trainees.

upgrading of the necessity of the courses. The main objections were on the contrary directed towards the contents of the courses. 'One did not learn very much', was the typical verdict.

In contrast to the rhetoric which says that taking courses only is an excuse to avoid 'real work' and/or a reward allowing the employees some stimulating intermission in the daily toil, we can conclude that in effect only some courses are questioned, and for quite other reasons. By juxtaposing teachable knowledge and knowledge acquired by 'real work' the rhetoric seems to reveal a process similar to the 'learning to labour' that Paul Willis made known in his painfully enthralling description of the British working class. The contempt for book-knowledge and the refusal to accept the subordinate position as a student during the process of education is seen in Willis's work to regenerate the working class from its own rank and file.[40] Turning to Hagalund we can conclude that neither the merciless scorn for 'sissy' white-collar jobs, nor the cruel means and methods of keeping the mates loyal to their kind can be seen to find their counterparts in the yard. The rhetoric is present, but it veils the reality rather than describes it.

The truth is that despite derogatory and depreciatory comments about 'courses' the shunting community acts collectively like a sponge when it comes to learning. When learning how to drive the remote controlled engines, or to operate the switch plant, or to go to class and do the 'Technical Coach Service' is on the agenda, almost everyone wants to be first. Those few who opt out, regardless of what they state as their motive for doing so, will be suspected of doubting their own abilities to pass the course.

The resistance comes when the courses infringe upon skills that are considered to be learnt 'by themselves' in the context of the daily work and social intercourse, skills which are heavily dependent on individuality and personal abilities. To become a good foreman (*arbetsledare*) cannot be learnt at a course, it is thought. 'You learn it through experience, if you learn it at all. Some people are just not suitable for that task and if they do not learn how to deal with people after twenty years at Hagalund they will never learn, even if they were sent to a hundred courses.' Such views are often aired, at least they **were** before the new manager stated that in appointing the new *tkm* the participation and success at such courses would seriously be taken into consideration.

This declaration from the manager entailed that the crucial work skills were being redefined by the management and what more, they were being

---

40 Cf. WILLIS,*passim.*

appropriated by the management. The earlier principle of strict seniority had meant that promotion formally was befalling everybody in their due time, while in effect many persons chose to stand back. They felt that they were not suited for the job indoors, that they would not stand up to the expectations from the shunters, or that they did not like the idea for some other reason. The long years in the yard had made their position clear and the ones who insisted on their place as indoor Tkm, despite obviously being unsuited for the job, constituted a small minority. Evil tongues said that they were just as badly suited to work in the yard, too, and that in the office they were at least out of the way.

Defining the requirements for promotion in terms set up and controlled by the management not only changes the nature of the *tkm* office and alters the choice of persons appointed (probably tending to reduce the age of the appointed *tkm*, thus blocking the possibility for many ever to qualify, leading to an enhanced segregation between indoor and outdoor). It also reflects back into the yard as it denies the importance of the evaluation and re-evaluation of skill, affecting the self-appeciation as well as the appreciation of others, which is going on there. It radically changes the conditions for the constant shaping of one's position.

Just as the changing conditions in the switch plant were met by different attitudes and strategies, we can assume that the novelties in the yard are encountered in various manners. This has been the case, and we are now only able to account for the initial reactions as the process is only in its infancy when we leave the yard.

The different reactions among the shunters highlight the immanent conflict between the teachable knowledge, favoured and promoted by the management and the tacit, experiental knowledge, always present in the consciousness of the shunters in their view of their work – not under the label 'tacit knowledge', but rather as: 'to know what it's all about', 'to feel it in the spinal marrow', 'to know how things work here in Hagalund', as well as 'to have psychology', 'to know how to deal with people' – in short: 'to know what you're doing'.

It is also evident that the management is associated with education and all that belongs to the field of formalized knowledge, such as schooling and courses, as well as all oral or written 'info'. The superiority of the management is felt to be marked by eloquence and the ability to annihilate criticism and forward own plans by an oral display, confronting the adversary with a shower of figures and numbers, experiential 'facts' from outside the yard and organizational postulates and limitations. The shunters may be verbal and outspoken, but they do not have the same polished and controlled oral versatility. They often do not speak out until they are quite agitated and then explode in a rather uncontrolled and fierce way, using language which may be very strong, catchy and amusing, but which could not be put down in print without losing its value by the mere contact with the literary contagion that would inevitably follow from such a translation.

The shunters, practitioners of skills that cannot be put into words, born and bred into a code that distrusts and discredits scholarly credits, are told that thirty years of practice counts little in comparison to a three-week management course. A shunt leader who through decades of work has earned himself a solid reputation for being 'cool', fair and reliable, or a *tkm* who says the only thing that ever interested him about the work is the opportunity to learn how to deal with all the different, and often amusingly weird, characters that the yard seems to attract, such seniors are now at a course put in front of their fellow foremen, and asked to turn pages on a huge flip chart displaying odd shapes badly fit into squares, and asked to read aloud: 'Some are big (turning one page to the next figure), some are small (turn of page), some are edgy (turn of page), some are chequered (turn of page), some are spotted (turn of page)...' supposedly drawing the foremen's attention to the existence of different personalities among their staff.

The shunters are not only devoid of a language that could criticize the purpose and use of such education, the context puts them in a position that effectively stops them from doing so, as all criticism will be turned back on them as evidence of their wanting in 'positive', cooperative spirit, displaying exactly the 'oldfashioned' and backward ways that the course sets out to uproot.

Consequently some shunters play along, grudgingly or with silent scepticism. The course only confirms their view of 'courses' and education. They may appreciate the ambition on the part of the management to ameliorate relations between different sections and divisions ('some could really better their ways'), but the faulty parties will not change because of a course. Unfit foremen might even do well at the course, and then go back and behave in just the same way as before. Good foremen might on the other hand do less than well in the course, just because they are not used to 'talk a lot of rubbish', but prefer to get on with their work.

Other shunters find the course rewarding, in that finally they are given the opportunity to further themselves and get credit for their skills as foremen. The course confirms that the ability to deal with people is evaluated by the management – even if it remains doubtful whether this actually could be learnt at the course. It rather endorses and testifies to skills already obtained and works therefore as a way to separate the sheep from the goats. But it does promote a good ambiance, tying foremen at different sections together. You are less likely to shout and yell over the telephone at people you have established a personal relationship to at a course.

These two main attitudes correspond to different alliances. The first group – just like those operators in the switchboard plant who stress **inter**-yard rather than **intra**-yard contacts – approach the point of view that is considered to be the company view. According to this view management is not only a question of performing a task, functionally defined and separate from all other tasks. It is a question of bringing out the best qualities in the subordinates, and thereby being responsible and taking the credit or blame, as the case may be.

The foreman course stressed the role of the foreman as 'the face of the group' towards other groups and towards the outside world. No doubt this is a description of loyalty, where the interests of the group should come second to company cohesion and company interests. The old antagonistic foremen, who questioned demands and refused to comply to those they thought were 'unnecessary', should give way to 'service-minded' foremen, who gladly would take on all tasks, not at least because the new system of accountancy meant that every order brought money to the group.

The position as foreman was to be transformed from being the final stop before retirement to a job to which 'talented' persons were selected, in order to be trained and educated for a longer career. There was a new and higher status in the job and a closer cooperation 'upwards'. It demanded a certain style, and the manager stressed that wearing a tie was a matter of being polite towards others, not a matter of pretence. Soft chairs, a little kitchenette of their own, nice manners on the phone and keeping the greasy shunters out of the office, preferably communicating through the shutter, signalled the new status rather clearly. The indoor *tkm* had a hectic job to do, and had no time for shunters who came in to chat or, even worse, to create a noise by copying stupid pictures on the copying machine. The shunters were to do their job and let the foremen do theirs. A line was drawn and the foremen were looking upwards. Maybe the *tkm*-office no longer represented the end of the career, but the beginning of a new one.

The other strategy among the foremen was, again just like among the switchboard plant operators, to look on the company jargon with scepticism. They felt that they already had been forced to work more for less money. Now they were locked to constantly ringing telephones. After all, they were foremen for the yard and their task was to see to it that the shunters could work without trouble from their instructions. The slips had to be correct. That was more important than all fancy talk and courses about square and round persons. To work calmly and correctly, to treat people with normal decency and to defend the group when accusations and unfair demands were put to them – that was more important than suave eloquence, ties and SJ-policy. Just to do indoor work did not mean that one was not a worker like the others out in the yard. Every decade had its fads and fancies, managers came and went, but what remained in all this was the job, to conjure up carriages from the blue in order to keep the trains rolling. In this the shunters were on their own relying on one another and no courses could help them out. Work, not the airy ideas of SJ management, decided who were in the same boat. The sharp line between workers and management was to be kept simply because, despite all EGS (*'Effektivitet Genom Samverkan'*, 'Effectivity Through Cooperation') groups it was the manager who decided and they who had to obey.

By defining the character of the indoor foreman's task and by setting a new standard in the selection of *tkm*, the management not only changes the character of the *tkm*-office and the relation between foremen and the outdoor shunters, they do in effect change the prospects for success for every shunter in the yard. By incorporating the shunting career into a world of documented merit the silently established and indirectly communicated skills are circumvented and pushed into insignificance. Orality is here not in conflict with writing, but with tacitness, with all which cannot be exhibited by a theoretical stopgap, but only disclosed in demonstration in the original and real context.

Shunters, feeling uncomfortable with all re-presentations of work that courses and tests require, judging themselves as lacking in oral as well as in written exercises, clearly identify the demand for documented and measurable skill as a demarcation line between 'doers' and 'do-nothings', between workers and management. The contempt for those with an ambition to cross this line – especially if the ambition is accompanied by signs of estrangement in clothing and patterns of sociability – makes it even less attractive actively to strive for ways of improving oneself by theoretical and discursive education.[41]

We do on the other hand remember the massive interest for working in the switchboard plant, or rather for giving it a try. The high salary for operators

---

[41] The slight irony is that the manager himself confesses to be a man of action rather than theory, but his personal inclinations and values matter little in comparison with his position as the prime judge of others, the skills of whom he can only assess by partial or indirect evaluation, such as speed of work and amount of damage to materials on one hand and hearsay and performance in courses on the other hand.

was undoubtedly a strong incentive, but several shunters were interested in 'learning about computers', which was thought to be embraced by training for the plant. Computers, being associated with the future, signified a step forward, learning a skill which crossed the boundaries of the yard and its ancient work process.

There were also a couple of shunters who saw a future in mastery of technical knowledge in engine driving and in rolling stock.

Only time can tell which of the strategies will turn out to be good investments. Will there be shunting at all, or will automatic coupling make the skills of the shunters obsolete? Or will the shunters 'take over' a larger part of Hagalund, as envisioned by the manager, replacing the troubled employer-worker relations in other parts with their cooperative and 'sensible' spirit.

It seems that the only thing we can say with some certainty is that the closed world of the shunters will no longer be the silent pond it was for so long. Ditches are dug, fresh water is streaming in, connecting the pond to bigger waters.

Conclusions

The reorganization meant a rearrangement of physical as well as symbolic space. Organizational limits which had been insignificant were marked by walls and distances, while other aspects of hierarchy were downplayed and construed so as to invite contact and sociability.

New technology meant approximation in the case of the remote controlled engines, where the team more than earlier could work as one, and where the persons handling of the work processes stood in close contact with the persons controlling them. As a result speed and flow were increased.

Concerning the other major piece of new technology, the switchboard plant, the effect was the adverse. Distance between co-workers, in this case distance between the persons handling the physical process and the persons controlling crucial parts of it – lining the switches – was extreme and managed through radio contact. Flow and speed were reduced. The distance in physical space made it possible to turn control of the switchboard into control over people.

Time, as an aspect of advancing at work, was also given a new meaning as seniority now could be overruled by individual suitability. While such a rule is seen as sensible **in principle**, as it easily can be argued that the best thing for an organization is to have the right people in the right positions, it nevertheless creates a different perspective for the individual shunter and for the relation between shunters. What is 'suitability' and how will I, and the work I perform, be judged? What information is being passed on, and by whom?

Judging the new perspectives of work is not easy and the strategies to cope diverge. But behind even the most optimistic outlook there is the insight that shunting is an outmoded trade, which one day will be replaced by new technological solutions. Shunters are relics from an era which belongs to the history books. Every step forward in shunting technology is a step towards effacing the world of the shunters.

Shunt leader showing 'slow'.

10. SUMMARY

Ida Simpson described the 1930s-50s as a 'golden age' of industrial sociology. It was a time, she said, when the worker, the social relations in the workplace, and work itself were in focus. In 1989 she saw a very different trend in research and she asked: 'Where Have the Workers Gone?' adding: "We now study [the workers'] earnings, comparable worth, skills, human capital markets, and the labor process that abstracts work from the worker and turns it into an economic commodity." She expressed a wish for studies that "[...] try to understand how workers actively go about dealing with forces they can and cannot control and how they experience them".[1]

There were times when anthropologists, too, could have been accused of neglecting the worker, although the occupational division of labour between sociology and social anthropology always granted a space for the worker in the latter field, even during the most 'economistic' era in the 1960s-70s.[2] Now there is a vast literature which sets out to kill the 'technological beast'. Technology as such does not exist, 'the technological is social', Bijker and Law state.[3] This does not always mean that the worker is brought in. Skill has still been a 'beast', a thing external to the worker, something which the worker must acquire. Only recently the worker has come to be seen as an agent in relation to his/her own skills.[4]

Bringing the workers into the study of work and skill does not mean adding ethnographic description, though this may be necessary. The perspective is one which cannot exclude the worker simply because it assumes, and claims, that worker, work, skill and technology constitute a complex whole, which can be studied as such.[5]

---

[1] Cf. SIMPSON, 563 f., 579.

[2] The contributions to the ASA volume *Social Anthropology of Work* offer a range of perspectives, a few of which include the worker . Cf. e.g. SEARLE-CHATTERJEE, MURRAY.

[3] Cf. BIJKER & LAW, 4.

[4] Studies of apprenticeship, of the so called 'skipper effect', and of tacit knowledge are examples from a vide range of such approaches. Cf. COY & al., PÁLSSON, PERBY.

[5] I must say that I always found James Frazer's comment in the preface to Malinowski's 'Argonauts of the Western Pacific' both significant and touching (coming from one of the last 'armchair' anthropologists). Sir James writes: "It is characteristic of Dr. Malinowski's method that he takes full account of the complexity of human nature. He sees man, so to say, in the

This book has aspired to such a holistic view. My starting point has been simple. I have asked what work is all about in a particular shunting yard. What is good work? Therefore, I have seen skill, the aquisition of skill, and the workers' conceptions of skill, as the key to an understanding of the relation between workers, work and technology.

The shunters believe that in order to perform work well one should possess a well developed 'split vision', an ability to cooperate and plan ahead, and, not at least, one should 'have psychology'. But the shunters see skill as something more than only the ability to work well. One has to **keep on** working well. Shunting is a protracted test, which not every individual with all the above mentioned abilities will pass. One should possess a good deal of tenaciousness, and not too serious an attitude to work and life. It is thought that the only way to endure the cold, the wind, the sleet and the ardour is to laugh at it. It is therefore only practice, in a long perspective, that will decide who is a good shunter. Skill implies relating to a context, but this context must also include a future, if our perspective aspires to contribute to a theory of practice.

Many of the aspects of skill, implied in the shunters' views, are also reflected in the ways anthropologists, sociologists and philosophers have treated the subject of skill. Skills 'residing in the man himself' have been distinguished from skills that the job demands (Cockburn) and skills that are judged by others (Rolf, More). Skills that follow rules have been seen as different from skills that allow transformation of the rules (Rolf; know-how versus competence). Tacit, as opposed to verbally transmissible, skills have been defined (Janik, Perby). Skills have been seen as inherently variant, constantly reconceptualized and dependent on cooperation and context (Engeström, Ingold, Lave & Wenger, Pálsson).

Although I have found myself disagreeing with some of these writers at some points, it is on the whole not the criticism of the definitions of skill that has been the ultimate purpose of this book. My aim has been to step further and not only characterize skill as, for example, defined by the context, but actually try to see **how** it is defined by the context. As the context changes we may expect change in the definition of skill, too.

If I can be said to have reached any new insights at all, they stem not from a new definition of skill, but from studying skill in its various roles in the formation of social relations in the shunting yard. Skill can be constituted as an ideal, as what good shunting should be like, but it also represents a

round and not in the flat." FRAZER, IX. I believe this still should serve as a lodestar for social inquiry.

'tradition' in the yard.[6] 'The way shunting has always been done here in Hagalund' is a strong precedent, not because it is defined or definable, but because it is imprecise and vague.

It is not surprising, then, that the emerging picture of the meaning of skill has not been one of consistency, but rather of change and flux. Conceptions of skill depend on conceptions of what is technologically given and possible, as well as on conceptions of how division of labour could and should be organized. In the shunting yard we have seen how hierarchical team organization was considered to be technologically determined and therefore accepted and seen as self-evident. The concept of shunting became equated with the work done by three shunters; the shunt leader, the B-member and the C-member. This strict hierarchy, where the duties of every member were so specific that orders almost became superfluous, stood in strong contrast to another aspect of good work; the egalitarian ethos. This is not an ideology endogenous to the shunting yard, but a part of Swedish working class culture,[7] and as such naturally influenced by ideological currents in society at large.

When the new order in the teams was forced upon the shunters it was quickly accepted (although some managed to cling to the old ways) and even seen as inherently satisfying. There can be no doubt that the fact that the new organization agreed with the egalitarian ideal made it acceptable as a good order.

Conflicts between collective ideals and individual interests were also inherent in the team-work. The firm belief in 'the ways things are done here in Hagalund' encompassed ideas about adaptability to the collective and traditional ways of thinking. This came to clash with the individualistic right to establish a personal work style (as well as an eccentric life style), when teams no longer were established through individual choice and long time socialization, but through a forced mix of idiosyncratic styles. The VIK-list, which rotates its members between all teams, functioned then, as always, as a hamper on such conflicts, because the clashes of styles were reduced to temporary encounters. Here time can be seen as a mediator between (permanent) individualistic styles and (temporary) agreements about 'the Hagalund way of working'.

---

[6] Nyíri says: "[...] what we need is not so much definitions as much rather a detailed examination of the ways in which traditions in all their forms and varieties function at the different levels and in the different spheres of social life[...]" NYÍRI, 32.

[7] The 'Swedish Model', which was a political ambition concerning regulations on the labour market, was built on egalitarian ideals, held by the Social Democratic Party and the trade union movement. It can be seen to have strenghtened, but not created, an already existing egalitarian ethos. Cf. LINDGREN, 39 ff, 731. ROSENDAHL, 54 f.

The 'Hagalund way of working' is something the beginner must incorporate in his/her work repertoire. Lacking regulative rules, this style, as all other styles, must be learnt in everyday work through the long process of learning to see a pattern; to 'see something **as** something'. Relating to this picture or pattern the beginners adopt various approaches in order to incorporate it to their own styles of working. However, the character of the picture, as well as the nature of the approach, depends on the point of observation, which, in its turn, is not given by the immediate context. It is given by the embodied history; the habitus.

I have distinguished between two learning strategies, representing two types of habitus, calling them paraphrastic and mimetic, respectively. They could be said to result from relating male and female habitus to a workplace which is seen to be male through and through. Heavy machinery, arduous physical work – and a long tradition of male workers, and a military organization – has an ideological weight which cannot be balanced by undifferentiated treatment.

The different learning strategies imply a different appropriation of work, and a different way of relating to the shunting community. To show off, to mark oneself as an able shunter is an assurance that work proceeds without risk, but it is also a means of communication. The able shunter is part of the process, of good flow, of the team and the shunting community.

This book has tried to show that relations between people and technology and between people and work cannot be separated from the social relations between people. In fact, the relations to skilled work, to handling of carriages and to operating switchboards are part of the relations between people. This must not be taken to mean that, for example, skill, and the transmission of skill through learning and teaching, are construed in accordance with social relations; they are, and constitute, ways of relating.

Therefore, this book is not only about studying work, worker and technology from an external point of view, creating a new 'beast' external to consciousness, but to see how work, worker and technology are related through the ways they are conceived of by the workers themselves.

We have seen how the shunters conceive of their history, as well as their future. We cannot kill the beast without looking at their ideas about what work has been, what it should be, what it could be and what it will be in the years to come

Recently one of the shunters said, looking out over the yard from the switchboard plant: 'Everything here at Hagalund is exactly the same as thirty years ago.' If the reader has a different understanding of this statement after reading this book than he/she would have had before reading it, I have managed to convey an important part of my message.

UNPRINTED SOURCES

Minutes from the local union club meetings.
Rangieren ohne Risiko. An educational film from DB. Doderer, Kircher, Müller.
Taped interviews (INT 1-22).

BIBLIOGRAPHY

ADAM, Barbara 1990. *Time and Social Theory.* Cambridge: Polity Press.
ARISTOPHANES 1955. III (Transl.: Benjamin Bickley Rogers.) London &
    Cambridge MA: Loeb.
Årsredovisning 1995 SJ-koncernen. SJ Stab Information, Stockholm.
ARVASTSON, Gösta 1985. Tombola as a model of reality. *Ethnologia
    Scandinavica.*
————1987. *Maskinmänniskan: Arbetets förvandlingar i 1900-talets
    storindustri.* Göteborg: Bokförlaget Korpen.
BACK, Les 1993. Gendered participation: Masculinity and fieldwork in a south
    London adolescent community. *Gendered Fields.* (Eds: Bell, Diane,
    Pat Kaplan & Wazir Jahan Karim) London & New York: Routledge.
BARTHES, Roland 1981. *Mythologies.* (Transl.: Annette Lavers) London,
    Toronto, ...: Granada.
BIJKER, Wiebe E. & John LAW 1992. General introduction. *Shaping
    Technology/Building Society: Studies in Sociotechnical Change.*
    (Ed.: Bijker, Wiebe E. & John Law) Cambridge MA & London: The
    MIT Press.
BOURDIEU, Pierre 1977. *Outline of a Theory of Practice.* Cambridge, London,...:
    Cambridge Univ Press.
————1981. Men and machines. *Advances in Social Theory and Methodology:
    Toward an Integration of Micro- and Macro Sociologies.* (Eds:
    Knorr-Cetina, Karin & Aaron.V. Cicourel) Boston, London...:
————1989. *Distinction: A Social Critique of the Judgement of Taste.* (Transl.:
    Richard Nice) London: Routledge & Kegan Paul Ltd.
————1990a. *The Logic of Practice.* (Transl.: Richard Nice) Cambridge: Polity
    Press.
————1990b. The Scholastic Point of view. *Cultural Anthropology,* 5 (4).
BROADY, Donald 1991. *Sociologi och epistemologi. Om Pierre Bourdieus
    författarskap och den historiska epistemologin.* Stockholm: HLS
    Förlag.
The Cassell Concise English Dictionary. 1989 (Ed.: Betty Kirkpatrick) London:
    Cassell.
CICOUREL, Aaron V. 1981. Notes on the integration of micro- and macro-levels of
    analysis. *Advances in Social Theory and Methodology: Toward an
    Integration of Micro- and Macro Sociologies.* (Eds: Knorr-Cetina,
    Karin & Aaron.V. Cicourel) Boston, London...: Routledge & Kegan
    Paul.
COCKBURN, Cynthia 1981. The Material of Male Power. *Feminist Review,* 9.
————1984. *Brothers: Male Dominance and Technological Change.* London:
    Pluto Press.

COCKBURN, Cynthia & Susan ORMROD 1993. *Gender and Technology in the Making*. London, Thousand Oaks...: Sage.

COHEN, Anthony P. 1979. The Whalsay croft: Traditional work and customary identity in modern times. *Social Anthropology of Work* (Ed.: Sandra Wallman) London, New York...: Academic Press.

————1992. *The Symbolic Construction of Community*. London & New York: Routledge.

COLLINS, H. M. 1993. Expert systems and the science of knowledge. *The Social Construction of Technological Systems: New Directions in the Sociology and History of Technology*. (Eds: Wiebe E. Bijker, Thomas P. Hughes & Trevor Pinch) Cambridge MA & London: The MIT Press.

COLLINSON, David L. 1988. 'Engineering humour': Masculinity, joking and conflict in shop-floor relations. *Organization Studies*, 9 (2).

COOLEY, Charles H. 1956. *The Two Major Works of Charles H. Cooley: Social Organization; Human Nature and the Social Order*. Glencoe Ill.: Free.

COOPER, Eugene 1989. Apprenticeship as field method: Lessons from Hong Kong. *Apprenticeship: From Theory to Method and Back Again* (Ed.: Michael W. Coy) Albany, NY: State Univ of New York Press.

COTTRELL, W.F. 1939. Of time and the railroader. *American Sociological Review*, 4 (2).

COY, Michael W. 1989a. From theory. *Apprenticeship: From Theory to Method and Back Again* (Ed.: Michael W. Coy) Albany, NY: State Univ of New York Press.

————1989b. Being what we pretend to be: The usefulness of apprenticeship as a field method. *Apprenticeship: From Theory to Method and Back Again* (Ed.: Michael W. Coy) Albany, NY: State Univ of New York Press.

CSIKSZENTMIHALYI, Mihaly 1990. *Flow: The Psychology of Optimal Experience*. New York: Harper Perennial.

D'ANDRADE, Roy 1995. *The Development of Cognitive Anthropology*. Cambridge, New York...: Cambridge University Press.

DILLEY, R. M. 1989. Secrets and skills: Apprenticeship among Tukolor weavers. *Apprenticeship: From Theory to Method and Back Again* (Ed.: Michael W. Coy) Albany, NY: State Univ of New York Press.

DOUGLAS, Mary 1986. *Risk Acceptability According to the Social Sciences*. London: Routledge & Kegan Paul.

————1994. *Risk and Blame: Essays in Cultural Theory*. London & New York: Routledge.

EDELMAN, Birgitta 1993. Acting cool and being safe: The definition of skill in a Swedish railway yard. *Beyond Boundaries: Understanding, Translation and Anthropological Discourse*. (Ed.: Gísli Pálsson) Oxford: Berg.

EHN, Billy 1981. *Arbetets flytande gränser: En fabriksstudie*. Stockholm: Prisma.

ENGESTRÖM, Yrjö 1989. *Developing Thinking at the Changing Workplace: Toward a Redifinition of Expertise*. [Chip 130] Center for Human Information Processing. University of California, La Jolla.

FARNELL, Brenda M. 1994. Ethno-graphics and the moving body. *Man* (N.S.) 29 (4).

322

Föreskrifter angående fordringarna med avseende på kropps- och sinnesbeskaffenheten hos personalen vid Statens Järnvägar. SJ's Författningssamling, 9 A. (no date)

FOUCAULT, Michel 1993. *Surveiller et punir: Naissance de la prison.* Paris: Gallimard.

FRAZER, James G. 1961. Preface. *Argonauts of the Western Pacific: An Account of Native Enterprise and Adventure in the Archipelagoes of Melanesian New Guinea.* (Bronislaw Malinowski) New York: Dutton.

GAMST, Frederick C. 1978. *Position Explanation for Railroad Operating Employees...* Report No. FCG-SP-78-3.

—————1980. *The Hoghead: An Industrial Ethnology of the Locomotive Engineer.* New York: Holt Rinehart, and Winston.

—————1985. *The industrial relations of seniority, with particular reference to railroad crafts.* Report No. FCG-UC-85-1.

—————1986. Women as operating and clerical railroaders: Some considerations on enculturation and intrinsic and external barriers. *Urban Anthropology,* 15 (3-4).

—————1989. The railroad apprentice and the 'Rules': Historic roots and contemporary practices. *Apprenticeship: From Theory to Method and Back Again* (Ed.: Michael W. Coy) Albany, NY: State Univ of New York Press.

GARFINKEL, Harold 1956. Conditions of successful degradation ceremonies. *American Sociological Review,* 61.

GARSTEN, Christina 1994. *Apple World: Core and Periphery in a Transnational Organizational Culture.* [Stockholm Studies in Social Anthropology 33] Stockholm: Almqwist & Wiksell.

GEERTZ, Clifford 1973. *The Interpretation of Cultures.* New York: Basic Books Inc.

—————1983. *Local Knowledge: Further Essays in Interpretive Anthropology.* New York: Basic Books.

GELL, Alfred 1996. *The Anthropology ot Time: Cultural Constructions of Temporal Maps and Images.* Oxford, Washington D.C.: Berg.

van GENNEP, Arnold 1969. *The Rites of Passage.* Chicago: Univ of Chicago Press. (Transl.: Wizedom Monika B. & Gabrielle L. Caffee)

GIDDENS, Anthony 1978. *The Class Structure of the Advanced Societies.* London: Hutchinson & Co Ltd.

—————1979. *Central Problems in Social Theory.* Berkeley & Los Angeles: Univ of California Press.

—————1987. *Social Theory and Modern Sociology.* Cambridge & Oxford: Polity Press.

—————1990. *A Contemporary Critique of Historical Materialism.* Basingstoke: MacMillan.

GOFFMAN, Erving 1972. *Relations in Public: Microstudies of the Public Order.* Harmondsworth & Victoria: Penguin.

—————1976. *The Presentation of Self in Everyday Life.* Harmondsworth, New York ...: Penguin.

GRAVES, Bennie 1989. Informal aspects of apprenticeship in selected American occupations. *Apprenticeship: From Theory to Method and Back Again* (Ed.: Michael W. Coy) Albany, NY: State Univ of New York Press.

323

GUSTAFSSON, Bo 1986. Conflict, confrontation and consensus in modern Swedish history. *Economics and values.* (Ed.: Lennart Arvedson & al.) Stockholm: Almqvist & Wiksell.

GULLESTAD, Marianne 1992. The transformation of the notion of everyday life. *The Art of Social Relations: Essays on Culture, Social Action and Everyday Life in Modern Norway.* Oslo: Scandinavian Univ Press.

GUNNARSSON, Ewa 1989. *Kvinnors arbetsrationalitet och kvalifikationer.* Arbetsrapport nr 6 i Qvistprojektet. Stockholm: Arbetslivscentrum.

HAAS, Jack 1989. The process of apprenticeship: Ritual ordeal and the adoption of a cloak of competence. *Apprenticeship: From Theory to Method and Back Again* (Ed.: Michael W. Coy) Albany, NY: State Univ of New York Press.

HANNERZ, Ulf 1983. *Över gränser: Studier i dagens socialantropologi.* Lund: Liber.

————1992. *Cultural Complexity: Studies in the Social Organization of Meaning.* New York & Chichester: Columbia Univ. Press.

HERITAGE, John C. 1987. Ethnomethodology. *Social Theory Today.* (Ed.: Giddens, Anthony & Jonathan H. Turner) Cambridge: Polity Press.

HOHN, Hans-Willy 1984. *Die Zerstörung der Zeit: Wie aus einem göttlichen Gut eine Handelsware wurde.* Frankfurt a. M: Fischer Alternativ.

HOLMSTRÖM, Björn 1992. *Stora kortspelsboken.* Prisma.

INGOLD, Tim 1990. Society, nature and the concept of technology. *Archaeological Review from Cambridge.* 9.

————1995. Building, dwelling, living: How animals and people make themselves at home in the world. *Shifting Contexts.*(Ed.: Marilyn Strathern) London: Routledge.

JANIK, Allan 1988. Tacit knowledge, working life and scientific method. *Knowledge, Skill and Artificial Intelligence.* (Eds: Göranzon, Bo & Ingela Josefson) London: Springer-Verlag.

————1990. Tacit knowledge, rule-following and learning. *Artificial Intelligence, Culture and Language.* (Eds: Göranzon, Bo & Magnus Florin) London, Berlin...:Springer-Verlag.

JENKINS, Timothy 1994. Fieldwork and the perception of everyday life. *Man* (N.S.) 29 (2).

JOHANNESSEN, Kjell S. 1990. Rule-following and intransitive understanding. *Artificial Intelligence, Culture and Language.* (Eds: Göranzon, Bo & Magnus Florin) London, Berlin...:Springer-Verlag.

KALLEBERG, Arne L. 1989. Linking macro and micro levels: Bringing the workers back into the sociology of work. *Social Forces,* 67 (3).

KANTER, Rosabeth Moss 1972. *When Giants Learn to Dance; Mastering the Challenges of Strategy, Management, and Careers in the 1990s.* London: Simon & Schuster.

KEMNITZER, Luis.S. 1977. Another view of time and the railroader. *Anthropological Quarterly,* 50.

KIMBALL, Solon T. 1969. Introduction.*The Rites of Passage.* Chicago: Univ of Chicago Press.

Kompletterande föreskrifter och anvisningar till säkerhetsordningen (säok). SJF 010.1. Utgåva 3. SJ Huvudkontoret, Stab trafiksäkerhet.

LAVE, Jean & Etienne WENGER 1991. *Situated Learning: Legitimate Peripheral Participation.* Cambridge: Cambridge Univ Press.

LÉVI-STRAUSS, Claude 1966. *The Savage Mind.* Chicago: Chicago Univ Press.

324

LINDGREN, Antony 1994. *Arbete, skola och familj i Sverige på 1900-talet.* [151 D]. Tekniska Högskolan i Luleå: Luleå.
LOCKE, John L. 1989. Babbling and early speach: Continuity and individual differences. *First Language*, 9.
LYMAN, M. & M. SCOTT 1967. Territoriality. *Social Problems*, 15.
MACKAY, Hughie & Gareth GILLESPIE 1992. Extending the social shaping of technology approach: Ideology and appropriation. *Social Studies of Science*, 22.
MAUSS, Marcel 1980. Les techniques du corps. *Sociologie et Anthropologie*. Paris: Presses Univ de France.
McCLELLAND, Keith 1989. Time to work, time to live: Some aspects of work and the re-formation of class in Britain, 1850-1880. *The Historical Meanings of Work* (Ed.: Patrick Joyce) Cambridge, New York...: Cambridge Univ. Press.
McKENNA, Frank 1980. *The Railway Workers 1840-1970.* London & Boston: Faber & Faber.
MEHLER, Jacques & Emmanuel DUPOUX 1994. *What Infants Know: The New Cognitive Science of Early Development.* (Transl.: Patsy Southgate) Oxford & Cambridge, MA: Basil Blackwell.
MELLSTRÖM, Ulf 1995. *Engineering Lives: Technology, Time and Space in a Male-Centred World.* Linköping: Linköping University.
MOORE, Henrietta L. *Feminism and Anthropology.* 1994. Cambridge & Oxford : Polity Press.
MOORE, Wilbert E. 1947. *Industrial Relations and the Social Order.* New York: The MacMillan Company.
MORE, Charles 1980. *Skill and the English Working Class, 1870–1914.* London: Croom Helm.
MUMFORD, Lewis 1973. *Interpretations and Forecasts: 1922-72: Studies in Literature, History, Biography, and Contemporary Society.* London: Secker & Warburg.
MUNN, Nancy D. 1992. The cultural anthropology of time: A critical essay. *Annual Review of Anthropology*, 21.
MURRAY, Colin 1979. The work of men, women and the ancestors: Social reproduction in the periphery of Southern Africa. *Social Anthropology of Work.* (Ed.: Sandra Wallman) London, New York...: Academic Press.
NIEMANN, Linda 1990. *Boomer: Railroad Memoirs.* Berkeley, Los Angeles...: Univ of California Press.
NYÍRI, J.C. 1988. Tradition and practical knowledge. *Practical Knowledge: Outlines of a Theory of Traditions and Skills.* (Eds: Nyíri J. C. & Barry Smith) London: Croon Helm.
NYSTRÖM, Örjan 1991. *Järnvägar och järnvägare: En bok om järnvägens historia om framtid – men mest om arbetet på Göteborgs godsbangårdar från 30-tal till 70-tal.* Vänersborg: Tre Böcker.
NØRRETRANDERS, Tor 1991. *Märk världen: En bok om vetenskap och intuition.* (Transl.: Jan Wahlén) Stockholm: Bonnier Alba.
PÁLSSON, Gísli 1994. Enskilment at sea. *Man* (N.S.) 29 (4).
PÁLSSON, Gísli & E. Paul DURRENBERGER 1990. Systems of production and social discourse: The skipper effect revisited. *American Anthropologist*, 92 (1).
På tre år och 100 punkter ska SJ bli bättre. SJ Stab Information.

325

PERBY, Maja-Lisa 1995. *Konsten att bemästra en process: Om att förvalta yrkeskunnande.* Smedjebacken: Gidlunds förlag.

PERSSON, Nils-Erik 1986. *Växlingsarbete. Olycksfall: uppkomst och konsekvenser. Rapport om omfattning och utveckling av arbetsolycksfall i växlingsarbete 1976-1985.* (AFS 1986:11) SJ, PAH.

PFAFFENBERGER, Bryan 1988. The social meaning of the personal computer: or, why the personal computer revolution was no revolution. *Anthropological Quarterly.* 61 (1).

———1992. Technological dramas. *Science, Technology, and Human Values.* 17 (5).

POGREBIN, Mark R. & Eric D. POOLE 1988. Humor in the briefing room: A study of the strategic uses of humor among police. *Journal of Contemporary Ethnography,* 17.

PYE, David 1968. *The Nature and Art of Workmanship.* Cambridge: Cambridge Univ Press.

PYLYSHYN, Zenon 1991. Rules and representations: Chomsky and representational realism. *The Chomskyan Turn.* (Ed.: Asa Kasher) Oxford & Cambridge, MA: Basil Blackwell.

ROGOFF, Barbara 1990. *Apprenticeship in Thinking: Cognitive Development in Social Context.* New York, Oxford: Oxford Univ Press.

ROLF, Bertil 1991. *Profession, tradition och tyst kunskap: En studie i Polanyis teori om den pofessionella kunskapens tysta dimension.* Övre Dalkarlshyttan: Nya Doxa.

ROSENDAHL, Mona 1985. *Conflict and Compliance: Class Consciousness among Swedish Workers.* [Stockholm Studies in Social Anthropology 14] Stockholm: Department of Social Anthropology, University of Stockholm.

RYLE, Gilbert 1990. Collected Essays 1929-1968.*Collected Papers, 2.* Bristol: Thoemmes.

SAHLINS, Marshall D. 1968. *Tribesmen.* Englewood Cliffs: Prentice-Hall.

Säkerhetsmeddelanden 7. SJ Huvudkontoret, Stab Trafiksäkerhet.

Säkerhetsordning (säo). SJF 010. Utgåva 13. SJ Huvudkontoret, Stab Trafiksäkerhet.

SCHELER, Max 1973. *Formalism in Ethics and Non-Formal Ethics of Values.* (Transl.: Frings M. S. & R. L. Fuenck) Evanston: Northwestern Univ Press.

SEARLE-CHATTERJEE, Mary 1979. The polluted identity of work: A study of Benares sweepers. *Social Anthropology of Work.* (Ed.: Sandra Wallman) London, New York...: Academic Press.

SECKMAN, Mark A. & Carl J. COUCH 1989. Jocularity, sarcasm, and relationships; An empirical study. *Journal of Contemporary Ethnography,* 18 (3).

SHARMA, Ursula 1996. Bringing the body back into the (social) action. Techniques of the body and the (cultural) imagination,. *Social Anthropology,* 4 (3).

SIMPSON, Ida Harper 1989. The sociology of work: Where have the workers gone? *Social Forces,* 67 (3).

SMITH, Barry 1988. Knowing how vs. knowing that. *Practical Knowledge: Outlines of a Theory of Traditions and Skills.* (Eds: Nyíri J.C. & Barry Smith) London: Croon Helm.

326

SÖRBOM, Göran 1966. *Mimesis and Art: Studies in the Origin and Early Development of an Aesthetic Vocabulary.* Stockholm: Bonnier.
STARKEY, Ken 1988. Time and work organization: A theoretical and empirical analysis. *The Rhythms of Society.* (Eds: Young, Michael & Tom Schuller) London: Routledge.
Svensk-engelsk ordbok. 1935. Stockholm: Svenska bokförlaget.
Svensk ordbok. 1986. Uppsala: Esselte.
THOMPSON, E. P. 1978. *The Poverty of Theory, and other Essays.* London: Merlin Press.
TRICE, Harrison M. & Janice M. BEYER. 1993. *Cultures of Work Organizations.* Englewood Cliffs.: Prentice Hall.
TURNER, Jonathan H. 1987. Analytical theorizing. *Social Theory Today.* (Ed.: Giddens, Anthony. & Jonathan H.Turner) Cambridge: Polity Press.
TURNER, Victor W. 1974. *The Ritual Process.* Penguin.
VAUGHT, Charles & David L. SMITH 1980. Incorporation and mechanical solidarity in an underground coal mine. *Sociology of Work and Occupations,* 7 (2).
WAJCMAN, Judy 1991. *Feminism Confronts Technology.* Cambridge: Polity Press.
Växlingsinstruktion (vxi). SJF 010.3. Utgåva 3. SJ Trafikavdelningen, Säkerhetssektionen.
WICKENS, Peter. 1987. *The Road to Nissan: Flexibility, Quality, Teamwork.* Basingstoke: Macmillan Press.
WILLIS, Paul E. 1978. *Learning to Labour: How Working Class Kids Get Working Class Jobs.* Westmead: Saxon House.
WITTGENSTEIN, Ludwig 1992. *Philosophical Investigations.* (Transl.: G.E.M. Anscombe) Oxford & Cambridge MA: Basil Blackwell.
WOOD, Stephen J. (1991). Post-Fordism and the Japanization of the labour process theory: Where goes the skilling debate. *Work and Welfare: Papers from the Second Karlstad Symposium on Work June 18-20, 1990 at the University of Karlstad.* Research Report 91:7. University of Karlstad.
ZIJDERVELD, Anton C. 1968. Jokes and their relation to social reality. *Social Research,* 35.

NOTATION

I have used the term 'shunter' instead of the rather common 'switchman'. This is because I find it easier to talk about 'female shunters' than 'female switchmen' – or 'switchwomen'. I have retained a lot of Swedish terms. Swedish readers will find it easier to understand what I talk about, while other readers, hopefully, will understand this sociotechnical system on its own terms, and not draw instant parallels to other railways.

There is a distinction between two types of quotations.

' ...' is used for common expressions (or short quotations from texts) and for quotations which I have taken down in my notes some time after they were uttered.

"..." is used for verbatim quotations (sometimes translated though). The source is either a text or an audio tape.

Bold face indicates emphasis, while non-English words are written in *italics*.

I have used pseudonyms for the persons in this book.

GLOSSARY AND ABBREVIATIONS

Å95	*Årsredovisning 1995 SJ-koncernen*. SJ Stab Information, Stockholm.
AFS	Arbetarskyddsstyrelsens kungörelse AFS 1986:11 'Växlingsarbete'.
air brake hose	Rubber hose connecting coaches to the air brake system. (If broken the air will leak out and the coach will be brought to a halt.)
A-member	(See: shunt leader)
avhängare	(See: C-member)
avkopplare	(See: C-member)
bangårdsgruppen	The Yard Group, i.e. the shunting group.
bas, -ar	(See: *tkm*)
between (stand, to be in)	The term for standing between coaches, buffers and the rails of a track. Necessary position when coupling or uncoupling coaches and air brake hoses. To go between, or to 'enter', is to take such a position.
B-member	Member of shunting team who is stopping and attending to kicked coaches. (Am.: herder)
boss (indoor/ outdoor)	(See: *tkm*)
bottle-neck	(*flaskhalsen*) Part of track in Hagalund where most ingoing and outgoing traffic must pass. The b. is in addition in the middle of the lead in the South.

brake heel	(*bromssko*, or *doja*) Mobile brake implement, which is put on the track in order to stop kicked coaches, or to secure coaches that are left temporarily.
brake hose	(See: air brake hose)
brake shoe	(*bromsklots*) Iron blocks that seize the wheels when brakes are applied.
bromssko	(See: brake heel)
cab	Driver's workplace on engine. (Engines have driver on left-hand side, as Swedish railways has left-hand traffic)
CCE	The Cassell Concise English Dictionary.
coach recorder	Person checking *littera*, weight and brake weight of departing trains.
C-member	Member of shunting team who does most of the coupling and uncoupling. Also called coupler or coupling-boy.
composition plan	Book containing descriptions ('train pictures') of how every train should be composed.
couple	(*koppla*) To connect two coaches. (See: coupling)
coupler 1)	(See: C-member)
	2) Part of traction contrivances; the 'eye'-part of the clasp and eye.
coupling	1) (*koppel*) Mechanism allowing two coaches to be connected, consisting of a large hook and eye. The coupling is tightened by means of a screw mechanism.
	2)(*ge koppel*) To give a coach or a cut of coaches a push with an engine, in order to make the buffers contract and enable coupling or tightening of the coupling.
	3) (*visa 'koppel'*) To signal that 2) should be made.
coupling boy	(*koppelpojke*) (See: C-member)
Cst	The Central Station
cut	Two or more coaches coupled.
dra (about coaches)	(See: pull)
dra (about coupling)	(See: draw)
draw	To tighten a coupling.
draw (or connect) for good	To tighten couplings and connect cables and hoses according to regulations for coaches that are to go in traffic.
drudger	(*gnetare*) Person who is working extra skifts or who is known to be willing to work extra shifts.
electric post	(*värmepost*) Pillar at the end of each track, to which electric cables from the engineless trains are connected in order to provide light and heating.
emellan	(See: between)
engine foreman	(See: shunt leader)
Englishman	1)Native or naturalized inhabitant of England, but also
	2)Double switch

330

extension track	*(utdragsspår)* Track which extends far behind the last switch, in the yard enabling long cuts to be shunted. Ends in a stopbar.
FAF	*Föreskrifter angående fordringarna med avseende på kropps- och sinnesbeskaffenheten hos personalen vid Statens Järnvägar.*
fast	(See: steady)
fieldman	(See: B-member)
flat spot	Damage to wheel created by friction between locked wheel and track, due to heavy braking or frozen brake shoe.
flaskhalsen	(See: bottle-neck)
footplate	platform for engine driver (here on shunt engine)
foreman	(See: *tkm*)
fridagsnyckel	('free-time key') Schedules for work days and days off for VIK as well as persons working on steady lists.
gnetare	(See: drudger)
gnetlista	List of extra shifts available for volunteers.
göra rätt för sig	To earn one's pay, to do one's share.
gubbtur	'Old man's shift'. Easy shift.
heel	(See: *bromssko*)
herder	(See: train-puller)
'highball'	(Am.) signal for all clear, 'get going'.
hjulplatta, -or	(See: flat spot,-s)
INT	Taped interview.
kabyl	Old railway argot for beginner.
key	1) schedule of work, often implying exact hours of shifts, but also used to signify days of work only, as in: 2) (See: *fridagsnyckel)* 3) Removable handle to switch supply of electricity on/off from engine to coaches behind it.
kick	1)*(skjutsa)* To shove one or a cut of coaches with force of the engine so that they roll ahead when the engine is stopped. 2)*(skjuts)* Coaches shoved as in 1) 3)*(visa 'skjuts')* To show 'kick'. To signal that 1) should be performed.
knackare	(See: knocker)
knocker	Person preparing trains for shunting by raising bridges, disconnecting air brake hoses and electric cables, and loosening the coupling. He also drains the air from the airbrake system (Am.: to 'bleed' a car).
koppelstång	Long metal bar, used to unhook the coupling from outside the buffers. If available it will lie on the engine ledge and is only used for disconnecting shunting engine and first coach.
lämna av	(See: report)
lapparna	(See: slips)

lead (working lead, running track)	*(växelgata)* Track where shunting takes place. Forks out into all the different sidings.
ligger, det	Lit.: 'it lies'. The track is lined (up). (See: line)
line	To turn the switches in order to allow movement on a track. (See also: line behind)
line behind	To turn back the switch after passing through it.
littera	type of coach
mainline	*('linjen')* Track for trains in scheduled traffic. Not to be found in Hagalund.
Middle Yard	*(Mellanbangården)* Auxiliary yard South of the Southern part of the main yard.
MTÖ-B	Official abbreviation for the Yard Group, *bangårdsgruppen.*
North	*(Norr, norra bangården)* Northern part of the main yard. Shunted by two shunting teams.
obekväm arbetstid	Inconvenient working hours, unsocial hours (compensated according to different rates of extra payment, depending on hour and calendar day, such as Sun- or Holidays).
OC	(See: Order Centre)
Order Centre	Centre for information. Announces departures on loud speaker system to train-pullers and informs outdoor *tkm* about trains that are ready to be pulled.
Ordercentralen	(See: Order Centre)
P3	*På tre år och 100 punkter ska SJ bli bättre.*
palt	Hand lantern, used for signalling when it is dark or foggy.
points	(See: switch)
pull	To pull out a train to a lead in order to start to connect and disconnect coaches.
report	Task of outdoor boss to indoor boss. Sums up what the shunting team has accomplished during the shift. Could be considered as an updating of the inventory of the coaches in the yard.
reserve	1) tracks for spare coaches 2) reserve-list (See: VIK)
rykare	'Smoker', i.e. a hard kick. To make a hard joint.
sammansättningsplan	(See: composition plan)
SÄM	*Säkerhetsmeddelanden.*
SÄO	*Säkerhetsordning (säo),* Security Regulations. 'The Rule Book'.
SÄOK	*Kompletterande föreskrifter och anvisningar till säkerhetsordningen (säok).* The commentaries to SÄO.
S-E O	*Svensk-engelsk ordbok.*
shunt leader	leader of a shunting team (sometimes, but very rarely, called A-member)
siding	*(sidospår)* Auxiliary tracks. Here, somewhat improperly, used for all tracks in the yard, except the leads and the extension track.

signalgivare	(See: signaller)
signaller	Person who is in charge of initiating the signals to the driver. Often, but not always, the shunt leader.
SJ	*Statens Järnvägar*, The Swedish State Railways
SJF 010.3	*Växlingsinstruktion (vxi)*, Shunting instructions.
skjuts	(See: kick)
skjutspassare	(See: B-member)
skubben (gå på)	The VIK-list, to work as a VIK. (See: VIK)
slips	Work orders for the shunting teams, but also lists of arriving and departing trains, used by train-pullers.
SO	*Svensk ordbok.*
South	*(Söder, Södra bangården)* Southern part of the main yard. Shunted by one (earlier two) shunting teams.
ställa upp	'Play ball', i.e. not to let the other(s) down.
steady, go	To work on a fixed schedule. The opposite of working as a VIK.
steady list	The list of persons who go steady. (Also the work schedule of these persons.) (See: steady)

stins, stationsinspektör Obsolete titel, approx. station-master.

stinsex. (stinsexpeditionen) Office for communication concerning ordering of extra coaches, etc. 'Telegrapher', working with telephones and computers.

stop-bar	*(stoppbock)* Bar with buffers, marking the end of a track.
switch	*(växel)* Implement allowing movement from from one track to another when being thrown, (or turned or lined). There are manual (turned by hand), half-manual (turned by pressing a button on the ground) and automatic (operated from the swithboard plant) switches in Hagalund. The manual ones have a big red and yellow sphere, indicating whether the switch is lined 'right ahead' (yellow half turned up) or 'to the side' (red half turned up). Many switches are heated in order to prevent that they will be clogged by snow.

switch-blindness Inability to judge how the switches are lined. Considered to be incurable.

switchboard plant Computerized signal and switch system, operated by one or two switchboard operators. The computer lines all the switches to a track, as well as it lines nearby switches in safety positions. Appropriate signals, 'dwarfs', are also lit, allowing and prohibiting movement.

trunk line	*(stambana)* Priority mainline.
tågdragare	(See: train-puller)
tåglots	(See: train-puller)
tastatur	Electric keyboard, directly connected to Cst, on which train and engine numbers can be reported in the right order of their departure from Hagalund. Operated by train-pullers.

Technical Coach Service 2-week further education for shunters, now included
in the introductory course.

Teknisk vagntjänst   (See: Technical Coach Service)

tkm   (trafikmästare) Come in two kinds; indoor and outdoor. Also
called boss,-es *(bas,-ar)*.

trafikmästare   (See: *tkm*)

train pilot   (See: train-puller)

train-puller   Train guide with responsibility for movements of trains and
engines, other than those controlled by shunters, inside
Hagalund area.

uppkopplare   (See: knocker)

vagnupptagare   (See: coach recorder)

VIK   The list of deputies, i.e. persons who do not work on a
steady list as team-members, train-pullers, knockers, coach
recorders, switchboard operators or *tkm*. Depending on
individual qualifications they may replace any of these during
holidays, etc. VIK personnel are steady employees, but their
exact time-table can be changed without notice up to two
weeks before the shift.

vikarielistan   (See: VIK)

värmepost   (See: electric post)

växelgata   (See: lead)

växelledare   (See: shunt leader)

work order   (See: slips)

yard conductor   (See: shunt leader)

Yard Group   *(bangårdsgruppen)* The shunting group at Hagalund. An
administrative entity as well as a social group.

yardmaster   (See: *tkm*)

334

INDEX

Available from Almqvist & Wiksell International